GW00659169

THE
PRICE
WE PAID

THE PRICE
WE PAID

The Extraordinary Story
of the Willie & Martin
Handcart Pioneers

ANDREW D. OLSEN

DESERET
BOOK

SALT LAKE CITY, UTAH

Illustrations on pages 4–5, 74, and 214–15 courtesy LDS Church Archives, Salt Lake City, Utah.

Photos on pages 8, 37, 53, 66, 67, 69, 98, 122, 124, 133, 158, 231, 245, 261, 262, 271, 283, 311, 338, 381, and 419 courtesy LDS Church Archives, Salt Lake City, Utah.

Engravings on pages 23, 103, 175, and 307 by Frederick Piercy, in *Route from Liverpool to Great Salt Lake Valley* (1855).

Photo on page 39 courtesy Spence Lloyd.

Photo on page 147 courtesy Riverton Wyoming Stake.

Photo on page 201 courtesy Mark Seethaler.

Photos on pages 250 and 365 courtesy Drusilla Smith.

Painting on page 344, *The Blue Angel—Joseph Angell Young,* by Julie Rogers, courtesy Julie Rogers.

Photo on page 427 of *She Stood Tall on Her Knees,* bronze sculpture by Jerry Anderson of Leeds, Utah, courtesy Southern Utah University Photo Services.

Photo on page 457 courtesy Karen Barker.

All other photos by the author.

© 2006 Andrew D. Olsen

All rights reserved. No part of this book may be reproduced in any form or by any means without permission in writing from the publisher, Deseret Book Company, P. O. Box 30178, Salt Lake City, Utah 84130. This work is not an official publication of The Church of Jesus Christ of Latter-day Saints. The views expressed herein are the responsibility of the author and do not necessarily represent the position of the Church or of Deseret Book Company.

DESERET BOOK is a registered trademark of Deseret Book Company.

Visit us at DeseretBook.com

Library of Congress Cataloging-in-Publication Data
Olsen, Andrew D.
    The price we paid : the extraordinary story of the Willie and Martin handcart pioneers / Andrew D. Olsen.
        p.   cm.
    ISBN-10: 1–59038–624–8
    ISBN-13: 978–1–59038–624–8 (hardbound : alk. paper)
    1. James G. Willie Emigrating Company—History. 2. Edward Martin Emigrating Company—History. 3. Mormon handcart companies—History. 4. Church of Jesus Christ of Latter-day Saints—History. 5. Mormon Church—History. 6. Mormon pioneers. I. Title.
    BX8611.O47 2006
    289.309'034—dc22   2006018246

Printed in the United States of America
Publishers Printing, Salt Lake City, UT

10   9   8   7   6

CONTENTS

PREFACE vii

MAPS xii

INTRODUCTION: ONWARD TO ZION 1

PART 1
THE STORY OF THE WILLIE HANDCART PIONEERS

1   FROM ENGLAND TO IOWA CITY 7

2   THE CALL TO GATHER 14

3   THE HANDCART PLAN 21

4   ADVANTAGES AND MISGIVINGS 27

5   AN ENTHUSIASTIC RESPONSE 36

6   MAKING PREPARATIONS 48

7   CHALLENGES FOR THE WILLIE COMPANY IN IOWA CITY 57

8   FROM IOWA CITY TO FLORENCE, NEBRASKA 71

9   DIFFICULT DECISIONS IN FLORENCE 77

10   FROM FLORENCE TO FORT LARAMIE 86

11   FROM FORT LARAMIE TO INDEPENDENCE ROCK 102

12   THE RESCUE BEGINS 114

13   FROM INDEPENDENCE ROCK TO FIFTH CROSSING 124

14   THE RESCUERS ARRIVE 131

15   CROSSING ROCKY RIDGE 146

16   FROM ROCK CREEK TO FORT BRIDGER 163

17   ACCUSATIONS AND REPRIMANDS IN SALT LAKE CITY 166

18   FROM FORT BRIDGER TO SALT LAKE CITY 172

19 AFTER THE TREK: DIFFICULTIES AND BLESSINGS 177
20 REMEMBER 209

PART 2
THE STORY OF THE MARTIN HANDCART PIONEERS

21 FAREWELL TO THEE, ENGLAND 217
22 FROM BOSTON TO IOWA CITY 227
23 AN ENTHUSIASTIC RESPONSE 243
24 FROM IOWA CITY TO FLORENCE, NEBRASKA 273
25 DIFFICULT DECISIONS IN FLORENCE 282
26 FROM FLORENCE TO FORT LARAMIE 295
27 FROM FORT LARAMIE TO THE LAST CROSSING
    OF THE PLATTE RIVER 312
28 LAST CROSSING OF THE PLATTE RIVER 316
29 SNOWBOUND AT RED BUTTES 327
30 THE RESCUERS ARRIVE 337
31 AT DEVIL'S GATE 353
32 TAKING SHELTER IN MARTIN'S COVE 358
33 LEAVING MARTIN'S COVE AND DEVIL'S GATE 369
34 HELP FROM EPHRAIM HANKS 381
35 SOME OF THE RESCUERS TURN BACK 388
36 FROM THE PLAINS OF WYOMING TO THE MOUNTAINS
    OF UTAH 391
37 ARRIVAL IN SALT LAKE CITY 398
38 AFTER THE TREK: DIFFICULTIES AND BLESSINGS 403
39 THE HEARTS OF THE FATHERS 467

CONCLUSION: A TRAIL OF TEARS, A TRAIL OF HOPE 470
NOTES 481
SOURCES 519
INDEX 525

PREFACE

This book had its beginning in my first visits to Rock Creek Hollow and Martin's Cove. These are places made sacred by the sacrifices of the Willie and Martin handcart pioneers. I have known the stories of these pioneers for most of my life. But when I visited these places, I realized that I knew them in only a vague, distant way. Almost immediately I felt a compelling need to know them better.

In researching these stories, I found them to be even more tragic than I had known before. But for me the most profound discovery, shining through all the heartbreak and misery, is their boundless capacity to instruct and inspire. This power is comparable to the stories in the scriptures. The intent of this book is to contribute to a greater understanding of the Willie and Martin handcart stories. My hope is that as they become better known, their power to teach and bless will continue to increase.

Many of the misunderstandings about these handcart companies come from the traditional combining of their accounts. Although the groups were similar in some ways, they were usually about 100 miles apart, and their experiences differed significantly. Toward the end of the trek, for example, the Willie company stretched so far ahead that they were entering the Salt Lake Valley on the same day the Martin company was leaving Martin's Cove, 325 miles away.

In an effort to tell these stories as clearly as possible, this book has separate sections for the Willie and Martin companies. Each section provides brief updates on the other company at key points. The Willie section also includes background information that applies to both handcart companies, covering subjects such as the gathering, the origin of the handcart plan, and the beginning of the rescue. The Martin section includes information about the Hodgetts and Hunt wagon companies, which traveled closely with the Martin handcart company and shared in their experiences. Both sections tell of the rescue, which differed considerably for the two groups.

Woven into the overall stories of these handcart companies are stories of the people—the emigrants, their leaders, and their rescuers. Before this study, I knew very few of them by name and knew even less about their lives before and after the handcart experience. In a day when conviction often concedes to convenience, when sacrifice often concedes to self-indulgence, I have found that there is much to learn from these people.

I have learned not only from their faithfulness but also from their imperfections. Along with stories of people helping those who fell behind are stories of people who did not receive the help they needed. Providing a counterpoint to those who shared their scanty rations are those who gave in to their desperate hunger and pilfered. Even many of those who later expressed gratitude for their trials sometimes felt doubt and despair. To see these people doubt and then rally their faith, to see them err and then make amends, to see them triumph despite their weaknesses is an important source of the power in these stories.

Most accounts of the Willie and Martin pioneers end with the rescuers leading them into the Salt Lake Valley, but the stories do not really end there. What were the lives of these people like after the handcart ordeal? What were the long-term effects of the experience? This book addresses these questions for many members of each company. This part of the story is as instructive and inspiring as anything that happened during the handcart trek.

SOURCE NOTES

The research for this book draws heavily on the journals kept by members of the Willie and Martin handcart companies, the Hodgetts and Hunt wagon companies, and the rescuers. On their own, however, these journals have some limitations. Not many exist, most of the entries are brief, and few of them continue after the October storms began. To supplement the journals, I have used recollections and reminiscences. Because some of these were written more than 50 years later, they often contain inaccuracies about such facts as places, dates, and names. Nevertheless, these sources are valuable in providing personal feelings and insights.

When quoting unpublished sources, I have occasionally made minor spelling, grammar, and punctuation changes so the accounts read more clearly. When encountering differences in spellings and dates, I have used what seemed to be the most credible source for such information.

As with any historical study, some interpretation of the sources has been necessary in assembling these accounts. If there are errors in the interpretation or analysis, I bear responsibility for them. If readers have information that would correct errors or provide additional insights, I welcome it. The following e-mail address is available for providing such information or any other feedback: handcarts@hotmail.com.

ACKNOWLEDGMENTS

I am grateful for the support of my wife, Linda, during this project. She has encouraged me even as I have used evenings, weekends, and vacations to research and write—and even as the completion date kept extending for months. She has also shared valuable insights and suggestions while reading the manuscript. Many times I have felt her prayers answered on behalf of this project. Some of her ancestors were in the Martin company, and one of them, George Barnes, died on the journey, most likely at Martin's Cove.

Our children, Jessie, Eric, and Scott, have also given support and encouragement. As we have knelt together at night, they have prayed for me to receive help. They constantly inquire about my progress. And they never seem to tire of handcart stories for family home evening.

I am also grateful to my parents, Richard and Alma Olsen, for their counsel and encouragement. Throughout her life, my mom has demonstrated the same faith and sacrifice that the handcart pioneers did. My dad has also been a spiritual guidepost. At one point during this project I asked if he would give me a father's blessing the next time we were together. Rather than waiting for what I expected would be a month, the next Sunday afternoon he and my brother Ryan drove from Idaho in a snowstorm so he could give me the blessing. It has been a constant source of strength.

I would not have started this book, much less finished it, without the help of my friend Rob Perry. He encouraged me to put the first words on paper. He read the manuscript at least twice and commented extensively. His questions and insights have influenced many of the chapters. Almost everyone who knows Rob has felt his rescuing embrace. I have especially felt it whenever I needed help during this project. One of the Martin company's rescuers, Arza Hinckley, is Rob's kinsman. Rob Perry is no less a rescuer.

I am grateful to many others who have provided essential help. Robert Scott Lorimer, former president of the Riverton Wyoming Stake, and his wife, Desiree, have been generous in their assistance. Jolene S. Allphin, author of *Tell My Story, Too,* has likewise been generous in reading and critiquing the manuscript and sharing information. Gordon and Margaret Nebeker have also provided important assistance in reviewing the manuscript. Cory Maxwell and Suzanne Brady of Deseret Book have been especially helpful in guiding the preparation of the manuscript and refining the final product. I also appreciate the assistance of Don H. Smith and Stewart Glazier, who readily responded to many questions, and William Slaughter for help with most of the photographs and illustrations. I am also grateful to Julie Rogers for permission to use her painting of rescuer Joseph Young riding into the Martin company's camp.

Many of the sources in this book have come from the archives of The Church of Jesus Christ of Latter-day Saints and the History Department of the Daughters of Utah Pioneers. I am grateful for access to these materials and for permission to use them.

Finally, I am grateful for the members of the Willie and Martin handcart companies, the Hodgetts and Hunt wagon companies, and their rescuers. They will never be just names to me again. Their example and influence have guided me almost daily since I began to study their lives. I have often wondered if they had any idea of the far-reaching, long-lasting impact of their sacrifice. I believe that the good resulting from what they did will only continue to multiply.

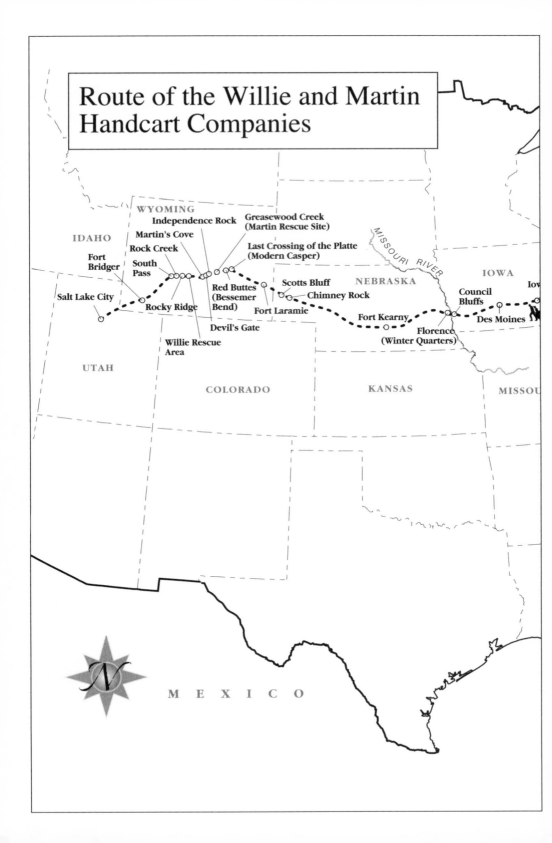

Route of the Willie and Martin Handcart Companies

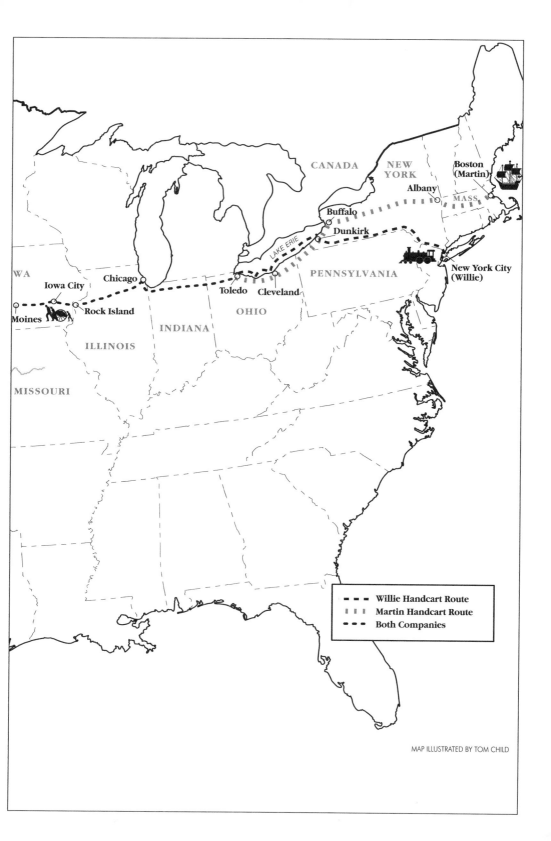

MAP ILLUSTRATED BY TOM CHILD

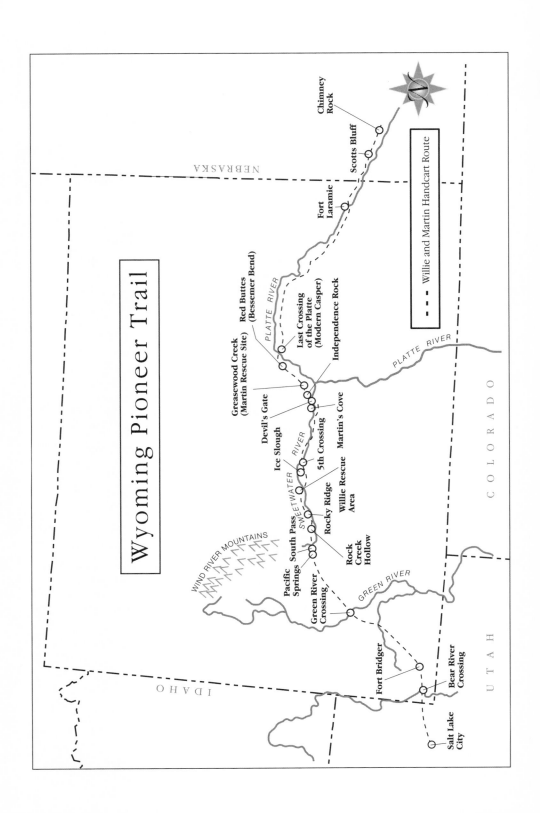

ONWARD TO ZION

Francis Webster had already traveled the world when he left England for good in 1856. When he was 18, he had gone to Australia, then to New Zealand, and then to California, where he prospected for several years during the Gold Rush. After enjoying moderate success, he returned to England in 1855 and began to seek a different kind of fortune. He married, renewed his baptismal rites as a member of The Church of Jesus Christ of Latter-day Saints, and answered the call of Church leaders to gather to Zion.

During his years in California, Francis Webster had accumulated enough gold to get a comfortable start in life. Wanting to be well outfitted for the journey to Salt Lake City, he placed $500 with a Church emigration agent a few months before leaving England. With this money the agent would buy a wagon, oxen, and camp equipment and have it ready for the Websters in Iowa City, the point of departure for the trek west.

But plans soon changed. The number of converts who wanted to emigrate in 1856 exceeded any previous year. More than 2,000 of them were too poor to pay their own expenses, and Church resources to assist them were limited. To help solve this problem, Church leaders asked those who had money to help pay the emigration expenses of the poor. Hearing this counsel, Francis Webster canceled his wagon order and elected to cross the trail in a much less expensive way—by handcart. Without elaborating on the cost of this sacrifice, he simply said, "[I paid] the fare for nine persons besides myself and wife to Salt Lake City."[1]

Francis and Betsy Webster sailed with the last large company of

Latter-day Saint emigrants to leave England in 1856. Their group was also the last to arrive in Iowa City, where most of them were organized into the season's fifth and last handcart company, led by Edward Martin.

Traveling by handcart instead of wagon exposed the Websters to the worst extremities. Even before they were struck by winter storms, they suffered greatly. While still in Nebraska, Betsy was weak from having a baby and Francis was weak from dysentery. Describing this affliction, Francis wrote, "[It was] so bad that I have sat down on the road and been administered to by the Elders and [then] gotten up and pulled my handcart with renewed vigor."[2] Later, Francis's feet became severely frozen. And as for his comfortable start in life, by journey's end this one-time prospector who had traveled the world seeking his fortune had nothing left but his tattered clothes.

Francis Webster could have lived the rest of his life lamenting his losses. He could have become bitter toward Church leaders, even toward God. Instead, two days after arriving in Salt Lake City he continued another 240 miles south to Cedar City, where he raised a large family and lived a long, productive life of Church and civic service.

Decades later, when Francis Webster was an old man, he was sitting quietly in a Sunday School class in Cedar City as some people were criticizing Church leaders for the handcart tragedy. When he could bear the criticism no longer, he stood and asked the people to stop. Speaking calmly but with emotion, he acknowledged that it was a mistake to send the handcart companies so late. He also acknowledged that he and others in these companies had suffered greatly. Nevertheless, he bore testimony that he had found a pearl of great price in the experience:

"We suffered beyond anything you can imagine, and many died of exposure and starvation. . . . [But we] came through with the absolute knowledge that God lives, for we became acquainted with Him in our extremities.

"I have pulled my handcart when I was so weak and weary from illness and lack of food that I could hardly put one foot ahead of the other. I have looked ahead and seen a patch of sand or a hill slope and I have said, I can go only that far and there I must give up, for I cannot pull the load through it. I have gone to that sand, and when I reached it, the cart began pushing me. I have looked back many times to see who was pushing my cart, but my eyes saw no one. I knew then that the angels of God were there.

"Was I sorry that I chose to come by handcart? No. Neither then nor any minute of my life since. The price we paid to become acquainted with God was a privilege to pay, and I am thankful that I was privileged to come in the Martin handcart company."[3]

In pulling handcarts to Zion, Francis and Betsy Webster were part of what has been called "the most remarkable travel experiment in the history of Western America."[4] Between 1847 and 1869, some 70,000 members of The Church of Jesus Christ of Latter-day Saints came to Utah by overland trail. Most of them traveled in wagon companies, but approximately 3,000—4 percent of the total—came by handcart.

In all, ten companies of handcart pioneers made the journey to Utah between 1856 and 1860. Although pulling handcarts was arduous even in the best conditions, eight of these companies made the journey more quickly and with fewer deaths than the typical wagon company. The other two handcart companies—the Willie and Martin companies—suffered a tragedy that President Gordon B. Hinckley described as "without parallel in the western migration of our people."[5] They paid what he called "a terrible, terrible price."[6]

This price included some 200 deaths, numerous amputations of frozen limbs, the widowing of many women, and the orphaning of many children. It included broken hearts and broken dreams of families who had left Europe with the hope of living together in Zion.

And yet, as Francis Webster attested, the price was not paid in vain, nor for that which does not satisfy. In a way made possible only by the power of faith and the grace of God, the payment of this price has brought everlasting blessings not only to those who paid it but also to generations that have followed.

PART 1

THE STORY OF THE
WILLIE HANDCART PIONEERS

CHAPTER 1

FROM ENGLAND TO IOWA CITY

In one night, thirteen of [the Willie] company died and were buried in a common grave, and two others died the next morning. We remember them with appreciation and gratitude. . . . We feel in our hearts the great redeeming power of Thy Son, who saved them as He has saved all men through His atoning sacrifice. . . . We know that they came to know Thee in a particular way in the dire circumstances in which they found themselves those early winter days in 1856. . . .

O God, our Eternal Father, we thank Thee for the great inheritance that is ours, that we come of the strain of noble people who valued faith more than life itself, who were willing to work and sacrifice—even to give their lives in death—for the cause in which they believed. Help us to be true to the faith, and help all the generations who shall follow to remain true to the faith, that they may keep the trust which became so much a part of the lives of those who died here and elsewhere along this trail of tears.

—President Gordon B. Hinckley
dedicatory prayer at Rock Creek Hollow, Wyoming, 23 July 1994

The events that brought President Gordon B. Hinckley to Rock Creek, Wyoming, in 1994 had their beginning in Liverpool, England, in 1856. On May 4 of that year, 764 members of The Church of Jesus Christ of Latter-day Saints set sail on the ship *Thornton,* bound for America. Most of them were converts to the Church, responding to the call to gather to Zion.

Franklin D. Richards, a member of the Quorum of the Twelve Apostles, oversaw the emigration as president of the European Mission. At age 35, he was serving his third mission to England and was mission president for the second time. Some of his missionaries were returning home on the *Thornton,* and he appointed one of them, James G. Willie, to preside over the Saints on the ship. Ten

Franklin D. Richards

weeks later, most of this group would be organized into the fourth handcart company, with James Willie appointed to continue as their leader. By the time he began this long journey home, James Willie had been away from his wife and three small children for nearly four years.

ACROSS THE ATLANTIC

Crossing the Atlantic in the 1850s could be daunting. Although steam-powered ships were available, Church leaders chartered sailing vessels because of tight finances. Going west, these ships typically had to battle contrary winds that made the voyage last six weeks or longer. During these seemingly endless days, emigrants had to endure cramped, poorly ventilated berths, some of them three levels below deck. Berths for two people were 6 feet long, 4.5 feet wide, and 2 feet high.[1] The food was monotonous and often unsavory, and the water was sometimes so bad the people would drink it only in desperation. New to the sea, most emigrants retched with seasickness for at least a few days, some of them for weeks. Diseases were always a risk and would spread quickly. A few deaths—sometimes many—were almost a certainty. Rough treatment of passengers by the captain and crew was not unusual.

The Saints on the *Thornton* experienced many of these challenges but faced them with fortitude and generally had a good voyage. The company journal frequently tells of their unity and good spirits. As the ship neared America, 31-year-old Anna Tait wrote to some friends back home, "I have been blessed with the living Spirit of our God all the time, and have never found the moment but what I could thank my God with all my heart for the privilege of going across the Atlantic."[2]

The company journal also tells of good relations with Captain Collins and his crew, who gave "kind attentions" and made every effort to make the passengers comfortable.[3] One reason the captain liked them was because they were clean and orderly compared to other groups. "Great order prevailed," the journal records, and "the Captain was much pleased."[4] Anna Tait wrote that the captain was so cordial that he "often joined in [singing] the songs of Zion. . . . I have often thought that President F. D. Richards must have breathed his spirit on him at Liverpool."[5]

The company journal tells of three births, three marriages, and eight deaths at sea. The first birth occurred before the ship even left the dock, when a son was born to Janet and Thomas McNeil. The first marriage occurred on the first day, when Allan Findlay was married to Jessie Ireland. The first death, of 75-year-old Rachel Curtis, occurred on the third day. The journal records the poignant feelings that attended her burial the next morning:

"At 10 A.M. the bell tolled as a signal that the hour had arrived when we were to consign the remains of our beloved Sister Curtis to the sea to await the resurrection of the just. Great solemnity prevailed among all present. President J. G. Willie offered up a prayer to the Almighty. She was buried in the mighty deep."[6]

Feelings were especially tender for George Curtis, Rachel's husband. A person can see this aged, grieving man watching his wife's body disappear in the ocean and continuing to look longingly into the water. The community of Saints, diverse but already united, tries to console him. Left alone while still so close to home, did George Curtis wish he could turn back? This story will later show that his wife's death only seemed to steel his desire to reach Zion.

THE MORMON EMIGRANT SHIP

"A Mormon charter ship differed . . . sharply from the usual emigrant vessel," wrote historian Wallace Stegner. "I have seen emigrant ships before . . . , and these people are so strikingly different from all the other people in like circumstances whom I have ever seen," wrote

Charles Dickens, a contemporary of the handcart pioneers. While neither of these authors was specifically describing the Saints on the *Thornton,* both could have been. A brief description of the organization and deportment that characterized the Saints on these emigrant ships is useful in understanding this part of the journey—and forecasting the rest of it.

Wallace Stegner continued: "A Mormon charter ship . . . was organized to the smallest corner and to the ultimate quarter-hour. [Leaders] divided the ship into wards and created bishops to head them. The elders worked out a sequence of duties, [including] rising, cleaning quarters, disposing of refuse over the side, prayer; then breakfast in orderly groups [in] the galley. . . . Throughout the day [there were] instructive talks by the elders, prayer meetings, fairly often a wedding, sometimes a baptism, occasionally a burial, then another orderly [meal in] the galley and another spell of cleaning; in the evening [there was] music or a dance or group singing; at eight or nine, by bugle or bell, prayers."[7]

Charles Dickens's firsthand impressions were equally favorable. In 1863 he spent a day on a ship that was preparing to carry Latter-day Saint emigrants to America. Although most of these people were from lower economic classes, he was so impressed by their organization, industry, and cooperation that he described them as "the pick and flower of England." When he asked the captain for more information about them, he was told:

"Most of these came aboard yesterday evening. They came from various parts of England in small parties that had never seen one another before. Yet they had not been a couple of hours on board, when they established their own police, made their own regulations, and set their own watches at all the hatchways. Before nine o'clock, the ship was as orderly and as quiet as a man-of-war."[8]

More contemporary with the *Thornton* was the *S. Curling,* which had brought one group of Saints to New York in 1855 and another group just a few weeks before the *Thornton* in 1856. Reporting on the arrival of the *S. Curling* the previous year, a writer from the *New York Tribune* observed:

"A large majority of the passengers are of the poorer classes of British peasantry. [They] appear to enjoy good health and spirits. The vessel was the cleanest emigrant ship we have ever seen; notwithstanding the large number of her passengers, order, cleanliness, and comfort prevailed on all hands. The between decks were as sweet and well ventilated as the cabin, and the orlopdeck [lowest deck] was as white as scrubbing brush and holystone could make it. It would be well if the packet-ships that ply between this port and Liverpool were to imitate the system of management that prevailed on board this ship."[9]

Arrival in New York City

After six weeks at sea, the *Thornton* arrived in New York City on June 14. "This has been such a day of rejoicing," wrote Anna Tait. Fifteen-year-old George Cunningham felt similar excitement and gratitude: "How well I remember the first step that I took on American soil. How thrilled I was to be in the land of the free—the land of promise! . . . I felt like thanking God for the blessing I then enjoyed."[10]

At the end of the voyage, the passengers adopted a testimonial commending Captain Collins. When James Willie presented it to him, Anna Tait recalled that "he received it with tears of gratitude and came forward and addressed the Saints. He said that he had done nothing but his duty, that he never crossed the sea with so good a company of passengers before—they had always been willing to do anything he wanted. . . . He wished the Saints prosperity in all their future works, and said he would remember them with the warmest feelings as long as he lived. He asked God to bless them. Here his feelings overcame him, and he had to stop speaking."[11]

The arrival of the *Thornton,* like that of the *S. Curling,* was noteworthy enough to attract the attention of the New York newspapers. Describing the group, one reporter wrote, "They are mostly families, and appear to belong to the better class of emigrants." After speaking with the ship's captain and some of the leaders and passengers, the reporter commended James Willie and the other elders for keeping the passengers "clean, orderly, and pious." Early in the story the reporter told of the births at sea, and later he elaborated, perhaps with tongue in cheek, "The only accident that happened was the three births aforesaid, and this the Elders state resulted from causes above and beyond their control."[12]

The reporter also commented on the demographics of the group, an important factor as these people would soon begin one of the most physically demanding journeys in the history of America's western migration: "There seemed to be a preponderance of females among them. . . . The number of children, too, is very large, there being nearly one hundred under six years of age."[13]

The group's demographics were likewise noted by Anna Tait, whose letter provides additional detail that forecasts the challenges this group would soon face: "I believe there has never before been a company with so many old and young, halt, blind, and lame, from so many nations, [that] crossed the sea."[14] Anna would travel nearly 5,000 miles from her home in Glasgow, Scotland, before succumbing near Rocky Ridge, just 270 miles short of Zion.[15]

FROM NEW YORK TO IOWA CITY

After arriving in New York, the emigrants had to travel another 1,200 miles to get to the handcart outfitting site in Iowa City. This was not an express journey even by the standards of the 1850s. Rather, it was an arduous 11-day ordeal by rail, steamboat, and ferry, often in difficult conditions. Sometimes the Saints traveled in baggage or cattle cars to reduce expenses.

According to historian Stanley Kimball, these trains had no eating or sleeping facilities, averaged only 20 miles an hour, and operated on erratic schedules.[16] They had "bad ventilation, dim lighting, marginal sanitary facilities, . . . a lack of drinking water; loud noise, strong smells, jolting, shaking, vibration . . . ; an abundance of dirt, lice, soot, sparks, smoke, and fire; gamblers, thieves, tramps, drunks, marauding soldiers, impolite railroad personnel . . . ; and such other inconveniences as . . . animals on the tracks, derailments, accidents, wrecks, [and] delays."[17]

From New York City the group went by train across the state to Dunkirk, southwest of Buffalo. Next they traveled by steamboat across Lake Erie, disembarking at the railroad station in Toledo, Ohio. There, the company journal records, railroad authorities "manifested a very unkind spirit towards us, putting us to all inconvenience in their power."[18]

From Toledo the group traveled by train the rest of the way across Ohio, across Indiana, and into Chicago, where the conductor treated them roughly and left them on the street for the night. Eventually a railroad superintendent gave them space in a warehouse.[19]

Because of an insufficient number of rail cars, the group was divided for the journey across Illinois. The first day they were delayed by a broken-down bridge and had to sleep on the train. They finally reached the Mississippi River at 11:00 the next night, stopping at Rock Island, a town 50 miles north of Nauvoo. They spent another night on the train, ferried across the river the next morning, and then boarded another train that took them the final 50 miles to Iowa City, where the rail ended and the handcart journey would begin.

In discussions of the handcart companies, the Willie company is often closely connected with the Martin company, as though they were together. However, the Saints who would form the Martin company left England three weeks later, and during most of the handcart journey they were 8 to 10 days behind the Willie company. They fell three weeks behind in the last month. The only time the two groups were together was in Iowa City, when they overlapped for about a week while getting outfitted.

President Franklin D. Richards's role with the Willie company did not end with arranging for their voyage and seeing them leave the shores of England. He would continue to be one of the central figures in the story of this company.

The outfitting site for the handcart companies was actually about three miles west of Iowa City, in present-day Coralville. A Mormon Handcart Park there memorializes the handcart pioneers.

CHAPTER 2

THE CALL TO GATHER

Janet McNeil was nine months pregnant with her seventh child when she boarded the *Thornton.* Doing so probably violated every maternal instinct. She knew the conditions for giving birth would be rather primitive. Surely she knew the risks of taking an infant on such a voyage and then crossing an unknown continent with him. She had to wonder how she would provide for the baby, whether she would be able to feed him. Nevertheless, the call to gather to Zion sounded so strongly in her heart that she and her family chose to emigrate despite these risks and uncertainties. "The time to go is now," Janet told her husband when he asked if it might be better to emigrate in a different year. "Something may come up to hinder us if we wait. I will put my trust in God, and He will see me through."[1]

Rachel Curtis, the 75-year-old woman who died on the third day of the voyage, had been in declining health before leaving Liverpool. Given her age and health condition, she likely knew that she had only a small chance of seeing Zion. But she boarded the ship anyway, willing to leave everything behind, sail across the ocean, and walk 1,300 miles.

"THE FIRE OF EMIGRATION BLAZES"

For many years, Church leaders used stirring prose and oratory to encourage converts to gather to Utah. "Emigrate as speedily as possible," Brigham Young wrote in 1847.[2] "Come! and help us to build and grow, until we can say, enough—the valleys of Ephraim are full," the First Presidency wrote in 1849.[3] Sometimes the call to gather was given with the force of a commandment, as in 1855 when President Franklin D. Richards wrote:

"The Lord never gave a commandment to His people, but what, if they would go to with full purpose of heart and try to obey it, they could do so. The commandment to gather out to the land of America is just as binding on the Saints, so far as it is possible for them to accomplish it, as it was in the first place to be baptized for the remission of sins. . . . Every impulse of the heart of the Saint, every hope of the future, says, 'Gather up to the land of America.'"[4]

The zeal to emigrate grew quickly until it was almost universal. William H. Kimball, a missionary in England who would later play a prominent role with the Willie company, described the feelings in his field of labor:

"The fire of emigration blazes throughout the Pastorate to the extent that the folks are willing to part with all their effects, and toddle off with a few things in a pocket handkerchief.

" . . . Verily there is power in 'Mormonism.' . . . People who once felt they would rather die than leave 'happy England,' . . . who looked upon other countries with supreme contempt, [now] sing with joyful hearts, 'There is a land beyond the sea / Where I should like to be; / And dearer far than all the rest, / Is that bright land to me.'"[5]

THE PUSH AND PULL TO EMIGRATE

What prompted this zeal to emigrate? Long before the pushing and pulling of handcarts began, converts felt both a push and a pull to gather to Zion. The "push," or the practical reasons, existed mainly for those who were poor, for whom emigration would provide an opportunity to improve their oppressive economic and social situations. Elder Millen Atwood, a missionary in England who later became one of the subcaptains of the Willie company, explained this further in his mission report:

"I did not go to England for gold or silver, but to preach the gospel and gather the poor. We started home with a goodly number on board the ship *Thornton,* and they were of the class that Br. Brigham wrote for when stating, 'If they have not a sixpence in the world, they are the ones to bring here.' The people that came from where I was were perfectly destitute. . . .

"They have prayed and fasted day after day, and night after night, that they might have the privilege of uniting with their brethren and sisters in these mountains. . . . When Br. Brigham offered his property so liberally, and the word came that they should gather from England, it ran like fire in dry stubble, and the hearts of the poor Saints leapt with joy and gladness; they could hardly contain themselves."[6]

One reason Brigham Young was so devoted to gathering the poor was his personal concern for them. Knowing their needs and fervent desires, he wanted to help them—and he wanted others to help also:

"The cry from our poor brethren in foreign countries for deliverance is great, the hand of the oppressor is heavy upon them, and they have no other prospect on earth through which they can hope for assistance. Many of them are long in the Church, and have been faithful in all things. . . . Shall we turn a deaf ear to their appeals and leave them to linger in the midst of wicked Babylon, where, year by year, the perplexity and distress of nations, their wickedness, abominations, and corruptions, wars, pestilence, and persecutions are multiplied by waxing greater and greater?"[7]

The "pull," or the spiritual reasons for emigrating, existed for converts of all economic levels. They wanted to gather to Utah so they could join the community of Saints in the common goal of building Zion. Rather than suffer constant prejudice and persecution, in Utah they hoped to raise their families and worship among people who shared the same beliefs and values. Just as the poor hoped to escape economic bondage by emigrating, converts of all economic levels had a very real feeling that they would escape spiritual bondage by doing so. In the words of John H. Latey of the Hodgetts wagon company, the Saints "rejoic[ed] in their emancipation from gentile bondage, and with the flattering prospect of speedily tasting the sweets of liberty in the beehive State of Deseret."[8]

HOW THE GATHERING BENEFITED THE CHURCH

Brigham Young's concern for the poor was not the only reason for his passion about the gathering. In addition to benefiting those who emigrated, the gathering benefited the Church in Utah. Bringing faithful Saints to the territory was necessary to build the latter-day Zion that Brigham Young envisioned. Franklin D. Richards explained, "In connection with building a Temple, and other objects equally necessary for the progress of the kingdom, the gathering of the poor from the nations of the earth is a subject of deep and abiding interest in the hearts of the First Presidency."[9]

During the earliest years in Utah, Brigham Young emphasized gathering those who had the skills and resources to help the Saints become self-sufficient. As he sought to settle the vast reaches of the Great Basin, develop its resources, build the temple, and establish public works, he simply needed more faithful people, whether they had skills and resources or not. LeRoy and Ann Hafen explained:

"To build their new empire—the Kingdom of God on earth— the Mormons soon realized that they would need more workers and an increased population. . . .

"The wisdom of the Gathering, for the advancement of the Church, was evident. Having established themselves in a desert country and undertaken there the building of a commonwealth, the Mormons were in need of more settlers to develop the resources of the land. Also, experience had proved that the Church thrived best when concentrated, and thus under the influence and encouragement of its leaders."[10]

Wallace Stegner saw additional practical purposes for such a strong emphasis on the gathering. It allowed Brigham Young, he said, to "quickly [people] his empire and [make] it strong against the inevitable renewed clash with the Gentile world."[11]

In addition to these practical benefits of the gathering, Brigham Young saw benefits that were more visionary. The entire world, he believed, would be spiritually blessed by gathering new converts to Utah. In a letter to Franklin D. Richards in 1855, he acknowledged

the benefit of bringing more people to "assist in the works of Zion."
But beyond that, he said, gathering the Saints to Utah "has a benefi-
cial influence in the world, and aids those who go on to proclaim the
Gospel, in obtaining hearers and believers."[12]

HELPING THE POOR EMIGRATE

Missionary work in Great Britain was so successful that by 1850
there were 30,747 Church members in Britain compared to only
11,380 in Utah.[13] While most of those Saints wanted to gather to
Zion, many were too poor to pay for their passage, barely subsisting
from week to week. By 1856, only 5 percent of those who wanted to
emigrate had been able to do so.[14]

"The Lord Helps Those Who Help Themselves"

Church leaders tried to remove impediments to the emigration
of the poor in two ways. First, they told even the poorest of Saints
that they must do all they could to help themselves. These Saints
were counseled to be frugal so they could save something each week
toward their emigration, if only a shilling. In an editorial in the
Millennial Star, the official Church periodical in England, President
Franklin D. Richards emphasized the importance of each person
making a plan for emigration and working to accomplish it:

"Have you, during the past season, made it your study and business to accomplish something towards your emigration? Or have you
carelessly passed it by, leaving it to some mere chance in the future?
Have you acted as though you expected the Lord to do that for you
which you have not considered worthy of your own exertions? Or
have you laboured faithfully to accomplish your own salvation? . . .

"As strong as the desire of the Saints is almost universally to
gather, there are comparatively few who have gone to work system-
atically to accomplish it."[15]

President Richards frequently taught, "The Lord helps those who
help themselves,"[16] and missionaries throughout the land echoed his

message. Some Church members in England scratched and saved for nearly 20 years before they were able to fulfill their desire to gather to Zion. Learning this principle of self-reliance while in England served them well many months later when they were crossing the plains and mountains of the American West.

This principle etched itself into the character of these Saints so strongly that many of them lived and taught it until the end of their lives. Sixty-three years after the handcart trek, one woman who wrote an account of her experiences concluded with this testimony:

"For the benefit of the youth of Zion who may read this, I bear testimony that I know God hears and answers prayers, and the Lord will help those who help themselves."[17]

The Perpetual Emigration Fund

The Perpetual Emigration Fund was the second way Church leaders tried to overcome impediments to emigration. Initiated in 1849, the fund was originally used to help the poor Saints from the United States gather to Zion. Beginning in 1852, it was used to assist those who lived abroad. Nearly two-thirds of those who sailed on the *Thornton* did so with the aid of the fund.[18]

Brigham Young said the purpose of the Perpetual Emigration Fund was "to deliver the honest poor, the pauper, . . . from the thraldom of ages, from localities where poverty is a crime, . . . where every avenue to rise in the scale of being to any degree of respectable joyous existence is forever closed."[19] Through this fund, the poor were advanced part of the money they needed for the journey to Utah. After arriving, they were expected to repay the fund in cash, commodities, or labor. The replenished fund could then be used to help others.

The necessity of this fund to help the poor emigrate is shown in a letter that Elder James Willie wrote to President Richards while presiding over the Southampton Conference:

"There is not one family in the Southampton Conference that has means to emigrate with to America, and in the Dorset

Conference there is but one family and two single brothers that [have] means to emigrate. . . . I am certain the only source the Saints here can look to for deliverance and escape from Babylon is the P. E. Fund. . . .

"To show you how the 'leaven of the Spirit' works amongst the Saints in emigration matters, I have concluded to mention a few cases out of many. At our Conference recently held, a brother agreed to donate £2 as a free offering, and another agreed to give 5 [shillings] per week to the first of January next, also as a donation to the P. E. Fund. Many others will do likewise, according to their circumstances.

"I can truly say the emigration spirit is universal here, and most of the Saints appear to be impressed with the belief that 'God helps them who help themselves.'"[20]

Today's Perpetual Education Fund is patterned after the Perpetual Emigration Fund. Under the leadership of President Gordon B. Hinckley, the Church established the fund in March 2001. Within five years, tens of thousands of students were receiving assistance from the fund to help them receive education they could not have afforded otherwise.

CHAPTER 3

THE HANDCART PLAN

If they were to come to Zion, they would have to walk, pulling a small cart
behind them.

—PRESIDENT GORDON B. HINCKLEY

As early as 1852, Brigham Young considered having emigrants
use handcarts for their journey to Utah. For a few years he set
the idea aside in favor of the traditional method of traveling in ox-
drawn wagon trains. In late 1855, however, he returned to the handcart plan because the number of emigrants was increasing and the
financial resources for assisting them were diminishing.

Conditions that prompted Brigham Young to reconsider the
handcart plan began to develop in 1854. That year a poor wheat harvest created food shortages and serious economic problems. Despite
these difficulties, emigration continued at a brisk pace in 1855. More
than 4,000 people emigrated from Europe that year, with 1,300
receiving assistance from the Perpetual Emigration Fund.[1] Expenditures from the fund exceeded the total of the previous three years.

Economic conditions in Utah declined further when the harvest
of 1855 was even worse than in 1854. A combination of grasshop-
pers and drought reduced the grain crop by one-third to two-thirds
throughout the territory.[2] Conditions grew worse still in the winter of
1855–56 when severe cold and heavy snow caused the death of thousands of beef cattle and other animals.[3] With grain and meat supplies
depleted, many people were in a state of semi-starvation. Some were
driven to digging pigweed and thistle roots to survive, as they had

done in 1849. President Heber C. Kimball described the conditions in early 1856 to his son William in England:

"Our winter has been extremely hard and has caused great loss among our cattle. I suppose one-half of the Church stock is dead. . . .

"There are not more than one-half the people that have bread, and they have not more than one-half or one-quarter of a pound a day to a person. A great portion of the people are digging roots, and . . . thousands, their teams being dead, are under the necessity of spading their ground to put in their grain. There is not any settlement or people, in any part of the Territory, but what feel the scarcity of food, money, cattle, horses, etc. . . .

"My family, with yours, have only one-half a pound of bread stuff to a person, a day. We have vegetables and a little meat. We are doing first rate, and have no cause but to be very thankful; still I feed hundreds of others, a little, or they must suffer. . . .

"I shall be very glad when you return home to take a little of my burden off my shoulders, for it has been extremely hard for me and your mother to calculate, devise, and administer to near[ly] one hundred that are dependent on us. . . . Your mother is very sympathetic, and it gives her much sorrow, not because your children and mine cry for bread, but because of others. There was no need of rationing my family, but I did it for the sake of keeping hundreds of others alive. I foresaw these times more than three years ago, and prepared myself. . . .

"This people have been told . . . to build store-houses and lay up grain to last seven years, and hundreds of other things. Have they done it? No. . . . I can say in my heart, I wish to God this people would all listen to counsel, and do at the start as they are told, and move as one man, and be one. If this were the case, our enemies never would have any more power over us, our granaries never would be empty."[4]

AN EMIGRATION DILEMMA

In late 1855, Brigham Young faced a dilemma as he looked ahead to the next year's emigration season. On one hand, he wanted to keep the flow of emigrants coming. On the other hand, with food and money scarce in the territory, perhaps it would not be wise or even possible to bring in large numbers of emigrants until conditions improved.

The emigration required large amounts of both of these scarce resources. Each year, emigrants were met on the trail with many tons of provisions that Brigham Young described as "gratuitous."[5] After arriving in Utah, the newcomers typically needed to be fed from the existing food supply for the first season.

Even if problems with the food supply could be resolved—

Brigham Young

perhaps with a good harvest in 1856—the territory's crippling economic problems seemed to preclude a large emigration that year. By the end of 1855, Brigham Young reported that the Perpetual Emigration Fund, the primary source of financial assistance for the gathering, was in debt.[6] Unless the condition of the fund improved, he said, "we shall be obliged to measurably suspend operations in the ensuing year. We have . . . almost entirely absorbed every available resource of the Church to aid in this matter."[7]

Brigham Young appealed to all Saints to be "liberal in their donations" to the Perpetual Emigration Fund. He also appealed to emigrants to be "prompt in paying what they owe, that the Fund may be sustained, and our next year's operation be not crippled for the want of means."[8]

Despite these appeals, the flow of money into the fund either from new donations or the payment of debts nearly stopped because of the economic problems.[9] While struggling for survival, most of the Saints had no way to make such contributions or payments. In 1856 the fund had receivables of more than $100,000 that earlier emigrants were unable to pay.[10]

HANDCARTS: A RESOLUTION TO THE DILEMMA

Despite the hardships of famine and finances, Brigham Young felt so strongly about the gathering that he wanted to hasten it rather than slow it down. To do so, he decided to implement the handcart plan he had considered in 1852. This plan, he believed, presented the best opportunity to accelerate the emigration for two reasons. First, more people would be able to pay their own emigration expenses because the cost would be greatly reduced. Second, the limited resources of the Perpetual Emigration Fund could be extended to help more of those who could not pay their own way—thousands more, Brigham Young said.[11] Outlining the handcart plan in a letter to Franklin D. Richards, Brigham Young wrote:

"We cannot afford to purchase wagons and teams as in times past. I am consequently thrown back upon my old plan—to make handcarts and let the emigration foot it, and [carry] upon them the necessary supplies, having a cow or two for every ten [people]. They can come just as quick, if not quicker, and much cheaper. . . .

"The carts can be made without a particle of iron, with wheels hooped, made strong and light. . . . I think we might . . . save [the] enormous expense of purchasing wagons and teams—indeed we will be obliged to pursue this course, or suspend operations. . . .

"Their passage through to Iowa City . . . will not cost more than 8 or 9 dollars, and they will only have to be supplied with money for provisions and a few cows. . . . Of course you will perceive the necessity of dispensing with all wooden chests, extra freight, luggage, etc. They should only bring a change of clothing."[12]

A few weeks later in a general epistle, Brigham Young introduced the plan to the entire Church. More than just encouraging the Saints to pull handcarts to Zion, he announced that this was the expectation for those who received assistance from the Perpetual Emigration Fund:

"Let all the Saints, who can, gather up [to] Zion, and come while the way is open before them; let the poor also come, whether they receive aid or not from the Fund; let them come on foot, with handcarts or wheelbarrows; let them gird up their loins and walk through, and nothing shall hinder or stay them. . . .

"Let the Saints . . . who intend to immigrate [in] the ensuing year understand that they are expected to walk and draw their luggage across the plains, and that they will be assisted by the fund in no other way."[13]

According to the handcart plan, the emigrants would pull lightweight two-wheeled carts that had shallow boxes on top, about three feet wide by five feet long, for carrying their belongings. Five people would typically be assigned to each cart, and each of them would be allowed 17 pounds of personal belongings. The weight of the handcart itself would be 60 to 75 pounds, so the total weight, with luggage, would generally be about 160 pounds—not the unreasonable 500 pounds cited in some accounts.[14] Most of the carts would be heavier for a week or two in Nebraska since they would also be carrying 100 pounds of flour, but that would gradually diminish because it would be eaten before the flour carried on the wagons.[15] The plan also called for one supply wagon for every 100 people. These wagons would carry the heavy items—tents and most of the food—as well as the people who were sick or incapacitated.

Although traveling by handcart would lessen expenses, it would still require tens of thousands of dollars from the Perpetual Emigration Fund. With the fund in debt, and with few donations and repayments, where would this money come from? The words quoted previously from Millen Atwood allude to a large part of the answer:

"When Br. Brigham offered his property so liberally, and the word came that they should gather from England, it ran like fire in dry stubble, and the hearts of the poor Saints leapt with joy and gladness; they could hardly contain themselves."[16]

In late 1855, Brigham Young offered for sale $60,000 worth of his own property to help replenish the Perpetual Emigration Fund. This property included a large flour mill, houses, city lots, and farming land.[17] The largest single purchase of these assets was by a wealthy English convert named Thomas Tennant, who, while still in England, bought one of Brigham Young's homes for $25,000. As these proceeds and others were placed in the Perpetual Emigration Fund, President Richards could charter ships, and the gathering of the poor could proceed.

Thomas Tennant's story is told in more detail in the account of the Martin company. He, his wife, his son, and his wife's parents sailed from England on the Horizon, *leaving three weeks after the* Thornton. *In Iowa City they joined the Hodgetts wagon company, which traveled closely with the Martin handcart company. Unfortunately, Thomas Tennant never saw the home he bought, as he died in October near Scotts Bluff, Nebraska.*

CHAPTER 4

ADVANTAGES AND MISGIVINGS

Responsibility for getting the handcart plan underway fell primarily to President Franklin D. Richards. Following the lead of Brigham Young, he used every resource in his power—logic and labor, rhetoric and revelation—to promote the plan. To use a modern analogy, it may have seemed like offering bicycles when others had been given air-conditioned cars. Nevertheless, Brigham Young and Franklin D. Richards promoted the plan as not only viable but preferable to the traditional method of travel by ox-drawn wagons, for several reasons.

Speed. From Brigham Young: "They can beat any ox train crossing the plains."[1] From Franklin D. Richards: "The system of ox-trains is too slow and expensive. . . . In a short time emigrants will look back and wonder how they could have clung so long to this heretofore slow and laborious system of crossing the plains."[2]

Easier, more efficient preparation for the journey. From Franklin D. Richards: "It would be much more economical . . . in time, labour, and expense, if, instead of spending several weeks to obtain, and accustom to the yoke, a lot of wild, ungovernable cattle, impairing the health of many of the brethren by excessive labour and fatigue, . . . on the arrival of a company of Saints on the frontier they could have the necessary handcarts ready, and load them, and be 200 or 300 miles on their journey, with the same time and labour that would otherwise be expended in getting started."[3]

Less difficulty getting started each morning. From Franklin D. Richards: Those who traveled by ox-drawn wagon usually had to spend an hour or two every morning "driving up and yoking unruly cattle." While getting started each morning, they would typically "hear the word pass around that some brother has an ox missing, [and] then another hour, or perhaps half of the day, is wasted, . . . during which a company with handcarts would have performed the greater part of an ordinary day's journey."[4]

Less worry about animals. From Brigham Young: "In this way the expense, risk, loss, and perplexity of teams will be obviated."[5] From Franklin D. Richards: "There being but few animals in a handcart company, there will be less to tempt the cupidity of the Indians. A large share of that most laborious and harassing duty—guarding [animals]—can be dispensed with, and the time occupied with sleep and refreshment—with songs of rejoicing and prayer. The anxieties of mind about losing cattle by stampedes, poisonous water, and exhaustion will be avoided."[6]

Better health; fewer deaths. From Brigham Young: "After they get accustomed to it, they will travel 20, 25, and even 30 [miles] with all ease, and no danger of giving out, but will continue to get stronger and stronger; the little ones and sick, if there are any, can be carried on the carts, but there will be none sick in a little time after they get started."[7]

Brigham Young also believed that the intended route for the handcart Saints would help reduce the mortality rate from previous years. Before 1856, most emigrants traveled by ship to New Orleans and then went up the Mississippi and Missouri Rivers before getting outfitted. That route was plagued with cholera, malaria, and other deadly diseases.[8] The handcart plan would use a northern route to the outfitting camp. This route, Brigham Young believed, would help the Saints "escape the scenes of distress, anguish, and death which have often laid so many of our brethren and sisters in the dust."[9]

More timely arrival. Figuring the journey by handcart would take less time getting started and would cross the trail about two weeks faster than wagons, President Richards said emigrants would be able to arrive in the Salt Lake Valley by the middle of July. "They would then be in time to assist in gathering in the crops, and provide themselves with bread and necessaries for the winter."[10]

Less expense. A "well-finished, ironed, and painted" handcart cost $20. A "more primitive style, and without iron" cost only $10.[11] Wagons averaged $90, and oxen to pull them averaged about $70 a yoke, with three yoke required to pull a full wagon.[12] A wagon outfit, then, could cost $300.

Less personal indebtedness. Emigrants who traveled by handcart would be less indebted to the Perpetual Emigration Fund when they arrived in America. For some people, even repaying the relatively small loan they received to emigrate by handcart was burdensome.

"THE SCENES . . . PARTAKE LARGELY OF THE ROMANTIC"

While most of these advantages are defensible, the handcart plan may have been overpromoted at times. President Richards wrote, "When we allow our imaginations to wander into the future and paint the scenes that will transpire on the prairies next summer, they partake largely of the romantic."[13] Such idealizing was later criticized by John Chislett, who became one of the subcaptains of the Willie company. Instructions about the handcart plan, he said, "were published . . . with such a flourish of trumpets as would have done honour to any of the most momentous events in the world's history."[14]

Writing with the benefit of hindsight after the handcart tragedy, John Chislett also found fault with the emphasis that Church leaders placed on the plan's divine origin. In an early editorial, President Richards wrote, "The plan is the device of inspiration, and the Lord will own and bless it."[15] A few weeks later he wrote, "The mode [of travel] so nearly resembles that of ancient Israel in the wilderness that it must elicit the peculiar favour and blessing of the Lord upon it. . . . The present plan is peculiarly the Lord's."[16] John Chislett said that with such a declaration, "the word went forth to the faithful Mormons with the stamp of Divinity upon it."[17]

Not all of President Richards's editorials romanticized handcart travel, however. Occasionally he grounded his lofty language about the plan, exchanging it for a more realistic, pedestrian approach: "It is our constant desire not to mislead the Saints concerning the difficulties of the journey to Utah. We wish them calmly to make up their minds that it is not an easy task, and start with faith, . . . which will enable them to endure all things, and accomplish the desire of their hearts."[18]

RESERVATIONS ABOUT THE HANDCART PLAN

The most common reservation about the handcart plan was the difficulty of walking and pulling a cart so far. Another common reservation was the small luggage allowance. Many people worried that the limit of 17 pounds of personal luggage would prevent them from carrying even the necessities for a 1,300-mile trek. Others were troubled that they would not be allowed to take along heirlooms or other prized possessions.

A third reservation was the feeling that pulling handcarts would be degrading. Patience Loader of the Martin company recalled such feelings when she first learned of the handcart plan: "I could not see it right . . . to do such a humiliating thing. To be . . . harnessed up like cattle and pull a handcart loaded up with our bedding, cooking utensils, and our food and clothing and have to go through different towns to be looked at and made fun of as I knew we would be was very hurtful to my feelings."[19]

Responses of Brigham Young and Franklin D. Richards

Brigham Young responded to concerns about the handcart plan with typical candor: "If any apostatize in consequence of this [plan], so much the better, for it is far better that such deny the faith before they start, than to do so for a more trifling cause after they get here;

and if they have not faith enough to undertake this job, and accomplish it too, they have not faith sufficient to endure, with the Saints in Zion, the celestial law which leads to exaltation and eternal lives."[20]

Reflecting Brigham Young's feelings, Franklin D. Richards dismissed all worries about the handcart plan as "frivolous excuses."[21] In an early *Millennial Star* editorial on the subject, he wrote:

"Many men have traveled the long and weary journey of 2,000 miles from the Missouri River to California on foot, and destitute, in order to obtain a little of the shining dust [gold]—to worship at the shrine of Mammon. Who that appreciates the blessings of the Gospel would not be willing to endure as much and more, if necessary, in order to dwell with the righteous and reap the riches of eternal life?"[22]

Several weeks later President Richards responded to any lingering reservations by recalling a scriptural precedent:

"When ancient Israel fled from bondage into the wilderness, they had not even the privilege of taking provisions for their journey, but had to trust to the good hand of the Lord for their daily bread. . . .

"The Lord can rain manna on the plains of America just as easily as He did on the deserts of Arabia, or as He sent quails into the camp of the Saints on the Mississippi River in 1846. Ancient Israel travelled to the promised land on foot, with their wives and little ones. The Lord calls upon modern Israel to do the same."[23]

Reservations Illustrated: The James and Amy Loader Family

The typical reservations about the handcart plan are illustrated in the story of the James and Amy Loader family. James was 56 years old, Amy 53. They left England in December 1855 with 6 of their 13 children, ages 9 through 34. Like others at the time, the Loaders expected to travel the first part of the overland journey by train and the last part by wagon. After arriving in New York, they started working and saving while awaiting the time when wagon companies would be formed.

After a few weeks in New York, the Loaders received a letter from their son-in-law, John Jaques, saying they would be expected to travel by handcart rather than wagon. John worked closely with President Richards as the assistant editor of the *Millennial Star,* so his letter carried some authority. This news greatly distressed the family, and 28-year-old Patience Loader sent her brother-in-law a letter expressing their misgivings. She was emphatic that traveling by handcart would be physically impossible for them:

"Father and mother think this cannot be done, and I am sure I think the same, for mother cannot walk day after day, and I do not think that any of us will ever be able to continue walking every day. . . . If we girls were strong boys, then I think it might be done, but father is the only man in our family. I don't feel myself that I can go like this. . . . Mother, I am sure, can never go that way. She says herself that she cannot do it."[24]

The other complaint Patience expressed was that handcarts would require the family to leave behind too many of their possessions: "Why, we shall have to sell nearly all our clothes! And what shall we do for things to wear when we get to the Valley? Seventeen pounds weight is but very little."[25]

Patience also explained what it would take for her mother to have a change of heart about the plan: "Mother says that she must have a revelation before she can see this right."[26]

John Jaques's initial pleasure of receiving a letter from his wife's family turned to dismay as soon as he started reading it. He was so grieved that he "felt to weep . . . as Jesus did over the Jews."[27] In response, he wrote a scathing rebuke that he addressed not to Patience but to James, his father-in-law. "When your wife has heard this," he wrote, "I think she will fancy she has got revelation enough about the handcarts."[28]

The letter's indignant tone, which would be harsh even if it were directed to a recreant subordinate, begins in the first paragraph and rarely moderates:

"I could scarcely believe that you could have sent such a [letter]. There is not one atom of the spirit of Zion in it, but the very spirit of apostasy. I felt to exclaim in my heart, 'Who has bewitched you, and with whom have you been taking counsel, that you should so soon forget the goodness of the Lord in delivering you from this part of Babylon, and opening up your way to Zion?' . . .

"If I were to turn aside, on my way to Zion, for such trifling reasons as those in your [daughter's] letter, now that the Lord has so kindly given me the privilege of going, it seems to me that I ought to be damned. . . . As for me and my house, we will serve the Lord, and when we start we will go right up to Zion, if we go ragged and barefoot. Why do not you rise up as a man of God, and say that you and your house will serve the Lord, and will go up to Zion at all hazards?"[29]

As the letter continues, echoes of the words and tone of President Franklin D. Richards resound in nearly every sentence:

"Nothing has grieved me more for a long time than the light and contemptuous manner in which you speak of the handcart operation. Know ye not that it is the holy ordinance of the Lord, revealed through His Prophet Brigham, for the redemption of the humble, faithful poor, and that it will be blessed and sanctified of Him to the salvation of thousands who are not too proud to be saved in His appointed way? . . . The Lord has promised, through His servant Brigham, that the handcart companies shall be blessed with health and strength. . . .

"You have also thought of performing the journey in your own strength, forgetting that you should put your trust in the Lord. . . . You know that when He calls His Saints to do anything, if they will rely upon Him and do the best they can, He will fit the back to the burden, and make everything bend to the accomplishment of His purposes."[30]

Twice in her letter, Patience had said that rather than travel by handcart, the family thought it would be better to stay in New York or St. Louis until they could earn enough money to buy their own wagon. In New York, Elder John Taylor responded favorably to this idea,[31] but John Jaques gave it no accommodation:

"How can you expect the Lord to give you means to buy a

wagon when He has provided you a cart? He thinks that is good enough. Why should you think otherwise? Perhaps when you can buy a wagon, if you ever have the means, you will want to wait a little longer, till the railroad is made. And all this time your children will be growing up in all the wickedness of Babylon, and perhaps getting married among the Gentiles."[32]

John also gave Patience no sympathy over her concern about having to sell all her clothes:

"[Patience] seems very much afraid that she will not have clothes enough when she gets to Zion. Well, if she sets more store upon fine clothes than upon the counsel of the Lord and the blessings of living in Zion, I can say she is different to me. The fact is, she has too many clothes—they are a trouble to her, and she seems willing to hazard her salvation for them."[33]

In conclusion, John Jaques exhorted his father-in-law "to choose understandingly whom and what you will serve—Zion or Babylon, God or the devil. Greater consequences to yourselves, your children, and your ancestors hang on this decision than you can well imagine."[34] Making the wrong decision, he said, would "shipwreck your own salvation, and your children's too."[35]

What was the outcome of this spirited exchange? The Loaders must have been hurt by the letter's tone and accusations. Hurt must have been compounded by embarrassment when President Richards published both letters in the *Millennial Star* with little attempt to protect the family's identity. President Richards justified the risk of embarrassing or alienating the family by the belief "that others [who had similar feelings] might profit by the excellent and pertinent rebuke there administered."[36]

Hurt and embarrassment were no comparison for the next development from these letters. A returning missionary who passed through New York told the Loaders that people in England who read the letters thought the family was apostatizing.[37] Rather than create a rift with his son-in-law for allowing sensitive personal correspondence to become public, James Loader told his wife, "I cannot stand to be accused of apostasy. I will show them better. Mother, I am going to Utah. I will pull the handcart if I die on the road."[38]

Within a few days, all family members quit their jobs in New York and started for Iowa City. Soon after they arrived, John and Zilpah Loader Jaques arrived with the large group of Saints who sailed under the direction of Edward Martin. Patience says the reunion was happy, though it must have also been awkward.

The extended Loader and Jaques family would travel to Utah together as part of the Martin company. More of their story will be told in the account of that company. In brief, James Loader would die on the trail in Nebraska. His widow, Amy Loader, who had been so sure she could not make the journey, would become one of the stalwart examples of strength, leading and literally cheering on even her adult children through untellable difficulties. Flora Jaques, the two-year-old daughter of John and Zilpah, would die during the last week of the journey. Zilpah would also give birth to a son along the trail.

CHAPTER 5

AN ENTHUSIASTIC RESPONSE

Despite the difficulties the handcart plan would impose, thousands embraced it enthusiastically. President Franklin D. Richards later reported:

"We have not had much preaching to do to the people in the old countries to get them started out with handcarts. There were fifteen or twenty thousand waiting for the next year to roll around, that they may be brought out by the arrangement of the P. E. F. Company."[1]

Like Janet McNeil and Rachel Curtis, many who chose to emigrate risked everything to do so. The desire to gather to Zion was so fervent that people would go even if it meant leaving beloved family members or comfortable homes, even if it meant selling all their possessions, indeed, even if it meant pulling a handcart 1,300 dusty, difficult miles. Most of these Saints were willing to make any sacrifice for their religious convictions. The stories of a few of those who became members of the Willie handcart company are introduced in this chapter and further developed within the chronology of their westward trek. Summaries of their lives after they reached the Salt Lake Valley, along with some of their reflections on the handcart experience, are included in a later chapter.

EMILY AND JULIA HILL

Emily and Julia Hill, ages 20 and 23, were sisters who overcame great obstacles to join the Church and then gather to Zion. Emily tells how her preparation to hear the gospel began when she was young:

Emily (left) and Julia Hill

"When but a mere child I was much concerned about my eternal salvation and felt that I would make any sacrifice to obtain it. I asked all kinds of questions of my mother and sisters, seeking how to be saved, but could get no satisfaction from them nor from the religious body to which they belonged."[2]

Similar to Joseph Smith, in her youth Emily searched the scriptures for answers to her questions, "waiting for something, I knew not what." Her wait ended at age 12 when a cousin came to visit. Emily welcomed the visit because she expected to have some fun, but her cousin was "too full of a 'new religion' to do anything but preach." The next Sunday her cousin invited the family to a meeting that was being held in a village five miles away. Emily's family all declined, her brothers because of the distance and her sisters because they felt too respectable to attend a meeting "of such a primitive sect."[3] Laughing, Emily's sisters told her father, "Send Em, she will tell us all about it." Emily went, walking both ways. The meeting was held in a small house, and as the members bore their testimonies, Emily was touched by the Spirit and felt that she had found the truth. "It was indeed as though I had been brought 'out of darkness into marvelous light,'" she said.[4]

Overjoyed at finding what she had so long desired, Emily could hardly wait to get home to tell her family and friends. As soon as she entered the house, she said, "I astounded them all by the emphatic declaration that I knew the Latter-Day Saints were the right people and I would join them as soon as I was big enough."[5] This report displeased her parents, as they had been prejudiced against the Church. "I was never sent to 'take notes' of the Mormons again," Emily said, "but on the contrary was closely watched lest I should be led away."[6]

Emily showed remarkable strength in staying true to her convictions even though her parents refused to consent to her baptism. Criticized by those who said she was too young to judge such matters, she studied the scriptures so she could defend her faith. Within her family, Emily felt alone in her beliefs for some time until a missionary came to her home and bore such a powerful testimony that her older sister, Julia, wanted to join the Church. From that time on, Emily said, "I had a friend in the family, and we were both determined that cost what it might we would be true to the light within us."[7]

Emily and Julia were baptized in 1852, when Emily was 16 and Julia nearly 19. Soon after her baptism, Julia moved to Northampton, and a while later Emily went to visit her. Describing her time in Northampton, Emily wrote, "For the first time I enjoyed religious freedom, and there also I took my lessons of hard times, preparing me for greater hardships in store."[8]

Both sisters earnestly desired to gather to Zion, and both worked until they had earned enough money to emigrate. Despite their parents' objections, in May 1856 they joined the Saints on the *Thornton.* Eight years after Emily Hill had first heard the gospel, she was finally going to Zion.

JOSEPH AND EMILY WALL

Joseph and Emily Wall, two other siblings who were emigrating on their own, did so with the blessing of their parents. Joseph was 17 and Emily 16 when they left England, the oldest of nine children. Because the family could not afford to emigrate together, Joseph and Emily were sent ahead, and the rest of the family hoped to follow soon afterward.

Before Joseph and Emily left England, Elder Orson Hyde gave them a blessing in which he promised that they would complete their journey safely if they were faithful and obeyed the counsel of those in authority.[9] The fulfillment of this promise would require not only great faith but great sacrifice by Emily to help her brother.

SUSANNA STONE

Most people in the Willie company traveled with at least one other family member, and some traveled as large extended families. In contrast, Susanna Stone was the only member of her family to make the journey. Like Emily Hill, she studied the scriptures in her youth and yearned for more than her parents' church could provide. As she studied, she wished she could have lived in the days of apostles and prophets, not yet knowing that apostles and prophets were once again on the earth. When she was about 18, she learned of the Restoration and was baptized. "When I heard it preached, I hailed it with joy," she wrote.[10]

After joining the Church in 1848, Susanna wanted to gather to Zion. "My parents, relatives, and friends did all in their power to keep me from coming to America," she

Susanna Stone

wrote, "but I had the spirit of gathering and the Lord opened the way and I came to Utah in 1856 with a handcart company."[11]

Susanna was 25 years old at the time of the journey. Before it was over, she would be so buffeted that some who had known her in England would not recognize her. Despite these difficulties, she would later write, "I am thankful that I was counted worthy to be a pioneer and a handcart girl."[12] She would also testify that she was miraculously sustained by the power of God.

DAVID REEDER FAMILY

David Reeder, age 54, was emigrating with his son Robert (19) and his daughter Caroline (17). His wife had died in 1839. His daughter Eliza; her husband, James Hurren; and their children were also with the group. Robert gave the following explanation of the family's desire to emigrate:

"I left my old home where I was born and raised in the county of Suffolk, England, having embraced the gospel of Jesus Christ of Latter-day Saints some three years before that time, and being anxious to gather with the Saints in the valleys of the mountains, which I had heard talked and sung so much about. [I did not have] any idea or thought of the trials that would be in the way to contend with in completing the journey, but [was] moved solely by the spirit of gathering."[13]

The journey did not begin easily for Robert, as indicated by his description of the voyage across the ocean:

"I was very sick on the way and could not eat such food as they had on 'seafare,' which consisted of what they called sea biscuits and salt pork and salt beef, also brown sugar and vinegar and very little other food. I got very feeble living principally on sugar and vinegar for three weeks. I was glad when we arrived at Castle Garden, New York, where we could get a piece of bread once more."[14]

Despite his difficulty on the voyage, Robert would soon be the strongest member of his family. The challenges they faced—and the tragedies—will unfold in the pages that follow.

James and Eliza Hurren Family

James and Eliza Hurren were emigrating with their three daughters, Mary (7), Emma (4), and Sarah (2). When they left England, Eliza was expecting another child, who would be born on the journey. As mentioned above, the Hurrens were accompanied by Eliza's father, David Reeder; one of her brothers, Robert; and one of her sisters, Caroline. This family would soon face many sorrows and hardships. Their baby would die, and Mary's feet would freeze black. However, Eliza Hurren would later say, "We have never felt to murmur or complain or regret the steps we have taken."[15]

Ann Rowley Family

Ann Rowley was a widow who was emigrating with her seven children and one stepdaughter from her husband's first marriage. Sixteen years earlier, Ann and her husband, William, belonged to the United Brethren, a religious group that had broken off from the Wesleyans. After hearing Wilford Woodruff preach a "new gospel message," the Rowleys and all but one of the 600 members of the congregation were baptized. "We had only to hear him once and William and I knew with all our hearts that he was offering us a priceless treasure," Ann wrote.[16] Further showing the power of the gospel message, Ann said the Church of England sent a constable to one of the meetings to arrest Elder Woodruff. Instead, the officer was converted. The Church of England then sent two spies to attend the meetings and report back. "They too were converted," Ann wrote, "so the church dared not send anyone else."[17]

The Rowleys wanted to emigrate, but William died in 1849, and the family struggled to save enough money. "I knew that our parting was only temporary and that viewed from the eternities, this was but a fleeting moment," Ann wrote. "I also knew that no matter how fleeting a moment it was, I had to make the best of it. I had a very real job to do. The children had to be fed and clothed, but the big task and the one I must accomplish, is to get us all to Zion. I must be among the people of my faith and I must get the Temple work done for us."[18]

So urgent was Ann Rowley's desire to gather to Zion that after her husband died, all of her children who could earn money were put to work. Louisa and Elizabeth, ages 11 and 10 at the time, worked late into the night making gloves and doing needlework. John and Samuel, ages 8 and 6, worked in a brickyard tramping mud to be used for bricks. Finally, seven years after William Rowley's death, and with assistance from the Perpetual Emigration Fund, the family was ready to emigrate.

MARJORIE SMITH FAMILY

Marjorie Smith was another widow who was emigrating with her children. One son had already emigrated and strongly encouraged the rest of the family to follow. "He bids us to exert ourselves to emigrate," Marjorie told her children, "and says he will pray while we work."[19] The children who accompanied Marjorie were Jane (17), Mary (15), Betsey (13), and Alexander (6). Marjorie was also accompanied by a daughter from her first marriage, May Bain, and May's friend Euphemia Mitchell. Euphemia would later marry Marjorie's son who had already emigrated.

"The spirit of gathering to Zion was strong upon us," Betsey later wrote, "and we worked at our looms by day, our fancy work by night, and saved the proceeds. By this means, we gathered enough in six months to pay our passage across the sea; and in many ways we realized that God helps those who help themselves."[20]

As the Smiths left Liverpool on the *Thornton,* their native land tugged strongly at their hearts. Betsey wrote: "We finally took a last farewell of the sacred graves of our dead . . . and the heather hills of Scotland. [We left] the shores of Great Britain, our beloved native land, and dear old Scotland, for the gospel's sake."[21] This family would suffer greatly along the way. Despite these difficulties, Betsey would later write, "I will not dwell upon the hardships we endured, nor the hunger and cold, but I like to tell of the goodness of God unto us."[22]

William and Jane James Family

William and Jane James were emigrating with their eight children, ages 8 months to 19 years. Their three oldest daughters later wrote accounts of the journey: Sarah (19), Emma (16), and Mary Ann (11).

William James was a farm laborer in England. He struggled to provide for his family because of poor health, so his wife and older daughters worked to help the family subsist. When the missionaries came to their village in 1854, they were greatly impressed by the gospel message. Mary Ann recalled:

"The apostasy and restoration, unthought of before, appealed to [Mother], and she was led to prayer. The answer came and she was ready to leave all we had, and with an almost invalid husband and eight children, brave the journey to an unknown land and a wilderness."[23]

William James wanted to wait until his health improved to emigrate, but Jane felt they should go before their children began to leave home. She prevailed, and the family sailed to America on the *Thornton.* When they were nearly to New York, their baby daughter died. Mary Ann recalled: "My parents were called upon to part with their baby, . . . and we were obliged to place the precious bundle in a watery grave. Mother's heart strings were torn, but the brave little mother that she was felt not to murmur against the will of Him who gave."[24]

The difficulties for this large family would soon multiply. Jane James was a strong woman—in will, faith, and endurance. That strength would be needed both during the handcart trek and after the family settled in Zion.

George Cunningham

"As [I was born] on Sunday, I ought to be religious," George Cunningham wrote.[25] At age 15, George was emigrating with his parents, James and Elizabeth, and three sisters. An older brother would later emigrate with his own family in 1861. George's parents were the first converts in their district of Scotland.[26]

George Cunningham had endured a difficult childhood. To help sustain his family, he began working in a coal pit when he was 7 years old. Of this experience he wrote:

"I labored there for six years, often working twelve or fourteen hours a day, sometimes not seeing the light of heaven for a whole week, only on Sunday. . . . No one knows the dangers and privations experienced there, only those who have gone through the same."[27]

Living in such adverse circumstances, the Cunninghams were very thankful when they were given the opportunity to emigrate in 1856. "We sold our small effects and bade our friends farewell, took the train for Glasgow, and from there went by steamboat to Liverpool," George wrote.[28] A few days later they boarded the *Thornton*. George Cunningham was one person for whom pulling a handcart would perhaps be easier physically than his life in Great Britain.

SAMUEL AND ELIZA GADD FAMILY

Samuel Gadd joined the Church in 1841 and served as presiding elder at Bessems and Cambridge. Although the Gadds were "comfortably fixed farmer people" in England, Samuel was so moved by the spirit of gathering that he decided to uproot his family and join the Saints in Zion.[29] One unusual thing about the Gadd family was that Samuel's wife, Eliza, was not a member of the Church. Nevertheless, she agreed to emigrate so the family could stay together. Samuel and Eliza traveled to America with eight children, ages 2 to 19. The youngest were twin sons.

This family would have to endure many adversities, including three deaths. These anguishing difficulties would evoke remarkable responses from family members who survived.

John and Maria Linford Family

John and Maria Linford were emigrating with three sons, ages 11, 14, and 17. Two other children had died in infancy, and an older son, James, did not emigrate until 1861 because he was serving a mission at the time. Leaving him behind was especially hard because the family had been promised that if they emigrated, he would be released so he could go with them. "However," James later wrote, "when my parents received their notice of the time the ship would sail, my name was not on the notification. The only thing the family could do was to give up going or leave me to be a missionary. . . . It was a great disappointment to all of us, [but] I think I see the hand of the Lord in what occurred, for had I gone with my parents I might have died on the journey, as I was never healthy and strong and undoubtedly could not have withstood the hardships suffered by the handcart company."[30]

The Linfords had joined the Church in 1842 after hearing the gospel preached by Elder Joseph Fielding.[31] People in the Linfords' town of Gravely, England, were greatly prejudiced against the Church. Because John was a Church leader, serving as a counselor in the branch presidency and later as branch president, he and his family were especially persecuted. John had built up a good shoe-making business, but after he joined the Church his customers—even his relatives—tried to put him out of business. "If we cannot persuade him to give up Mormonism, we will starve him to it by withholding our work," they said.[32]

James Linford recalled that during these times of persecution and financial difficulty, "Father kept open house for the Elders as usual, and they never knew the straightened circumstances we were in. . . . My noble mother stood by my father without a murmur in this hour of trial. It was a dark outlook for a husband and father as financial ruin and starvation stared him in the face."[33] During this time the Linfords also paid donations to buy glass for the Nauvoo Temple, paid their tithing, and contributed to the support of their branch, which met every Sunday in their home.[34]

When the opportunity came to emigrate with assistance from the Perpetual Emigration Fund, the Linfords gladly took it. They sold their belongings for only £5 and left for Liverpool.

MARGARET KIRKWOOD FAMILY

Margaret Kirkwood was a widow from Scotland who was emigrating with her four sons, Robert (22), Thomas (19), James (11), and Joseph (5). Her husband and two daughters had died before the family emigrated.

Margaret and her oldest son would have to pull Thomas in the handcart during most of the trek. Margaret would often give 11-year-old James responsibility for 5-year-old Joseph. James and Joseph would face their ultimate test on Rocky Ridge, where Joseph would become unable to walk. This account will relate the extent of James's sacrifice for his brother, who would live another 77 years as a result of the ultimate expression of brotherly love.

JENS AND ELSIE NIELSON FAMILY

Approximately 100 Saints from Denmark joined the more than 600 from Great Britain who sailed on the *Thornton*. The Danish Saints included Jens and Elsie Nielson, their son Niels (nearly 6), and their friend Bodil Mortensen, who turned 10 during the journey. The Mortensens could not afford to emigrate together, so they entrusted Bodil to the Nielsons and hoped to join her in Utah the next year.

Jens and Elsie Nielson were very poor when they were first married, but soon they prospered. Jens wrote:

"The Lord blessed me on my right hand and on my left, and I was very successful, and prospects in temporal concerns were very bright. I was looked upon as a respectable neighbor and many times [was] invited to the higher class of society."[35]

In the fall of 1852, missionaries came to the Nielsons' neighborhood. Jens had heard only bad reports about the Church, but he decided to attend a meeting out of curiosity. "As soon as I saw these men's faces, I knew they were not the men as represented to be," he later wrote. "Before the meeting was out, I knew the testimony they bore was of God. We bought some few of their tracts and studied them for a few weeks and were perfectly satisfied the work was of God."[36]

Jens and Elsie were baptized in March 1854. "From that time on all my former friends turned against me and spoke all kinds of evil against me," Jens recalled. He and Elsie now had higher priorities than advancing in society. "All my possessions had no power over me," Jens wrote. "My only desire was to sell out and come to Zion."[37]

That year he found a buyer for his property, but before the sale was completed, a Church leader asked him to stay in Denmark for a time and serve a mission. Disappointed but obedient, Jens wrote:

"He told me I had been warned and it was my duty to warn others. That counsel came right in contact with my natural feelings, but the Spirit whispered [to] me I must obey, for 'obedience is better than sacrifice.' Then I was ordained a priest and sent out to preach with another young man holding the same priesthood."[38]

After Jens served a successful mission, he and his family prepared to emigrate. Jens sold his property and then took Elsie, Niels, and Bodil to England, where they joined the Saints on the *Thornton*. As they approached the New York harbor a few weeks later, the Nielsons made a great sacrifice. Many people needed financial assistance for the journey from New York to Iowa City. Elder Johan Ahmanson, who served as a counselor to James Willie and presided over the Danish Saints on the ship, appealed to those who had money to help those who did not. Jens and Elsie Nielson contributed part of their savings to assist those in need. Additional sacrifice would soon follow.

CHAPTER 6

MAKING PREPARATIONS

The gathering was not a haphazard operation. Church agents were responsible for every detail.

—PRESIDENT GORDON B. HINCKLEY

The commitment of Church leaders to the gathering is shown by their efforts to help people emigrate. Only a few Saints emigrated on their own—and Church leaders in fact discouraged them from doing so for their own well-being.[1] Most of those who came from Europe traveled in companies organized by the Church. To understand the story of the Willie company, it is helpful to have some knowledge of what was required to oversee the emigration of large groups of people in the 1850s.

PREPARATIONS IN LIVERPOOL

The Role of Missionaries

The Church's emigration efforts in Europe operated as part of the European Mission. The mission office in Liverpool included an Emigration Department, staffed largely by missionaries. In terms of effort and commitment of resources, the work of emigration was nearly as large as the work of finding and baptizing the converts in the first place. In terms of a missionary's duties, teaching and baptizing were just the beginning. Their work also included getting the converts on their way to Utah. The work of returning missionaries was not finished until they helped the converts reach the Salt Lake Valley. President Richards instructed these missionaries:

"We take this occasion to remind the Elders in these lands, who are expecting to go home during the coming season of emigration, that their mission is not done when they are released from their present fields of labour, nor yet when they leave the shores of Britain. You have been here preaching the Gospel—the principles of the gathering, and using every exertion to call into action the energies of the Saints to accomplish their deliverance; and it will devolve on you to aid those who emigrate [in] the coming season, to accomplish the task which lies before them.

"The poor have particular demands on you. On your journey home you should constantly seek how you can aid them by your experience, direct and comfort them by your counsels, cheer them by your presence, strengthen their faith, and keep the spirit of union and peace in their midst, that the destroyer may have no power over them.

"On your arrival in the United States, instead of feeling as though you had nothing to do but to get home yourselves, be in readiness to render any assistance or assume any responsibilities which those having charge of the emigration may see fit to place upon you. Make the interests of the gathering poor your interests, and be as anxious to see them safely home as yourselves.

"Travelling across the plains with teams has always been trying to the patience and perseverance of the inexperienced, and travelling with handcarts cannot be expected to be any less so. You cannot crown your mission with a labour more befitting your calling, or more consonant with the spirit of the Gospel you have been preaching, than to consider it your duty and privilege to assist the poor in gathering home."[2]

The Saints who would come to Utah in 1856 began leaving Liverpool on November 30, 1855. During the next six months, President Franklin D. Richards and those who assisted him oversaw the emigration of some 4,400 converts—the largest number of any year to that time.[3] Most of these emigrants traveled on eight ships, with the size of the groups ranging from 146 to 856.

Complexity of the Operation

The communication required for such mass emigration was daunting. Although most of those who emigrated in 1856 came from England, they also included converts from 14 other nations.[4] With communication rarely traveling faster than foot speed, President Richards and those who assisted him had to send information about emigration opportunities into every branch in Great Britain as well as other European nations. Then they had to gather applications and deposits from those who were emigrating, often on short notice. Next they had to communicate departure dates back to the field on notice of three weeks or less before departure.[5] And finally they had to receive confirmations and, in some cases, go through the entire process again to find substitutes.[6]

The scheduling associated with helping such large numbers of people emigrate was also complex. Based on the information President Richards gathered, he had to charter sufficient ships, a task that could be difficult because ships to the northern ports in America were sometimes in short supply. "We cannot expect to know the scarcity or plenitude of ships any great length of time before securing one," he wrote, explaining that "this depends upon the fluctuations of commerce, and also upon the winds, which at winter and spring seasons sometimes blow adversely for weeks."[7] The shortage of ships in 1856 was also a consequence of a severe winter and of the demand for vessels to transport men who were returning from the Crimean War, which had just ended. President Richards also had to coordinate scheduling with Church leaders in America who would oversee the overland travel.

The financial aspects of the emigration were similarly complex.[8] Accumulating enough money to charter ships was a constant challenge, especially because prices were escalating in 1856.[9] Accounting for this money was also a major task. It often came in small amounts, sometimes through appeals for generosity, sometimes through selling assets. Adding to the complexity, 2,012 of those who emigrated in 1856—nearly half the total—needed assistance from the Perpetual

Emigration Fund.[10] Because there were not enough resources to accommodate everyone who wanted to emigrate, sometimes President Richards had to make judgments about who merited such assistance and who should get priority.[11]

PREPARATIONS IN AMERICA

Making preparations in America was equally challenging. Historian Carol Cornwall Madsen explained:

"The organization required to coordinate sea, train, river, and overland travel for thousands of emigrants took masterful planning, especially in the days before the telegraph. LDS emigration agents . . . carried a tremendous responsibility for chartering ships, purchasing railroad tickets, preparing schedules, meeting emigrants at arrival and departure points, buying and distributing equipment and supplies, and keeping financial records in order."[12]

In America, the complexity of planning the 1856 emigration was compounded by the inauguration of the handcart plan. This plan was intended to make emigration faster and easier. However, because it was a new venture with new equipment and venues, the work required to get it started was enormous.

Implementation of the handcart plan in America was carried out largely by Church emigration agents, most of whom were missionaries returning from England. They were able, dedicated men who had considerable experience with emigration. They would work tirelessly with too little time and too few resources for a larger number of emigrants than they expected. They would work against circumstances that were beyond their control. Further complicating matters, they would work without the benefit of timely communication with those at the venues before and after them, usually hundreds or even thousands of miles away. Operations today that require a fraction of the complexity would seem impossible without hundreds of daily, instant communications.

New Venues: Iowa City and Florence

The handcart plan had four key venues: Liverpool; New York City (or Boston); Iowa City; and Florence, Nebraska. Liverpool was well established as the point of departure, and the affairs there were well organized under the direction of Franklin D. Richards. For the Willie company, New York City was the point of arrival, and the affairs there were well organized under the direction of another Apostle, John Taylor. But before the spring of 1856 the Church had virtually no presence in Iowa City or Florence, which were to be the key outfitting sites. Although Florence had been a major emigration base 10 years before, when Winter Quarters was established there, it had not been used for outfitting large companies for many years.[13] Therein lay the biggest challenge: Iowa City and Florence were probably the most important of all the emigration venues, yet the Church had no infrastructure or resources in either place for outfitting emigrant companies.

To prepare for the emigration of more than 4,000 people through Iowa City and Florence, agents had to do the following:

- Arrange for camping grounds and other property to be used for outfitting.
- Build handcarts (or contract to have them built) for each company.
- Obtain supply wagons and oxen for each company.
- Obtain cattle to provide beef and milk for the companies.
- Obtain tons of flour and other provisions, as well as tents and other equipment.

Profile of the Labors of a Church Emigration Agent

Missionaries began leaving England in February 1856 to prepare for the emigration; however, preparations in the Midwest had actually begun a few months before, with much of the work done by James McGaw and Andrew Cunningham.[14] James McGaw had gone to Florence and negotiated land to use for outfitting the companies.[15]

Later, as companies came through Florence, he would be the chief emigration agent there.

The first missionaries to leave England in 1856 were Elders William H. Kimball and George D. Grant. These men are perhaps best known for their efforts several months later in leading the rescue of the handcart companies, but their service to these companies began much earlier. Because their story parallels that of the Willie company, a profile of their preparatory labors is helpful in understanding the overall magnitude of their efforts during the year.

Elders Kimball and Grant arrived in New York City in late February. They met with Elder John Taylor to coordinate their assignments and then left for Iowa City. Arriving there in mid-March, they contracted to have 100 handcarts built.[16]

William Kimball then turned his attention to Florence. He traversed Iowa, a journey of 270 miles, and reached Florence on April 2. Building on the work of James McGaw, he immediately began calling on town leaders to make arrangements to bring large groups of Mormons back into the area. The next day he wrote to Elder John Taylor that he had succeeded in this key endeavor: "Met with proprietors of the town, with whom I have concluded satisfactory arrangements for making this the permanent starting point and outfitting place for our emigration."[17] With this, the approvals were in place for Florence—but the outfitting resources were still absent.

William Kimball's work was just beginning. In the next three days he had remarkable success in making other crucial arrangements. On April 7 he wrote to President Richards:

"Since I have been at this point, I have got some lands deeded to the Church at Florence, *alias* Winter Quarters, and am building a frame warehouse for the Church, 24 by 40 feet. I have also made arrangements for timber and fuel for

William Kimball

Church purposes, for the term of ten years, free of charge. I have also contracted our ferriage across the Missouri, Elk Horn, and Loup Fork rivers."[18]

In addition to all these arrangements, preparing Florence for the emigration also included fencing fields, putting in grain, building corrals, and assembling a supply of equipment and tools—all within about two months. A small group of men continued these preparations while William Kimball turned to his next assignment.[19]

Elder John Taylor had appointed William Kimball to purchase cattle for the emigration.[20] In mid-April, William left Florence and spent through the end of July crossing Iowa and Missouri several times to fulfill this assignment. In early May he was back in eastern Missouri. "Bought 2 mules for the emigration," he wrote on May 4. "Bought 48 oxen and branded them and started with them for Iowa City," he wrote on May 6.[21] It took him two weeks to get the oxen to Iowa City.

By late May, William Kimball was back in western Missouri, looking at cattle in Kansas City, St. Joseph, and elsewhere. He arrived in Florence with those animals in mid-June and then crossed Missouri again to St. Louis, arriving on July 10. Two days later he started west again for "the Bluffs," buying more oxen on the way. He arrived in Council Bluffs on August 2 and Florence on August 4. There he spent the next month assisting the handcart companies as they came through.

William Kimball finally left Florence for Utah on September 3, joining President Franklin D. Richards's small company of returning missionaries. Even after all this, the story will soon show that his service to the handcart companies was far from finished.

Arrival of Daniel Spencer in Iowa City

Elder Daniel Spencer, another missionary who was returning from England after four years of service, was appointed to be in charge of emigration in Iowa City. During part of his mission he had served as first counselor to President Richards in the mission presidency.[22]

Daniel Spencer left England in March 1856 with Elder John Van Cott and arrived in Iowa City on April 23. His first matter of business was finding a place for the emigrants to camp while they were getting outfitted. Hundreds of Saints were already on the Atlantic, and the first group would be in Iowa City in 19 days. He soon arranged to use some property on the Iowa River about three miles from town, negotiating a price of $50.

On his first day in Iowa City, Daniel Spencer examined the handcarts that were being built by contract laborers. In his journal he recorded this troubling assessment: "Examined the handcarts contracted by G. D. Grant which I did not much like."[23] Although he did not specify the problems, he probably thought the handcarts looked too frail to be trailworthy.

Daniel Spencer had earlier served as mayor of Nauvoo. After the exodus from Nauvoo in 1846, he served as a bishop of one of the wards in Winter Quarters. During the journey to the Salt Lake Valley in 1847, he had been president of two companies of 50.

Challenges in Building the Handcarts

Building handcarts was the most significant labor of the emigration of 1856. Unlike wagons, which could be purchased, every handcart had to be built new. Several problems were associated with this.

First, no one had built handcarts for such a purpose before, so the Saints had to design their own. In February 1856, C. R. Dana sent President Richards detailed specifications for the carts, outlining the materials required and the method of manufacture. "In this way I am confident that carts could be built that would be *substantial, light,* and *easy to draw*," he promised.[24] Regardless of how sound these specifications were in theory, however, they were still experimental. There was simply no way to know how well the carts would perform until they were tested on the trail. Four different designs were used in 1856, partly to see which one would work best.[25]

Second, emigration officials in America did not have a complete count of how many would be traveling by handcart. John Taylor said, "Not having been informed as to the exact numbers of the European emigrants who would want handcarts, I found it impossible to make any correct estimate as to the number that should be required."[26] He had contracted to have 100 built in St. Louis, and another 100 were being built in Chicago. These, together with the 100 that George Grant had contracted for in Iowa City, would accommodate 1,500 people. But the number of emigrants to travel by handcart kept growing until it reached 2,000, and the number of handcarts manufactured had to grow accordingly—to 400. To make up the difference, as well as to save costs, Daniel Spencer brought the construction of most of these extra handcarts in-house.[27] Chauncey Webb, a returning missionary who was a skilled wheelwright, supervised the construction.

A third problem in building the handcarts was procuring the proper wood. Brigham Young had instructed "that the best of seasoned lumber be used."[28] Seasoned lumber was essential for quality construction because green lumber would soon warp and split. Ideally, different types of wood were to be used for the axles (hickory), hubs (red or slippery elm), spokes and rims (white oak), and shafts and box (white ash).[29] Such lumber was apparently in short supply in Iowa City because the day after Daniel Spencer arrived, he sent John Van Cott all the way to Chicago—more than 200 miles—to obtain some.[30] John Van Cott returned on April 29, just 13 days before the first handcart emigrants would arrive.

Very soon the demand for seasoned lumber so greatly exceeded the supply that emigration officials began making costly compromises. Needing to hurry the handcart companies onto the trail, they began using green wood from trees they felled themselves. "Went with Bunker to the woods to chop logs for handcart timber 6 miles distant from camp," William Woodward wrote soon after arriving in Iowa City.[31]

CHAPTER 7

CHALLENGES FOR THE WILLIE COMPANY IN IOWA CITY

The tragedies the Willie and Martin companies would experience in October and November resulted from a conjunction of many causes, some of which occurred months earlier. One cause was their late departure from England. Another was the delay these companies experienced in Iowa City, where the handcarts, tents, and other equipment and supplies were not ready for them. Without these delays, the Willie company almost certainly would have arrived in Utah before the October storms, and the same is probably true for the Martin company. For this reason, the Iowa City delays merit careful examination, specifically of the following questions:

Why weren't the handcarts and other equipment ready?

Were the delays unreasonably long?

Could the delays have been prevented?

To what extent can these delays be blamed for the high mortality rate of these companies?

REASONS THE HANDCARTS AND OTHER EQUIPMENT WERE NOT READY

The season's first handcart emigrants arrived in Iowa City on May 12. The 534 people were divided into two companies, led by Edmund Ellsworth and Daniel McArthur. They took four weeks to outfit, leaving on June 9 and 11. Even before these first two companies left, another group of handcart emigrants arrived on June 2. They took more than three weeks to outfit before Edward Bunker led them out of Iowa City on June 25.[1] During the six weeks from May 12 to June 25, emigration leaders in Iowa City had worked tirelessly to equip and send off approximately 800 handcart pioneers in three companies.

On June 26, 1856, only one day after the third handcart company left, James Willie arrived with between 600 and 700 emigrants from the *Thornton*. Two weeks later, Edward Martin arrived with about 700 emigrants from the *Horizon*. Some of these Saints would be traveling in wagon companies, but 1,100 to 1,200 would be traveling by handcart. To outfit the handcart portion of these companies would require at least 250 handcarts, a dozen supply wagons, six dozen oxen, dozens of tents, 100 beef cattle and cows, 10 tons of flour, and other equipment and supplies.

Ideally, emigration leaders would have had all this ready when the Willie and Martin groups arrived, but they didn't. Why weren't they ready? The most common explanation is that there was miscommunication about the arrival of these groups; however, these leaders were not taken completely by surprise. They knew about the Willie group, with an approximate count of emigrants, at least two weeks before they arrived. They knew about the Martin group, again with an approximate count of emigrants, at least three weeks before they arrived.

In a June 11 letter to President Heber C. Kimball, William Woodward, who was clerk of the camp in Iowa City, announced the departure of the first two handcart companies and said, "We have heard that another ship of immigrants have arrived at New York by the ship *Thornton*, numbering when they left Liverpool 764 souls. We expect them at this point by the 16th or 17th of June."[2]

In a June 19 letter to Brigham Young, Daniel Spencer wrote, "I am looking every day for the arrival of the *Thornton* company, and in a few days for the last of the Fund Passengers by the *Horizon* [the ship that carried the Martin company]. They will together have nearly 1,200 souls to go by the handcarts."[3]

It is uncertain whether emigration leaders in Iowa City received word of these pending arrivals before June, and it could be argued that June was late to receive such information. However, even if these leaders had received word months in advance, there was little more they could have done to prepare for the Willie and Martin groups. Emigration leaders were already overextended in getting the first three handcart companies outfitted. The reason they were not prepared, then, seems to have more to do with their workload than with communication problems.

From the day the Willie group arrived to the day the Martin group left, the outfitting proceeded with all haste. Even inexperienced emigrants were put to work building and assembling handcarts. At the end of three weeks, the Willie company was ready to leave. One week later, Jesse Haven led the first half of the Martin company out of camp. After another few days, Edward Martin left with the other half. In the five weeks after the Willie group arrived, emigration leaders in Iowa City outfitted nearly 50 percent more handcart emigrants than in the previous six weeks. During this time they also helped finish outfitting the 400 members of the Hunt and Hodgetts wagon companies.

LENGTH OF THE DELAYS

Were the three-week delays for the Willie and Martin companies unreasonably long? Compared to the ideal expressed by Elder John Taylor, they were. When emigration agents had passed through New York in February, Elder Taylor had "emphatically stated that there must be no delay." In April he had written, "I wish the passengers, on their arrival at the place of outfitting, to be prepared to start the next day, or, in a day or two, at furthest."[4]

However, comparing these later handcart companies to the first three companies provides another perspective on this delay. As outlined earlier, those handcart companies had been delayed in Iowa City even longer than the Willie and Martin companies—about four weeks each—despite being much smaller. A modern comparison can also provide perspective on this delay. Today's trek reenactments usually take several months and a dozen committees to prepare, even though most of them have far fewer participants, last only three days, use handcarts that are already built, travel a total of 12 to 25 miles, and have the convenience of refrigerated trucks and motor homes nearby.

Considering the logistical challenges of preparing 1,100 to 1,200 people for such a difficult journey, and given that some of these preparations had to start with uncut lumber and fabric, finishing them in only five weeks for the last two companies of 1856 is perhaps one of the most underappreciated efforts of the entire handcart experience.

PREVENTION OF THE DELAYS

Could the delays in Iowa City have been prevented? Perhaps, but only if emigration leaders had been able to have everything ready for the first handcart companies when they arrived in May. Once those companies were delayed, the arrival of the other companies in such rapid succession made it impossible to get ahead in preparing for them. In any case, it seems unlikely that better communication about the coming of the Willie and Martin companies could have prevented the delay they each experienced.

EFFECT OF THE DELAYS ON THE MORTALITY RATE

To what extent can the delays in Iowa City be blamed for the high mortality rate of these companies? The two main causes of death would be lack of food and early winter storms. As will be shown later, the handcart companies probably would have run low on food regardless of the delays in Iowa City. But again, if everything had been ready when the Willie and Martin companies arrived in Iowa City, they probably would have made it to Salt Lake City before the winter storms. So the delays were indeed costly. But as costly as they were, Brigham Young would later imply that the delays were not the main cause of the tragedy. The main cause, he said, was the decision to send the emigrants on from the Midwest despite the lateness of the season (see page 167).[5]

SUMMARY OF EFFORTS TO PREPARE FOR THE EMIGRATION

This account may seem unusually sympathetic toward Church emigration agents and others who were sent to prepare for the emigration. Criticism of their efforts is more common, as represented in the words of John Chislett:

"Preparations on the frontiers were altogether inadequate to the number of emigrants, as indeed were the preparations throughout the entire journey west of New York. For instance, several hundred emigrants would arrive at Iowa City, expecting to find tents or some means of shelter, as agents had been sent from Liverpool to purchase tents, handcarts, wagons, and cattle, and to prepare generally for the coming flood of emigrants. But they were doomed to disappointment. There were no wagons or tents and, for days after their arrival, no shelter but the broad heavens. They were delayed at Iowa City for some weeks . . . while carts were being made, and this, too, when they should have been well on their way."[6]

Despite John Chislett's assessment, the evidence presented here suggests that emigration leaders in Iowa City did the best they could under the circumstances—and perhaps as well as or better than anyone else could have done.

POOR LIVING CONDITIONS

While the Willie company was in Iowa City, the lack of equipment and supplies was not the only problem. Living conditions were often trying. The response of the Saints to these discomforts, many of which they could have felt were the result of bad planning and organization, reveals much about them.

At first there was a severe shortage of tents, leaving many people without shelter from daily thunderstorms. On the first night, George

Cunningham recalled, "the sky began to gleam with lightning streaks, followed in rapid succession until some parts of the firmament seemed entirely in a flame. The rain commenced to fall in torrents, [and] the wind blew most terrible. We were there without the least particle of shelter, no tent, no cover whatever."[7]

Despite these heavy rains, the company journal records that "the Saints [were] all cheerful and . . . doing the best they can without tents."[8] When rains returned that night, the journal records that "the Saints bore it with fortitude, perfectly resigned to the will of Heaven. Union and love seem to prevail with all." Even after a week of sewing tents, many people were still without shelter. "The tents not being done, we had [another] good soaking," the journal reports.[9]

While most people endured the poor living conditions with "little discontent,"[10] George Cunningham recalled some murmuring:

"Such storms continued for several successive nights. Of course, some growled and repined about the good homes they had left. Indeed, many felt like the ancient Israelites, who looked back and moaned after their leeks and onions of Egypt. But after a few days, cloth was procured and tents were made and things went along much better."[11]

The heat compounded the problems caused by the rain. Afternoon temperatures in the tents approached 110 degrees. "The Iowa heat was steamy," wrote Wallace Stegner. "Reared in England's gray cities, the pale novices sweltered, crowded three or four families to a tent. Children whined with prickly heat, . . . and when the heat wave finally broke, the rain came with such a rush of thunder, lightning, and wind that it trampled their tent town as if stampeding elephants had run over it."[12]

The poor living conditions also contributed to illness. Thirteen-year-old Betsey Smith, who emigrated with her widowed mother, three sisters, and a brother, became so ill with scarlet fever in Iowa City that she could not open her eyes. A baby had just died in camp, and Betsey overheard one of the women saying, "I am sorry she is dying; another death in camp soon."[13] When Betsey's mother brought her some broth a while later, Betsey was scared and crying because of what she had heard. "Mother, they think I am dying; I want to live and go to the Valley," Betsey said. Her mother immediately brought some elders to administer to Betsey. "[They] rebuked the disease," Betsey recalled, "commanding it to leave both me and the camp. My recovery was rapid. I was able to travel."[14]

LACK OF EXPERIENCE

Wallace Stegner identified another kind of challenge the Saints faced in Iowa City: their background and lack of experience. The following description is of the first handcart companies, but it applies equally well to the Willie group:

"In all its history, the American West never saw a more unlikely band of pioneers than [those] who were camped on the bank of the Iowa River at Iowa City in early June, 1856. Looking for the brown and resolute and weather-seasoned among them, you would have seen instead starved cheeks, pale skins, bad teeth, thin chests, all the stigmata of unhealthy work and inadequate diet. There were more women than men, more children under fifteen than either. One in every ten was past fifty, the oldest a woman of seventy-eight; there were widows and widowers with six or seven children. They looked more like the population of the poor farm on a picnic than like pioneers about to cross the plains.

"Most of them, until they were herded from their crowded immigrant ship . . . and dumped here at the brink of the West, had never pitched a tent, slept on the ground, cooked outdoors, built a campfire. They had not even the rudimentary skills that make frontiersmen. But as it turned out, they had some of the stuff that makes heroes."[15]

Stegner goes on to describe the handcart emigrants as "casualties of the industrial revolution, . . . to whom Mormonism had brought its irresistible double promise of a new start on earth and a guaranteed Hereafter."[16] What was it, then, that helped these people become heroes? That many of them came from such a low condition and would show such strength and courage in the most extreme adversity is not merely a manifestation of the will to survive. It is perhaps even more an indication of the transforming power of the gospel of Jesus Christ.

SACRIFICES IN PREPARING FOR THE JOURNEY

Jens and Elsie Nielson Sacrifice Their Savings

Although Jens and Elsie Nielson were not wealthy, they had sold their property before emigrating and had more means than many others. As their ship approached the New York harbor a few weeks earlier, they had been encouraged to give part of their savings to help the poor. They had generously done so.

That was just the beginning of the Nielsons' sacrifice. In Iowa City another call was issued to help the needy. "I had money enough to come to Utah," Jens later wrote, "but we were counseled to let all the money go we could spare and cross the plains with handcarts."[17] At a time when the Nielsons could have been justified in keeping enough money to ensure the security of their family and perhaps even provide a modest start in Utah, they followed their leaders' counsel and gave nearly all the rest of their savings to help those in need. Describing this sacrifice, one of the Nielsons' descendants wrote:

"Upon arriving at the end of the railroad in Iowa, Jens Nielson obtained a victory which to most of us is the most difficult of all, that of parting with money and security. He had the money from the sale of his farm, and [he] let all of [it] go to the Church except enough to buy a handcart and to stock it with 15 pounds of belongings per person. Thus, he could have obtained wagons, horses, stacks of food, and other supplies and traveled west in style and comfort, and early enough to beat the winter.

"He gained the great victory over selfishness by parting with his life's savings and demonstrated his unyielding faith [in order] that those Saints who had nothing might at least have a handcart. . . . Jens [and his family] were left with a handcart, poorly constructed of green lumber, and unfit for the journey."[18]

This sacrifice would require an immense cost. The full extent of it will be detailed as the rest of the Willie company story unfolds.

Ann Rowley Chooses Zion

For even the poorest of the handcart pioneers, such as Ann Rowley, a widow traveling with eight children, the luggage limit of 17 pounds meant leaving behind things they valued greatly. Ann recalled that in Iowa City "everything that even hinted of being a luxury [had to] be eliminated. There were many keepsakes that I wanted to take but couldn't. But there was one thing I didn't consider a luxury and that was my feather-bed. I had hung onto that beloved item from the time of the auction in England and now clearly there was no room for it. It wouldn't be so bad to walk 1,300 miles if one had a feather-bed to sleep on at night, but no matter how I folded it, it was too bulky. Wouldn't it just be wonderful, I thought, if I could deflate it in the morning and inflate it at night, so it would pack compactly. But a feather-bed is a feather-bed, and when it came to choosing between Zion and a feather-bed, well it was a little too late to turn my back on Zion, so I ripped it open and emptied the feathers on the ground and used the tick to cover the supplies on the handcart."[19]

FORMAL ORGANIZATION OF THE WILLIE COMPANY

On July 12, Daniel Spencer organized most of the Saints who had sailed on the *Thornton* into "the 4th Division of the P. E. F. Handcart Company."[20] James Willie was appointed to continue as their leader. Millen Atwood, Levi Savage, William Woodward, John Chislett, and Johan Ahmanson were appointed subcaptains who would each oversee 100 people.

James G. Willie

James G. Willie

James G. Willie was returning from a mission to England. Born in England in 1814, he was well educated in an English boarding school and then learned the mercantile business. When he was 21, he went to America to seek his fortune, settling in New York. Six years later, in 1842, he obtained a different kind of wealth when he joined the Church. The next year he served a mission in the East.

In 1846, James Willie and his fiancée, Elizabeth Pettit, left New York and traveled to Nauvoo. They hoped to receive their temple endowment and be sealed, but Nauvoo was nearly deserted when they arrived because the Saints had been forced to leave earlier than expected. James and Elizabeth were married civilly and traveled across Iowa to Winter Quarters, where they spent the winter of 1846–47. In the summer of 1847 they left for the Salt Lake Valley, arriving just three months after the first pioneer company.

In August 1852, James Willie heard his name announced from the pulpit, calling him to return to England as a missionary. The next month he left Elizabeth and three small children to preach the gospel in his native land. He was formally released from his mission in February 1856, but like other returning missionaries, he was told that his mission would not be complete until he helped the emigrating Saints arrive in Zion.[21]

Millen Atwood

Like James Willie, Millen Atwood was returning from a mission to England. Born in Connecticut, he went to Nauvoo in 1841 and joined the Church. He knew the Prophet Joseph Smith personally and fulfilled many important Church assignments. In 1847 he traveled to the Salt Lake Valley under the direction of Brigham Young and returned to Winter Quarters that same year. Like James Willie, he was called to serve a mission to Great Britain in 1852. After laboring in several areas of Scotland and England, he was released in 1856. He had served as a counselor to James Willie during the voyage on the *Thornton*.[22]

Levi Savage

Levi Savage was born in Ohio in 1820 and grew up in Ohio and southern Michigan. His father and some other family members were baptized in 1843 by missionaries who went to Michigan from Nauvoo. Levi affiliated with the Church but was not baptized until 1846, just before enlisting in the Mormon Battalion.[23]

After completing his battalion service in 1847, Levi Savage started for the Salt Lake Valley to find his family. Arriving in October, he found his father and some other family members there, but his mother had died near Council Bluffs, Iowa.

Levi Savage married Jane Mathers in 1848, and they had a son, Levi Mathers Savage, in January 1851. Eleven months later, Jane died. Ten months after that—when his son was not yet two years old—Levi was called on a mission to Siam (Thailand). He left his son with his sister, departed from Salt Lake City in October 1852, and sailed from San Francisco to Calcutta and then to Burma (Myanmar). Twice obstructed in his efforts to get to Siam, he served in Burma for nearly two years. He tried to teach the gospel to the native people but struggled to learn Burmese, had no Church materials

Levi Savage

in the language, and found the people uninterested. In May 1855 he wrote to President Richards:

"I have been . . . labouring under the most adverse and trying circumstances, with no other view but the advance of our Redeemer's cause, but with very little success. My faith has failed me, and I have become discouraged, and intend to leave for Zion as soon as possible."[24] Surely his thoughts and heart were turned to his 4-year-old son in Utah, who had been without a parent for two and a half years.

Levi Savage was returning from his mission at the time he was made a subcaptain in the Willie company. He had sailed from Burma to Boston and then traveled to Iowa City, arriving just four days before the Willie company would depart. That day he wrote in his journal: "I reported myself to Brother Daniel Spencer, the agent for forwarding the saints. He requires my assistance, and I commenced."[25] The next day he was appointed captain over the second hundred of the Willie company. He was one of the few who kept a daily journal of the trek. His story would become one of the most compelling of any in the company.

William Woodward

William Woodward was born in England in 1833, joined the Church in 1848, and emigrated to America in 1850. Soon after arriving in Salt Lake City, he returned to England as a missionary. When he was released in 1856, he sailed on the *S. Curling* with those who would compose the third handcart company, led by Edward Bunker. Instead of traveling with the Bunker company, though, he remained in Iowa City for a few more weeks, serving as clerk of the camp and helping outfit the companies before being assigned to the Willie company. Like Levi Savage, he kept a daily journal of the journey. In October he was assigned to keep the Willie company journal.

John Chislett

John Chislett was born in England in 1834. He joined the Church as a young man and was called directly from his homeland to serve as a missionary. After completing his missionary service, he and his fiancée, Mary Ann Stockdale, emigrated together on the *Thornton*. They and a few other couples in the handcart companies were postponing marriage until they arrived in Salt Lake City because they wanted to be sealed in the recently completed Endowment House.

John Chislett

Although John Chislett did not keep a daily journal, he later wrote a detailed account of the journey that is cited frequently in these pages.

Johan Ahmanson

Johan Ahmanson has already been introduced as the counselor to James Willie who presided over the Danish Saints on the *Thornton* (see page 47). He was among the first people to receive the gospel in Denmark. After he was baptized, he served as a missionary in Denmark and Norway. For part of his mission he was assigned to be a traveling elder throughout all the conferences of the Scandinavian Mission. In April 1856 he led 162 emigrants from Denmark over the North Sea to Liverpool.[26]

Johan Ahmanson planned to make the journey from Iowa City by wagon, but before he left Liverpool, President Richards asked him to serve as a subcaptain in the handcart company. "Emigrants of larger means naturally preferred to travel in the customary way [by wagon], and that is what I [planned] as well," he wrote. "But F. D. Richards had requested me to escort the indigent Danes with their train of handcarts, since I was the only one of them who had any competence in English."[27]

In Iowa City, Johan Ahmanson arranged for his wife and young son to travel with the Hodgetts wagon company while he fulfilled his assignment with the handcarts. His handcart division, he said, "consisted of 93 Scandinavians, for which I was appointed leader; but the honor connected with this post was slight, and the advantages even less than that."[28] Indeed, like Captain James Willie, each of the sub-captains made significant sacrifices to fulfill their assignments.

CHAPTER 8

FROM IOWA CITY TO FLORENCE, NEBRASKA

After spending nearly three weeks getting ready for the journey, the Willie company left Iowa City on July 15. It consisted of nearly 500 people, 120 handcarts, 25 tents (each sleeping 20 people), 5 supply wagons (carrying food and tents), 24 oxen (for pulling 4 of the wagons), 5 mules (4 were used to pull the other wagon), and 45 beef cattle and milk cows.[1]

"All seemed in first rate spirits," the daily journal recorded as the members of the Willie company began pulling handcarts.[2] Sub-captain John Chislett said the group "presented a singular, and sometimes an affecting appearance" as they pushed and pulled their way across Iowa toward Florence, Nebraska, some 270 miles away:

"The young and strong went along gaily with their carts, but the old people and little children were to be seen straggling a long distance in the rear. Sometimes, when the little folks had walked as far as they could, their fathers would take them on their carts, and thus increase the load that was already becoming too heavy as the day advanced. But what will parents not do to benefit their children in time of trouble? The most affecting scene, however, was to see a mother carrying her child at the breast, mile after mile, until nearly exhausted. The heat was intense, and the dust suffocating, which rendered our daily journeys toilsome in the extreme."[3]

Almost immediately the pulling of handcarts began to separate those who were truly committed from those who were not. The company journal tells of at least 15 people who turned back within the first 10 days of leaving Iowa City. The journal entries are made in a matter-of-fact tone, giving no explanations and leaving unanswered what prompted the change of heart and what became of those who left:

"Sister Adelaid A. Baker left us and this morning came and took her luggage and two of her children away with her."[4]

"Charles Peat and family, with Martha and four children from Worcester, England, left us this morning."[5]

Millen Atwood, one of the subcaptains, gave one explanation for the people leaving:

"The Saints found . . . a wide difference between singing about going to Zion, and actually going. You would almost have thought that they would take wings and fly like doves, . . . but when they really got into the work, the tune was a little different; but the great majority stuck to it."[6]

REACTIONS OF IOWA RESIDENTS

Rather than following the same river for any considerable distance, the handcart route across Iowa used existing roads to travel what has been called the "river to river route."[7] These roads passed through beautiful prairie land with abundant grass and, in most places, wood.

Iowa was the most populated part of the handcart route, so the companies also passed through many towns. Experiences with the residents of these towns were mixed. "The inhabitants are generally very kind, but others manifest more of the mobbing spirit," Levi Savage wrote.[8] At first, threats and disturbances occurred almost daily. One night a group of 30 men came and caused trouble. The next evening a posse of men came with a warrant to search the supply wagons, having heard "that the women were detained contrary to their wishes with ropes."[9] Sometimes when the company passed through towns, residents would try to persuade the women to leave. At other times the people who came to visit the handcart camp were, in Levi Savage's words, "very civil."[10]

Millen Atwood recalled the humiliating treatment that occasionally occurred during this part of the journey: "The gentiles . . .

laughed us to scorn and ridiculed the idea of men and women traversing 1,200 miles with handcarts." For all their scorn, though, "they marveled to see the Saints travel on so cheerfully" and were deeply curious about the motivating power behind this movement. Millen Atwood explained:

"They were astonished, and wanted to know what kind of a doctrine we preached to them to make them willing to undertake such a task. I told them that we administered the same kind of medicine to all, and it united them together."[11]

George Cunningham, who was 15 at the time, also recalled the negative comments:

"People would mock, sneer, and deride us on every occasion for being such fools as they termed us, and would often throw out inducements to get us to stop. . . . When we went through a town or settlement pulling our handcarts as we always had to do, people would turn out in crowds to laugh at us, crying 'gee-haw' as if we were oxen."[12]

It would be reasonable to expect a 15-year-old to shrink with embarrassment at such treatment. But George Cunningham showed remarkable strength of resolve:

"We told them that we were going to Zion and would not stop on any account," he said. "This did not discourage us in the least, for we knew that we were on the right track."[13]

One showing of goodwill occurred about halfway across Iowa in Des Moines. A gentleman named Charles Good gave James Willie 15 pairs of children's boots for the company. James Willie wrote, "I readily accepted [them] as he seemed to be interested by a sincere desire to do good."[14]

John Chislett seemed to recall more good treatment than bad while traveling through Iowa:

"The people in Iowa were very good in giving to those who asked for food, expressing their sympathy for us whenever they visited our camp—which they did in large numbers if we stopped near a settlement. They tried to dissuade us from going to Salt Lake in that way, and offered us employment and homes among them.

Handcart company passing through Iowa

A few of our company left us from time to time, but the elders constantly warned us against 'the Gentiles' and by close watching succeeded in keeping the company tolerably complete."[15]

SHORT FLOUR RATIONS

Flour was the dietary staple of the handcart pioneers, with adults typically receiving a daily ration of one pound. A pound of flour has about 1,600 calories—not much compared to the estimated 4,000 calories a day it takes to pull a handcart. The flour was supplemented by meat from the cattle and from wild game.

Members of the Willie company were given a daily flour ration of only 10 ounces for the trek across Iowa, likely because outfitters thought they could obtain additional food along the way. Levi Savage gave this succinct assessment of the ration: "It is not enough."[16] John Chislett was more expressive:

"Our rations consisted of ten ounces of flour to each adult per day, and half that amount to children under eight years of age. Besides our flour we had occasionally a little rice, sugar, and bacon. But these items (especially the last) were so small and infrequent that they scarcely deserve mentioning. Any hearty man could eat his daily allowance for breakfast. In fact, some of our men did this, and then worked all day without dinner, and went to bed supperless or begged food at the farmhouses as we travelled along."[17]

Breakdowns

Handcart breakdowns were a problem for all the companies of 1856. Because the construction of handcarts was a new undertaking, there had not been an opportunity to identify the flaws by trial and error and resolve them. Daniel McArthur, who had led the second company across Iowa a few weeks earlier, described the problems with his group's handcarts:

"Our carts, when we started, were in an awful fix. They moaned and growled, screeched and squealed, so that a person could hear them for miles. You may think this is stretching things a little too much, but it is a fact, and we had to eternally patch—mornings, noons, and nights."[18]

The Willie company's 120 handcarts were probably even worse than the McArthur company's. They had been built more hastily, using more unskilled laborers, and using more unseasoned wood. John Chislett described the constant breakdowns of the Willie handcarts and the various remedies that were tried:

"The axles and boxes being of wood, and being ground out by the dust that found its way there in spite of our efforts to keep it out, . . . had the effect of breaking the axles at the shoulder. All kinds of expedients were resorted to as remedies for [this], but with variable success. Some wrapped their axles with leather obtained from boot-legs; others with tin, obtained by sacrificing tin-plates, kettles, or buckets from their mess outfit.

"Besides these inconveniences, there was felt a great lack of a proper lubricator. Of anything suitable for this purpose we had none at all. The poor folks had to use their bacon (already totally insufficient for their wants) to grease their axles, and some even used their soap, of which they had very little, to make their carts trundle somewhat easier."[19]

MARKING THE WAY WITH WOODEN HEADBOARDS

Two members of the Willie company died on the journey across Iowa. One of them was Selena Hurren, who was born the day before the company left Iowa City and died just two weeks later. Her body was covered with a small cloth and buried in a grave that her parents and three older sisters would never visit again. Four-year-old Emma Hurren remembered that her father lifted her to his shoulder so she could see the burial of her baby sister.[20]

Wallace Stegner described the feelings of those who were left to carry on after the deaths of loved ones, often leaving the same day as the burial: "They marked their way with wooden headboards, and on mornings when one of those graves must be left behind, there were men and women who went numbly, head down, pushing like sleepwalkers at the crossbars and feeling the heaviness of the cart drag like the total weight of what they there gave up."[21]

CHAPTER 9

DIFFICULT DECISIONS
IN FLORENCE

The Willie company pulled into Florence, Nebraska, on August 11. They had taken nearly a month to travel the 270 miles from Iowa City. With only two deaths and few people turning back, the handcart experience was looking like a success. Wallace Stegner observed that to that point, the walking was more beneficial than detrimental—just as Brigham Young and other Church leaders had said it would be:

"They had pulled and pushed their carts nearly three hundred miles in less than a month. The sun had burned them brown, [and] camp life and hard walking had toughened their muscles. As Brigham had prophesied, there were fewer sick. The children . . . had already hardened into health."[1]

This does not mean the walking was easy, however. Agnes Caldwell described how it felt on her 9-year-old legs:

"Although only tender years of age, I can yet close my eyes and see everything in panoramic precision before me—the ceaseless walking, walking, ever to remain in my memory. Many times I would become so tired and, childlike, would hang on the cart, only to be gently pushed away. Then I would throw myself by the side of the road and cry. Then realizing they were all passing me by, I would jump to my feet and make an extra run to catch up."[2]

Even the ever-determined Emily and Julia Hill struggled with the endless walking. Emily recalled:

"My sister broke down and was unable to walk, and I remember asking myself (footsore and weary with the first week of walking and working) if it was possible for me, faith or no faith, to walk twelve hundred miles further. The flesh certainly was weak but the spirit was willing."[3]

DELAYS IN FLORENCE

After Iowa City, Florence was the most important stop for the handcart pioneers. There they received assistance and supplies for the final thousand miles of the journey. Starting with almost nothing a few months earlier, emigration agents had established a bustling way station in Florence. They had built workshops, a warehouse, and other supply buildings. They had also established a large encampment for the Saints and had built corrals for the animals. As emigrant companies came through Florence, it became a flurry of activity.

The first two handcart companies had been delayed in Florence for two weeks to rest and repair handcarts, the third company nearly as long.[4] The Willie company would also need time in Florence for repairs. Some of the carts required new axles, and all of them needed iron on the wheels because the wood was wearing away.[5]

Just as procuring materials had been a challenge in building the handcarts, it remained so in repairing them. The journal of William Woodward, one of the subcaptains, reveals a glimpse of what it took to obtain these materials in Florence. Although he was sick with fever, the second day after arriving he went six miles south to Omaha to purchase hoop iron for the wheels. After trying all day without success, he crossed the river and spent the night in Council Bluffs. The next day he was finally able to buy 61 pounds of iron. Although this was probably not as much as he hoped for, he hurried back to Florence, and the men immediately began to put it on the wheels.[6] Time of delay: two valuable days.

Like the delays in Iowa City, the delays for repairs along the Iowa trail and in Florence are often cited as contributors to the forthcoming tragedy. These delays were not unusual, however, and giving them undue culpability minimizes the tremendous success in reducing them. The Willie company had not only moved out of Iowa City more quickly than the first three companies but crossed Iowa a little more quickly, and they would be delayed in Florence for a much shorter time. The same is true for the Martin company, which was 11 days behind the Willie company at the time. In fact, from the date of arrival in Iowa City to the date of departure from Florence, the Willie company would take 52 days and the Martin company 50. The first three companies had taken 69, 73, and 60 days, respectively.

Despite these increased efficiencies, the Willie company was losing the race against the earth's vernal turn. Summer was ebbing, and with it their margin of safety. Mid-August was late for a large company, traveling on foot, to leave Florence. The Salt Lake Valley was still 1,031 miles away, and this span included the most difficult parts of the trail. Constant stream and river crossings, inhospitable terrain, ascents of thousands of feet in elevation, and sandy and rocky trail conditions would try even the best-equipped companies in the best weather.

The Pleadings of Levi Savage

In addition to being a repair and resupply stop, Florence was also a potential site for spending the winter. The Church had established Winter Quarters there after the exodus from Nauvoo 10 years earlier. For shelter, the Saints had quickly built hundreds of cabins and had excavated dugouts. More than 3,500 stayed there that winter, and some 400 died from cold, hunger, and disease.[7] Winter Quarters then became the staging ground for the first pioneer companies that traveled west in 1847.

The Church abandoned Winter Quarters after 1848 because of an agreement with the Indians to do so. In 1854 the Nebraska Territory was opened for settlement, and real estate developers changed the name of Winter Quarters to Florence. By 1856 the property around Florence had all been claimed. Without sufficient property rights, the Saints would have had to make special arrangements with landowners to stay the winter. Today Florence is a suburb north of Omaha. A pioneer cemetery is located there, and the Church has built a temple and a visitors' center adjacent to it.

Members of the Willie company gave some consideration to staying in Nebraska until spring—in Florence, at the Elkhorn River, or at Wood River[8]—but for most of them it was only token consideration. The company journal suggests that James Willie and most of the group were single-minded about continuing on. This assumption seems clear in the entry for August 12, the first full day in Florence: "Brother Willie addressed the Saints and gave them some needful instructions and advice before proceeding on the remainder of the journey."[9]

On the evening of August 13, another meeting was held. Far from an ordinary camp meeting, this one had high drama with life-or-death stakes. James Willie and two of his subcaptains, Millen Atwood and Levi Savage, bore their testimonies and gave their opinions on the upcoming journey.[10] James Willie continued to urge everyone forward, but Levi Savage spoke strongly against proceeding so late in the season. Although he was a man of faith, Levi Savage also felt that reason and experience should factor into the decision. Knowing the risks of starting so late in the season, he advised the group to stay in Florence through the winter and resume the journey in the spring. His own account of the meeting, written contemporaneously, not in hindsight, reads:

"August 13, 1856, Wednesday, Florence, Nebraska Territory. Today we continued preparations for starting. Evening we held [a] meeting in camp. Brother Willie exhorted the Saints to go forward regardless of suffering even to death. After he had spoken, he gave me the opportunity of speaking. I said to him that if I spoke, I must speak my mind, let it cut where it would. He said certainly to do so.

"I then related to the Saints the hardships that we should have to endure. I said that we were liable to have to wade in snow up to our knees and shovel at night, lay ourselves in a thin blanket and lie on the frozen ground without a bed. [I said it] was not like having a wagon that we could go into and wrap ourselves in as much as we liked and lie down. No, said I, we are without wagons, destitute of clothing, and could not carry it if we had it. We must go as we are.

"The handcart system I do not condemn. I think it preferable to unbroken oxen and inexperienced teamsters. The lateness of the season was my only objection to leaving this point for the mountains at this time. I spoke warmly upon the subject, but spoke truth."[11]

John Chislett recalled that in speaking these words, "Levi Savage used his common sense and his knowledge of the country. He declared positively that to his certain knowledge we could not cross the mountains with a mixed company of aged people, women, and little children so late in the season without much suffering, sickness, and death. He therefore advised going into winter quarters without delay."[12]

Recalling Levi Savage's words and demeanor, George Cunningham wrote: "He counseled the old, weak, and sickly to stop until another spring. The tears commenced to flow down his cheeks, and he prophesied that if such undertook the journey at that late season of the year, . . . their bones would strew the way."[13]

"GO FORWARD REGARDLESS OF CONSEQUENCES"

Through his tears, Levi Savage looked into the faces of the people and saw fear and confusion. They had put their destinies in the hands of their leaders, and these men were giving conflicting counsel on matters of life and death. Sensing that Levi Savage's words might have planted doubts, James Willie retook the offensive. Levi Savage recalled:

"Elder Willie then spoke again in reply to what I had said, evidently dissatisfied, and said that the God he served was a God that was able to save to the uttermost, . . . and he wanted no Job's comforters with him."

With these words, James Willie questioned not only Levi Savage's loyalty but also his faith. Nevertheless, when Levi Savage spoke again, he did not retreat:

"I then said that what I had said was truth, and if Elder Willie does not want me to act in the place where I am, he is at full liberty to place another man in my stead, and I would not think hard of him for it, but I did not care what he said about Job's comforters. I had spoken nothing but the truth, and he and others knew it."[14]

The words of Levi Savage caused some to worry and even some to stay in Florence, but the majority of the company decided to proceed.[15] The reasons were numerous. One was that most members of the company were anxious to get to Zion and be settled there, in many cases with family and friends who were awaiting them. Another reason was that resources were lacking to sustain a large company at Winter Quarters or the other Nebraska sites. Securing adequate employment, shelter, food, and fuel for the winter would have been difficult or perhaps impossible.[16]

Another factor in the desire to continue was that most of the emigrants did not know how harsh the climate and territory ahead of them could be. Despite the warnings of Levi Savage, in the heat of a Midwestern summer it would have been hard for them to anticipate the extremities they could face on the high plains of Wyoming.

Some people wanted to proceed simply because they didn't feel they had much choice. Emma James recalled that this was true for her parents: "I can remember that when [Brother Savage] finished, there was a long time of silence. I was frightened. Father looked pale and sick. I turned to Mother to see what she was thinking, and all I saw was her old determined look. She was ready to go on tomorrow. There were many others like her. We really didn't have much choice. There was no work here for us to keep ourselves through the winter, and our family had to live. 'We must put our trust in the Lord, as we have always done,' said mother, and that was that."[17]

As mentioned by Emma James's mother, trust in the Lord was another factor in the decision to continue. The Saints had been promised a safe journey if they were obedient. Surely, they seemed to feel, they were doing God's will, so he would protect them.

Trust in their leaders also influenced the decision to continue. Levi Savage recalled that when the Willie company arrived in Florence, "Brothers McGaw, Kimball, Grant, and Van Cott addressed the Saints [and] exhorted them to go forward regardless of consequences."[18] John Chislett had a similar recollection:

"The emigrants were entirely ignorant of the country and climate—simple, honest, eager to go to 'Zion' at once, and obedient as children to the 'servants of God.' Under the circumstances it was natural that they should leave their destinies in the hands of the elders. . . .

"There were several at Florence superintending the emigration, among whom elders G. D. Grant and W. H. Kimball occupied the most prominent position. These men all . . . favoured going on. They prophesied in the name of God that we should get through in safety. . . . Even the elements he would arrange for our good. . . . One elder even declar[ed] that he would guarantee to eat all the snow that fell on us between Florence and Salt Lake City."[19]

Subcaptain Johan Ahmanson singled out William H. Kimball for his role in urging the company forward: "The oldest son of [Heber C.] Kimball . . . delivered a speech in which he sternly rebuked those of little faith, and he promised that he would 'stuff into his mouth all the snow they would ever get to see on their journey to the valleys!' With this of course every doubt had to vanish altogether."[20]

The encouragement and promises from their leaders, John Chislett said, "had a telling effect on the people—to them it was 'the voice of God.'"[21] Wallace Stegner drew the following conclusion about the influence and motives of these leaders:

"Like many others, they were intoxicated with zeal to prove the handcart plan sound. They joined, and to some extent probably strengthened, the eagerness of the tenderfeet to press on. These told themselves that they had not come this far only to winter in a dugout along the Platte. They had come to join the Saints in Zion, and they had come by God's own plan."[22]

Emigration leaders may have had another motivation too. Because most of them were returning from missions after years away from their families, they were anxious to get home themselves.

"IF NECESSARY, I WILL DIE WITH YOU"

How did Levi Savage react to the decision to continue? How did he react to being "rebuked by the other elders for want of faith"?[23] He must have felt that his position as subcaptain was compromised. In his mind he must have questioned why other leaders dismissed life-threatening realities they knew to be true.

The natural reactions to such a situation include rebellion, withdrawal, bitterness, backbiting, perhaps even forming a personal following. Instead, Levi Savage issued this peerless statement of loyalty and love:

"Brethren and sisters, what I have said I know to be true; but seeing you are to go forward, I will go with you, will help you all I can, will work with you, will rest with you, will suffer with you, and, if necessary, I will die with you. May God in his mercy bless and preserve us."[24]

Unfortunately, more difficulties lay ahead for Levi Savage. There would be more criticism. Within two months the winter storms would begin and the hardships he warned about would come to pass. How would he react then? Would he murmur or become bitter? Would he remind everyone that he had been right and the leaders should have listened to him? Would he withdraw and leave the other leaders to work out the problems they had brought upon themselves?

John Chislett said that only four men in the Willie company had previously been all the way across the pioneer trail: James Willie, Levi Savage, Millen Atwood, and William Woodward.[25] *But Levi Savage had not crossed the trail before. In 1846 he broke off the trail in Council Bluffs, Iowa, when he joined the Mormon Battalion and marched to California. After completing his enlistment with the battalion in 1847, he went to Utah from California. When he left on his mission in 1852, he sailed from California.*

Because Levi Savage had never crossed the plains of Wyoming or the mountains of Utah, how could he warn so forcefully about the dangers of a late departure? First, he had several thousand miles of trail experience.

Second, when crossing the Sierra Nevada range in 1847 after his battalion service, he encountered the grisly remains of the Donner Party. In 1846 this California-bound company had reached the Sierra Nevada late in the season and become snowbound. Approximately half the company died from starvation and cold. Descriptions by battalion members who came upon the scene several months later are ghastly. Some of the dead still had not been buried, so a few men from the battalion buried them. The recollection of this sight likely influenced Levi Savage's graphic warning that if the handcart Saints left so late in the season, "their bones would strew the way."

CHAPTER 10

FROM FLORENCE TO
FORT LARAMIE

The first and second hundreds of the Willie company left Florence on August 16 after taking just five days to repair their handcarts. The rest of the company left the next day. This group had consisted of 500 people and 120 handcarts when it left Iowa City, but it was down to 404 people and 85 handcarts when it left Florence because some had turned back in Iowa and many others decided to stay in Florence.[1] Another change in Florence was the assignment of a small independent company of four wagons and 20 people to travel with the Willie company. The captain of these wagons, Andrew Siler, operated under the presidency of James Willie.[2] The Willie company was also given two more supply wagons and some additional oxen, beef cattle, and milk cows.[3]

A reporter from the *Council Bluffs Bugle,* located across the Missouri River from Florence, wrote with admiration about the Willie company as they started into the vast westward expanse of Nebraska toward Fort Laramie, 522 miles distant:

"Having seen several handcart trains pass through this city, and cross the ferries at Elk Horn and Loup Fork, we could not help but remark on the enthusiasm which animated all classes and ages. . . .

"It may seem, to some, that these people endure great hardships in traveling hundreds of miles on foot, drawing carts behind them. This is a mistake, for many informed me that after the first three days' travel, it requires little effort for two or three men or women to drag the light handcart. . . . It is also a fact that they can travel farther in a day, and with less fatigue, than the ox trains. . . .

"This is enthusiasm—this is heroism indeed. Though we cannot coincide with them in their belief, it is impossible to restrain our admiration of their self-sacrificing devotion to the principles of their faith."[4]

John Chislett also recalled the good spirits as the Willie company left Florence: "We moved gaily forward full of hope and faith. At our camp each evening could be heard songs of joy [and] merry peals of laughter [concerning] our condition and prospects. Brother Savage's warning was forgotten in the mirthful ease of the hour."[5]

The Willie company had relatively good traveling for the next two weeks. The day after leaving Florence, Millen Atwood spoke to the company about the "grumblers" and "double-minded" who had left them in Iowa.[6] He said that if any others had similar feelings, this was their last chance to leave. The company journal does not record a single person turning back during the six weeks it took to cross Nebraska and reach Fort Laramie.

Two days after the Willie company left Florence, the company of handcarts led by Jesse Haven arrived. Three days later, on August 22, the company led by Edward Martin arrived. That night, President Franklin D. Richards combined these two companies and placed Edward Martin in charge of the entire group. After repairing handcarts, the Martin company left Florence on August 25, eight days after the last of the Willie company.

Brothers and Sisters Helping Each Other

Betsey and Alexander Smith

The handcart trek includes many stories of brothers and sisters helping and sacrificing for each other. Betsey and Alexander Smith, ages 13 and 6, were emigrating with their widowed mother (see page 42). Walking 10 to 15 miles a day was especially hard for children like Alexander, who was too young to fully understand the purpose of all the difficulty. He probably complained from time to time, which could have annoyed others in the family. But rather than be irritated, Betsey helped him through each mile. She later recalled, "[Alexander] used to travel that distance by me taking his hand to encourage him, and by telling him stories of the future and the good things in store for us."[7]

Joseph and Emily Wall

Joseph and Emily Wall were siblings ages 17 and 16 whose parents had sent them to America on their own because the family could not afford to emigrate together (see page 39). Sometime after leaving Florence, they faced a serious challenge. During one of the river crossings, Joseph nearly drowned. When he was going under the water for the third time, he was rescued by someone who grabbed his hair.

Joseph soon became too ill to walk, and company leaders wanted him to stay behind and wait for the next company. Emily refused to leave her brother, so she promised to pull him in the handcart if they would be permitted to continue. With the help of a young girl, Emily pulled Joseph for several days.[8]

THE GREAT PLATTE RIVER ROAD

On August 20, four days after leaving Florence, the Willie company arrived at the Platte River. They would follow this river most of the way across Nebraska and well into Wyoming—a period of 51 days and a distance of more than 600 miles.

Traveling westward along the Platte, the Willie company would slowly climb from the prairie lands to the arid high plains, where grass was shorter and wood less abundant. About 200 miles from Florence, they would reach Fort Kearny and begin crossing the part of the trail known as the Great Platte River Road, so named because trails on both sides of the river were traveled by an estimated 350,000 emigrants between 1841 and 1866.[9]

The journey across Nebraska would be more toilsome than across Iowa. Factors contributing to the increased difficulty included heavier carts (100 pounds of flour had been loaded onto them in Florence), the gain in elevation, and the ubiquitous Platte Valley sand. "Had heavy sandy roads," Levi Savage would write after an especially hard day's travel. "Both people and teams are much fatigued by the heavy sandy roads," he would write a few days later.[10] "Very bad sandy roads throughout the day which, combined with a very high wind, rendered it the most arduous day's trip up to this point," the company journal would report the next day.[11]

Cattle Lost in a Stampede

Perhaps the biggest turning point in the Willie company's journey occurred on the evening of September 3 or the early morning of September 4, when the group was about halfway across Nebraska. The company journal records, "30 head of cattle had strayed away (most probably in a stampede) during the night."[12] Levi Savage recorded, "Some time last night, 30 of our best working cattle left us. We had a guard around them, but no one knows when or where they went."[13]

Central Nebraska was buffalo country. "There are large herds to be seen in all directions," Levi Savage wrote the day before the cattle were lost.[14] Stampedes were not unusual in the area, especially if something frightened the buffalo. Describing one of these stampedes, 16-year-old Emma James wrote: "It sounded like thunder at first, then the big black animals came straight for our carts. We were so scared that we were rooted to the ground. . . . They went past us like a train roaring along."[15]

Apparently on the night of September 3, a violent storm arose that prompted another stampede—and this one frightened away the cattle. Emma James recalled:

"As the sun went down, a terrible storm came up. A strong wind tore the tents out of our hands and sent everything flying in all directions. The thunder and lightning was like nothing we had ever seen before. We had all we could do to keep track of each other. The noise terrified the children so that they ran for any shelter they could find.

Soon we all did, for the rain came down in torrents, and in a matter of minutes we were soaked to the skin."[16]

Most or all of the missing cattle were the oxen that pulled the supply wagons. The importance of these animals is shown by the effort made to find them. The group stopped and searched for three days. The searchers struggled to track the animals because the rain had washed away all traces of them. The entries in the company journal reveal an almost doomed disappointment when these men came back empty-handed:

September 4: "Different brethren under the command of Capt. Savage, Siler, and Christianson started in different directions. Capt. Siler with his company returned about 5 and Captains Savage and Christianson with theirs about 8 P.M. after a fruitless search."[17]

September 5: "This morning Prest. Willie sent out together Capt. Savage in command of a mule company and Captain Christianson in command of a foot company in search of the missing cattle, but the 2 parties returned at dark together this evening and reported a complete failure."[18]

On the third day after the stampede, Captain Willie decided the company had to move on. "It was evident to all that our provisions were getting very short," George Cunningham recalled. "We had between six and seven hundred miles to travel to accomplish our journey, which we would be compelled to do or perish in the mountain snows."[19] Joseph Elder and Andrew Smith were left behind to continue searching for the cattle.[20]

Only 12 of the company's oxen remained, leaving two for each ox-drawn supply wagon typically pulled by six oxen.[21] Emma James recalled the last-resort improvising as the company tried to get started again: "With no oxen or mules to pull the wagons, it was necessary to hitch the milk cows to the wagons. It was a sorry sight which started out [again] on the trail."[22]

John Chislett provided more detail about this circumstance: "We at last reluctantly gave up the search and prepared to travel without [the oxen] as best we could. We had only about enough oxen left to put one yoke to each wagon; but, as they were each loaded with about 3,000 pounds of flour, the teams could not of course move them. We then yoked up our beef cattle, milch cows, and, in fact, everything that could bear a yoke—even two-year-old heifers. The stock was wild and could pull but little, and we were unable, with all our stock, to move our loads. As a last resort we again loaded a sack of flour on each cart."[23]

In consequence of the stampede, then, not only did the people lose three valuable days, as well as many of their oxen, but they also had to expend extra energy to pull heavier carts. Ann Rowley summed up the devastating chain reaction of problems caused by the loss of these animals:

"This was the beginning of our great hardships and probably was the cause of most of them, for we had spent valuable time looking for the oxen. This loss in turn reduced our meat supply, and because there weren't enough cattle to pull the supply wagons, a hundred pounds of flour was placed in each handcart. Our handcarts were not designed for such heavy loads and were constantly breaking down."[24]

Despite the problems the stampede caused, Ann Rowley also found reason to give thanks. As usual, things could have been worse: "I thanked the Lord, that our lives had been spared, for we all could have been killed."[25]

Levi Savage also tried to be optimistic. Two days after some of the wild cows had been yoked to pull the wagons, he seemed pleasantly surprised by their performance. "Surely the hand of the Lord is with us yet," he wrote.[26]

Still, the situation was dire, and it led to increased strife. "The patience and faith of the good honest people were shaken somewhat by this (to them) hard stroke of Providence," John Chislett recalled. "Some complained openly; others, less demonstrative, chewed the bitter cud of discontent."[27]

Captains Willie and Atwood urged unity and obedience, confession and forgiveness. Captain Willie "said he would like to see all the grumblers, pilferers, liars, and so forth, if any were still so in their hearts, immediately stand by themselves, aside from the rest, so that the brethren might better know them."[28]

Captains Willie and Atwood also appealed to the Siler wagon company to consecrate their wagons and teams to provide assistance. The handcart captains even asked members of the wagon company to help pull the overburdened handcarts.[29] This small wagon team would travel with the Willie company as far as Fort Laramie, assisting them along the way. At Fort Laramie, Andrew Siler would stop his wagons so he could "recruit and strengthen his teams."[30] His group would complete the last part of the journey with the Hodgetts wagon company.

John Chislett recalled that although travel was difficult, most members of the company soon showed their usual resilience:

"The belief that we were the spiritual favourites of the Almighty, and that he would control everything for our good, soon revived us after our temporary despondency, and in a day or two faith was as assuring as ever with the pilgrims. But our progress was slow, the old breakdowns were constantly repeated, and some could not refrain from murmuring in spite of general trustfulness. It was really hard for the folks to lose the use of their milch cows, have beef rations stopped, and haul 100 pounds or more on their carts. Every man and woman, however, worked to their utmost to put forward toward the goal of their hopes."[31]

Could the loss of cattle have been avoided? Because of similar losses in previous years, leaders of emigrating companies were counseled to chain or tie up their cattle, especially in buffalo country. If this precaution had been taken, the outcome for the Willie company might have been different. The company would have been at least three days closer to the rescuers—and probably more.[32] Leaders of the Willie company apparently learned from the mistake of leaving the oxen unsecured. "We chained our oxen to the wagons," Levi Savage wrote on September 15.[33]

ARRIVAL OF PRESIDENT FRANKLIN D. RICHARDS

The Willie company trudged across Nebraska, following the Platte River. On September 12, about a week after the stampede, they received a lift when the company of President Franklin D. Richards caught up with them. In England, President Richards had overseen the emigration of most members of the Willie company. Nearly three months after bidding them farewell, he left Liverpool with a small group consisting mostly of returning missionaries. They had journeyed by steamship across the ocean, by express train to St. Louis, by riverboat up the Missouri to St. Joseph, and by stagecoach to Florence, taking only 26 days to travel the same distance that took the handcart companies three months.[34] In Florence President Richards's group had met up with the Martin company and the Hunt and Hodgetts wagon companies. After helping them get back on the trail, they hurried homeward and soon overtook the Willie company.

The Willie company had traveled 320 miles from Florence and was a couple of days west of modern-day North Platte, Nebraska, when President Richards caught up with them. An understandably envious tone can be detected in John Chislett's description that the group was traveling in "a grand outfit of carriages and light wagons."[35] The company journal more evenly records: "This evening President Franklin D. Richards and suite . . . arrived just before dusk in 3 carriages and 2 wagons. They were loudly greeted by the hearty hurrahs of the Saints."[36]

Further showing how essential the lost oxen were, the two men who had been sent to look for them did not return to the company until six days later when they arrived with President Richards. They had found no sign of the animals.

Soon after arriving, President Richards addressed the Saints. The company journal records that he "express[ed] his satisfaction at their having journeyed thus far, and more especially with handcarts. . . . He promised in the name of Israel's God and by the authority of the Holy Priesthood that no obstacle whatever should come in the way of this camp but what they should be able, by their united faith and works, to overcome, God being their helper. And, that if a Red Sea should interpose, they should by their union of heart and hand walk through it like Israel of old, dryshod. On the same conditions he promised that though they might have some trials to endure as proof to God and their brethren that they had the true 'grit,' [neither] heat nor cold nor any other thing should have power to seriously harm any in the camp but that we should arrive in the valleys of the mountains with strong and healthy bodies."[37]

John Chislett recalled that when President Richards caught up with the Willie company in Nebraska, he "gave us plenty of counsel to be faithful, prayerful, obedient to our leaders, etc., and wound up by prophesying in the name of Israel's God that 'though it might storm on our right and on our left, the Lord would keep open our way before us and we should get to Zion in safety.' "[38]

These were bold promises, but they were not unusual. When President Richards arrived in Salt Lake City less than a month later, he suggested that many such promises had been made:

"Every time we got to talking about the handcarts in England, and on the way, we could not talk long without prophesying about them. On shipboard, at the point of outfit, and on the plains, every time we spoke we felt to prophesy good concerning them."[39]

How can these promises be reconciled with the tragedy that would soon unfold?

Wallace Stegner stands on one extreme in assessing these promises, saying that President Richards himself must have understood that they were "mainly tactical encouragement" rather than inspired pronouncements.[40] Stegner's assessment of President Richards's expectation that God would deliver the handcart pioneers safely to Zion is both sympathetic and stark: "If he had been God's worst enemy, instead of the essentially good man that he was, God could not have denied his expectations more harshly."[41]

Although Wallace Stegner's assessment of these promises is understandable, it is not the only defensible conclusion. His assessment removes all spiritual basis from the promises, essentially classifying them as motivational tactics. If that were the case, the promises would have been fraudulent, which is inconsistent with President Richards's character.

It is more likely that these promises were prompted by many

strong spiritual impressions. Such impressions do not usually come as explicit scripts from heaven. More often they require interpretation, and in that process they may be filtered through human experience and hopes. With all his heart, President Richards wanted the handcart plan to succeed. He believed that God had inspired the plan and would ensure its success. The spiritual feelings and fortuitous events that attended the handcart effort from its inception would be easy to interpret as heavenly confirmation of this belief.

A likely factor in how President Richards interpreted spiritual impressions was his conviction that the Lord helps those who help themselves. President Richards apparently expected the Lord to compensate for the late start because those involved in the emigration had given their best effort. He expressed this feeling with an explicit *therefore* in a letter he wrote the day he left Florence:

"From the beginning we have done all in our power to hasten matters concerning the emigration; therefore, we confidently look for the blessing of God to crown our humble efforts with success, and for the safe arrival of our brethren . . . in Utah, though they may experience some cold."[42]

From another perspective, it could be argued that President Richards's promises would be fulfilled to a remarkable degree. Although these Saints would suffer terribly, this story will show that the hand of God would be miraculously manifested many times in the survival not only of individuals but of most members of both the Willie and the Martin companies.

ANOTHER CHALLENGE FOR LEVI SAVAGE

On September 13, the morning after President Richards and his group arrived, the handcarts were packed and the teams were hitched to the wagons and ready to start when an unexpected meeting was called. Levi Savage summarized the meeting in his journal:

"A meeting of the Saints was called, not on the campground as usual but a short distance [away]. I supposed it was for prayers. After singing and prayer, Brother Richards commenced to speak, and I soon perceived that the meeting was called in consequence of the wrong impressions made by my expressing myself freely at Florence, concerning our crossing the plains so late in the season. The impression left was that I condemned the handcart system, which is wrong. I never conveyed such an idea, nor felt to do so."[43]

Another incident that prompted the meeting had occurred more recently, when Captain Willie and Levi Savage had disagreed about the placement of Andrew Siler's wagons on the trail. In the words of Levi Savage:

"Someone, unknown to me, informed Brother Richards of the disagreeable words that took place between Bro. Willie and myself concerning Brother Siler's teams traveling between the handcarts and fund wagons, which I supposed was settled when I asked Bro. Willie's and the Saints' forgiveness for all that I had said and done wrong. Brother Richards reprimanded me sharply. Bro. Willie said that [was] the spirit that I had manifested from Iowa City. This is something unknown to me and something he never before expressed. I had always the best of feelings toward him and supposed he had toward me until now."[44]

William Woodward and John Chislett also mentioned this incident in their accounts.[45] John Chislett recalled: "In the morning a general meeting was called. Apostle Richards addressed us. He had been advised of the opposition Brother Savage had made, and he rebuked him very severely in open meeting for his lack of faith in God."[46]

George Cunningham provides the most detailed account of this meeting, along with interesting commentary and insight. He said that Captain Willie reproved not only Levi Savage but also Millen Atwood for "rebellious talk and not upholding him in his place." When President Richards spoke, he reproved not just these brethren but the entire company "for the dissensions that had been allowed to creep into camp. He said that the hand of God had been heavy upon us for this cause. Brother Savage was called up and was told that he would have to take back what he said at Florence . . . or be tried for his fellowship. He was forced to do so. But it reminded me of Galileo, the great Italian philosopher, who discovered that the sun stood still. He was hauled up before the Roman inquisition for teaching heresy and made to swear by everything that was holy that he would never teach such doctrine again, but while rising off his knees, he was heard to mutter in an undertone, 'The earth, the earth does revolve for all that.' "[47]

The rebuke blindsided Levi Savage. A month had passed since his plea in Florence for the Saints to wait until spring to continue the journey. His other disagreement with Captain Willie had occurred two weeks earlier. In his mind, these matters had already been settled. He had expressed himself, been overruled, and supported his leaders' decisions anyway.

What did Levi Savage say in his defense? What prompted him to continue on despite this public criticism? Except for the feeling of surprise shown above, his journal is silent on these matters. He simply appears to have borne the rebuke meekly. Nothing in his written words shows any indignation for how this incident was handled, for his brethren holding grudges they would not front with him openly, for being criticized behind his back to President Richards, or for being reprimanded in public. Still to be seen, though, was whether this latest criticism would affect his actions—and the pledge he had made in Florence to do everything he could to assist the company, even to the point of giving his life if necessary.

Departure of President Richards

After the meeting, President Richards and his group forded the Platte and hurried on toward Salt Lake City, promising to send additional supplies as soon as possible. President Richards later described the company's morale as he left:

"Never was there a more soul-stirring sight than the happy passage of this company over that river. Several of the carts were drawn entirely by women, and every heart was glad and full of hope."[48]

JOSEPH ELDER: "I'LL GO WHERE YOU WANT ME TO GO"

One notable absence from President Richards's group was Joseph Elder. His decision to stay with the Willie company marked the third time during the emigration that he had agreed to an abrupt change of plans so he could serve where Church leaders said he was most needed.

Joseph Elder, age 21, had joined the Church in the Midwest in 1855. In 1856 he was attending McKendree College in Lebanon, Illinois. On April 11 of that year he wrote, "Today I left McKendry College with peculiar feelings and started to visit the saints in Saint Louis."[49] Heeding those "peculiar feelings" led to some unexpected changes in his life.

The next day, Joseph Elder met with Church leaders in St. Louis, who proposed ordaining him an elder. Before his ordination, he pledged "to perform every duty and bear every burden that God through his holy priesthood is willing to lay on my shoulders."[50] His ordination was a powerful spiritual experience. "I felt the Spirit of God moving upon my heart," he wrote. Accordingly, he sought the counsel of Church leaders about what he should do. He recorded their response—and his—in his journal:

"Their opinion and decision was that I should return home and arrange my business the best I could and leave old McKendry and go to the valley of the great S. Lake, [but that first] I should return as soon as possible and accompany

Joseph Elder

Broths. Grant and Kimball in buying cattle, horses, mules, etc. for the emigrants to cross the plains with, and this seemed to me just to be my duty, and I accordingly determined to set about it in good faith."[51]

Joseph Elder returned to McKendree, sold his scholarship (though not easily), met with the school president to announce his intent to leave (a difficult encounter), concluded other business, and, most difficult of all, bade his family and friends good-bye. Feelings were understandably tender as he was leaving so suddenly and going so far:

"I bade adieu to my sisters and mother, and oh how my heart did almost break to leave them when they with tears and sobs and entreaties pled to the last for me to stay. But God had use for me in other places and I must go, so I spoke a few kind words to them and embraced them and parted, not knowing when we should see each other again, and I took up my line of march for the valleys of Ephraim 2,000 miles distant."[52]

Two days later, Joseph Elder was back in St. Louis, and three days after that he was on his way across Missouri to meet up with Elders Grant and Kimball. After finding them, he helped buy cattle and herd them to Florence, where he stayed to assist the handcart companies. He planned to remain in Florence until early September and then join with President Franklin D. Richards and most of the emigration leaders for the rest of the journey to the Salt Lake Valley. Soon after the Willie company arrived on August 11, however, plans changed again for Joseph Elder. Emigration officials wanted to provide the Willie company an extra wagon to carry provisions and supplies for the first part of their journey. On August 15 they approached Joseph Elder in the corral and asked him to leave immediately with the Willie company and drive this wagon. Joseph Elder's response, written in his journal, reflects a model of willing obedience:

"They proposed my starting with the present handcart company on the morrow and drive their team until they overtook us on the plains. Short notice. However, I determined to start for Utah."[53]

In less than two days, Joseph Elder was on the trail with the

Willie company. During the journey across Nebraska, he quickly proved faithful and competent, prompting Captain Willie to give him important assignments. For example, as mentioned earlier, he was one of the men who was asked to keep searching for the lost cattle when the rest of the company moved on. During the search, Joseph Elder met President Richards's group, which was moving homeward after concluding the season's emigration business in Florence. He traveled with this group until they caught up with the Willie company two or three days later.

Originally emigration leaders asked Joseph Elder to stay with the Willie company only until President Richards overtook them. When President Richards arrived, however, Joseph Elder received a third abrupt change of plans. Sensing that the Willie company would continue to need help, President Richards asked him to remain with the handcarts for the rest of the journey.

Again Joseph Elder agreed to what was surely a difficult request. He must have been disappointed that he would not finish the journey with Elders Grant and Kimball. Many people would have resented being left behind with the plodding handcarts while their friends hurried ahead in relative comfort and ease. Many would have sulked, feeling left out or taken advantage of. But in his journal, Joseph Elder does not indicate any of these feelings. Rather, he again shows a simple, understated willingness to serve at any time, in any place, and in any way his leaders felt he was needed:

"I had made arrangements such as to go on [to the Salt Lake Valley] with them, that is, the missionaries, but owing to the advice of Brother Franklin and others, I chose to remain with the handcart company and assist them all that I could."[54]

William Kimball would later praise his friend's selfless service, as Joseph Elder recorded in his journal:

"He said that I had not only been a talker but an actor, that I had imparted freely of all that I had, both money, property, time, and talent to the emigration, and that every word and action proved that I was determined to do the will of God and do all that I was able to help build up the kingdom of God in these last days."[55]

Joseph Elder was not a person who viewed Church assignments as a buffet from which he chose only what suited him at the time. He was not a person who set conditions in serving the Lord, accepting only certain assignments, fulfilling them only for so long, or working only with certain people (or not with others). He was not a person who was prone to negative feelings when an assignment changed and became more demanding or difficult than when he accepted it. Because he served willingly wherever the Lord needed him, he would soon play a pivotal role in the survival of most of the Willie company.

CHAPTER 11

FROM FORT LARAMIE TO INDEPENDENCE ROCK

The Willie company arrived at Fort Laramie on October 1, nearly three weeks after President Richards passed them in Nebraska. They had traveled the 522 miles from Florence to Fort Laramie in six weeks. With the exception of the loss of cattle, the journey had gone relatively well. The six deaths were not unusually high, especially given the proportion of elderly people in the company. Even wagon companies could expect about the same mortality rate. Fewer people died during these six physically demanding weeks than died during the six sedentary weeks on the ocean.

The deaths that did occur, mostly of the old and the very young, were painful even if they were not statistically high. Elizabeth Ingra was 75, leaving behind a husband who would continue another lonely month before succumbing himself. William Haley, age 66, died of "general decay," leaving his wife to continue the journey alone. Ann Bryant, age 69, also died of "general decay of constitution." Richard Turner was 67. William Leason, age 2, died of "canker in the stomach," leaving his grieving mother to travel alone, with no one to reach up for her hand. Jesse Empy, age 31, died of scrofula (tuberculosis of the lymph glands, especially in the neck), leaving his wife to bear the burdens of the journey with four young children, one of whom would later die along the trail.[1]

Although the number of deaths was not yet excessive, Levi Savage was beginning to see some ominous signs. Toward the end of September he recorded, "The old appear to be failing considerably."[2] The daily walking, which made some of the Saints more strong and fit, seemed to be hastening the demise of those who were older and

Fort Laramie

weaker. They would have little left to sustain them when food supplies were reduced and the winter storms arrived.

Fort Laramie is about 80 miles northeast of present-day Laramie,
Wyoming. It was founded in 1834 by fur traders and was purchased in
1849 by the U.S. military. In the 1850s, one of the main duties of the
troops at the fort was to patrol and maintain the security of a lengthy
stretch of the Oregon Trail. Today Fort Laramie is a national monument.
 When the Willie company arrived at Fort Laramie on October 1,
the Martin company was about 110 miles behind them, midway
between Ash Hollow and Chimney Rock in western Nebraska.

STATUS OF THE FOOD SUPPLY

The Willie company's food supply had been insufficient for the
journey across Iowa,[3] and the journey from Florence to Salt Lake
City had potential for much greater problems. One complication was
the distance: 1,031 miles, compared to 270 miles across Iowa. A
second complication was the lack of any reliable sources of additional

supplies along the way. These complications led to a third: because the distance from Florence to Salt Lake City was more than three times the distance across Iowa, the Willie company had to carry three times more flour. This was no small burden.

Brigham Young initially suggested the handcart companies take 90 days' worth of rations from Florence, even though he thought they could make the journey in 60 to 70 days.[4] However, a 90-day supply of flour—36,000 pounds for the Willie company—would far exceed the company's carrying capacity. To avoid overburdening the handcarts, the people who pulled them, and the supply wagons, emigration officials decided to provide 60 days' worth of rations from Florence.[5] It was possible to travel from Florence to Salt Lake City in 60 days—but only by averaging 17 miles a day, including Sundays. None of the 10 handcart companies would maintain that pace. The fastest time was 65 days, and the Willie company would need 83 days.

The 60-day supply was admittedly "scanty" and did not allow for any margin of error.[6] To ensure that the handcart companies did not run out of food, Church leaders in Salt Lake City planned to send resupply teams to meet them partway.

The Willie company had left Florence with a full load of about 24,000 pounds of flour—enough for each person to receive one pound a day for 60 days. The company's seven supply wagons carried most of it, with a capacity of about 3,000 pounds each, which also included the weight of the tents.[7] The rest of the flour was carried in the 85 handcarts, with one sack placed in most of the carts, adding 100 pounds to the weight each cart had carried across Iowa.[8] Even though Levi Savage saw the carts and wagons sagging under this load, he sensed it would not be enough: "We yet want 25 hundred or more [pounds of flour] and have no wagon nor can purchase one to haul it in."[9]

By the time the Willie company reached Fort Laramie, the halfway point between Florence and Salt Lake, they had used 70 percent of their flour. If they continued to travel at the same pace of about 12 miles a day, they would need another 42 days for the final 509 miles to the Salt Lake Valley. If they continued to use their flour at the normal rate, their supply would expire in 18 days, leaving them 24 days or nearly 300 miles short of their destination (by John Chislett's estimate, they would run out of flour 350 miles short of their destination).[10] Having already lost two-thirds of their cattle, the company would be in a dire condition unless they received resupply.

THE PROMISE OF RESUPPLY

The promise of resupply was such a certainty that the pioneers even sang about it in "The Handcart Song." The familiar song of "Some must push and some must pull / As we go marching up the hill" also includes this verse:

> But ere before the valley gained
> We will be met upon the plains
> With music sweet and friends so dear
> And fresh supplies our hearts to cheer.[11]

As promised, fresh supplies had been delivered to the first three handcart companies a few weeks earlier. Brigham Young sent the first resupply wagons to these companies on July 28, as soon as wheat was harvested and milled.[12] Some of the teams traveled as far as Deer Creek, which was within 100 miles of Fort Laramie. At Deer Creek and also at South Pass, they provided the first handcart companies with thousands of pounds of flour. Even though these companies were relatively small, traveling at a good pace, and enjoying favorable weather, the resupply proved essential to them. Such provisions would be even more important for the Willie company, which was nearly twice the size, was experiencing numerous delays, and would soon face brutal winter storms.

"THE PROVISIONS WERE NOT THERE FOR US"

The Willie company hoped for and even expected a resupply at Fort Laramie. The words of John Chislett and Levi Savage have a haunting spareness in describing what they found instead. From John Chislett: "The provisions, etc., which we expected were not there for us."[13] From Levi Savage: "Brother Richards has no cattle provided for us here and no other provisions made."[14]

There were two potential sources of resupply at Fort Laramie. One was the fort itself. Although the fort could not be counted on for substantial assistance, members of the Willie company hoped for moderate help. When President Richards left the group in September, he had said he would try to purchase flour at Fort Laramie and leave it for the company to pick up.[15] But President Richards had not left any flour at the fort because very little was available. Captain Willie was able to buy only a small amount of flour—less than a day's supply for less than half of the company—at the expensive price of 20 cents a pound. By comparison, flour had been 3 to 3.5 cents a pound in Iowa and 4.5 cents a pound in Florence.[16] Flour was also scarce later along the trail at Fort Bridger, though only 12 cents a pound.[17]

As mentioned earlier, wagons from Salt Lake City were the other potential source of resupply. Before the Saints left England, Brigham Young wrote that resupply wagons might extend as far east as Fort Laramie.[18] But at Fort Laramie a letter from President Richards was waiting with bad news about these wagons. According to John Chislett, the letter said the company should not expect to meet supplies until they got to South Pass—about 280 miles away.[19] Levi Savage also mentions this letter twice in his journal, though he names Pacific Springs as the potential resupply site, approximately four miles west of South Pass.[20] Both sites were beyond the range of the company's remaining food supply.

President Richards had passed through Fort Laramie on September 19, twelve days before the Willie company. Because he had not met any eastbound companies to that point, his naming of South Pass as the resupply site could not have been based on firsthand information but was simply an estimate. When the Willie company reached Fort Laramie,

President Richards was still three days away from Salt Lake City. The first rescue team would not start toward them for another week.

One little-known part of this story is that three small resupply teams were closer to the Willie company than President Richards knew when he wrote this letter. One or two of these teams were on the trail at least a month before Brigham Young mobilized the rescue effort in October. They seem to have left Utah as a matter of routine with the intent to resupply any of the several companies on the trail, not specifically the handcart companies. When the Willie company arrived at Fort Laramie, the closest of these small teams was within three or four days of them, assuming the wagons and handcarts continued to travel toward each other.

President Richards met the first of these teams on September 24, five days after leaving Fort Laramie. The meeting point was Independence Rock, about 180 miles west of Fort Laramie. This team consisted of Patriarch John Smith and two other men "who had come out with flour for the companies."[21] President Richards reported that "Br. Smith returned with us," but the wagons apparently continued forward. They did not proceed far enough to meet the Willie company, however.

Three days later, on September 27, President Richards met William Smith and two men who had "2 wagons of flour for the companies."[22] These men were 15 miles east of Pacific Springs, or about 255 miles from Fort Laramie. President Richards specifically "counseled them to cache their flour and go on to meet Br. Willie and his company, which they agreed to do."[23] Like the first team, however, they stopped short of the Willie company.

President Richards met a third small resupply team near the Big Sandy crossing, 330 miles from Fort Laramie. "We gave [them] the same counsel, to go on with [their] teams to help Br. Willie," President Richards reported.[24] Like the others, however, this team also stopped short of the Willie company.

Would the outcome for the handcart companies have been different if these resupply teams had gone far enough to meet them?

These teams could easily have reached the Willie company two weeks before the first rescuers arrived. One wagon load of flour could have fed the company for a week. Although that would not have been enough to sustain them all the way to Salt Lake City, these teams could have provided enough flour to save many lives.

These resupply teams knew the handcart companies were on the trail, so why did they not keep going until they met them? A partial explanation may be that they resupplied one or more wagon companies they met first. The Abraham Smoot wagon company was about a week ahead of the Willie company, and they too were dangerously low on flour. A report from the Smoot company on October 2, when they were at the last crossing of the Platte River, reads, "We met here a relief wagon with flour, which we received, and the wagon left for the Valley."[25] If this was one of the wagons belonging to John or William Smith—and the timeline suggests that it was—it was turned around when it was just 115 miles away from the Willie company.

Another reason these resupply teams stopped short of the handcarts may be that they did not know how desperate these groups were becoming.

Yet another reason is suggested in the journal of Robert T. Burton of the first rescue team. On October 13, six days into their race toward the handcart companies, these rescuers met some supply teams that were returning home. Robert Burton wrote that these teams were returning because they "got tired of waiting."[26]

WHAT HAD GONE WRONG?

Why wasn't a substantial resupply effort mobilized for the Willie and Martin companies? The most likely explanation lies in the previously cited letters that emigration officials in Iowa City had sent to Brigham Young and Heber C. Kimball in June (see pages 58–59). These letters had arrived in Salt Lake City in late July. They mentioned that the Saints who sailed under the direction of James Willie and Edward Martin would soon be arriving in Iowa City. They also mentioned that these groups "will together have nearly 1,200 souls to go by the handcarts."[27] In addition, one of these letters reported that some wagon companies would soon be leaving for Salt Lake City. However, neither letter stated—and apparently authorities in Utah did not expect—that the late-arriving handcart emigrants would try to get all the way to the Salt Lake Valley that year.

With crucial matters left unstated in these letters, and with no way for leaders who were half a continent apart to get timely clarification, each group made assumptions about the decisions of the other. Those in Iowa City and Florence, who sent the Willie and Martin companies ahead late in the season, apparently assumed that resupply teams would be sent to provide help—for that was the plan. Those in Salt Lake City, who had completed the resupply effort for the season, apparently assumed that authorities in Iowa City and Florence would not allow handcart emigrants to leave so late—for that was also the plan. These assumptions, while reasonable on both ends, played a central part in the tragedy that would soon unfold.

Difficulties between Fort Laramie and Independence Rock

The Willie company continued past Fort Laramie on the same day they arrived, October 1. Although they could not obtain much additional flour at the fort, they did negotiate the purchase of 400 pounds of "hard bread," or crackers, which Levi Savage said were extremely costly.[28] While that amount may seem substantial, it was only a day's supply for the company.

Rationing Begins

Captain Willie knew the company did not have enough food to get to the Salt Lake Valley. His more pressing concern was that they would not have enough even to get to South Pass. As mentioned earlier, the company had an 18-day supply of flour, but South Pass was 280 miles away—a 22-day journey if they kept traveling at the same pace as they had traveled during the previous six weeks.

On the evening of October 2, the day after leaving Fort Laramie, Captain Willie called the company together to propose reducing each person's daily ration of flour so the remaining supply would last until they reached South Pass.[29] John Chislett recalled:

"Captain Willie called a meeting to take into consideration our circumstances . . . and prospects, and to see what could be done. It was ascertained that at our present rate of travel and consumption of flour, the latter would be exhausted when we were about 350 miles from our destination. It was resolved to reduce our allowance from one pound to three-quarters of a pound per day, and at the same time to make every effort in our power to travel faster. We continued this rate of rations [for 177 miles] from Laramie to Independence Rock."[30]

Just as rationing began, the trail got even more arduous. Between Fort Laramie and Independence Rock, the Willie company began moving into mountain country, with more climbing and a rougher road. Grasses and other forage became more sparse as sagebrush, greasewood, and cactus became more dominant. And perhaps most difficult, during the last 50 miles before Independence Rock, the company would have to leave the Platte River for an overland drive that had very little water—and even less that was fit to drink because it was tainted by alkali.

More People Leave; Difficulties of Reduced Rations

Although the Willie company's most severe trials were still nearly three weeks away, the fires of affliction were intensifying. Most people remained faithful, but the lack of assistance and the endless, difficult miles tried the faith of some. The company journal records that several women left the camp and took up residence at Fort Laramie. Another woman left the camp with an apostate.[31] Joseph Elder recorded:

There was "quite a fussing in camp. Some grunted. Some lied. Some apostatized. Some followed us after we were gone and begged the captain to receive them again into the company."[32]

The one-pound flour ration had barely been adequate for subsistence. Reducing that ration was so hard that some people resorted to desperate measures. Levi Savage reported, "Some stealing is practiced by some; consequently, we put all the provisions into three wagons and placed a guard over them."[33]

Death of David Reeder

The reduced flour ration, together with the effort to increase the pace, multiplied the signs of weakness that Levi Savage had seen the previous week. During the first week of October, six people died—the same number as the previous six weeks combined. The weather conditions were not yet a factor. Rather, some people finally reached a point of utter exhaustion. This seemed to be the case for David Reeder, whose son Robert recalled:

"My father, David Reeder, would start out in the morning and pull his cart until he would drop on the road. He did this day after day until he did not arise early on October [1], 1856. He was found dead in his bed. . . . Sister Eliza wrapped a cherished sheet around him, and we placed him in a shallow grave, hoping the wolves would not disturb. We must go on our way in silent mourning and in a weakened condition."[34]

Death Strikes the Gadd Family

Tragedy also began to multiply for the Gadd family the first few days of October. On October 4, one of the family's two-year-old twins died. His oldest brother, 19-year-old Alfred, who made a brief entry in his diary nearly every day, used the same tone to record the death of his brother as he used to record the day's mileage: "We went three miles and camped. My brother Daniel (aged 2) died this afternoon."[35]

Five days later, Samuel Gadd, the father of this family, the man who wanted to lead them to Zion even though his wife was not a member of the Church, died a few miles east of present-day Casper, Wyoming. Alfred wrote: "We went eighteen miles. My father was dying before we left this morning, but they put him in a wagon, and when we saw him at noon, he was dead."[36] Alfred's only words in his diary the next day are even more brief: "We buried Father this morning." Through all these difficulties, Alfred does not record one word of complaint in his diary.

The death of Samuel Gadd left his wife, Eliza Chapman Gadd, to finish a pilgrimage she had no religious connection to. Death would soon strike another of her children, 10-year-old Samuel Jr., her husband's namesake. Months earlier, Eliza had agreed to emigrate because she wanted to keep her family together. Now she was losing her family, with three deaths in three weeks. Eliza herself would at one point become snowblind for three days and have to be led by her 8-year-old daughter, Mary Ann.[37] This story will later tell of her reaction to all these difficulties—whether she would become bitter and resentful, condemn the experience as ill-advised folly, and return home with her surviving children, or eventually find a home in Zion.

Condition of the Animals

Like the people, the animals were becoming emaciated and were failing due to inadequate feed. "This morning one of our best oxen belonging to the P. E. Fund died," wrote William Woodward in the company journal on October 8. "This loss impaired us much," wrote Levi Savage.[38] Three days later William Woodward recorded, "Several of our cows gave out that were hauling wagons."[39] Levi Savage was more specific: "Three of our working cows gave out, and one died. The remainder of our oxen were nearly overcome."[40] The next day William Woodward recorded in the company journal, "A cow was killed that was not fit to travel."[41]

When cattle were killed earlier in the journey, each person generally received about one-half pound of meat.[42] Now, however, with little flesh left on the animals, people were happy to receive bones or even pieces of hide—anything to help relieve the sharp hunger that afflicted everyone.

Ann Rowley Feeds Her Family with Two Sea Biscuits

Ann Rowley, a widow who had eight children to feed, felt a mother's pain in their hunger. "It hurt me to see my children go hungry," she wrote. "I watched as they cut the loose rawhide from the cart wheels, roast[ed] off the hair, and chew[ed] the hide."[43] One evening she felt the providence of God in helping feed her children:

"Night was coming and there was no food for the evening meal. I asked God's help as I always did. I got on my knees, remembering two hard sea biscuits that . . . had been left over from the sea voyage. They were not large, and were so hard they couldn't be broken. Surely, that was not enough to feed 8 people, but 5 loaves and 2 fishes were not enough to feed 5,000 people either, but through a miracle, Jesus had done it. So, with God's help, nothing is impossible. I found the biscuits and put them in a dutch oven and covered them with water and asked for God's blessing. Then I put the lid on the pan and set it on the coals. When I took off the lid a little later, I found the pan filled with food. I kneeled with my family and thanked God for his goodness. That night my family had sufficient food."[44]

CHAPTER 12

THE RESCUE BEGINS

Stories of their rescue need to be repeated again and again. They speak of the very essence of the gospel of Jesus Christ.

—PRESIDENT GORDON B. HINCKLEY

While the Willie company was in the area of Fort Laramie, the first three handcart companies were arriving in Salt Lake City. The Ellsworth and McArthur companies arrived on September 26, and the Bunker company on October 2. Brigham Young and other Church leaders met the first two companies at the foot of Little Mountain and escorted them into the city. Members of these companies pulled their carts in a procession through town as brass bands played and spectators thronged to cheer them. When they stopped, Brigham Young addressed them and gave them a blessing. The *Deseret News* reported:

"This journey has been performed with less than the average amount of mortality usually attending ox trains; and all, though somewhat fatigued, stepped out with alacrity to the last, and appeared buoyant and cheerful. . . .

"And thus has been successfully accomplished a plan, devised by the wisdom and forethought of our President, for rapidly gathering the poor."[1]

Although the journey had been difficult, it was celebrated as a great success. Wilford Woodruff recalled:

"I must say my feelings were inexpressible to behold a company of men, women, and children, many of them aged and infirm, enter the City of the Great Salt Lake, drawing 100 handcarts . . . with

which they had traveled some 1,400 miles in nine weeks, and to see
them dance with joy as they travelled through the streets, complain-
ing of nothing. . . .

"As I gazed upon the scene, meditating upon the future result, it
looked to me like the first hoisting of the floodgates of deliverance
to the oppressed millions. We can now say to the poor and honest in
heart, come home to Zion, for the way is prepared."[2]

Despite a few setbacks and delays, the travels of these first handcart companies had gone as well as could be expected. The treks had
been orchestrated simultaneously from points 5,000 miles apart, as
well as points in between. Agents had been working in Iowa City
even before emigrants had left Liverpool. Resupply wagons had been
sent from Salt Lake City the same week the first companies left
Florence. Given the speed of communication at the time, it was an
outstanding effort.

THE REPORT OF FRANKLIN D. RICHARDS

Two days after the third handcart company arrived in Salt Lake
City, the mood of celebration about the handcart plan suddenly
changed. On October 4, President Franklin D. Richards and his
group reached the city. It was a warm day, the temperature in the
upper 70s. Summer was just two weeks past. But when President
Richards met with Brigham Young that day, thoughts turned to
winter.

President Richards reported that two large handcart companies
and two wagon companies—some 1,300 people—were still on the
trail, hundreds of miles from the Salt Lake Valley. Brigham Young
was stunned. "We had no idea there were any more companies upon
the Plains, until our brethren arrived," he wrote to Elder Orson Pratt
later that month. He had presumed that emigration leaders "would
consider their late arrival in America and not start them across the
Plains until another year."[3]

Although it was still two weeks before the first winter storm
would arrive, Brigham Young immediately sensed the potential for a

disaster. He knew that winter storms could strike the high plains of
Wyoming and the mountains of Utah in October. He knew that by
necessity the handcart companies were traveling with a minimum of
clothing, bedding, and food—and therefore would not have adequate protection from the elements or adequate food to sustain them
all the way to Salt Lake City. He also knew that there were not sufficient resupply wagons on the trail to provide the assistance that
would be needed.

"Bring in Those People Now on the Plains"

The minutes from the meeting where President Richards gave
his report do not show any great alarm. They matter-of-factly out-
line how many tons of flour and how much clothing the late companies would need.[4] When Brigham Young convened the general
conference the next morning, however, his tone changed to one of
great urgency. Perhaps this change occurred because he felt the need
for "savvy rhetoric, or because he had worried overnight, or because,
as he told the people, urgency was the dictation of the Holy Ghost
to him."[5]

"I will now give this people the subject and the text for the
Elders who may speak," Brigham Young said. "It is this. On the 5th
day of October, 1856, many of our brethren and sisters are on the
plains with handcarts, . . . and they must be brought here, we must
send assistance to them. The text will be, 'to get them here.' I want
the brethren who may speak to understand that their text is the
people on the plains, and the subject matter for this community is
to send for them and bring them in before winter sets in.

"That is my religion; that is the dictation of the Holy Ghost that
I possess. It is to save the people. . . . This is the salvation I am now
seeking for, to save our brethren that would be apt to perish, or suffer
extremely, if we do not send them assistance.

"I shall call upon the Bishops this day. I shall not wait until
tomorrow, nor until the next day, for 60 good mule teams and 12 or
15 wagons. I do not want to send oxen. I want good horses and

mules. They are in this Territory, and we must have them. Also 12 tons of flour and 40 good teamsters, besides those that drive the teams. . . .

"I will tell you all that your faith, religion, and profession of religion, will never save one soul of you in the celestial kingdom of our God, unless you carry out just such principles as I am now teaching you. Go and bring in those people now on the plains, and attend strictly to those things which we call temporal, or temporal duties, otherwise your faith will be in vain; the preaching you have heard will be in vain."[6]

President Franklin D. Richards and Daniel Spencer, who had returned together the previous day, also spoke during the conference. Having managed much of the emigration, they seemed to feel a special responsibility for these Saints; however, while expressing concern that the emigrants were late, they seemed to feel that all would be well with them.

From Franklin D. Richards: "The Saints that are now upon the plains, about one thousand with handcarts, feel that it is late in the season, and they expect to get cold fingers and toes. But they have this faith and confidence towards God, that he will overrule the storms that may come in the season thereof and turn them away, that their path may be freed from suffering more than they can bear. They have confidence to believe that this will be an open fall."[7]

From Daniel Spencer: "The emigration is late, quite late. But it is useless for me to undertake to explain why it is so. They are late, but the faith of those that have been associated with them is that the God of heaven will control the elements, providing that you, my brethren and sisters, render them that assistance which He has given you ability to do. . . .

"We feel for those brethren and sisters that are still upon the plains, for we have been in the old countries and seen their faith and diligence, and now we feel to plead with you to assist them."[8]

In the next morning's conference session, Brigham Young accelerated the theme of urgency:

"I feel disposed to be as speedy as possible in our operation with regard to helping our brethren who are now on the plains. Consequently I shall call upon the people forthwith for the help that is needed. I want them to give their names this morning, if they are ready to start on their journey tomorrow. And not say, 'I will go next week, or in ten days, or in a fortnight hence.' For I wish to start tomorrow morning.

"I want the sisters to have the privilege of fetching in blankets, skirts, stockings, shoes, etc. for the men, women, and children that are in those handcart companies. . . . I will give you the privilege of bringing hoods, winter bonnets, stockings, skirts, garments, and almost any description of clothing. Our brethren and sisters could not bring much with them on the plains, even if they had had it. . . .

"I now want brethren to come forward, for we need 40 good teamsters to help the brethren on the plains. You may rise up now and give your names."[9]

The blacksmiths in the congregation were then dismissed so they could shoe the horses and repair the wagons of those who were about to leave. Many men came to the pulpit. And some of the sisters, rather than wait until they got home to find warm clothing to send, "stripped off their petticoats, stockings, and everything they could spare, right there in the tabernacle" to be packed into the wagons.[10]

SACRIFICES REQUIRED BY THE RESCUE

In issuing the call to rescue, Brigham Young must have wondered how much more he could ask the Saints to sacrifice. They had just endured two years of drought and famine. Although the harvest of 1856 was better, resources were still scarce. To help ensure survival for another year, every hand was needed to prepare for winter and plant wheat for the next season. LeRoy and Ann Hafen described this circumstance—and the Saints' response in spite of it:

"Only nine years removed from the stark desert it had settled upon with empty wagons and bare hands, the Mormon community was not yet one of surpluses. But the religious and human tie that bound the Saints in the Valley to those who soon might be freezing and starving on the Plains transcended the instinct for personal safety.

"Families of moderate means and the poorest individuals contributed from their meager stores. One lent a horse, one a wagon, one a tent; another, two bales of hay and a sack of barley. Some gave iron camp kettles, dutch ovens, brass buckets, tin cups and plates. Women darned socks and shawls; patched underwear, trousers, and dresses; faced quilts, sewed together pieces of blankets; and took clothes from their own backs. Families brought out from their scant cellars sacks of flour, sides of home cured bacon, bags of beans, dried corn, packages of sugar and rice."[11]

From Wallace Stegner's perspective, the rescue effort would show "the priesthood and the people of Mormonism . . . at their compassionate and efficient best."[12]

COUNTING THE COST OF THE RESCUE

As admirable as these sacrifices were, Brigham Young was displeased that they were necessary—and wanted to make sure they would not be needed again. Ever practical, he had long said he wanted emigrants to leave their homelands early enough so they could arrive in Utah by August. That would allow them, he said, to "aid in the harvest and have an opportunity to lay up some provisions for winter; . . . whereas now a great portion have to be sustained by charity almost a year before they can do much for themselves."[13]

Instead of contributing to the general economy, late-arriving emigrants could seriously strain the territory's resources. In 1856 the first three handcart companies had already arrived relatively late. Now two more companies would not only be arriving late but would draw away hundreds of the best men and teams for the rescue effort. Brigham Young calculated the cost of this too:

"This people are this day deprived of thousands of acres of wheat that would have been sowed by this time, had it not been for the misconduct of our immigration affairs this year, and we would have had an early harvest, but now we may have to live on roots and weeds again before we get the wheat."[14]

In a letter to Orson Pratt, who succeeded Franklin D. Richards as president of the European Mission, Brigham Young emphasized the need for the next year's emigration to start early—and continued to count the cost of late arrivals:

"The immigration is too late; this is an evil that must be remedied in the future. We now give you positive instructions [that] you are not to permit any company to leave the Missouri river [Florence] later than the first of August, and it is far more preferable that they leave early in June or May. . . .

"Every year, large numbers of men and great quantities of provisions are sent back to meet the immigration; this is an outlay which is now considered, as it always has been, gratuitous; but it is a heavy task upon the people and is becoming a serious public detriment. It prevents thousands of acres of wheat from being sown in the fall, which would . . . save an immense amount of labour in watering, besides producing a larger amount of wheat, earlier harvest, and of superiour quality."[15] Earlier arrivals, Brigham Young concluded, would benefit not only the emigrants but "all Israel."

PROPHETIC FORESIGHT IN THE CALL TO RESCUE

Brigham Young knew the pioneer trail well, having crossed it three times. That experience surely influenced his reaction to President Richards's news. But his reaction also seems to be a result of prophetic foresight and inspiration. For example, the weather in Wyoming could be expected to get cold and even snowy in October, but subzero temperatures with the capacity to kill in just hours were more a possibility than an expectation. Yet Brigham Young seemed to anticipate the severity of the weather even though the winter storms were still two weeks away.

Prophetic foresight was also evident in the urgency of Brigham Young's call to rescue. This urgency may have seemed unreasonable at the time. Given the magnitude of the mission—rescuing more than a thousand people, hundreds of whom were more than a three-week journey away—the rescuers could have justifiably expected to have a few days to get ready. Instead, Brigham Young called for volunteers to come to the pulpit the day of conference and expected the first team to be on the trail within a day. As the story will soon show, each additional day probably would have cost many lives.

The inspiration behind this sense of urgency is even more remarkable in light of the report of Franklin D. Richards. As mentioned earlier, President Richards had known the handcart companies would need help, but his promises to them suggest that he thought they would be all right. Ever optimistic, he thought the Willie company would be much closer than they actually were. It is therefore understandable that his report to Brigham Young would express concern but not extreme urgency. The uncompromised urgency of Brigham Young's call to rescue seems to show foresight that they were much farther away and in a more precarious condition than reported.

In summary, the call to rescue illustrates a fundamental characteristic of Brigham Young. Franklin D. Richards and others had promised—and were expecting—that miracles from heaven would deliver the handcart companies safely to Zion. Brigham Young also looked for help from heaven, but he was not a person who waited upon such miracles.

DEPARTURE AND PROGRESS OF THE FIRST RESCUE TEAM

The first rescue team left the Salt Lake Valley on October 7. Led by Captain George D. Grant, this group consisted of 27 men and 16 wagons loaded with food and supplies.[16] By the end of October, at least 250 relief wagons would be headed east as part of the rescue effort.[17]

Six members of this first rescue team had been part of Franklin D. Richards's group that had just returned to Salt Lake City after long service abroad. After being home less than three days, these

George D. Grant

six men left again, undertaking a mission that would subject them to miserable conditions and put their lives at risk. They included Captain George D. Grant, Joseph A. Young (son of Brigham Young), Cyrus Wheelock, William H. Kimball, James Ferguson, and Chauncey Webb. Joseph Young and Cyrus Wheelock had traveled with President Richards all the way from England after concluding their missions. The other four men had returned from their missions earlier in the year and spent several months in the Midwest assisting the handcart companies before joining President Richards's group when it left Florence.

George Grant and William Kimball may have felt a special obligation to help with the rescue because they had urged the companies forward a few weeks earlier in Florence. Perhaps Brigham Young imposed that sense of obligation on them. Or perhaps they felt it in their own consciences, though they could not have known the magnitude of the error when they embarked on the rescue. Whatever their motivations, all six of these men were the ultimate example of sacrificing comfort and convenience to duty and concern for others.

The first rescue team reached Fort Bridger on October 12, having traveled 113 miles in six days. In Salt Lake City, Franklin D. Richards had estimated that the Willie company might be as near as Fort Bridger. However, Captain Grant found no sign of them. The next day the rescue team traveled to Black's Fork, and two days later, October 15, they arrived at the Green River crossing. President Richards had thought the Willie company would be no farther away than the Green River, but there was still no sign of them.[18] Perhaps sensing that the handcart pioneers were in serious trouble, one of the rescuers recorded, "Our hearts began to ache when we reached Green River and yet no word of them."[19]

Not finding the Willie company as far along as expected, Captain Grant decided to send an express team to find them, let them know that help was on the way, and report back. Departing on October 14, this team consisted of Cyrus Wheelock, Joseph Young, Stephen Taylor, and Abel Garr.[20]

How far away was the Willie company? On October 14, the day the express went ahead of the main rescue team to find them, they were just arriving at Independence Rock, more than 160 miles away from where the rescuers expected them to be. Here was one of many examples of the rescuers going the extra mile, having to travel much farther than expected when they left their families and set out for the rescue.

There is a disparity in Franklin D. Richards's estimates on the meeting point for the resupply. In his letter to James Willie, he had estimated the meeting point to be South Pass (231 miles from Salt Lake City). For the rescuers who left Salt Lake City, he apparently estimated the meeting point to be as close as Fort Bridger (113 miles away) or no farther than the Green River (169 miles away). Both estimates were optimistic in favor of the different audiences for them. The actual meeting point would be east of Rocky Ridge, some 270 miles from Salt Lake City.

FROM INDEPENDENCE ROCK
TO FIFTH CROSSING

O n October 14 the Willie company arrived at the Sweetwater River, crossed it for the first time, and camped near Independence Rock. They had taken two weeks to travel the 177 miles from Fort Laramie, continuing to average about 12.5 miles a day. The Sweetwater was a welcome sight, as the previous 50 miles had been almost without water and were considered some of the most difficult of the entire trail.

The headwaters of the Sweetwater River are in the Wind River Mountains in western Wyoming. The Sweetwater flows into the North Platte River, which now goes through Pathfinder Reservoir.

Independence Rock is a smooth, rounded mass of granite at the eastern end of the Sweetwater valley, about 50 miles southwest of Casper and five miles east of Devil's Gate. It was one of the most prominent landmarks on the trail.

Independence Rock

RATIONS REDUCED AGAIN

Although the Willie company had been on reduced rations for two weeks, trying to conserve their flour, by the time they reached Independence Rock they were down to a four- or five-day supply. The resupply assistance they hoped for at South Pass was 100 miles away—and uncertain. Trying not to run out of flour before that point, James Willie and the other leaders decided to reduce rations even more drastically. Men would receive 10.5 ounces each day, women 9 ounces, and children 3 to 6 ounces depending on their age and size.[1] For adults, this would be the approximate equivalent of 6 or 7 slices of bread for the entire day.

From Independence Rock the trail generally follows the Sweetwater River for nearly all of the 100 miles to the Continental Divide at South Pass. The Willie company would have to cross the river eight more times and average at least 20 miles a day to get to South Pass before their flour was gone. During this time, the adults would have a dietary deficit of about 3,000 calories a day.

"THE PEOPLE ARE GETTING WEAK, AND FAILING VERY FAST"

On October 15, the first day of twice-reduced rations, the Willie company traveled 16 miles from Independence Rock. The burden of this journey was heavy in Levi Savage's journal entry that night: "The people are getting weak, and failing very fast, a great many sick. Our teams are also failing fast, and it requires great exertion to make any progress." The burden was also evident in the script of this journal entry. To that point, Levi Savage's writing had always been tidy, the letters tight and lines straight. On that day the letters were coarse, the lines ragged, as though he hardly had strength to hold a pen.

The problems of short rations began to be compounded by colder weather. Although the days were still mild, the nights chilled the life out of some people, and the mountains in the distance showed ominous signs. John Chislett described the challenges the company faced during these days along the Sweetwater:

"We had not travelled far up the Sweetwater before the nights, which had gradually been getting colder since we left Laramie, became very severe. The mountains before us, as we approached nearer to them, revealed themselves to view mantled nearly to their base in snow, and tokens of a coming storm were discernible in the clouds which each day seemed to lower around us.

"In our frequent crossings of the Sweetwater, we had really 'a hard road to travel.' The water was beautiful to the eye, as it rolled over its rocky bed as clear as crystal; but when we waded it time after time at each ford to get the carts, the women, and the children over, the beautiful stream, with its romantic surroundings (which should awaken holy and poetic feelings in the soul, and draw it nearer to the Great Author of life), lost to us its beauty, and the chill which it sent through our systems drove out from our minds all holy and devout aspirations, and left a void, a sadness, and—in some cases—doubts as to the justice of an overruling Providence.

"Our 17 pounds of clothing and bedding was now altogether insufficient for our comfort. Nearly all suffered more or less at night from cold. Instead of getting up in the morning strong, refreshed, vigorous, and prepared for the hardships of another day of toil, the poor 'Saints' were to be seen crawling out from their tents looking haggard, benumbed, and showing an utter lack of that vitality so necessary to our success."[2]

Not yet a husband or father himself, John Chislett was moved by the devotion of those who were husbands and fathers, trying to care for their wives and children in such extreme circumstances:

"It was surprising to an unmarried man to witness the devotion of men to their families and to the faith, under these trying circumstances. Many a father pulled his cart, with his little children on it, until the day preceding his death. I have seen some pull their carts in the morning, give out during the day, and die before next morning. These people died with the calm faith and fortitude of martyrs. Their greatest regret seemed to be leaving their families behind them, and their bodies on the plains or mountains instead of being laid in the consecrated ground of Zion. The sorrow and mourning of the bereaved, as they saw their husbands and fathers rudely interred, were affecting in the extreme, and none but a heart of stone could repress a tear of sympathy at the sad spectacle."[3]

The sacrifices that many people made, even for others who were not their kin, impressed 15-year-old George Cunningham. "Some would sacrifice themselves by giving their food or perhaps some old blanket that covered them," he wrote. "In common cares, we cannot tell what our friends and neighbors are, but there are circumstances which undoubtedly proved them."[4]

"Death's Stamp Could Be Traced upon Their Features"

As the Willie company proceeded on short rations, the carts "dragged like millstones at their heels."[5] Wallace Stegner described the changes these conditions brought about:

"Now those who wore out were as often as not their strongest, the men who had labored all the way to protect the families and the weaker members. These days, they stumbled into camp with their faces drawn and set, and sometimes if they rested a few minutes before putting up the tents, they lay down and died without ever knowing how completely exhausted they were."[6]

John Chislett's firsthand account confirms Stegner's words:

"Cold weather, scarcity of food, lassitude, and fatigue from over-exertion soon produced their effects. Our old and infirm people began to droop, and they no sooner lost spirit and courage than death's stamp could be traced upon their features. Life went out as smoothly as a lamp ceases to burn when the oil is gone. At first the deaths occurred slowly and irregularly, but in a few days at more frequent intervals, until we soon thought it unusual to leave a campground without burying one or more persons.

"Death was not long confined in its ravages to the old and infirm, but the young and naturally strong were among its victims.

Men who were, so to speak, as strong as lions when we started on our journey, and who had been our best supports, were compelled to succumb to the grim monster. These men were worn down by hunger, scarcity of clothing and bedding, and too much labour in helping their families. Weakness and debility were accompanied by dysentery. This we could not stop or even alleviate, no proper medicines being in the camp; and in almost every instance it carried off the parties attacked."[7]

Struggles of William James

William James, who was emigrating with his wife and eight children, was in poor health even before leaving England. At this point of the journey, his health declined even further. Laleta Dixon vividly describes how William James and others were suffering as a result of inadequate food, clothing, and footwear:

"Many were weakening from the lack of nourishing food. The young and the old and the weak began to die quietly. Even the strong men, who were secretly giving their portion to their families, pulled their carts until they died. Soon rations were cut again. Clothing was in rags, especially shoes. Any piece of rag, burlap, or canvas was tied around the feet. All too soon this was chewed through by the torturous terrain. It was not uncommon to take clothing from the dead to cover the living. Many lives were saved in this way."[8]

Nineteen-year-old Sarah James was more specific about her father's condition:

"Father was white and drawn. I knew that Mother was worried about him, for he was getting weaker all the time and seemed to feel that there was no use in all the struggle. Mother had taken as much of the load off his shoulders as she could in pulling the cart. We girls and [13-year-old] Reuben did most of the work so that Father could rest a lot. Mother didn't have much to say, and I wondered if she remembered that council meeting in [Florence] and wished that we had taken the advice of the more experienced people. I am sure that many of us had those thoughts."[9]

Although there was little meat left on the cattle, Sarah James received rations of bones and hides with gratitude. Recalling the desperate hunger, she wrote:

"How good the soup tasted made from the bones of those cows although there wasn't any fat on them. The hides we used to roast after taking all the hair off of them. I even decided to cook the tatters of my shoes and make soup of them. It brought a smile to my father's sad face when I made the suggestion, but mother was a bit impatient with me and told me that I'd have to eat the muddy things myself."[10]

"Each Death Weakened Our Forces"

The Willie company reached the Fifth Crossing of the Sweetwater on October 18. They had traveled 44 miles in four days from Independence Rock, an impressive effort given that they were weakening with each step. But they were down to a one-day supply of food with 56 miles to go before they could hope for a resupply at South Pass, and people were dying every day.

Death of Caroline Reeder

The Reeder family was the first to suffer a death between Independence Rock and the Fifth Crossing. David Reeder, the father of the family, had died two weeks earlier. His 17-year-old daughter Caroline died on October 15 near Independence Rock. Her brother Robert recalled that she died while doing her duty of gathering firewood:

"Our rations were growing shorter, and we reduced them by common consent from day to day. Nights were getting colder, and some would sit down by the roadside and die. My younger sister, Caroline, 17 years old, after traveling all day and seeing the camp being made for the night, took off her apron to tie some sagebrush in to bring into the camp. She sat down to rest, leaning on her bundle, exhausted. They found her chilled and dying and carried her to camp. She died without gaining consciousness. She, too, was placed in an unmarked grave. . . . Her death was another real loss to us, but we must hurry on."[11]

Death of George Curtis

George Curtis, an elderly man, had been the first member of the Willie company to suffer the death of a loved one on the journey. His wife, Rachel, had died three days after leaving England and was buried at sea (see page 9). Rather than weakening George's resolve, her death seemed to intensify his yearning for Zion, as though he needed to keep going for her as well as himself. With each step a burden and a hope, he continued the lonely journey for five months after his wife's death. Then on October 16, just beyond Independence Rock, his journey also ended. He was only three weeks away from Zion.

Two others died on October 16, another the next day, and another the next. John Chislett recalled the effects of these deaths on the company:

"Each death weakened our forces. In my hundred I could not raise enough men to pitch a tent when we encamped, and now it was that I had to exert myself to the utmost. I wonder I did not die, as many did who were stronger than I was. When we pitched our camp in the evening of each day, I had to lift the sick from the wagon and carry them to the fire, and in the morning carry them again on my back to the wagon. When any in my hundred died, I had to inter them, often helping to dig the grave myself. In performing these sad offices I always offered up a heartfelt prayer to that God who beheld our sufferings, and begged him to avert destruction from us and send us help."[12]

CHAPTER 14

THE RESCUERS ARRIVE

While the Willie company was toiling westward, the first rescue team was racing east toward them. The express from the rescue team was averaging about 27 miles a day since being sent ahead of the rest of the group, which averaged about 20 miles a day. Along the way this group, which started with only 27 men and 16 wagons, received small reinforcements.

On October 18 the express rescuers were camped near the Sixth Crossing of the Sweetwater. The remainder of the rescue team was about 35 miles behind them, camped on the Sweetwater River 3 miles east of South Pass. Captain George Grant decided to establish a relief station at this site to provide fresh supplies and assistance as the handcart companies came through. He assigned Reddick Allred to take charge of the station and left him with a few men and wagons. The next day, October 19, Captain Grant and the rest of his team hurried forward. They would not get far.

FIRST WINTER STORM ARRIVES;
FIRST RESCUERS ARRIVE

On October 19, members of the Willie company awoke to face one of the hardest days of the trek. It was a Sunday—but not a day of rest. The company had only a one-day supply of flour and was desperate to reach the potential resupply at South Pass, still 56 miles away. Camped at the Fifth Crossing of the Sweetwater, they would have to travel 16 miles, all the way to the Sixth Crossing, the first day. Stopping short of the Sixth Crossing was out of the question because there was no water or wood along the way.[1]

After issuing the last ration of flour, the Willie company started out on one of the most bleak, exposed sections of the trail. Midway through the day, the first winter storm blasted in, the snow accompanied by a shrill, furious wind. Almost immediately, as if this were the last adversity the company could bear, hope arrived. Near a place called the Ice Slough, the express rescuers finally found the Willie company. In the appendix to the Willie company journal, William Woodward recorded:

"C. H. Wheelock and Joseph A. Young with two other brethren met us a short distance west of 'Ice Springs' and brought us the cheering intelligence that assistance was near at hand; that several wagons loaded with flour, onions, and clothing, including bedding, [were] within a day's drive of us."[2]

John Chislett recalled: "As we were resting for a short time at noon, a light wagon was driven into our camp from the west. Its occupants were Joseph A. Young and Stephen Taylor. They informed us that a train of supplies was on the way, and we might expect to meet it in a day or two. More welcome messengers never came from the courts of glory than these two young men were to us."[3]

There is a historical marker at the Ice Slough along Highway 287. The Ice Slough is also called Ice Springs in some accounts.

These messengers provided hope, but because they were traveling light, they did not have the supplies to provide much help. They shared some flour and onions and then hurried on in search of the Martin company, who, John Chislett correctly assumed, "were even worse off than we were."[4] Indeed, on this same day the Martin company and the Hodgetts and Hunt wagon companies were approximately 100 miles behind the Willie company and were having their own severe trials in the same storm at the last crossing of the Platte River.

Before leaving, Joseph Young pulled a small onion from his pocket and gave it to 20-year-old Emily Hill, whom he had known while serving as a missionary in England. Emily and her sister, Julia, had joined the Church as teenagers and were emigrating on their own (see pages 36–38). When Joseph Young saw Emily, he burst into tears. "Why do you cry, Brother Young?" she asked. "Oh, because you look so starved, and the provision wagons are [miles] away," he replied. Rather than eat the onion, Emily held on to it. That night she saw a man near the fire who appeared to be dying. Emily gave him the onion, and he later said that it had saved his life.[5]

Joseph A. Young

Of necessity, the Willie company pressed on toward the Sixth Crossing of the Sweetwater and finally reached it after dark. John Chislett recalled:

"We pursued our journey with renewed hope and after untold toil and fatigue, doubling teams frequently, going back to fetch up the straggling carts, and encouraging those who had dropped by the way to a little more exertion in view of our soon-to-be improved condition, we finally, late at night, got all to camp—the wind howling frightfully and the snow eddying around us in fitful gusts. But we had found a good camp among the willows, and after warming and partially drying ourselves before good fires, we ate our scanty fare, paid our usual devotions to the Deity, and retired to rest with hopes of coming aid."[6]

Describing this first night of sleeping in the snow, William Woodward wrote: "A snow fell on us that night about a foot deep. It was a sorry sight, over 400 people with handcarts, short of bedding, and to sleep on the cold ground. One thought is enough for a lifetime."[7]

The Mormon Handcart Visitors' Center at Sixth Crossing is located near the junction of Highways 287 and 135. The precise site of the Sixth

Crossing is not known, but it is thought to be a few miles upstream of this point.

THE STORM INTENSIFIES; MORE PEOPLE DIE

On the morning of October 20, from four to twelve inches of snow had accumulated. Continuing with John Chislett's account:

"Our cattle strayed widely during the storm, and some of them died. But what was worse to us than all this was the fact that five persons of both sexes lay in the cold embrace of death. The pitiless storm and the extra march of the previous day had been too much for their wasted energies, and they had passed through the dark valley to the bright world beyond. We buried these five people in one grave, wrapped only in the clothing and bedding in which they died. We had no materials with which to make coffins, and even if we had, we could not have spared time to make them, for it required all the efforts of the healthy few who remained to perform the ordinary camp duties and to look after the sick—the number of whom increased daily on our hands, notwithstanding so many were dying."[8]

Because the company's last ration of flour had been issued the previous morning, all they had left in the commissary were a few pounds of sugar and dried apples, a partial sack of rice, and the hard bread that Captain Willie had obtained at Fort Laramie.[9] This was hardly enough for a one-day supply, but it was distributed as far as it would go. In addition to the last food from the commissary, two of the skin-and-bones cattle were killed and issued for beef. "With this," John Chislett recalled, "we were informed that we would have to subsist until the coming supplies reached us."[10]

CAPTAIN WILLIE LEAVES TO FIND THE RESCUERS

The express rescuers had said that relief wagons were a day or two away. On the morning of October 20, with the Willie company camped at the Sixth Crossing of the Sweetwater and their food supply exhausted, Captain Willie decided that circumstances were so desperate that he would go search for these wagons. He took the ever-willing Joseph Elder with him. John Chislett recalled:

"Being surrounded by snow a foot deep, out of provisions, many of our people sick, and our cattle dying, it was decided that we should remain in our present camp until the supply train reached us. It was also resolved in council that Captain Willie with one man should go in search of the supply train and apprise its leader of our condition, and hasten him to our help. When this was done we settled down and made our camp as comfortable as we could. As Captain Willie and his companion left for the West, many a heart was lifted in prayer for their success and speedy return."[11]

Days of Terrible Suffering

The time it would take for Captain Willie to find the rescue team and return with them was filled with terrible suffering. John Chislett's account vividly describes the sickness and death:

"The scanty allowance of hard bread and poor beef . . . was mostly consumed the first day by the hungry, ravenous, famished souls.

"We killed more cattle and issued the meat, but eating it without bread did not satisfy hunger, and to those who were suffering from dysentery it did more harm than good. This terrible disease increased rapidly amongst us, . . . and several died from [it].

"Before we renewed our journey, the camp became so offensive and filthy that words would fail to describe its condition, and even common decency forbids the attempt. Suffice it to say that all the disgusting scenes which the reader might imagine would certainly not equal the terrible reality. It was enough to make the heavens weep. The recollection of it unmans me even now. . . .

"During that time I visited the sick, the widows whose husbands died in serving them, and the aged who could not help themselves, to know for myself where to dispense the few articles that had been placed in my charge for distribution. Such craving hunger I never saw before, and may God in his mercy spare me the sight again.

"As I was seen giving these things to the most needy, crowds of famished men and women surrounded me and begged for bread! Men whom I had known all the way from Liverpool, who had been true as steel in every stage of our journey, who in their homes in England and Scotland had never known want; men who by honest labour had sustained themselves and their families, and saved enough to cross the Atlantic and traverse the United States, whose hearts were cast in too great a mould to descend to a mean act or brook dishonour; such men as these came to me and begged bread.

"I felt humbled to the dust for my race and nation, and I hardly know which feeling was strongest at that time, pity for our condition, or malediction on the fates that so humbled the proud Anglo-Saxon nature. But duty might not be set aside by feeling, however natural, so I positively refused those men bread! But while I did so, I explained to them the painful position in which I was placed, and most of them acknowledged that I was right. Not a few of them afterwards spoke approvingly of my stern performance of duty. It is difficult, however, to reason with a hungry man; but these noble fellows, when they comprehended my position, had faith in my honour. Some of them are in Utah today, and when we meet, the strong grip of friendship overcomes, for the moment at least, all differences of opinion which we may entertain on any subject. May the Heavens ever be kind to them, whatever their faith, for they are good men and true. And the sisters who suffered with us—may the loving angels ever be near them to guard them from the ills of life."[12]

Death of John Linford

In addition to the five people who were found dead on the morning of October 20, four others died during the day and four more the next two days.[13] One of these was John Linford, who left behind his wife and three sons. He had been ill for most of the journey across the Midwest and gradually got worse until he needed to be pulled in the handcart. Despite his poor condition, he fulfilled his assignment as tent leader, taking responsibility for 20 people.

Showing his concern for each individual, he wrote their names and ages in his small leather-bound notebook. Among those under his care was the Gadd family, who had already suffered two deaths.

When Levi Savage saw John Linford in such a weakened condition, he again did all he could to be of service, sacrificing his own last ration of flour. John Linford's youngest son, 11-year-old Amasa, recalled, "While father was sick and just before he died of starvation, Levi Savage emptied his flour sack to make him some skilly as it was called; after eating this he died."[14]

Just before John Linford died, his wife asked if he was sorry they had undertaken the journey. Taking the long-range view, he said, "No, Maria. I am glad we came. I shall not live to reach Salt Lake, but you and the boys will, and I do not regret all we have gone through if our boys can grow up and raise their families in Zion."[15]

After John Linford died, one of his sons made the following entry in his father's little leather notebook: "Brother Willie went to meet the wagons on a mule, and father died the 21st of October 1856 down by the Sweetwater river at 5 o'clock in the morning. He had been ill from Florence, first the fever and ague and then weakness and the diarrhea. The journey was too much for him."[16]

The rescue team would arrive later on the day John Linford died.

The Thread of Life Was Nearly Exhausted

Concerning these dark days of death, George Cunningham applied the Apostle Paul's words of hope about the Resurrection in an almost despairing way to describe the condition of the Willie company: "One old writer said, 'O death, where is thy sting? O grave, where is thy victory?' It had gone too far to dread death, for the thread of life had by this time been nearly exhausted. Neither had the grave much victory to boast of, for many did not feel like going one step out of its way."[17]

CAPTAIN WILLIE FINDS THE RESCUERS

Captain Willie and Joseph Elder expected to find the rescuers a few miles away and return before evening on the same day they left, October 20.[18] But after traveling 10 to 12 miles to the base of Rocky Ridge, they hadn't found them.[19] So they had to ascend the ridge—one of the hardest parts of the trail—in snowy, freezing weather. "The snow and an awful cold wind blew in our faces all day," Joseph Elder wrote.[20]

After climbing Rocky Ridge, Captain Willie and Joseph Elder still saw no sign of the rescuers. They kept going, perhaps wondering if somehow they had bypassed the team or, in all the snow, lost the trail. Finally, near nightfall, and after traveling what Joseph Elder said was 27 miles, they saw a marker that pointed off the trail.[21] Captain Willie and Joseph Elder followed the marker and soon found Captain Grant and his men camped in a thicket of willows. The rescuers had gone there the previous day to seek protection from the storm.

Harvey Cluff's Signboard

That Captain Willie found the rescuers is something of a miracle—and another example of someone going the extra mile. After the rescuers set up camp off the trail, they realized that if the express team returned with word about the handcart companies, they would be unable to see the camp and would pass by it. Harvey Cluff, a 20-year-old member of the rescue team, recalled:

"I volunteered to take a signboard and place it at a conspicuous place at the main road. This was designed to direct the express party who was expected to return about this time, so they would not miss us. In facing the northern blast up hill, I found it quite difficult to keep from freezing. I had only been back to camp a short time when two men rode up from Willie's handcart company. The signboard had done the work of salvation.

"Had Captain Willie and his fellow traveler from his company continued on the road, they certainly would have perished as they would have reached the Sweetwater where the storm first struck us. [They said] the handcart company was then 25 miles from our camp. As they [Willie and Elder] had traveled that distance without food for themselves or horses and no bedding, they must have perished. I have always regarded this act of mine as the means of their salvation."[22]

Harvey Cluff's act of service had an influence that reached far beyond his expectations. His sign was the means of salvation not only for James Willie and Joseph Elder but perhaps also for the Willie company. Had James Willie and Joseph Elder bypassed the camp, the rescuers might have stayed there another two or three days while awaiting better weather. If they had waited even two more days and then taken another day or two to cross Rocky Ridge and reach the handcart camp, the Willie company would have been three or four days without a particle of food.

A Pace That Stretched Every Man to the Breaking Point

It is natural to wonder why Captain Grant's team, which had been traveling at top speed for nearly two weeks, did not try to make any progress on the 20th. The storm made traveling difficult, but James Willie and Joseph Elder had traveled all day in it. The best explanation seems to come from John Chislett, who said that until Captain Willie and Joseph Elder arrived, the rescuers did not know "that we were so utterly destitute"—that they were literally perishing just a few miles away.[23] On this issue, Rebecca Bartholomew and Leonard J. Arrington concluded:

"Had anyone in the relief party foreseen the condition of either of the handcart companies, they would have . . . traveled day and night until their animals broke. It was just as well they did not know, for the relief effort would already require more strength and supplies than they carried. [As it was,] their pace would already stretch every man to the breaking point. Captain Burton had seen rigorous action in Tooele County while chasing Indian marauders; his company had been caught in summer with no water and in winter with no tents, bedding, or warm coats. But of the present campaign he would later state, 'This was the hardest trip of my life.' "[24]

ARRIVAL OF THE RESCUE TEAM

Early on October 21, the morning after Captain Willie found the rescue team, they hitched up their wagons and began pushing their way over Rocky Ridge toward the Willie company. They traveled as fast as they could in the conditions, retracing the grueling miles that Captain Willie and Joseph Elder had traveled the previous day. One of the rescuers, Harvey Cluff, recalled:

"The depth of the snow made traveling extremely difficult, and the whole day was spent before we reached the camp. . . . Arriving within the confines of this emigrant camp, a most thrilling and touching scene was enacted, melting to tears the stoutest hearts. Young maidens and feeble old ladies threw off all restraint and freely embraced their deliverers, expressing in a flow of kisses the gratitude which their tongues failed to utter.

"This was certainly the most timely arrival of a relief party recorded in history, for the salvation of a people. [Four] hundred people with handcarts, a scanty supply of clothing, bedding, and less supply of provisions, upon the plains in snow ten inches deep. . . . Think of it, ye mountaineers. [Three] hundred miles from any possible supply of provisions. You no longer wonder at the joy manifested by that perishing people when they saw salvation pull into their camp."[25]

Daniel W. Jones, another member of the rescue team, recorded that what he saw "would stir the feelings of the hardest heart. They were in a poor place, the storm having caught them where fuel was scarce. They were out of provisions and really freezing and starving to death. The morning after our arrival nine were buried in one grave. We did all we could to relieve them. The boys struck out on horseback and dragged up a lot of wood; provisions were distributed, and all went to work to cheer the sufferers."[26]

John Chislett's account of the rescue team's arrival is unrestrained in its expression of relief and gratitude:

"Just as the sun was sinking beautifully behind the distant hills, on an eminence immediately west of our camp, several covered wagons, each drawn by four horses, were seen coming toward us. The news ran through the camp like wildfire, and all who were able to leave their beds turned out en masse to see them. A few minutes brought them sufficiently near to reveal our faithful captain slightly in advance of the train.

"Shouts of joy rent the air; strong men wept till tears ran freely down their furrowed and sunburnt cheeks, and little children partook of the joy which some of them hardly understood, and fairly danced around with gladness. Restraint was set aside in the general rejoicing, and as the brethren entered our camp the sisters fell upon them and deluged the brethren with kisses. The brethren were so overcome that they could not for some time utter a word, but in choking silence repressed all demonstration of those emotions that evidently mastered them. Soon, however, feeling was somewhat abated, and such a shaking of hands, such words of welcome, and such invocation of God's blessing have seldom been witnessed.

" . . . That evening, for the first time in quite a period, the songs of Zion were to be heard in the camp, and peals of laughter issued from the little knots of people as they chatted around the fires. The change seemed almost miraculous, so sudden was it from grave to gay, from sorrow to gladness, from mourning to rejoicing. With the cravings of hunger satisfied, and with hearts filled with gratitude to God and our good brethren, we all united in prayer, and then retired to rest."[27]

Mary Hurren, who was only 7 years old at the time, 70 years later recalled the arrival of the rescue team in vivid detail:

"Captain Willie went ahead through the snow to meet the relief wagons and urge them to hurry as the people were freezing and starving to death. If help had not come when it did, there would have been no one left to tell the tale. As a small girl I could hear the squeaking of the wagons as they came through the snow before I was able to see them. Tears streamed down the cheeks of the men, and the children danced for joy. As soon as the people could control their feelings, they all knelt down in the snow and gave thanks to God for his kindness and goodness unto them. The last supply of food in the camp had been given out two days before the relief wagons came. They came just in time to save our lives."[28]

"How Nobly, How Faithfully, How Bravely They Worked"

Earlier in his account, John Chislett had criticized William Kimball and George Grant for encouraging the Willie company to press on to Salt Lake City rather than stay in Florence. When John Chislett saw these men back on the trail leading the rescue, his heart overflowed with gratitude toward them:

"Among the brethren who came to our succor were elders W. H. Kimball and G. D. Grant. They had remained but a few days in the Valley before starting back to meet us. May God ever bless them for their generous, unselfish kindness and their manly fortitude! They felt that they had, in a great measure, contributed to our sad position; but how nobly, how faithfully, how bravely they worked to bring us safely to the Valley—to the Zion of our hopes!"[29]

Unlike John Chislett, Johan Ahmanson expressed lingering resentment toward William Kimball in his account of the arrival of the rescuers. Twice he called him the "snow prophet," an allusion to the promise he had made in Florence to eat all the snow that would fall on the Willie company. His account then described the change in William Kimball when he saw the Willie company snowbound and distressed: "His courage was hardly as great now as it had been in Florence."[30]

Like others who oversaw the emigration, William Kimball had made some well-meaning but costly errors in judgment. He knew that despite giving his best efforts for six months to help the emigrants, he had contributed to their plight. How his heart must have ached when he first saw them in such a pitiful condition. He had known and loved many of these people since his mission in England. These were the people he had said were so filled with the spirit of gathering that they were "willing to part with all their effects, and toddle off with a few things in a pocket handkerchief."[31] Now many of them had died far short of Zion, others were dying, and others would be maimed. Getting any of them safely to Salt Lake City must have seemed impossible, given their physical condition and the brutal cold.

William Kimball was not a person who left others to make amends for his errors. Rather than shrink with guilt and shame, he would spend seven weeks in the rescue effort, working tirelessly to help those who were suffering because they had followed the counsel that he and other leaders had given. Such a response from William Kimball, as well as the other five missionaries who got back on the trail so soon after returning home, drew the admiration of Wallace Stegner:

"[Their presence] was significant. They were the missionaries who had converted a good many of the handcart emigrants in the first place. They had worked in Iowa City and Florence to get them outfitted. They had contributed to possible disaster by encouraging the tenderfeet to set out so late from Winter Quarters. They may have felt partially responsible, or have felt the Church to be responsible, for the delays at Iowa City. Whatever may be said of their excessive zeal in the first place, they were neither indifferent nor cowardly once they knew the handcart companies might be in distress. Separated from their families for two years or more, restored to the valley no more than 48 hours, they turned unhesitatingly around and drove out again with the rescue wagons."[32]

RAINING MANNA ON THE PLAINS OF AMERICA

Before the handcart pioneers left on their journey, President Franklin D. Richards had told them, "The Lord can rain manna on the plains of America just as easily as He did on the deserts of Arabia."[33] Was this an example of a tendency to issue idealistic promises? Or was the promise in some measure fulfilled? Although manna had not fallen from the sky, the flour from the rescuers was bread from heaven nevertheless. Although its arrival was not an inexplicable supernatural miracle, it was a miracle in its own right, having been initiated by an inspired prophet and carried out by people who sacrificed greatly to bring it. Without it, most members of the company probably would have perished.

THE RESCUE IS TOO LATE FOR SOME

The arrival of the rescuers was just in time to save hundreds from death by starvation and exposure. Some people, however, were too far declined for the rescuers to help. On the day after the rescuers arrived, two members of the company died, including Eliza Philpot, whose husband had died five days earlier. Their two daughters, ages 14 and 11, were suddenly orphans in a strange, inhospitable land. John Chislett wrote:

"Timely and good beyond estimate as the help which we received from the Valley was to our company generally, it was too late for some of our number. They were already prostrated and beyond all human help. Some seemed to have lost mental as well as physical energy. We talked to them of our improved condition, appealed to their love of life and showed them how easy it was to retain that life by arousing themselves; but all to no purpose. We then addressed ourselves to their religious feelings, their wish to see Zion; to know the Prophet Brigham; [we] showed them the good things that he had sent out to us, and told them how deeply he sympathized with us in our sufferings, and what a welcome he would give us when we reached the city. But all our efforts were unavailing; they had lost all love of life, all sense of surrounding things, and had sunk down into a state of indescribable apathy.

"The weather grew colder . . . , and many got their feet so badly frozen that they could not walk, and had to be lifted from place to place. Some got their fingers frozen; others their ears; and one woman lost her sight by the frost. These severities of the weather also increased our number of deaths."[34]

THE RESCUE TEAM DIVIDES; THE JOURNEY RESUMES

The first rescue team had reached the Willie company on October 21. Early the next morning, the rescuers divided, some staying to help the Willie company and others going on to search for the Martin company. In John Chislett's words:

"The small company which came to our relief divided: one half, under G. D. Grant, going east to meet Martin's company, and the other half, under W. H. Kimball, remaining with us. From this point until we reached the Valley, W. H. Kimball took full charge of us."[35]

The first rescue team had left Salt Lake City with only 27 men and 16 wagons, and they had received small reinforcements along the way—few resources for rescuing some 1,300 people. The Willie company journal records that the rescue team arrived with 14 wagons. Of those wagons, only 6 stayed with the Willie company. Captain George D. Grant took the other wagons east to find the Martin, Hodgetts, and Hunt companies.

A monument that memorializes the rescue of the Willie company is located at the eastern base of Rocky Ridge, about 14 miles from the Sixth Crossing visitors' center (for directions to the monument, see pages 158–59). When President Gordon B. Hinckley dedicated this monument in 1992, he said members of the Willie company "danced on frozen limbs with gladness for those who had come to rescue them."[36]

CHAPTER 15

CROSSING ROCKY RIDGE

As I walked over Rocky Ridge, I wondered if I have sacrificed enough. In my generation, I have not seen so much sacrifice by so many. I wonder what more I should have done, and should be doing, to further this work.

—PRESIDENT JAMES E. FAUST

A fter the rescue team divided on the morning of October 22, William Kimball and the other rescuers who stayed with the Willie company somehow got them going again. According to the company journal and the daily journal of Levi Savage, that day the group traveled 10 or 11 miles to a camp near the base of Rocky Ridge.[1] "The wind blew bleak and cold, and firewood [was] very scarce," Levi Savage wrote. In his next words a person can feel the cold, hard ground that members of the company slept on that night: "The Saints were obliged to spread their light bedding on the snow, and in this cold state endeavored to obtain a little rest."[2]

Whatever rest the members of the Willie company got that night must have come only because of complete exhaustion. The next morning, October 23, they awoke to face their biggest challenge yet: the ascent of Rocky Ridge, which at one point climbs 700 feet in two miles. Because only six rescue wagons had stayed with the Willie company, relatively few people could ride. Somehow most of them would have to arise from being near death and not only walk over Rocky Ridge but do so in arctic conditions while pulling their hand-carts.

The trek over Rocky Ridge would cover 15 or 16 miles and take some of the people 20 hours, ending at Rock Creek.[3] Every step of

A section of the trail at Rocky Ridge

these miles would be through 18 inches of snow and into a fierce northwest wind that dropped windchill temperatures below zero. Rocky Ridge has been called a "forced march"[4]—because everyone was forced to keep moving or die.

Rocky Ridge was the ultimate trial for the Willie company. Joseph Elder, who had already crossed Rocky Ridge twice in the previous three days to find and return with the rescuers, described how much harder it was when the entire company made the ascent:

"That was an awful day. Many can never forget the scenes they witnessed that day. Men, women, and children weakened down by cold and hunger, weeping, crying, and some even dying by the roadside. It was very late before we all got into camp. Oh, how my heart did quake and shudder at the awful scenes which surrounded me."[5]

Along with being the ultimate trial, Rocky Ridge was a tremendous triumph of faith and courage. That any of the company made it through that day, given their already weakened condition and the brutal elements, can be explained in no other way.

On the day the Willie company crossed Rocky Ridge, the Martin company arrived at Red Buttes, their last camp on the Platte River, approximately 115 miles behind them. Even the express members of the rescue team would not reach the Martin company until October 28, nine days after they had found the Willie company.

TRAGEDY FOR THE WILLIAM JAMES FAMILY AT ROCKY RIDGE

William James had been in poor health before leaving England. As the company traveled along the Sweetwater, his health declined further to the point that his wife and children pulled the handcart. Despite his weak condition, on the morning of October 23 he was asked to help bury the dead before beginning the ascent of Rocky Ridge. His oldest daughter, Sarah, recalled:

"It was a bitter cold morning in October as we broke camp. As usual, there were dead to be buried before we could go on. Father and Reuben were with the burial detail. Mother, who was helping pull the heaviest cart, had stayed behind until they could finish their sad work.

"After a short service, we . . . ran ahead to catch the rest of the company, and mother and Reuben started to follow. Father collapsed and fell in the snow. He tried two or three times to get up with mother's help, then finally he asked her to go on and when he felt rested, he would come on [later]. Mother knew in her heart that he had given out, but perhaps, she said, in a few minutes with some rest he could come on."[6] Thirteen-year-old Reuben stayed with his father.

Mary Ann James, who was 11 years old at the time, spelled out the dilemma her mother faced: "Mother was placed in an awful position, her husband unable to go farther, and her little children far ahead hungry and freezing; what can she do? Father said, 'Go to the children; we will get in if we can.'"[7]

Exhibiting the strength that has been cited earlier, Jane James took the handcart and hurried to catch up to her children. Sarah recalled:

"She found us on the river bank. We were too frightened and tired to cross alone. We had forded this river before many times, but it had never seemed so far across. It was about 40 feet, I guess, to the other bank. Mother soon had us on our way. The water was icy, and soon our clothing was frozen to our bodies. Our feet were frozen numb. Cold and miserable, we reached the other bank, put on dry clothing, and joined the rest of the company.

"When we stopped for the night, we made inquiries about [Father and Reuben], but nothing had been heard of them. Since there were some who had been a few hours behind us, we felt they would come with the next group. All night we waited for word. Toward morning some of the captains who had gone out to gather up the stragglers came into camp bearing the dead body of my father and the badly frozen body of my brother Reuben. His injuries were so bad that he would suffer from them for the rest of his life.

"When morning came, father's body, along with others who had died during the night, were buried. . . . Brush was thrown in and then dirt. A fire was built over the grave to kill the scent to keep the wolves from digging up the remains.

"I can see my mother's face as she sat looking at the partly conscious Reuben. Her eyes looked so dead that I was afraid. She didn't sit long, however, for my mother was never one to cry. When it was time to move out, mother had her family ready to go. She put her invalid son in the cart with her baby [four-year-old John], and we joined the train. Our mother was a strong woman, and she would see us through anything."[8]

Mary Ann James also paid tribute to her mother's strength: "Imagine, if you can, my mother only a young woman of forty-one, her husband lying dead in a frozen wilderness, with seven little children, starved and freezing, crying for comfort. Her physical and mental endurance was surely nothing short of miraculous."[9]

JOHN CHISLETT'S ACCOUNT OF THE ROCKY RIDGE CROSSING

John Chislett was one of the captains referred to by Sarah James who worked late helping the "stragglers" to camp. His account also tells of the death of Sarah's father, William James:

"The day we crossed the Rocky Ridge it was snowing a little—the wind hard from the northwest—and blowing so keenly that it almost pierced us through. We had to wrap ourselves closely in blankets, quilts, or whatever else we could get, to keep from freezing. Captain Willie still attended to the details of the company's travelling, and this day he appointed me to bring up the rear. My duty was to stay behind everything and [see] that nobody was left along the road.

"I had to bury a man who had died in my hundred, and I finished doing so after the company had started. In about half an hour I set out on foot along to do my duty as rear-guard to the camp. The ascent of the ridge commenced soon after leaving camp, and I had not gone far up it before I overtook a cart that the folks could not pull through the snow, here about knee-deep. I helped them along, and we soon overtook another. By all hands getting to one cart we could travel; so we moved one of the carts a few rods, and then went back and brought up the other. After moving in this way for a while, we overtook other carts at different points of the hill, until we had six carts, not one of which could be moved by the parties owning it.

"I put our collective strength to three carts at a time, took them a short distance, and then brought up the other three. Then by travelling over the hill three times—twice forward and once back—I succeeded after hours of toil in bringing my little company to the summit. The six carts were then trotted on gaily down hill, the intense cold stirring us to action. One or two parties who were with these carts gave up entirely, and but for the fact that we overtook one of our ox-teams that had been detained on the road, they must have perished on that Rocky Ridge."

John Chislett assisted those who lagged behind as well as he could. But this group kept increasing in number until he had to leave them and hurry on to the main camp for help. He recorded:

"We travelled along with the ox-team and overtook others, all so laden with the sick and helpless that they moved very slowly. The oxen had almost given out. Some of our folks with carts went ahead of the teams, for where the roads were good they could out-travel oxen; but we constantly overtook some stragglers, some with carts, some without, who had been unable to keep pace with the body of the company. We struggled along in this weary way until after dark, and by this time our 'rear' numbered three wagons, eight handcarts, and nearly 40 persons. With the wagons were Millen Atwood, Levi Savage, and William Woodward, captains of hundreds, faithful men who had worked hard all the way.

"We finally came to a stream of water which was frozen over [Strawberry Creek]. We could not see where the company had crossed. If at the point where we struck the creek, then it had frozen over since we passed it. We started one team to cross, but the oxen broke through the ice and would not go over. No amount of shouting and whipping could induce them to stir an inch. We were afraid to try the other teams, for even should they cross we could not leave the one in the creek and go on. There was no wood in the vicinity, so we could make no fire, and were uncertain what to do.

"We did not know the distance to the camp, but supposed it to be three or four miles. After consulting about it, we resolved that someone should go on foot to the camp to inform the captain of our situation. I was selected to perform the duty, and I set out with all speed. In crossing the creek I slipped through the ice and got my feet wet, my boots being nearly worn out. I had not gone far when I saw someone sitting by the roadside. I stopped to see who it was and discovered [William] James and his little boy [13-year-old Reuben]. The poor man was quite worn out.

"I got him to his feet and had him lean on me, and he walked a little distance. I partly dragged, partly carried him a short distance farther, but he was quite helpless, and my strength failed me. Being obliged to leave him to go forward on my own errand, I put down a quilt I had wrapped around me, rolled him in it, and told the little boy to walk up and down by his father, and on no account to sit down, or he would be frozen to death. I told him to watch for teams that would come back, and to hail them when they came. This done I again set out for the camp, running nearly all the way and frequently falling down, for there were many obstructions and holes in the road. My boots were frozen stiff, so that I had not the free use of my feet, and it was only by rapid motion that I kept them from being badly frozen. As it was, both were nipped.

"After some time I came in sight of the campfires, which encouraged me. As I neared the camp I frequently overtook stragglers on foot, all pressing forward slowly. I stopped to speak to each one, cautioning them all against resting, as they would surely freeze to death. Finally, about 11 P.M., I reached the camp almost exhausted. I had exerted myself very much during the day in bringing the rear carts up the ridge and had not eaten anything since breakfast. I reported to Captains Willie and Kimball the situation of the folks behind. They immediately got up some horses, and the boys from the Valley started back about midnight to help the ox teams in. The night was very severe and many of the emigrants were frozen. It was 5 A.M. before the last team reached the camp.

"I told my companions about [William] James and his little boy. They found the little fellow keeping faithful watch over his father, who lay sleeping in my quilt just as I left him. They lifted [his father] into a wagon, still alive, but in a sort of stupor. He died before morning."[10]

LEVI SAVAGE'S ACCOUNT OF THE ROCKY RIDGE CROSSING

"We buried our dead, got up our teams, and about 9 o'clock A.M. commenced ascending the Rocky Ridge," Levi Savage wrote with the tone of someone to whom burial duty was becoming routine. "This was a severe day. The wind blew awful hard and cold. The ascent was some five miles long and some places steep and covered with deep snow. We became weary, sat down to rest, and some became chilled and commenced to freeze. Brothers Atwood, Woodward, and myself remained with the teams, they being perfectly loaded down with the sick and children, so thickly stacked I was fearful some would smother.

"About 10 or 11 o'clock in the night, we came to a creek [Strawberry Creek] that we did not like to attempt to cross without help, it being full of ice and freezing cold. Leaving Brothers Atwood and Woodward with the teams, I started to the camp for help. I met Brother Willie coming to look for us. He turned for the camp, as he could do no good alone. I passed several on the road, and after about four miles [of] travel I arrived in camp, but few tents were pitched, and men, women, and children sat shivering with cold around their small fires.

"Some time elapsed when two teams started to bring up the rear. Just before daylight they returned, bringing all with them, some badly frozen, some dying, and some dead. It was certainly heartrending to hear children crying for mothers and mothers crying for children. By the time I got them as comfortably situated as circumstances would admit, . . . day was dawning. I had not shut my eyes for sleep, nor lain down. I was nearly exhausted with fatigue and want of rest."[11]

ANN ROWLEY'S ACCOUNT OF THE ROCKY RIDGE CROSSING

Ann Rowley was a widow who emigrated with her seven children and one stepdaughter from her husband's first marriage. Part of her commitment to get to Zion was to "be among the people of my faith and [to] get the Temple work done for us."[12]

The Rowleys suffered the same privations as everyone else on the journey. Ann explained how they endured the hunger, the illness, the exhaustion, the cold: "I was grateful for my faith in God, for it was only through this faith that I was able to carry on at all. I confess, it seemed at times, the Lord had deserted us. . . . However, the Lord had not deserted us, and I was ashamed for thinking for a moment he had."[13]

"I always thought, I shall be the happiest person, if I could reach Zion with all my children alive," Ann wrote. It was not to be, however, as her stepdaughter died the day the first winter storm arrived.[14] "Her long journey was at an end, but ours had a long way yet to go," Ann wrote.[15] Three days later when crossing Rocky Ridge, Ann's two oldest sons, including 15-year-old John, whom she had relied on most heavily, were being overwhelmed by the exposure. Ann recalled:

"In traveling at night, in the frost of that altitude, [10-year-old] Thomas' right hand froze while he was pushing on the back of the cart, and when we stopped at night and his hand got warm, it swelled up . . . 'like a toad.' John could finally go no farther, and I felt my heart would break as I saw him laying beside the trail, waiting for the sick wagon. By the time he was picked up, his body was frozen in two places. That night 12 people died, and the next morning 3 people joined them."[16]

This was likely the night when John Rowley's hair froze to the ground. "He lay there waiting to die," the family history records. "One of the company captains came along and gave him a painful kick. When he groaned, they realized he was still alive and placed him in the sick wagon, preserving his life."[17]

SACRIFICE OF ARCHIBALD MCPHAIL AT ROCKY RIDGE

Archibald McPhail was from Scotland. His first wife died in 1847, and he remarried in 1854. He was emigrating with his second wife, Jane; a daughter from his first marriage, Henrietta; and three other family members. Unlike most people, who waited many years to emigrate, the McPhails left for Zion the same year they joined the Church. During the journey, Archibald was given responsibility for the people in his tent. Two of the women often lagged behind, and after crossing Rocky Ridge he noticed that one of them was missing. His daughter Henrietta related this story to her granddaughter, who recounts it as follows:

"A terrible blizzard had been raging all day, and when they reached camp, [Archibald] found that one of his group was missing. [He] felt it was his duty to go back after her. It was indeed an undertaking for one so exhausted by the lack of food and nearly perishing cold, but he cheerfully accepted his responsibility and went in search of the woman. He found her sitting by the wayside on the other side of a frozen stream they had crossed earlier. He pleaded with her to come on, but she refused, saying she was going to stay there and die. There was nothing to do but cross the stream and get her. He picked her up, and as they crossed the stream the ice broke and he was soaked with icy water to the waist.

"By the time he reached camp, his clothes were frozen to him and he was taking heavy chills. The air was cold and wet, and the men were so weak and hungry they could not go in search of dry wood to make a fire. Without anything warm to eat or drink, he was placed in a cold bed with the covering of a handcart pitched over him for a tent. There was a strong wind . . . which blew it over three times, and they stopped trying to keep it up. He was in high fever, and Henrietta [his 16-year-old daughter] sat by his bed brushing the snow from his face as he lay dying."[18]

In his weakened condition, Archibald McPhail was taken into the wagons after that night. He was never able to regain his strength, however, and two weeks later he died at the Bear River crossing south of Evanston, Wyoming. His wife, Jane, often told the following story of his death, as recorded by her descendants:

"She was sitting in the wagon that night beside her husband in the dim light of a small tallow candle. She prayed fervently that the candle might last until his suffering had ended. Her prayer was answered, for the light of the candle and the life of her husband went out at the same moment. At the time of his death he was just thirty-nine years of age."[19]

TRIALS OF THE JENS NIELSON FAMILY AT ROCKY RIDGE

In Iowa City, Jens and Elsie Nielson had sacrificed their savings to help others. This sacrifice left them without enough money to buy a wagon, so they were traveling by handcart. With them were their 6-year-old son, Niels, and 10-year-old Bodil Mortensen, the daughter of some friends. Traveling by handcart instead of wagon exposed all of them to the worst extremities.

During the climb over Rocky Ridge, Jens Nielson was failing.

His feet became so frozen that he could not walk another step. Biographer Albert Lyman described the pathetic scene:

"In the fury of those storms which raged around them, [Jens] and his faithful wife toiled through the frozen snow till his feet were shapeless and useless with frost—he could walk no farther. What was to be done? Should he sink in the snow to die of despair? His young wife . . . looked at him—how desolate the world would be without him. 'Ride,' she urged. 'I can't leave you—I can pull the cart.'"[20]

Jens and Elsie survived the trek over Rocky Ridge, but their only son, 6-year-old Niels, did not. He was buried with 12 others in the common grave at Rock Creek. Jens later said of this ordeal, "No person can describe it. It cannot be comprehended or understood by any human in this life, but only those who were called to pass through it."[21]

STORY OF BODIL MORTENSEN CROSSING ROCKY RIDGE

The other child with Jens and Elsie Nielson, 10-year-old Bodil Mortensen, also had a terrible struggle up Rocky Ridge. Bodil's parents had entrusted her to the Nielsons for the journey because they did not have enough money for their entire family to emigrate together.

Bodil fought her way through the snow, wind, and freezing temperatures to get over Rocky Ridge. President James E. Faust told the rest of her story in a general conference talk: "When they arrived at camp, she must have been sent to gather firewood. She was found frozen to death leaning against the wheel of her handcart, clutching sagebrush."[22] Along with little Niels Nielson, Bodil was buried in the common grave at Rock Creek Hollow.

JAMES KIRKWOOD CARRIES HIS BROTHER
OVER ROCKY RIDGE

Margaret Kirkwood was a widow who was emigrating with her four sons, Robert (22), Thomas (19), James (11), and Joseph (5).

Her husband and two daughters had died before the family left Scotland. President James E. Faust told the story of her two youngest sons, James and Joseph, crossing Rocky Ridge:

"On the trip west, James was accompanied by his widowed mother and three brothers, one of whom, Thomas, was 19 and crippled and had to ride in the handcart. James's primary responsibility on the trek was to care for his little [5]-year-old brother, Joseph, while his mother and oldest brother, Robert, pulled the cart.

"As they climbed Rocky Ridge, it was snowing and there was a bitter cold wind blowing. It took the whole company [20] hours to travel 15 miles. When little Joseph became too weary to walk, James, the older brother, had no choice but to carry him. Left behind the main group, James and Joseph made their way slowly to camp. When the two finally arrived at the fireside, James 'having so faithfully carried out his task, collapsed and died from exposure and over-exertion.'"[23]

GATHERING AND BURYING THE DEAD

John Chislett described the grim scene in camp on October 24, the day after crossing Rocky Ridge:

"There were so many dead and dying that it was decided to lie by for the day. In the forenoon I was appointed to go round the camp and collect the dead. I took with me two young men to assist me in the sad task, and we collected together, of all ages and both sexes, 13 corpses, all stiffly frozen. We had a large square hole dug in which we buried these 13 people, three or four abreast and three deep. When they did not fit in, we put one or two crosswise at the head or feet of the others. We covered them with willows and then with the earth.

"When we buried these 13 people, some of their relatives refused to attend the services. They manifested an utter indifference about it. The numbness and cold in their physical natures seem to have reached the soul, and to have crushed out natural feeling and affection. Had I not myself witnessed it, I could not have believed that suffering would have produced such terrible results. But so it was. Two others died during the day, and we buried them in one grave, making 15 in all buried on that campground. . . . I learned afterwards from men who passed that way the next summer, that the wolves had exhumed the bodies, and their bones were scattered thickly around the vicinity."[24]

There is a monument at Rock Creek with the names of the dead on it, as well as a monument to the entire Willie company. Some groups that reenact the Rocky Ridge handcart trek start near Sixth Crossing and pull over Rocky Ridge, ending their journey here. Others make a shorter trek that starts at the Sage Campground.

Directions to Rock Creek Hollow: From I-80, exit to Highway 191 at Rock Springs. Follow Highway 191 north to the junction with Highway 28 in Farson. Follow Highway 28 northeast toward Lander. After about 45 miles, look for a Rock Creek/Willie Rescue Site sign. Turn east at the sign and follow the gravel road about 11 miles to Rock Creek Hollow. When the road forks to the left for Atlantic City, stay to the right.

Directions to Rocky Ridge: From Highway 287, take the Hudson–Atlantic City Road south. The junction of these roads is between mile markers 46 and 47, five miles west of the Sixth Crossing visitors' center. Follow this gravel road for 11 miles to the Sage Campground. Just before

Rock Creek Hollow

reaching the campground, look for a large staging area to the left. Turn into this area and follow a rougher road about two miles to the Lower Monument. These roads are closed in the winter and should be avoided in rainy weather.

Located at the eastern base of Rocky Ridge, the Lower Monument memorializes the rescue of the Willie company. Another monument is located about two miles up the trail on top of the ridge. Motor vehicles are not permitted on Rocky Ridge.

ASSISTANCE FROM REDDICK ALLRED

Brigham Young wanted the rescuers to set up stations along the trail to distribute supplies to the handcart companies as they came through. Captain Grant had established one such station on October 19 when he left a small group of men, wagons, and supplies near South Pass. He assigned Reddick Allred to be in charge of this camp and be ready to provide assistance when called upon (see page 131). It was an unenviable assignment, requiring weeks of waiting while enduring the wrath of the storms at one of the highest elevations on the trail. Reddick Allred wrote:

"Capt. Grant left me in charge of the supplies of flour, beef cattle, four wagons, the weak animals, and 11 men for guard. I killed the beef cattle and let the meat lay in quarters where it froze and kept well as it was very cold and storming almost every day. We were reinforced by 3 wagons and 6 men loaded with flour."[25]

On October 23, the day the rescuers helped the Willie company over Rocky Ridge, William Kimball sent an express to Reddick Allred, asking him to come and meet the company with assistance.[26] The next day, Reddick Allred and some of his men traveled to Rock Creek, arriving just before the last of the stragglers came into camp. In his journal that day he wrote:

"I took 6 teams and met them 15 miles below in such a hard west wind that they could not travel facing the drifting snow even if they had been ready for duty. I found some dead and dying laying over the camp in the drifting snow that was being piled in heaps by the gale and burying their dead. We set in with the rest to make them as comfortable as possible and remained in camp till [the] next day."[27]

After helping the Willie company get back on their way, Reddick Allred was instructed to return to his station and be ready to assist the Martin company. For three tedious, uncertain weeks he waited for any word about the company and his fellow rescuers. During that long wait, some of the men returned to Salt Lake City, presuming that members of the Martin company had died or had found a place to stay for the winter. These men tried to persuade Reddick Allred to go with them. He recorded the following exchange when John Van Cott and Claudeus Spencer arrived at his station in November and learned that there had been no word from the Martin company:

"Bro. Spencer tried to induce me to break up camp and return to the city. I declined his proposition, and he said he would return. I advised him to stay, for the lives of the company depended up[on] us. He then said that he moved that as I was president of the station, they center their faith in me, that I should get the word of the Lord to know what we must do. To this I objected as [the Lord] already said what he would [have us] do. They returned [the] next day."[28]

Because of Reddick Allred's determination to remain at his post, he was known as the "Bulldog." Elder Henry B. Eyring spoke of his heroic steadfastness in a general conference:

"There are few comforts so sweet as to know that we have been an instrument in the hands of God in leading someone else to safety. That blessing generally requires the faith to follow counsel when it is hard to do. An example from Church history is that of Reddick Newton Allred. He was one of the rescue party sent out by Brigham Young to bring in the Willie and Martin Handcart Companies. When a terrible storm hit, Captain Grant, captain of the rescue party, decided to leave some of the wagons by the Sweetwater River as he pressed ahead to find the handcart companies. With the blizzards howling and the weather becoming life-threatening, two of the men left behind at the Sweetwater decided that it was foolish to stay. . . . They decided to return to the Salt Lake Valley and tried to persuade everyone else to do the same.

"Reddick Allred refused to budge. Brigham had sent them out, and his priesthood leader had told him to wait there. The others took several wagons, all filled with needed supplies, and started back. Even more tragic, each wagon they met coming out from Salt Lake they turned back as well. They turned back 77 wagons, [some of which returned] all the way to Little Mountain [before they were turned around]. . . .

"Those with the faith of Reddick Newton Allred will keep offering friendship even when it seems not to be needed or to have no effect. They will persist. When some[one] reaches the point of spiritual exhaustion, they will be there offering kind words and fellowship. They will then feel the same divine approval Brother Allred felt when he saw those handcart pioneers struggling toward him, knowing he could offer them safety because he had followed counsel when it was hard to do.

"While the record does not prove it, I am confident that Brother Allred prayed while he waited. I am confident that his prayers were answered. He then knew that the counsel to stand fast was from God. We must pray to know that. I promise you answers to such prayers of faith."[29]

Finally, more than three weeks after Reddick Allred helped the Willie company, his steadfastness would be vindicated. On November 18, Captain Grant would arrive at his station with the Martin company. Again Reddick Allred would provide life-sustaining aid. Captain Grant would be so happy to see him that he would greet him with a cheer: "Hurrah for the Bulldog. Good for hanging on."[30]

What makes Reddick Allred's work in the rescue effort even more remarkable is that he was suffering from a severe case of pleurisy, a painful inflammation of the membrane that lines the lungs. Reddick Allred described the intensity of the pain in his journal entry for October 8: "I took cold and it gave me a severe pain in my breast that lasted one month that was almost like taking my life."[31] After reaching Fort Bridger five days later, he wrote, "I suffered much from plurisy or a pain in my breast and side."[32]

That Reddick Allred gave such dedicated service despite this illness reveals much about his character. But perhaps even more is revealed by considering when the illness began. If it had struck while he was at South Pass, he would have had little choice but to stay with the rescue team until their work was done. But instead, it struck the day after he left Salt Lake City. Since he was so close to home at the time, it would have been easy—and justifiable—for him to return home to protect his health. Surely he knew that rest was an important part of the remedy, yet he persisted at a pace that nearly broke the health of those who were well. Then he endured several weeks of hard winds, snows, and subzero temperatures at the crest of the continent with only a wagon cover for protection.

Would the Willie company have been better off to bypass Rocky Ridge? They could have done so by using an alternate route known as the Seminoe Cutoff, which had opened two years earlier. The cutoff leaves the main trail near the Ice Slough, a few miles west of the Fifth Crossing of the Sweetwater, and rejoins it west of Rocky Ridge. One probable reason the Willie company stayed on the main trail was that no one was familiar with the new route. Another reason may be that company leaders thought they would miss the rescuers if they took an alternate route. The company still could have taken the route after the rescuers found them, but doing so would have required backtracking several miles. Finally, in the opinion of some people, the cutoff was not necessarily an easier route than Rocky Ridge.

CHAPTER 16

FROM ROCK CREEK TO
FORT BRIDGER

On October 25, two men were sent as an express from Rock Creek to inform Church leaders of the tragedy that was occurring. They arrived in Salt Lake City on October 31, bringing the first word on the condition of the Willie company since Franklin D. Richards's optimistic report nearly four weeks earlier, a report that had been based on the company's condition when he left them on September 13. Wilford Woodruff was among those who heard the report. His words describe well the desperate situation of the Willie company:

"They bring bad news of that company; through starting so late in the season they have got caught in the snow storms and many have died. When the teams sent out at Conference arrived at this camp, there had been 20 deaths . . . and while with them in one day there were 15 burials; and when the messengers left there had been 55 deaths. . . . Men would dig graves for their brethren and before night die themselves. . . .

"At least 250 teams have been sent out to meet those companies and several tons of flour and great quantities of clothing."[1]

After resting for a day at Rock Creek, the Willie company resumed their journey the next morning, October 25. Although the company was assisted by a small group of rescuers, most of the emigrants had to continue pulling their handcarts until they reached Fort Bridger—another 133 miles. Besides the 15 people who had been buried at Rock Creek, many more were near death after the exposure and exhaustion they suffered on Rocky Ridge. Nevertheless, they somehow kept going, grinding out these miles in 10 days.

On the first day they traveled about 15 miles toward Reddick Allred's station near South Pass, where they found a few rescuers with supplies of food. Despite improved rations, however, more people died. John Chislett's account continues:

"During the day we crossed the Sweetwater on the ice, which did not break, although our wagons were laden with sick people. The effects of our lack of food, and the terrible ordeal of the Rocky Ridge, still remained among us. Two or three died every day. At night we camped a little east by north from the South Pass, and two men in my hundred died. It devolved on me to bury them. This I did before breakfast. The effluvia [odors] from these corpses were horrible, and it is small matter for wonder that after performing the last sad offices for them I was taken sick and vomited fearfully. Many said my 'time' had come, and I was myself afraid that such was the case, but by the blessing of God I got over it and lived. . . .

"Near South Pass we found more brethren from the Valley, with several quarters of good fat beef hanging frozen on the limbs of the trees where they were encamped. These quarters of beef were to us the handsomest pictures we ever saw. The statues of Michaelangelo, or the paintings of the ancient masters, would have been to us nothing in comparison to these life-giving pictures."[2]

At South Pass, the trail crosses the Continental Divide at an elevation of 7,412 feet. The Willie company crossed the pass on October 26. As the weather improved and more help arrived, the company's outlook improved somewhat. John Chislett recalled:

"After getting over the Pass, we soon experienced the influence of a warmer climate, and for a few days we made good progress. We constantly met teams from the Valley, with all necessary provisions. Most of these went on to Martin's company, but enough remained with us for our actual wants."[3]

Levi Savage had the thankless task of overseeing the company's slow, deteriorating animals. On the night of October 31, after the rest of the company had crossed the Green River, the journal records,

"Brother Savage, with the ox and cow teams, did not get to camp this evening."[4]

On November 2 the Willie company arrived at Fort Bridger, Wyoming. They were within 113 miles—and one week—of the Salt Lake Valley.

CHAPTER 17

ACCUSATIONS AND REPRIMANDS IN SALT LAKE CITY

As the rescue teams and the Willie company got closer to the Salt Lake Valley, word spread about the tragedy. Many people in Utah had friends or relatives in the handcart companies, and some of the residents were so upset about what happened that they began to blame the First Presidency for it. On Sunday, November 2, while the Willie company was a week away from the Valley and the location and condition of the Martin company were still unknown in Salt Lake City (they were just about to seek shelter in Martin's Cove), both Heber C. Kimball and Brigham Young took the offensive against such criticism.

In a meeting held in the old Tabernacle, President Heber C. Kimball said, "There is a spirit of murmuring among the people, and the fault is laid upon brother Brigham."[1] The criticism apparently had two fronts: first, the concept of emigrating by handcart; and second, the late start. President Kimball flayed both criticisms: "Three handcart companies have arrived in safety and in good season, and with much less sickness and death than commonly occur in wagon companies," he said.[2] Addressing the late start, he continued, "If the immigration could have been carried on as dictated by brother Brigham, there would have been no trouble."[3]

When Brigham Young stood to speak, he was indignant. "There is not the least shadow of reason for casting such censure upon me," he said.[4] "There is no ground or room for . . . suspecting that my mismanagement caused the present sufferings on the Plains," he continued, citing evidence in his defense.[5]

The real source of the problem, President Young said, was the "ignorance and mismanagement" of the emigration officials.[6] First he criticized them for not starting the emigrants early enough from Europe: "Our elders abroad say, by their conduct all the time, that we here in the mountains do not understand what is wanted in the east, as well as they do. [But] if they had sent our immigration in the season that they should have done, you and I could have kept our teams at home."[7]

Next, President Young reproved emigration officials for allowing the companies to leave the Midwest so late in the season:

"Here is brother Franklin D. Richards [and] here is brother Daniel Spencer. . . . I do not know that I will attach blame to either of them. But if, while at the Missouri river [Florence], they had received a hint from any person on this earth, or if even a bird had chirped it in the ears of Brothers Richards and Spencer, they would have known better than to rush men, women, and children on to the prairie in the autumn months . . . to travel over a thousand miles. [If] they would have stopped and considered for one moment, they would have stopped those men, women, and children there until another year."[8]

Three times in this address, Brigham Young said emigration leaders could have made the right decision if only a bird had chirped it in their ears. He concluded by saying that a spirit of pride and arrogance is what had caused "men and women to die on the Plains, by scores."[9] How were pride and arrogance manifested? By expecting God to mitigate the consequences of an unnecessarily risky decision.

The reprimands—and the opinions about the role of faith in continuing the journey late in the season—had come full circle since the warnings of Levi Savage a few weeks earlier in Nebraska. Back then, he had been rebuked for lacking faith that God would deliver the company safely. Now, while Levi Savage was still out on the trail, Brigham Young was reprimanding emigration leaders for asserting such faith. Brigham Young effectively agreed with Levi Savage that leaving so late was an error of judgment, not a demonstration of faith. He essentially said that while faith is good, faith combined with good judgment is better.[10]

Further vindicating the position of Levi Savage, Brigham Young issued a mandate that would prohibit late starts in the future: "Hereafter I am going to lay an injunction and place a penalty, to be suffered by any Elder or Elders who will start the immigration across the Plains after a given time; and the penalty shall be that they shall be severed from the Church, for I will not have such late starts."[11]

The tendency of the Saints in Salt Lake City to criticize Church leaders for the handcart tragedy is in marked contrast to the response of the handcart Saints themselves. Based on journals and other contemporaneous sources, the handcart pioneers were much less likely to criticize Brigham Young or other Church leaders.

One biographer of Brigham Young, Eugene England, has written that the "speech of rebuke" cited here "is fairly standard in tone and color" with some of Brigham Young's other speeches.[12]

ASSESSMENT OF THE EFFORTS OF
PRESIDENT FRANKLIN D. RICHARDS

Franklin D. Richards had been a key figure in the handcart emigration of 1856. Though not involved in the day-to-day details of the journey, he had been the primary promoter of the plan and had overseen its implementation. When the first three companies arrived safely in Salt Lake City, his efforts seemed successful beyond expectation. When tragedy struck the next two companies, those same efforts were criticized.

Before judging Franklin D. Richards too harshly for his role in the Willie and Martin tragedies, it is important to understand the context of his words and actions. Why was he so sure about the plan that he perhaps overreached in promoting it and making promises about it? One reason was that the plan had come from Brigham Young, the prophet of God, and Franklin D. Richards was a man who did all he could to support the prophet. Another possible explanation for President Richards's boldness about the handcart plan was that Brigham Young had been similarly bold. The words of

President Richards almost always take their cue from those of Brigham Young—with very little embellishment.

In promoting the plan, Brigham Young had said that people who pulled handcarts could out-travel any ox-drawn wagon train. He had said that pulling handcarts would make people stronger, not weaker. He had also said that pulling handcarts would cause less distress, anguish, and death than traveling by wagon.[13] In making promises about traveling by handcart, Brigham Young had written in a general epistle, "Let them gird up their loins and walk through, and nothing shall hinder or stay them."[14] With these words from Brigham Young, it is easy to see why Franklin D. Richards could feel justified in expressing similar confidence about the handcart plan—and perhaps even feel a mandate to do so.

It might seem easy for President Richards to promote pulling handcarts while writing editorials from his office in Liverpool, knowing he wouldn't be pulling a handcart himself. It also might seem easy for President Richards to ride up to the handcart companies on the trail in Nebraska and promise them safe passage when he would speed comfortably ahead of them the next day in his carriage. Was this a case of a leader enjoying comfort and privilege that put him out of touch with the experience of the common people? Given his life to that point, probably not. President Richards was no stranger to sacrifice and suffering.

During his first 9 years as a member of the Church, Franklin D. Richards served five missions in the United States. Over the next 10 years he served three missions in England and was away from his family for more than 7 of those years. Of the first 14 years of his marriage, he spent 10 years away on missions. During those missions he often "laboured under great bodily debility and weakness."[15] Indeed, he was familiar with sacrifice.

Franklin D. Richards was also familiar with suffering. His mission calls took him away from his family for long periods at the most inopportune times. He left on his first mission to England during the exodus from Nauvoo, when his wife was several months pregnant and his little daughter, Wealthy, was in precarious health. His first night in Liverpool, he wrote, "How comfortable I could be if I knew that my dear Jane and the family were well and happy."[16] Soon afterward he wrote, "I have felt very solicitous about my family yesterday and today. I wonder if they are sheltered from the still more piercing winds of the cold, bleak prairies. O Lord, my Heavenly Father, I entreat thee, do not leave them to suffer."[17]

That Franklin D. Richards was sacrificing so much to serve the Lord did not provide any guarantees that all would be well at home. He would soon find out that near Mount Pisgah, Iowa, his wife had given birth to a son who died almost immediately. He would also learn that three-year-old Wealthy died a few weeks later at Winter Quarters, leaving Jane childless and despondent. Then he would learn of the death of his 17-year-old brother, Joseph, who had been mustered into the Mormon Battalion. The depth of both his grief and his faith are revealed in the following writings from that time:

"Am I such a sinner that the Lord should take from me my two children, or cause me or my family to be afflicted as we have been during our absence from each other? . . . Father, I own thy dealings just; thy blessings have been more than [I deserve]; and do I not know that thy goodness never fails? I have feared that I should feel thy hand against me. But now I trust that in this also thou wilt reveal thy hidden stores of goodness and blessings, to counterpoise the deep sorrow of separation from my dear companions and tender babes."[18]

In 1848, Franklin D. Richards concluded his first mission in England and started for America, where he no longer had a home. He found Jane waiting for him at Winter Quarters, and together they made the trek to the Salt Lake Valley. They arrived in October and lived in their wagon that winter.

A few months later, in February 1849, Franklin D. Richards was called to be a member of the Quorum of the Twelve Apostles. He was 26 years old. In June 1849, Jane gave birth to another son. Then in October, after only a year back home, Elder Richards was called to serve another mission to England. Again his heart ached as he left Jane alone to face the rigors of pioneer life with a little child, living in a one-room adobe hut with a canvas roof and earthen floor. During his second mission to England, he succeeded Orson Pratt as mission president. He returned home in 1852 and then returned to England as mission president from 1854 to 1856. He later served a fourth and final mission to England from 1866 to 1868.

In addition to showing that Franklin D. Richards knew sacrifice and suffering, these accounts of his missionary service show that he was a person who responded to the prophet's words with his whole heart, regardless of difficulty or inconvenience. This characteristic provides insight into why he gave Brigham Young's handcart plan not only his support but his passion.

A biography of Franklin D. Richards, written by a grandson 25 years after Elder Richards's death, includes only one paragraph on the handcart experience and does not mention his personal involvement with it.[19] This omission may seem to distance President Richards from the tragedy, but he did not try to insulate himself from the sorrow and suffering that so many experienced. When the Martin company arrived in the Salt Lake Valley at the end of November, President Richards took the family of John Jaques into his own home, helped comfort them after their two-year-old daughter had died during the last week of the journey, and nurtured them back to health.[20]

Franklin D. Richards's service as a member of the Quorum of the Twelve spanned 50 years. In 1898 he became President of the Quorum, a position he held until his death in 1899. During his lifetime, he oversaw the emigration of more than 30,000 converts.

CHAPTER 18

FROM FORT BRIDGER TO SALT LAKE CITY

When the Willie company reached Fort Bridger on November 2, they were greeted by a happy sight. John Chislett explained: "At Fort Bridger we found a great many teams that had come to our help. The noble fellows who came to our assistance invariably received us joyfully, and did all in their power to alleviate our sufferings. May they never need similar relief!"[1]

The rescue teams at Fort Bridger were sufficient to allow all members of the company to ride in wagons for the final 113 miles to the Salt Lake Valley. For most of the emigrants, this was the first opportunity to ride in a wagon since the handcart trek began. "The entire distance from Iowa City to Fort Bridger I walked," John Chislett wrote, "and [I] waded every stream from the Missouri to that point, except [the] Elkhorn, which we ferried, and [the] Green River, which I crossed in a wagon."[2]

Although members of the Willie company did not have to pull handcarts from Fort Bridger, many of them were in a precarious condition. During the last week of the journey, one or two continued to die each day. The milder weather lasted only briefly as winter storms returned, causing limbs to freeze. "The people are much exposed to cold from lying on the cold ground," William Woodward wrote in the company journal.[3]

On November 4, William Kimball, who had been leading the rescue of the Willie company, led an express to Salt Lake City to "report on the condition of things."[4] He returned on November 8, bringing a timely load of provisions. The next day, November 9, 1856, he led the Willie company into the Salt Lake Valley. The company had suffered 74 deaths since leaving Liverpool.[5]

The Martin company was in even worse circumstances on November 9, as they were just leaving Martin's Cove, 325 miles away. Brigham Young still had not received any word on their location or condition, so on November 11 he sent William Kimball, Hosea Stout, Joseph Simmons, and James Ferguson to find them and report back.[6] Brigham Young also gave these men another important assignment. He had just learned that some of the rescue teams that were supposed to be assisting the Martin company had turned around and were returning to Salt Lake City. William Kimball and the others were assigned to turn them back around (see pages 388–90).

William Kimball's participation in this assignment is especially noteworthy. He had been working tirelessly on behalf of the emigrants since concluding his mission in England earlier in the year. He had left England in February and had gone to the Midwest to make preparations for the companies and then to help outfit them. After working for several months to complete that assignment, he left Florence with President Richards in early September and traveled to Salt Lake City. Three days after returning home, he left Salt Lake City with the first rescue team, led by George D. Grant. After finding the Willie company, he led them back to Salt Lake City. Having spent more than a month in the rescue effort, he was home for only two days when Brigham Young sent him on another assignment that would take him hundreds of miles into the maw of winter. Indeed, William Kimball had made errors in judgment during the emigration, particularly in Florence, when he urged the companies forward. But no one worked harder or accepted more accountability to help those who were suffering.

Kindness of the Saints in Salt Lake City

Although there were no bands, parades, or cheering spectators to greet the Willie company when they entered the Salt Lake Valley, as there had been for earlier handcart companies, hundreds of people gathered to greet them and show compassion. The final entry of the Willie company journal, made on November 9, records one death (of 10-year-old Rhoda Rebecca Oakey), tells of President Franklin D. Richards and others coming to meet the group "on the bench," and then concludes:

"As soon as the company arrived in the City of Great Salt Lake, the Bishops of the different wards took every person that was not provided a home and put them in comfortable quarters. Hundreds of persons were around the wagons on our way through the city, welcoming the company safely home."[7]

John Chislett concluded:

"When we left Iowa City we numbered about 500 persons. Some few deserted us while passing through Iowa, and some remained at Florence. When we left the latter place we numbered 420, about 20 of whom were independent emigrants with their own wagons [the Siler company], so that our handcart company was actually 400 of this number. Sixty-seven died on the journey, making a mortality of one-sixth of our number. Of those who were sick on our arrival, two or three soon died.

"President Young had arranged with the bishops of the different wards and settlements to take care of the poor emigrants who had no friends to receive them, and their kindness in this respect cannot be too highly praised. It was enough that a poor family had come with the handcarts, to insure help during the winter from the good brethren in the different settlements. My old friend W. G. Mills and his wife received me and my betrothed most kindly, so I had no need of Church aid.

"After arriving in the Valley, I found that President Young, on learning, from the brethren who passed us on the road, of the lateness of our leaving the frontier, set to work at once to send us relief. It was the October Conference when they arrived with the news. Brigham at once suspended all conference business, and declared that nothing further should be done until every available team was started out to meet us. He set the example by sending several of his best mule teams laden with provisions. Heber Kimball did the same, and hundreds of others followed their noble example. People who had come from distant parts of the Territory to attend conference volunteered to go out to meet us, and went at once. The people who had no teams gave freely of provisions, bedding, etc.—all doing their best to help us."[8]

Initial Reactions to the Salt Lake Valley

Most people create a mental picture of places they hear about but have never seen. How did the handcart pioneers picture Zion before they left Europe? How did the reality compare? Some were disappointed, surprised to see that Salt Lake City was such a fledgling, desolate community. Despite any negative impressions, however, most were happy to see the Salt Lake Valley because it meant they were finally at the end of their journey.

Joseph Elder described his first sight of Salt Lake City as follows: "At last we emerged from amongst the mountains, and the beautiful valley with all its loveliness spread itself out before our view. My heart was filled with joy and gratitude. The lovely city of G. S. Lake lay about 5 miles distant in full view. We entered it. The houses at first looked odd being built of adobes or sundried brick. Truly it is unlike anything I ever before had seen. The journey was over at last and the

Salt Lake City in the early 1850s

people were soon distributed amongst the several wards, and I put up with my old friend Wm. Kimball."[9] Like his friend William Kimball, Joseph Elder would soon go back on the trail to help the Martin company.

Johan Ahmanson described what the city looked like from a mountain viewpoint above the valley: "Many forgot the tribulations they had endured upon glimpsing this sudden vista. . . . From that distance the city with its light gray adobe houses looked like a huge encampment, and the Salt Lake Valley, which had a breadth of about thirty miles from east to west, resembled a basin or dried up lake, with its huge mountain masses ranging upward on all sides. Although the vegetation was now dead, and the eye of the observer met only a desolate treeless valley, surrounded by bare, reddish mountains, yet the impression made by the whole scene was still very pleasing."[10]

CHAPTER 19

AFTER THE TREK: DIFFICULTIES AND BLESSINGS

Think not, when you gather to Zion,
Your troubles and trials are through,
That nothing but comfort and pleasure
Are waiting in Zion for you:
No, no; 'tis designed as a furnace,
All substance, all textures to try,
To burn all the "wood, hay, and stubble,"
The gold from the dross purify.

—ELIZA R. SNOW

After all the handcart pioneers had suffered, something in human nature yearns for them to have rest from their trials for a season. But the suffering for most members of the Willie company did not end when they reached the Salt Lake Valley; indeed, for many it would continue throughout their lives. Despite their afflictions, however, most of those who survived the handcart ordeal lived at least the normal lifespan for the 1800s, and many far exceeded it.

Refined in the fire of affliction, most of these handcart pioneers also remained true to the faith. The common belief that none of them ever apostatized is not correct, however. Two subcaptains and a few other members of the Willie company later left the Church. Aside from these few exceptions, many of those who left records said they were strengthened by the experience, and some even expressed gratitude for it.

Not only would the sufferings of these Saints continue but so would the sacrifices they would be asked to make in building Zion.

Having endured the difficulties of the handcart journey did not exempt them from hard assignments in the future. Many would be sent to colonize some of the most inhospitable parts of the west. Just as they would make one place begin to feel like home, they would be assigned to a new one. Perhaps it was the refinement that came through their handcart experience that made them good candidates for such assignments.

JAMES WILLIE

James Willie's oldest son, eight-year-old William, had not seen his father for four years. When he learned that his father was about to arrive home, he was so excited that he walked to the mouth of Emigration Canyon to meet him. It was an emotional meeting for both father and son. James lifted William into the wagon, and they rode into town together.[1]

Young William may have been troubled to see his father's condition. James Willie's feet and legs were badly frozen and wrapped in burlap sacks. For a time it looked as though his feet would have to be amputated, but both were saved. His wife, Elizabeth, believed that "there was nothing but his faith and the power of the priesthood and administration that saved his legs."[2]

What kind of leader was James Willie on the handcart trek? His service is best summed up by George Cunningham: "Our captain . . . did his duty. He was badly frozen and came very close to dying. . . . [He] showed us all a noble example. He was furnished a mule to ride on our start from Iowa City, but he said, 'I will never get on its back. I shall show the example; you follow it.' He did so, and the captains of hundreds followed him. They would crowd on ahead to be the first into the streams to help the women and children across. . . . They waded every stream, I might say, a dozen times between Iowa City and Green River, with the exception of the Missouri River. [Toward the end] they were completely exhausted and had to be hauled the balance of the way, some of them not being able to stand on their feet."[3]

Mary Hurren also paid tribute to James Willie: "We all loved Captain Willie. He was kind and considerate and did all that he could for the comfort of those in his company. Many times he has laid his hands upon my head and administered to me."[4]

James Willie must have felt worn out after four years of missionary service and the four-month handcart ordeal, but he had little opportunity to rest. Six weeks after returning home, he was called to be bishop of the Salt Lake 7th Ward. He served in this position until the spring of 1859, when Brigham Young called him to help settle Cache Valley. He moved his family and made his home in Mendon, where he lived the last 36 years of his life. Using the training he had received as a young man, James Willie became superintendent and clerk of the local cooperative store. He also served in many civic positions, including mayor, water master, and postmaster.

James and Elizabeth Willie had two more children after James returned from his mission, for a total of five. James also had a daughter by a plural wife.

James Willie's Church service in Mendon was extensive and is well documented. He served in a bishopric and as a patriarch, among other callings. For many years, records from the Mendon Ward show him speaking in church nearly every month. He was considered an inspirational speaker whose life matched his words from the pulpit. A sampling of ward minutes that summarize these talks reveals much about James Willie's commitment to the gospel:

From September 23, 1888: "Not many [in the human family] can truly say, 'I know that my Redeemer lives.' . . . Many [Latter-day Saints] cannot say so [because] they have not taken the proper course to get this knowledge. It is our privilege to walk in the light that our God has made for us, for He is our guide and our deliverer. We must attend to our prayers and other duties, . . . else we will wither up and die spiritually."[5]

From January 5, 1890: "The God which I believe in is a God of revelation. It is a privilege to know the mind and will of God in relation to our various duties. How careful and guarded we should be in our language and actions. The Spirit of God will not rest in a person who will blaspheme the name of God. . . . The design of the gospel is to establish peace in the earth and to save all mankind and bring them back into the presence of God."[6]

From March 16, 1890: "It is beautiful to contemplate upon the majestic nature of this work, so noble, so powerful, so divine, yet so easily comprehended by those enjoying the Spirit of the Lord. We should magnify the priesthood which has been bestowed upon us and keep our covenants with God. He has given those principles to the earth which are calculated to save the human family, and we should yield to its influence and observe the truth contained in it."[7]

From March 30, 1890: "My earnest desire is that the Spirit of God may direct all my actions in life. It is highly necessary for us to set such an example before our youth that we will be pleased to see them follow our example. The gospel penetrates behind the veil and reaches into eternity."[8]

James Willie died in 1895, nearly 40 years after the handcart trek, at the age of 80. Showing the high esteem in which he was held, the people in Mendon closed their stores and came in from their fields for his funeral, with nearly everyone in town attending. James was buried in Mendon. A great-great-granddaughter wrote of what the example of James and Elizabeth Willie has meant to their descendants:

"James and Elizabeth faithfully lived the principles of the gospel. . . . Their example of obedience to the Lord and of love for their fellowmen continues to inspire to greater heights the lives of others."[9]

LEVI SAVAGE

The conclusion of the handcart journey marked the end of an eventful decade for Levi Savage. In 1846 he had joined the Church, and shortly afterward he joined the Mormon Battalion. After marching to California, he was discharged in 1847 and went to the Salt Lake Valley. In 1848 he married Jane Mathers. Early in 1851 his first son was born, but this joy turned to sorrow when his wife died later that year. The next year, 1852, Levi was called to serve a mission in

Siam. He departed in October, leaving his young son with his sister. After more than three years away from home in the most difficult circumstances, he sailed from Burma to Boston in 1856. On his way home he went through Iowa City, where he was appointed a subcaptain in the Willie company.

Levi Savage kept a daily journal through October 24, the day after crossing Rocky Ridge. After that he wrote only once more, summarizing the last 16 days of the journey with these exhausted words: "We commenced our march again. From this day I have not been able to keep a daily journal, but nothing much transpired except the people died daily."[10]

Levi Savage proved to be one of the great heroes of the trek.[11] Back in Florence, he had been remarkably accurate about the difficulties he foresaw for the Willie company. Although he disagreed with the decision to move forward, he not only supported it but pledged his life to minimizing negative consequences that might come from it. He worked tirelessly to keep that promise. Throughout the trek, he accepted the assignments given him, many of them undesirable. He also continued to be one of the most loyal and effective subcaptains, making personal sacrifices to help those most in need. John Chislett recalled that "no man worked harder than he to alleviate the suffering which he had foreseen."[12] Another subcaptain, William Woodward, later wrote, "Levi Savage, who was censured for his truthful statement at Florence, was I think the best help we had—resolute and determined. His whole soul was for the salvation of our company."[13] Some survivors owed their lives to him.[14]

Levi Savage was a hero not only for what he did but for what he did not do. Having leaders disregard his counsel that was later vindicated must have been difficult. But having them reprimand him and question his faith for giving this counsel must have been deeply humiliating. Despite all this, he never seems to have murmured or become bitter. He never seems to have volleyed I-told-you-so's back at his leaders. He never seems to have stopped supporting them even though their decision put him in a position of great personal risk and discomfort.

In addition to being silent the last two weeks of the journey, Levi Savage's journal has no entries for nearly two months after he returned home. The only documentation of his activities during this time is an invitation from Brigham Young to a Christmas dinner at his home. The invitation included an offer to bring his "lady," but Levi Savage had not remarried since his wife's death five years earlier.

Levi Savage finished the handcart trek with no resources other than the ragged clothes he was wearing. Unable to pay for his own residence, he and his son stayed with his sister and brother-in-law, Ira Eldredge. He tried to start a school, but it struggled because he had only a few students and had trouble collecting tuition. "I made out my school bills and presented some of them. Business is dull," he wrote on March 9. He was out trying to collect on his bills the very next day: "I endeavored to collect some of my school bills. In this I accomplished nothing."[15] Three months after he returned home, a journal entry painfully reveals his struggles to obtain even the most basic needs of life:

"I went to the business part of the city, intending to get credit for cloth for a pair of pants, but . . . in consequence of my indigent circumstances, I could not set a time of payment. I returned without the article."[16]

Two months later he wrote: "I have been trying for a month now to get a team [of oxen] and some employment but have failed in every attempt. What to do, I do not know. Myself and boy are yet living with Brother Ira Eldredge. I do not know that I ever shall be able to remunerate him for the trouble and expense that I have unavoidably caused him. May the Lord speedily relieve me from my present embarrassment."[17]

Ten days later, Levi wrote: "I went to the city and applied to Brother Rolley for work on the temple, stone cutting. For the want of steel to make tools, he could not set me at work. I am much disheartened. I have no team and am not able to engage in a very heavy labor, being weak in the loins. My son is yet at Brother Ira's. My not being able to provide a home for him . . . gives me much uneasiness. May the Lord bless Brother Ira and open the way for me."[18]

The next year Levi Savage married Ann Cooper, a widow from the Willie company who had two small girls. Ann had suffered the death of her first husband in 1854 and of a two-year-old daughter in Iowa City. The family soon moved to Holden, in Millard County, and Levi went into the stock business, tending sheep and cows on shares. Eventually he accumulated his own herd and a farm and ranch. At the call of Brigham Young, in 1863 he moved his stock to Kanab, where he plowed the first furrow and built the first home. Soon, however, settlers in the area were counseled to move because of troubles with the Indians. In 1866 Levi's family settled permanently in Toquerville after losing their land, improvements, and much of their stock in Kanab.

An incident in the 1870s again showed Levi Savage's commitment to the gospel. A dispute arose over the boundary of his property in Toquerville. The dispute was heard by several councils, both civil and ecclesiastical, and after six years was finally settled—against him. He again chose the better part, saying, "I had to comply to save my fellowship."[19] Again Levi Savage, a proud man, sacrificed his pride rather than allow it to damage his relationships or his standing in the Church. As Lynn Hilton observed, "He displayed an amazing persistence to defend what he felt was right and in the end was willing to accept an adverse decision."[20]

Levi Savage spent the last 45 years of his life in Toquerville. He died and was buried there in 1910, still strong in the faith at nearly 91 years old.

THE OTHER SUBCAPTAINS

Millen Atwood and William Woodward remained faithful throughout their lives, but John Chislett and Johan Ahmanson left the Church. John Chislett fell away a few years later; Johan Ahmanson left within a few months of arriving in Utah.

Millen Atwood

After returning home, Millen Atwood served on the high council of the Salt Lake Stake. He then served as bishop of the Salt Lake 13th Ward from 1881 until his death in 1890 at age 73.

Heber J. Grant, a future president of the Church who was born the same month the Willie company arrived in Salt Lake City, recalled the following powerful incident involving Millen Atwood. When Heber was 17 or 18 years old, he was studying grammar and was assigned to bring two examples of poor sentences, along with their corrections, to each class. Recalling a time he had heard Millen Atwood speak, Heber J. Grant later said:

"I wrote down his first sentence, smiled to myself, and said: 'I am going to get here tonight, during the thirty minutes that Brother Atwood speaks, enough material to last me for the entire winter in my night school grammar class.'"

Heber intended to correct this sentence and others while he listened to the sermon. "But I did not write anything more after that first sentence—not a word," he said. "And when Millen Atwood stopped preaching, tears were rolling down my cheeks, tears of gratitude and thanksgiving that welled up in my eyes because of the marvelous testimony which that man bore of the divine mission of Joseph Smith, the prophet of God, and of the wonderful inspiration that attended the prophet in all his labors.

"Although it is now more than sixty-five years since I listened to that sermon, it is just as vivid today, and the sensations and feelings that I had are just as fixed with me as they were the day I heard it. Do you know, I would no more have thought of using those sentences in which he had made grammatical mistakes than I would think of standing up in a class and profaning the name of God. That testimony made the first profound impression that was ever made upon my heart and soul of the divine mission of the prophet. I had heard many testimonies that had pleased me and made their impression, but this was the first testimony that had melted me to tears under the inspiration of the Spirit of God to that man."[21]

William Woodward

After the handcart trek, William Woodward taught school in Salt Lake City and Bountiful for a few years. In 1860 he was part of a group of pioneers that settled Franklin, Idaho. He lived there for the last 48 years of his life, working as a farmer, teacher, justice of the peace, city councilman, and postmaster. In the Church he was president of his seventies quorum for 40 years. He also returned to England on a brief genealogical mission in 1873. William Woodward died in Franklin in 1908 at age 75.

John Chislett

John Chislett wrote his eloquent account of the journey after he had fallen away from the Church. His account begins and ends bitterly. It criticizes Church leaders for being too ambitious, too presumptuous, and too willing to "experiment" with human life in the handcart tragedy.[22] But most of his account—even when describing the trials in graphic detail—does not exhibit this bitterness. Rather, feelings of gratitude to God and others, admiration for leaders and members of the company, empathy, and even faith and yearning for Zion dominate.

These positive excerpts from John Chislett's account have been quoted regularly in Church publications. The negative passages, which tend to occur whenever John Chislett breaks away from telling the story and begins to analyze it, are rarely cited. His final words on the subject are especially harsh:

"Immediately after the condition of the suffering emigrants was known in Salt Lake City, the most fervent prayers for their deliverance were offered up. There, and throughout the Territory, the same was done as soon as the news reached the people. Prayers in the Tabernacle, in the school-house, in the family circle, and in the private prayer circles of the priesthood were constantly offered up to the Almighty, begging Him to avert the storm from us. Such intercessions were invariably made on behalf of Martin's company, at all the meetings which I attended after my arrival.

"But these prayers availed nothing more than did the prophecies of [Franklin D.] Richards and the elders. It was the stout hearts and strong hands of the noble fellows who came to our relief, the good teams, the flour, beef, potatoes, the warm clothing and bedding, and not prayers nor prophecies, that saved us from death.

"It is a fact patent to all the old settlers in Utah that the fall storms of 1856 were earlier and more severe than were ever known before or since. Instead of their prophecies being fulfilled and their prayers answered, it would almost seem that the elements were unusually severe that season, as a rebuke to their presumption."[23]

John Chislett apparently had only a one-dimensional view of how these prayers could be answered—a narrow presumption on his part. To say that the survivors were saved only by the "stout hearts and strong hands" of the rescuers, and not by prayer, is a contradiction. Many in the company testified that the very presence of the rescuers was an answer to prayer.

Johan Ahmanson

Although Johan Ahmanson had planned to travel by wagon, he accepted an assignment from President Richards to be the sub-captain over the Danish Saints in the Willie company. Rather than subject his wife and young son to travel by handcart, he arranged for them to travel with the Hodgetts wagon company. After arriving in the Salt Lake Valley, he was very anxious for his wife and son, who were more than a month behind him. He tried to join with the relief teams but was not successful. Finally on December 17 he went on his own to Little Mountain to meet them. "Who could describe my joy at finding both of my dear ones in the best of health?" he wrote. "Forgotten were the hardships of the journey and the long separation, and joyfully we drove in to Zion."[24]

Unfortunately, during the winter these feelings of joy soon dissipated. In April 1857, just five months after arriving in Utah, Johan Ahmanson left the Church and moved to St. Joseph, Missouri. Two years later he moved to Omaha, where he lived until his death in 1891. In Omaha he worked as a hardware merchant, then as a grocer, and later as a doctor of homeopathic medicine.

In addition to the 17 pounds of luggage that Johan Ahmanson was allowed to carry on his handcart, he had arranged to have some additional belongings carried by the Hodgetts wagon company. He was probably dismayed when the wagons arrived in Salt Lake City without these goods. Like much of the other freight in the wagons, his property had been left at Devil's Gate when some of the wagons were unloaded so they could transport members of the Martin company. Johan Ahmanson tried to recover his belongings the next spring as he passed by Devil's Gate on the way to Missouri, but he was unsuccessful. In 1859 he filed a lawsuit against Brigham Young, demanding compensation for this property. His lawsuit also claimed that he should be paid $300 for his service as subcaptain. Nearly five years later, he and Brigham Young settled out of court for $1,000.[25]

Nineteen years after leaving Utah, Johan Ahmanson wrote a book in Danish that is critical of the Church, Brigham Young, and other leaders. The book includes a chapter on the handcart experience that refers to the handcarts as "infernal machines" and recounts a confrontation with William Kimball.[26] Ironically, however, the tone of the chapter is mostly neutral, even occasionally positive, rather than negative.

Emily and Julia Hill

Emily and Julia Hill, who had joined the Church and emigrated despite their parents' objections, both survived the journey. Three months after arriving in Utah, each married a man who had helped with the rescue. At least 15 other women in the Willie and Martin companies also married rescuers.

Julia became a plural wife of Israel Ivins. In 1861 they were called by Brigham Young to move south to help settle Utah's Dixie. Their wagon was one of the first to set camp in St. George. Many trials attended this assignment, but Julia endured them well. Of her eight children, four died in infancy.[27]

Emily married William G. Mills, but her marriage was not happy. After three years, William went on a mission to England, leaving Emily and one small child. After he had been away four years, during which time Emily struggled to provide for herself and her child, he sent word that he was not returning home. Stung by this rejection, Emily wrote, "No one can realize what such an ordeal is, unless they have passed through it. All that I had hitherto suffered seemed like child's play compared to being deserted by one in whom I had chosen to place the utmost confidence."[28]

In addition to the rejection, Emily was nearly destitute in the Zion she had sacrificed so much to come to: "Hard times stared me in the face, and I was almost overwhelmed. . . . I could not see how I should ever be able to keep 'the wolf from the door.' To add to my trouble, the house I occupied (and to which I had been led to believe I had some claim), was sold over my head, and thus I had the prospect of being homeless, at a time when rents were going up double and treble. One night when I was so weary with overwork and anxiety, pondering what to do, these words impressed me as if audibly spoken: Trust in God and Thyself."[29] Immediately Emily arose and composed four stanzas of poetry on that theme. With renewed faith, she soon found a way open up to resolve these problems.

This manifestation of Emily's poetic gift was a fulfillment of a blessing she had received while still a young girl in England. In that blessing, Elder John Halliday had promised that she would write prose and poetry that would comfort the hearts of thousands. Her writings that are well known today include the words to the hymn "As Sisters in Zion" and the Primary song "Let the Little Children Come."

Emily remarried in 1864 as a plural wife of Joseph Woodmansee, with whom she had eight children. Emily and Joseph suffered many setbacks and misfortunes, but both remained steadfast in the faith. Emily's most heartfelt desire was for her children to develop that same faith:

"I fervently hope that each and all of them may seek and obtain for themselves a knowledge of the truth (called Mormonism), for I know it can make them wise unto salvation, and may they be willing if needs be to endure reproach and privation for principle's sake.

I doubt not that all my troubles have been for my good, and today I am more than thankful for my standing in the Church of Jesus Christ of Latter-Day Saints."[30]

Given what Emily had been told about Zion before leaving England, and given what she sacrificed to gather there, it would have been reasonable for her to hope to find a kind of utopia where everyone was of one heart, where there were no poor, where everyone lived their beliefs. It is doubtful that she expected such realities as a brutal pilgrimage, fledgling settlements with scarce supplies, a husband who would desert her, and neighbors and landlords who were, at best, insensitive to her needs for the essentials of life.

Despite this disparity between hope and reality, Emily Hill remained true to the testimony she had first felt burn in her heart in a small home in England when she was 12 years old. Rather than become disillusioned, she seemed to understand that building Zion was a process. Far from a utopia where a person could just walk in and live happily ever after, Zion was a place where people were working out their salvation. They had flaws and imperfections, but the Lord was using them anyway in building his kingdom—as he always does.

JOSEPH AND EMILY WALL

Joseph and Emily Wall were teenage siblings emigrating on their own because their parents could not afford to have the entire family of nine children emigrate together. During part of the journey, when Joseph became too ill to walk, Emily pulled him in the handcart. In part due to this loving sacrifice, both Joseph and Emily made it to the Salt Lake Valley, as Elder Orson Hyde had promised in the blessing he gave them before they left England.

After arriving in Utah, Joseph and Emily Wall went to Manti. Emily then lived for a time in Salt Lake City with Amelia Young, one of Brigham Young's wives. In 1860, Joseph relocated to Gunnison, where he helped put in the first dam, plow the first field, and raise the first crop of grain.

In 1860, Emily married William Cowley, who had helped rescue the handcart companies four years earlier. During the rescue he had asked Emily if she would marry him someday, and she had said he would have to write to her mother in England to ask permission. After arriving in Salt Lake City, William was called away for three years to set up a printing press in San Bernardino. When he returned, he found Emily and asked if she remembered his proposal. She did, but she wanted to know if he'd written to her mother. He told her he had—and that her mother had said she would approve the marriage if William was a good man.[31]

The rest of Joseph and Emily's family finally made it to Utah in 1862. When Joseph met his family in Salt Lake City, he also met Selena Stevens, a friend of two of his sisters. Joseph and Selena were married in 1863 in the Endowment House. They went back to Manti, where Joseph worked in a grist mill.

Later in 1863 the Walls were among the first dozen families to answer Brigham Young's call to settle Glenwood, located a few miles east of Richfield in Sevier County. At first they lived in dugouts. Joseph and Selena's first child—and the first child born in Glenwood—came into the world in one of these small dugouts.

Joseph Wall and his father started to build a grist mill in Glenwood, but they and the other settlers encountered severe difficulties with the Indians, prompting Brigham Young to order them to leave the area for a time. The Walls went back to Sanpete County in 1866 and then returned to Glenwood in 1870. Joseph and his father built a home for the two families and started again to build a grist mill across the street. In 1874 they completed the mill, a three-story rock building that still stands today. Joseph Wall operated the mill until two years before his death, providing flour for most of the people in Sevier County.

Joseph and Selena Wall lived out their lives in Sevier County, strong in the faith. They had eight children, two of whom lived into their 90s. Their second child, Selena Ann, lived until 1962. Joseph died in 1898 at the age of 59 and was buried in Glenwood. His wife had died one year earlier, and his mother died one year later.

Emily and William Cowley became parents of 12 children. They lived in Logan for a time before moving to Salt Lake City and eventually settling near the rest of the family in Sevier County. Emily died in 1908 at age 68 in Venice, Sevier County, and was buried in Richfield. William Cowley died in 1915.

SUSANNA STONE (LLOYD)

Susanna Stone, age 25, was the only member of her family who was emigrating. During the trek she had felt miraculously sustained by the power of God. She later wrote:

"We traveled on, feeling that the Lord would protect his Saints, and so he did. Although we passed through many trying scenes, his protecting care was over us. . . .

"I often think of the songs we sang to encourage us on our toilsome journey. It was hard to endure, but the Lord gave us strength and courage. . . .

"We waded through the cold streams many times, but we murmured not, for our faith in God and our testimony of His work were supreme. And in the blizzards and falling snow we sat under our handcarts and sang, 'Come, come, ye Saints.'"[32]

Throughout the journey, Susanna was also sustained by the fellowship of the Saints. She wrote:

"Only once did my courage fail. One cold, dreary afternoon, my feet having been frosted, I felt I could go no further, and withdrew from the company and sat down to await the end, being somewhat in a stupor. After a time I was aroused by a voice, which seemed as audible as anything could be, and which spoke to my very soul of the promises and blessings I had received, and which should surely be fulfilled and that I had a mission to perform in Zion. I received strength, and was filled with the Spirit of the Lord and arose and traveled on with a light heart. As I reached camp, I found a search party ready to go back to find me, dead or alive. I had no relatives, but many dear and devoted friends, and we did all we could to aid and encourage each other."[33]

Susanna said that as the Willie company got close to the Salt Lake Valley, "we tried to make ourselves as presentable as we could to meet our friends. I had sold my little looking glass to the Indians for buffalo meat, so I borrowed one and I shall never forget how I looked."[34] Susanna said that the journey had taken such a toll that some of her old friends did not recognize her.

Susanna met her future husband the day she arrived in the Salt Lake Valley. Recalling this encounter, she wrote:

"Among others who came to meet their friends was a handsome young man, Thomas Lloyd, who had emigrated the previous year, 1855. . . . He had proved his integrity to his newly found faith by renouncing everything offered by a wealthy aunt who had raised him; his parents had died when he was but two years old, and he would have fallen heir to her fortune, but was cut off because he did not renounce Mormonism."[35]

Thomas Lloyd and Susanna Stone were soon married. They settled in Farmington for several years and then moved to Wellsville. They had 10 sons and 4 daughters. "All of them [are] healthy and all members of the faith," Susanna wrote late in her life, "and this is a joy to me in my declining years."[36]

Reflecting on the handcart experience, Susanna Stone Lloyd felt that she had received more than adequate compensation for the difficulties she had to endure:

"I am thankful that I was counted worthy to be a pioneer and a handcart girl. It prepared me to endure hard times in my future life. I often think of the songs we sang to encourage us on our toilsome journey. It was hard to endure, but the Lord gave us strength and courage. . . .

"My frosted feet gave me considerable trouble for many years, but this was forgotten in the contemplation of the great blessings the gospel had brought to me and mine."[37]

Susanna died in Logan in 1920 at 89 years of age. Drawing an application from her life, Mary Ellen Smoot, a former Relief Society general president, said:

"Having sold her own mirror to an Indian for a piece of buffalo meat, [Susanna] had not spent much time looking at herself. [When she did,] she did not recognize her own image. She was a different person, both inside and out. Over the course of rocky ridges and extreme hardship came a deep conviction. Her faith had been tried, and her conversion was concrete. She had been refined in ways that the very best mirror could not reflect. Susanna had prayed for strength and found it—deep within her soul.

"This is the kind of inner strength I would like to talk about. How do you and I become so converted to the truth, so full of faith, so dependent on God that we are able to meet trials and even be strengthened by them?"[38]

One answer to that crucial, universal question can be found in the life of Susanna Stone Lloyd.

DAVID REEDER FAMILY

David Reeder, whose wife had died before the journey, died along the trail, as did his daughter Caroline and a baby granddaughter. Of this family, only 19-year-old Robert Reeder survived, along with his older sister Eliza, who was married to James Hurren.

Robert Reeder married Lydia Wilkinson in 1861, and they were among the first settlers in Hyde Park, Cache County. Robert became the father of 14 children. He worked as a cattleman, deputy sheriff, and hay merchant. He died in 1917 at the age of 80 and is buried in the Hyde Park cemetery.[39]

JAMES AND ELIZA HURREN FAMILY

James and Eliza Hurren arrived safely in Utah with their three oldest daughters, Mary (7), Emma (4), and Sarah (2). Their losses were great, however. Their daughter Selena, who was born in Iowa City, died along the trail in Iowa. Eliza's father and sister, David and Caroline Reeder, also died during the journey, as did Mary's friend Bodil Mortensen.

Saving Mary's Legs (A Father's Love)

Surviving the journey was but the beginning of young Mary Hurren's trials. Her legs were so frostbitten that the family got her to a doctor as soon as they arrived in Salt Lake City. At first the doctor did not expect Mary to live more than a day or two. "She'll never get over this," Mary recalled the doctor saying. "There's nothing we can do here."[40] However, the next morning he returned and said the only way to save her life was to amputate her legs. "I will take her feet off, one above the knee and one below," he said; "then she will live for a while. That is all I can do with feet frozen as black as that."[41] Mary's father protested, "This little girl didn't walk a thousand miles across the plains to have her legs cut off. If she dies, she will die with her legs on."[42]

The family went to Brigham City to make their home. Mary recalled: "The flesh fell away from the calves of my legs, so that it was necessary to grow new flesh. My mother put sweet oil on my legs." A woman in town told Mary's parents that wrapping her legs in fresh steak would help them heal. Mary recalled the sacrifices her father made to try this remedy: "I remember that on several occasions after coming to Brigham City that father walked [20 miles] to Ogden to secure fresh beef to bind on my legs. It was three long years before I was able to walk."[43]

The Commandments of God Were Her Staff

Mary married Joseph M. Wight and became the mother of 13 children, 7 of whom preceded her in death.[44] During her lifetime she "nursed the sick and cared for the helpless. She took in a little orphan girl, age ten, with tuberculosis, and cared for her until she died four years later. She knitted lace, braided rugs, and on her 88th birthday, President Heber J. Grant came to her party. She remarked that she had shaken the hand of every modern-day prophet to that time, except Joseph Smith."[45]

Although Mary's feet did not have to be amputated, they hurt all her life. Concerning this pain, one of her granddaughters wrote,

"Her feet, aching, burning, full of constant pain and discomfort, took her through life, and she walked it proudly, each step a moan, sometimes a prayer, but she walked with a staff in her hands—the commandments of God."[46] Just before Mary died at age 89, she told those who surrounded her, "Just think, my feet don't hurt! I guess I have conquered those feet at last."[47]

Mary's Family Members

Mary's parents, James and Eliza, both lived to be 82, dying in Hyde Park, Cache County. Her two sisters who survived the journey, Emma and Sarah, lived to be 85 and 94. Although the family had suffered greatly, Eliza Hurren is reported to have often said, "With all our trials, [our] weary traveling, burying our loved ones, we have never felt to murmur or complain or regret the steps we have taken."[48]

ANN ROWLEY FAMILY

Ann Rowley was a widow who was emigrating with her seven children and one stepdaughter from her husband's first marriage. Her stepdaughter died three days before crossing Rocky Ridge, and two of her sons suffered from severe exposure, but none of her other children died on the journey.

After arriving in Salt Lake City, most of the family was sent to Nephi, where ward members provided for them. "I was grateful for the comparative comfort we enjoyed," Ann wrote, "but still owed our immigration fee and it was hard to accept charity."[49]

In the spring of 1857, Ann married Andrew Bastian, who paid the immigration fee that so concerned her. They moved to Parowan, which became home for most of the family for many years. Andrew Bastian died less than a year after their marriage, and in 1859 Ann married Luke Ford. He died in 1866, leaving Ann a widow for the third time. The last few years of her life, Ann lived with her son Thomas and his family in Huntington, Utah. She died in 1888 at age 81 and was buried in the Huntington cemetery.

Ann's oldest son, John, who had carried so much of the burden on the journey as a 15-year-old, later married Mary Ann Gadd, another member of the Willie company.[50] They lived in Nephi for most of their lives and had 12 children. In 1873 John entered into plural marriage and married Emma James, another member of the Willie company, who had been widowed the previous year.[51] They had two children. John died of pneumonia in 1893 at age 52. His last child was born a month after he died.[52]

Ann Rowley's second son, Samuel, had turned 14 during the journey. As an adult, he helped settle Panguitch.[53] In 1879, after he had returned to Parowan, he was called to help settle San Juan County. Like many other handcart pioneers, Samuel uprooted his family and left a comfortable home to accept another difficult assignment. They left Parowan in October 1879 and became part of the Hole-in-the-Rock expedition. After a grueling trek, they finally arrived in the San Juan area in April 1880. They helped establish the settlement of Bluff, and the Bluff Ward was organized under the shade of Samuel's tree, with Jens Nielson, another handcart pioneer, as bishop. "I furnished the bread . . . and officiated at the first sacrament," Samuel wrote.[54] Conditions in Bluff were so harsh that Samuel could not provide for his family, so after four years the Rowleys moved to Huntington. Samuel died in Huntington in 1928 at age 86.

MARJORIE SMITH FAMILY

Marjorie Smith was a widow who was emigrating with five of her children. In Iowa City her 13-year-old daughter Betsey had been miraculously healed. Somewhere along the trail after the snow began to fall, Marjorie herself became seriously ill. Betsey recalled her mother's faith and strength during this illness:

"My mother was taken very sick with cramp and cholera, a very fatal trouble in our weakened condition. We all felt bad about mother. I remember thinking, 'Many are dying; mother may die, and what a dark world it would be without our dear mother!' As I gathered the sage to burn on our campfire, I couldn't keep from crying. When I met mother, she asked me what was the matter. I told her how badly I felt.

"She said, 'Do not feel like that; pray for me. I have been out yonder in the snow praying to the Lord to spare our lives, that we might get through to the Valley. I will never murmur nor complain, whatever we pass through, when we get there.'

"God heard our prayers, and she kept her word. Even when, in years following, she went blind with age, she never murmured."[55]

Her mother's example of seeing with an eye of faith was a strong influence on Betsey, who later wrote concerning the journey, "I will not dwell upon the hardships we endured, nor the hunger and cold, but I like to tell of the goodness of God unto us."[56]

Marjorie Smith and all her children arrived safely in the Salt Lake Valley.[57] They settled in Lehi at first, because that was where Marjorie's oldest son was living.

Three years after arriving in Utah, Betsey married Isaac Goodwin. They made their homes in Cache Valley, Escalante, Wayne County, and Beaver. When Betsey wrote her account, she was 73 and had been a widow for 25 years. Her only other living sibling at that time was her older sister Jane, who was an ordinance worker in the Manti Temple. In the conclusion of her account, Betsey stated that her primary purpose for writing was to strengthen the youth of the Church. She also once again shared a teaching of President Franklin D. Richards that had been central in her life for 60 years:

"For the benefit of the youth of Zion who may read this, I bear testimony that I know God hears and answers prayers, and the Lord will help those who help themselves."[58]

WILLIAM AND JANE JAMES FAMILY

William and Jane James had started for Zion with eight children. Their youngest child died on the voyage, and William died on Rocky

Ridge. Jane led the rest of her children safely to Zion. Only 13-year-old Reuben, who had nearly frozen to death with his father on Rocky Ridge, suffered injuries that troubled him for the rest of his life.[59]

The three oldest daughters, Sarah, Emma, and Mary Ann, all wrote histories of the trek. The prevailing theme in these histories is the strength and determination of their mother:

On leaving England: "She was ready to leave all we had, and with an almost invalid husband and eight children, brave the journey to an unknown land and a wilderness."[60]

On the death of her baby daughter: "Mother's heart strings were torn, but the brave little mother that she was felt not to murmur against the will of Him who gave."[61]

During the meeting in Florence when deciding whether to continue the journey: "I was frightened. Father looked pale and sick. I turned to Mother to see what she was thinking, and all I saw was her old determined look. She was ready to go on tomorrow. . . . 'We must put our trust in the Lord, as we have always done,' said mother, and that was that."[62]

On helping her children over Rocky Ridge after her husband had given out: "[Mother] found us on the river bank. We were too frightened and tired to cross alone, [but] Mother soon had us on our way. The water was icy, and soon our clothing was frozen to our bodies. Our feet were frozen numb. Cold and miserable, we reached the other bank, put on dry clothing, and joined the rest of the company."[63]

On seeing her dead husband and frozen son brought into the camp at Rock Creek: "I can see my mother's face as she sat looking at the partly conscious Reuben. Her eyes looked so dead that I was afraid. She didn't sit long, however, for my mother was never one to cry. When it was time to move out, mother had her family ready to go. She put [Reuben] in the cart with [four-year-old John], and we joined the train. Our mother was a strong woman, and she would see us through anything."[64]

Jane's oldest daughter, Sarah, wrote that after they arrived in Salt Lake City, "the Saints took us in and were very kind to us. Bishop

[Aaron] Johnson of Springville sent word that he could take one family into his home for the winter, so we were sent South. We older children found work in the homes of the good people in the town, and mother moved into an unfurnished shack where she kept her younger children alive until spring with what work she could find."[65]

After four months in Springville, Sarah married Aaron Johnson. Emma married Aaron's brother Lorenzo on the same day. When Lorenzo died 15 years later, Emma became a plural wife of John Rowley, the son of Ann Rowley, another Willie company widow.

After a year in Springville, Jane and her younger children moved to Salt Lake City for four years. While there, Jane remarried. The marriage lasted only briefly, however, as her husband soon left both the Church and Jane, who was expecting a child at the time. When the baby was born, Jane named him William, after her husband who had died on Rocky Ridge.

Soon Jane moved back to Utah County, where she lived the rest of her life. She died in 1911 at age 96, having spent nearly all of her 55 years in Zion as a widow. Was Zion what she expected? Did she feel that all the sacrifice was worth it? Tributes from two of her daughters help answer these questions. Emma wrote, "She left a great posterity to revere her memory and give thanks that she had had the determination to come to Zion."[66] Mary Ann wrote, "She was one of the sturdy oaks of Utah, the like of which has made this dear old state 'blossom as the rose.' "[67]

Indeed, Zion was not a life of ease for Jane James. It often fell short of the ideal. But she seemed to accept that Zion was a process—and that she had not come merely to partake of it but to help build it.

George Cunningham

Fifteen-year-old George Cunningham, his parents, and his three sisters all made it to Utah alive. How the difficulties of the trek compared to laboring as a child for 14-hour days in a coal pit, six days a week, George does not say.

The Cunningham family was taken to American Fork, where they were cared for kindly. After family members regained their strength, they soon found employment and improved their poor circumstances. For George, though, easier times were not necessarily a blessing. "I soon forgot my past troubles," he later wrote, "and in a little more time found myself in the bloom of youth, hunting for worldly pleasures and vanities. It seemed to me that [these] worldly goods were made for those who lived upon it, and I concluded to enjoy them. . . . About this time of life, young people are very apt to take the wrong track and go after fascinations instead of stern realities and to idealize vain illusions and actions into heroic thoughts and deeds."[68]

George made trips to Fort Bridger and even back to the Sweetwater to sell and trade provisions with emigrants. He also transported grain for the overland mail company. Soon, though, he realized the folly of his free lifestyle:

"I was now twenty-one years of age, had sown quite a great deal of wild oats and reaped quite a crop of the same worthless seed. About this time I began to look back on the course of the life I had been pursuing, and before long I came to the conclusion like one of old, that it was all vanity and vexation of spirit. The pleasure that I had hunted for was all phantom and folly."[69]

When George was about 20 years old, he became attracted to Mary Wrigley for her "principles and amiability." "She was the same Mary Wrigley under all kinds of circumstances," he wrote.[70] It took Mary's parents two years before they would give consent for her to marry George.

George and Mary eventually had 13 children. In August 1885, when George was 45 years old, and just three weeks after his 11th child was born, he was called on a mission to the southern states and given only eight days' notice before he was to depart. "This found me in rather a straightened condition," he wrote. He was in debt and had a large family, "nine of them in petticoats."[71] However, he accepted the call and left for Chattanooga, Tennessee. "It had been pronounced upon my head by the servants of God that I would be useful in proclaiming the everlasting gospel, and I had often prayed and longed that it might come to pass," he wrote as he departed.[72]

George Cunningham died in March 1913 at age 72 and was buried in the American Fork cemetery. One of his descendants paid him this tribute: "[His] life was full and replete with personal sacrifices for the good of others, for the growth and advancement of the community in which he lived and the Church of which he formed a part. For more than forty years he labored as a public servant true to his convictions, sound in his judgment, and firm in his religious beliefs."[73]

George's mother, Elizabeth, died in American Fork in 1907, just two days before her 100th birthday. She had been a widow for 28 years.

SAMUEL AND ELIZA GADD FAMILY

Samuel Gadd and two of his sons died during the journey, the three graves spanning a distance of 150 miles in Wyoming. Only one of the graves is marked—that of Samuel Jr., who was buried with 12 others at Rock Creek. His mother said that of all her children, 10-year-old Samuel Jr. had been the most anxious to reach Zion.[74]

Eliza Chapman Gadd

Eliza Chapman Gadd and her six other children survived the journey. Rather than allowing these tragedies to alienate her from the Church, Eliza was baptized a week after arriving in Utah. In 1861, she and her children settled in Nephi. She worked as a midwife for more than 30 years, delivering 2,000 babies. Her charge for helping with the delivery and giving nine days' care was $2.[75] She also learned to weave and sew all the clothing worn by her family. In addition, she became a skilled hat maker, using straw she gleaned from the fields. Eliza died in 1892 at age 76 and was buried in Nephi. One of her granddaughters wrote, "She had proved herself a faithful Latter-day Saint and had earned the love and respect of the entire community, and many [were] proud to say they were one of her babies."[76]

Eliza's oldest son, Alfred, was 19 when he arrived in Utah. In 1862 he went to Omaha to help some emigrants, and while there he met and began to court Mary Ann Hobbs. They were married a year later and settled in Nephi. They had 11 children, seven of whom lived to maturity. Alfred Gadd was the first Juab County horticulturalist and introduced many new plants and bulbs.[77] In 1893, Alfred went on a mission to England. He died in 1909 at age 71 and was buried in Nephi.

Mary Ann Gadd, who turned eight during the journey and guided her mother during a time when she was snowblind, later married John Rowley, another member of the Willie company. She had 12 children and died in 1924 in Provo.

Isaac Gadd, the two-year-old twin who survived the journey, suffered bad breaks of both his legs several years later when a yoke of oxen bolted and threw him from a load of hay. In 1884 he was called to serve a mission to England. He was reluctant to leave his mother in her declining years, but she insisted that he go. When he returned, he married Martha Paxman. When their first child was born, Eliza helped with the delivery of her grandchild and also attended to Isaac, who lay sick with typhoid fever. Isaac struggled with problems in his legs for many years before one of them finally had to be amputated. He died in 1930 in Provo and was buried in Nephi.

Given the heavy losses the Gadd family suffered on the journey, did they feel that coming to Zion was worth it? Several of Eliza Chapman Gadd's grandchildren have written brief biographies of her, and none of them mentions any regret on her part for the price her family paid to come to Zion. Taking the long view, the sacrifices this family made to emigrate have blessed thousands. One family member who wrote in 1940 said that the known posterity of Samuel and Eliza Chapman Gadd at that time numbered 616.[78] It is likely that most of those people—and thousands more who have been added to their posterity since that time—have been blessed by the decision to come to Zion. One descendant expressed such feelings as follows:

"Even though Samuel's dream and desires to be in Utah never came to be, we are ever grateful to him for embracing the gospel of Jesus Christ. . . . He is loved and respected by those of us who never got to know him in this life and are thankful to him for his dedication and firm conviction of the truth of Mormonism and a strong hope of a glorious resurrection, and we shall hope to meet him then. We are ever grateful to him for bringing his family to America."[79]

JOHN AND MARIA LINFORD FAMILY

John Linford died near the Sixth Crossing of the Sweetwater, but Maria and their three sons who accompanied them on the journey arrived in Utah safely. The Linfords were taken to Centerville to recuperate.

In July 1857, Maria Linford married Joseph Rich, father of Apostle Charles C. Rich. He was kind and devoted to her and her sons, whom he called his own. In 1859, Maria was sealed to her deceased husband in the Endowment House by Brigham Young. Joseph Rich acted as proxy for John Linford.

In 1864 the Rich family was called to help settle the Bear Lake Valley. Joseph, Maria, and her two youngest sons moved to Paris, Idaho, where they lived in a wagon box the first winter. Soon afterward, Joseph suffered a stroke. He died in 1866, leaving Maria a widow for the second time. During her nearly 20 years in Paris, she served as Relief Society president and helped organize the Primary.

Maria died in 1885 in North Ogden while visiting her son George. In 1937 her descendants had a special headstone placed at her gravesite in the North Ogden cemetery. Elder George Albert Smith attended the ceremony and dedicated the marker. Before offering the prayer, he spoke to the family about their ancestors:

"[Maria] was filled with love, sacrifices, and devotion to family and church and great hardships endured for them. She never lost her faith as long as she lived. . . . My soul is stirred when I see all these younger generations. Will you live true to the faith of your ancestors? There is royal blood in your veins. Do strive to be worthy of all the sacrifices your ancestors have made for you."[80]

The Linfords' children remained true to their parents' legacy of faith. After completing his mission in England, James emigrated in 1861. He lived in Kaysville for 51 years, where he served in many Church and civic positions. He was later ordained a patriarch by President John Taylor. He outlived all his younger brothers, dying in 1925 at age 88. Toward the end of his life, he wrote the following testimony:

"I, James Henry Linford, being eighty-two years of age, in good health and sound of mind and body, bear the following testimony in the sincerity of my heart and leave it in writing, to my children, grandchildren, [and] all [my] descendants and kindred. . . . I bear this testimony as in the presence of my Maker, who knows the sincerity of my soul, that the Gospel as taught by The Church of Jesus Christ of Latter-day Saints is true; that it is the same that was taught by Jesus Christ and his Apostles; and that Joseph Smith was the instrument made use of by the Lord in restoring it in this dispensation. It was not made by man, neither was it named after man, but it was revealed to the Prophet by holy angels.

"I pray that the Lord will bless my family and all my kindred with the guiding influence of His Holy Spirit, and I bless them one and all from the depths of my heart with the blessings of this life, peace and prosperity, and trust that we may all meet again in the enjoyment of eternal life in the mansions of our Heavenly Father."[81]

The Linfords' second son, George, was 17 during the handcart journey. His mother said that at times he was the only able-bodied man in their company. He went to England to serve a mission in 1864, the same year his mother moved to the Bear Lake Valley. He later settled in North Ogden and raised a large family. He served in many Church and community positions, including president of the

Young Men's Mutual Improvement Association. He died in North Ogden in 1901.

Joseph Linford was 14 during the journey. In 1866 he married Mary Rich, his stepfather's granddaughter. In 1885 they moved to St. Charles, Idaho, where Joseph served for two years as county commissioner. He died in St. Charles in 1914.

The Linfords' youngest son, Amasa, was 11 during the journey. In 1867 he married Miranda Savage in the Endowment House and moved to Garden City, where he helped build the first school and the first meetinghouse. One time Amasa acted as an escort for President Brigham Young from Swan Creek to Blacksmith Fork Canyon. He moved to Logan in 1919 and died there in 1921.

In 1998, 250 descendants of John Linford dedicated a rock monument in his honor near the Sixth Crossing of the Sweetwater, where he died. This monument is located a few miles up the river from the Sixth Crossing Visitors' Center.

MARGARET KIRKWOOD FAMILY

Eleven-year-old James Kirkwood died after carrying his five-year-old brother Joseph over Rocky Ridge. His widowed mother, Margaret, and her sons Robert, Thomas, and Joseph finished the journey and were taken to American Fork. Robert worked as a merchant and later served as a city councilman in Provo, where he died in 1922 at age 88. He was the father of 27 children.[82]

Eighteen-year-old Thomas, who was crippled and had to ride most of the way in the handcart, died less than two years after arriving in Utah.

Joseph Smith Kirkwood lived to be 82, owing most of those years to the sacrifice of his 11-year-old brother James. He married Alice Pulley in the Endowment House. He became a successful farmer, chicken rancher, and dairyman who was known for his industry and honesty. He was also a faithful Latter-day Saint who did much to build his community.[83]

JENS AND ELSIE NIELSON

Jens and Elsie Nielson had planned to buy a wagon and team for the journey to the Salt Lake Valley. Then in Iowa City they sacrificed their savings to help others, retaining only enough to travel by handcart. What was the cost of this sacrifice? While crossing Rocky Ridge, Jens was saved from death only because Elsie pulled him in the handcart; their only child, 6-year-old Niels, died; and a young girl who was traveling with them, 10-year-old Bodil Mortensen, died. Recalling this time of terrible trial, Jens later wrote:

"It looked like we should all die. I remember my prayers as distinctly today as I did then, if the Lord would let me live to reach Salt Lake City, that all my days should be spent in usefulness under the direction of his holy priesthood. How far I have come short of this promise I do not know, but I have been called to make six homes, and as far as this goes I have fulfilled my promise."[84]

Having already endured the tragic handcart trek, Jens and Elsie Nielson would soon be given many additional difficult assignments. The "six homes" mentioned by Jens are a reference to their colonizing efforts in southern Utah, including Parowan, Paragonah, Circleville, Panguitch, and Cedar City. In 1879 the Nielsons moved again to build a sixth—and most difficult—home. They were called to help settle the San Juan area of southeastern Utah, the roughest, least charted portion of the territory. Jens was 59 years old at the time, an age when most people would think they were past their prime for such assignments, but he remembered his covenant and answered the call.

Jens Nielson became part of 250 people who composed the Hole-in-the-Rock expedition. Pioneers who had earlier participated in the trek west said the Hole-in-the-Rock expedition was even harder. The difficulty was compounded for Jens Nielson, who had been partially crippled by the handcart trek so that he limped with one foot at a right angle to the other.

After six months of winter travel that included constant trailblazing—only part of which was the treacherous descent down the

Hole-in-the-Rock—these pioneers stopped in April 1880 and established the settlement of Bluff. Five months later, Jens Nielson was called to be the bishop of Bluff, accepting an onerous responsibility for both the spiritual and temporal welfare of those who were struggling to make the settlement work.

Elsie Nielson and her two daughters did not accompany Jens on the original Hole-in-the-Rock expedition; however, another wife, Kirsten, and her six children did accompany him. After the expedition, one of these sons went back to Cedar City to pick up Elsie and her daughters and take them to Bluff.

Pioneers in Bluff had constant challenges with getting crops to grow. The San Juan River would rage and wash out their irrigation dams—and then get so low it could not be used for irrigation. In 1884 the river washed away the little town of Montezuma, east of Bluff. Most of the settlers in the area became discouraged and wanted to leave. Two Apostles, Joseph F. Smith and Erastus Snow, assessed the situation and initially thought the colony should move to another place. Then, Jens Nielson's biography states, they promised Jens "that if he would stay, the land would be blessed. At the time Jens was in debt, his team had died in a mudhole, and he was a poor man." Although many others left, the Nielsons decided to stay, and their fortunes soon changed. After building a brick home, Jens said, "This is the sixth home I have built in Utah, and when I move again I want to move on to the hill," meaning the cemetery.[85]

Jens Nielson remained in Bluff until his death in January 1906, just a few days before his 86th birthday. He had served as bishop until his death—a period of 26 years. His biographer recounted his final hours:

"When the end drew very near, so it was a matter of hours, to his loved ones around him he reviewed briefly his life mission, telling them again how the gospel had come to him in his native land, and how he had embraced it and cherished it always through tribulation. Again he declared in firmness to them that Joseph Smith was a prophet, and that through him the gospel of Jesus Christ has been revealed again."[86]

Elsie Nielson lived another eight years, dying in May 1914. Her son-in-law Kumen Jones, one of the scouts for the Hole-in-the-Rock expedition, paid her this tribute:

"Elsie Rasmussen Nielson will be better known for her real worth in and after the Resurrection than she was known here in mortality, except by her own family and close acquaintances. She lived the gospel, with its golden rule, to the fullest, forgetting herself . . . by making others comfortable and happy; industrious, careful, sensible, unpretentious, she plodded on, working for Eternal reward, while the great majority of her fellow mortal pilgrims were clamoring for the things that perish after this earthly life ends."[87]

Jens and Elsie Nielson clearly lived out their lives in fulfillment of the promise Jens had made to the Lord on Rocky Ridge.

CHAPTER 20

REMEMBER

We stand today as recipients of their great effort. I hope we are thankful. I hope we carry in our hearts a deep sense of gratitude for all that they have done for us. . . .

Our forebears laid a solid and marvelous foundation. Now ours is the great opportunity to build a superstructure, all fitly framed together with Christ as the chief cornerstone.

—PRESIDENT GORDON B. HINCKLEY

A century and a half later, the earth is subdued at Rock Creek Hollow, as though it still mourns. Our small group arrives late on a warm October afternoon. After parking, we walk in silence to a large rock monument and stop to read the plaque. Next to it we read a smaller, more modern granite marker that names each of the 15 people who were buried here, 13 of them in a common grave. After reading the names, my friend begins to weep and seeks solitude down in the willows. I look up the hill and try to consider all that occurred to make this otherwise unremarkable place become hallowed ground.

I picture the Willie company pulling their handcarts into the hollow after crossing Rocky Ridge. They begin to arrive late in the evening and continue through the night until 5:00 the next morning. Their clothing and eyebrows are white with frozen snow. They desperately try to start fires, with twigs of wet willows and sage their only fuel. Many huddle around these smoky, insufficient fires. Others just drop, exhausted and numb.

There is Jane James, finally pulling her handcart into camp

toward midnight. Her children had become scattered and disoriented in the whiteout on Rocky Ridge, but she has gathered six of them, and they arrive together. Somewhere back on the trail are her husband, William, and her 13-year-old son, Reuben. William had collapsed earlier in the day and sent Jane ahead to find the children. Reuben had stayed with his father. Over and over, Jane's children ask, "Will Father and Reuben be here soon? Do you think someone helped them?" All through the night the uncertainty gnaws. Finally, toward morning, one of the captains approaches Jane, bearing the dead body of her husband and the nearly unconscious body of her son. He tries to comfort her and then goes back to work. The look in Jane's eyes frightens her children, but she calls upon her deep reserve of faith and has her family ready to move on the next day.

There is five-foot Elsie Nielson pulling her husband, Jens, into camp in a handcart. Jens had also collapsed on Rocky Ridge, but Elsie had insisted that he ride in the handcart, and somehow she has made it to camp. Jens is cradling the frozen body of their only child, 6-year-old Niels. A few hours later, little Niels is placed in a common grave with 12 others.

Bodil Mortensen, the young girl who is traveling with the Nielsons, is exhausted from the day-long march but goes to gather firewood. Using the last of her strength, she shakes the snow from a sagebrush and pulls off some small branches. When she arrives back in camp, she sits down and leans against the wheel of a handcart to rest. It is a final rest. She is soon found frozen to death, sagebrush still in her hands.

Eliza Chapman Gadd, widowed two weeks earlier, is coming into camp with her children. Having already lost her husband and one son on the journey, she is pulling in her handcart the body of another son, 10-year-old Samuel. She is past tears.

Now 11-year-old James Kirkwood comes into the hollow. He is still carrying his 5-year-old brother Joseph, who had become too weary to walk. James sets Joseph down by his mother and then sits down to rest. I picture him as he takes his final breaths just a few minutes later.

Finally, soon after dawn, Reddick Allred comes from the west, bringing fresh supplies and assistance from his station 15 miles away on the Sweetwater. I see gratitude and relief in the faces of the short-handed rescuers as they see that Reddick Allred has faithfully remained at his post, ready to help.

Reflecting on these scenes, I sense a change in my feelings. More than suffering and death, I see sacrifice and faith, perhaps unparalleled, within these few sacred acres. The feeling that the earth mourns gives way to another feeling that is more subtle but just as real—a feeling that the earth rejoices. For what cause? Because of the sacrifices these people were willing to make for the gospel, for Zion. Because of the heroism of their rescuers. And even, perhaps, because of the power of these stories to teach and inspire. Certainly they teach important lessons about using good judgment and preparing carefully. But the overwhelming message that speaks from every breath of these stories is the power of faith in God and complete consecration to him.

REMEMBER

Late this October afternoon, even the wind is calm. In a glow of autumn gold, I walk to another granite monument. In one word, engraved in block letters that span the full width of the rock, this monument expresses a simple but profound imperative: *Remember.*

Remembering is the dominant theme in President Gordon B. Hinckley's extensive writings and addresses about the handcart experience. "Stories of the beleaguered Saints and of their suffering will be repeated again and again," he said. "Stories of their rescue need to be repeated again and again. They speak of the very essence of the gospel of Jesus Christ."[1]

Remembering, in this case, is more than a mental exercise. Rather, it implies an obligation, a call to action, as President Hinckley expressed in his prayer of dedication at Rock Creek Hollow:

"O God, our Eternal Father, we thank Thee for the great inheritance that is ours, that we come of the strain of noble people who valued faith more than life itself, who were willing to work and sacrifice—even to give their lives in death—for the cause in which they believed. Help us to be true to the faith, and help all the generations who shall follow to remain true to the faith, that they may keep the trust which became so much a part of the lives of those who died here and elsewhere along this trail of tears."[2]

To help us heed President Hinckley's plea to remain true to the faith, we can remember Bodil Mortenson.

We can remember James Kirkwood carrying little Joseph.

We can remember the rescuers who went back to help those who fell behind.

We can remember Betsey Smith, who, despite the terrible sufferings, said, "I will not dwell upon the hardships we endured, nor the hunger and cold, but I like to tell of the goodness of God unto us."[3]

We can remember Franklin D. Richards, who, after learning of the deaths of two children and a brother while he was serving a mission in England, wrote in his journal, "Father, I own thy dealings just; . . . do I not know that thy goodness never fails? I have feared that I should feel thy hand against me. But now I trust that in this also thou wilt reveal thy hidden stores of goodness and blessings."[4]

Finally, we can remember that the goodness of God, his grace and tender mercies, are found even in tragedies such as this, compensating eternally for any mortal suffering.

The Remember *monument is a six-foot granite marker that memorializes the Second Rescue, an inspired effort by members of the Riverton Wyoming Stake to research the names of the members of the Willie and Martin handcart companies and provide temple ordinances for them. For more information, see* Remember: The Willie and Martin Handcart Companies and Their Rescuers—Past and Present, *compiled by members of the Riverton Wyoming Stake, and* The Second Rescue, *by Susan Arrington Madsen.*

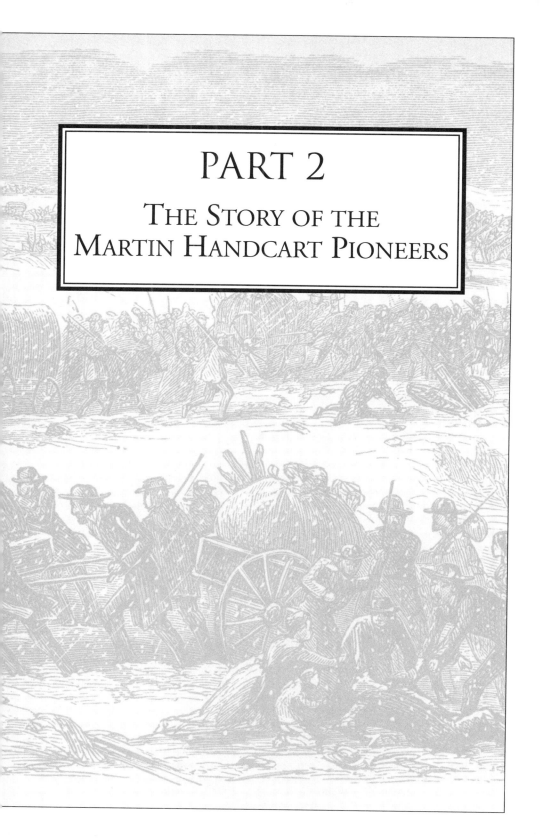

PART 2

THE STORY OF THE
MARTIN HANDCART PIONEERS

CHAPTER 21

FAREWELL TO THEE, ENGLAND

Terrible was the suffering of those who came here to find some protection from the heavy storms of that early winter. With their people hungry, cold, and dying from sheer exhaustion, they came up into this cove for shelter, and many died here. . . . They are buried somewhere in this earth. . . .

Father, we are so grateful for their faith—their faith in Thee and in Thy Beloved Son, their faith in the Prophet Joseph Smith and Thy work which was restored through him. They left their native [lands] to find refuge where they could worship according to their conscience with their associates in the Salt Lake Valley. Great was their suffering, terrible their tragedy.

—President Gordon B. Hinckley
dedicatory prayer for the Martin's Cove Monument, 15 August 1992

Louisa Mellor had higher expectations for her 16th birthday. Newly arrived in Liverpool with her parents and six younger siblings, she expected to celebrate aboard the ship that would take her family to Zion. But on the day the ship was to depart, Louisa's mother went into premature labor and was taken to a hospital, where she gave birth to conjoined twins. The babies lived only a few hours, and Louisa's mother, Mary Ann, was so close to death that she was unable to leave the hospital.

The Mellor family faced an agonizing dilemma. Their ship, the *Horizon,* would be carrying the last large company of Latter-day Saint emigrants to leave England that season. Unless the Mellors got on board, they would have to wait until another year to emigrate. But waiting would create other predicaments. The family had already given up their home and employment in Leicester and had sold most of their possessions. Having lived in poverty all their lives, they did not have the resources to wait out another year.

Another problem with waiting was the uncertainty of future emigration opportunities. Despite being industrious, the Mellors had not been able to save enough money to pay for the passage of their nine family members to America. Only by receiving a loan from the Perpetual Emigration Fund were they able to emigrate in 1856. There was no guarantee that such assistance would be available the next year. In 1856 the fund had been in debt—and its availability in doubt—until Brigham Young sold some of his own property to help replenish it.

Even in her weakened physical condition, Mary Ann Mellor was so committed to Zion that she saw only one way to resolve this dilemma. Although she could hardly bear to have her family leave, particularly in her time of need, she urged her husband to keep their places on the ship. Their passage had been arranged; their possessions were packed and ready for loading; she would go to America, some-how, when she recovered.

James Mellor reluctantly complied with his wife's request and took five of his children to the docks in Liverpool, where they boarded the ship. Two of the children stayed behind—16-year-old Louisa, who would look after her mother, and one of Louisa's 2-year-old twin sisters. Describing that 16th birthday on May 23, 1856, Louisa wrote, "A sad one it was for me, as I was left with a sick mother and a little sister 2½ years old, as my father had to take the rest of the family and go aboard."[1]

Louisa did not know when she would see her father again. She likely thought it would be at least a year—and maybe never. She likely worried that her mother might die, leaving her and her little sister on their own. But then to her great surprise, two days later her father returned to the hospital and said the ship's departure had been delayed. The ship had left the dock and was anchored in the River Mersey, but it would not be tugged out to sea until later that day. Although Mary Ann was still seriously ill, she decided she did not want her family to leave without her after all. Over the doctor's protests, James took her from the hospital on a stretcher and carried her onto the ship. The doctor predicted that sharks would follow the ship until she died. Seeing her condition, the captain predicted she would soon be food for the sharks.

Because Mary Ann was in such precarious health, some of the mission leaders who came aboard to bid the Saints farewell administered to her. In the blessing, Elder Cyrus Wheelock told Mary Ann that her mission on earth was not completed and that she would "see her seed in Zion."[2] What would be the outcome for this already beleaguered family as they made the arduous journey to Zion? The story of their experiences, as well as the stories of many others who became part of the Martin handcart company, will unfold in these pages.

The beginning of the Martin handcart company's story is similar to that of the Willie company. Both groups sailed from Liverpool, the Willie group leaving on May 4 and the Martin group on May 25, 1856. Both groups sailed on ships that had been chartered by the Church, the Willie group on the *Thornton* and the Martin group on the *Horizon*. Both companies consisted mostly of British converts, along with a smaller number of converts from other nations and a few returning missionaries.

Franklin D. Richards, a member of the Quorum of the Twelve Apostles, oversaw the emigration as president of the European Mission. Just as he had earlier appointed James Willie to preside over the Saints on the *Thornton,* he appointed another returning missionary, Edward Martin, to preside over those on the *Horizon*. Edward Martin's counselors on the ship were Jesse Haven, who was returning from a mission to South Africa, and George P. Waugh, a 68-year-old convert who was a veteran British soldier.

The *Horizon* carried 856 passengers, the largest company to leave England during the emigration season of 1856. The *Horizon* also carried the highest proportion of passengers who, like James and Mary Ann Mellor, received financial assistance from the Perpetual Emigration Fund. Nearly 75 percent—635 people—received such assistance.[3] By comparison, less than half of the other Saints who emigrated in 1856 received assistance from the fund,[4] and only about one-fourth of those who emigrated in 1855 had received it.[5]

The high proportion of Perpetual Emigration Fund passengers

is a significant factor in the story of the Martin company. Because the resources of the fund were limited, Brigham Young instructed President Richards to give priority to "those who have proven themselves by long continuance in the Church."[6] The people who received this assistance, then, were not only poor but also generally long-time members of the Church who had proven their faithfulness. Having a large number of such people would repeatedly evidence itself for the benefit of this company during the forthcoming journey.

"Farewell to thee, England—bright land of my sires." So begins a poem composed on the deck of the *Horizon* the day before it left Liverpool. Although the Saints were excited to be gathering to Zion, their homeland still tugged at them. The poem laments that never again would they see the scenes of their childhood. Never again would they see England's lush green beauty—its "moss-covered dells" and "blossomy bow'rs." But rather than lingering on losses, the poem turns abruptly to express loyalty to God:

> *I wish not to linger thy beauties among,*
> *I dare not be false to the God I adore,*
> *Henceforward my lute to His praises is strung,*
> *And to Him relinquish those memories of yore.*[7]

Indeed, most of the *Horizon*'s 856 passengers were on board because they felt it was God's will. With very few exceptions, they would make any sacrifice and endure any hardship to accomplish what they believed God wanted them to do.

JOURNEY ACROSS THE ATLANTIC

The journey of the *Horizon* across the Atlantic was similar to that of the *Thornton* (see pages 8–12). United by the gospel and the common hope of gathering to Zion, the Saints quickly formed a close community. Boundaries of class, blood, and culture that had existed for generations began to dissolve immediately. Four days into the voyage, John Jaques, a 29-year-old English convert who was the company's historian, wrote to President Franklin D. Richards: "Young and old are assembled on deck, with light hearts and cheerful faces. . . . I hear no murmuring or grumbling. All is peace and harmony in our floating town."[8]

The Saints on the *Horizon* were well organized and generally enjoyed a good relationship with Captain Reed and his crew. About a week into the voyage, John Jaques recorded that the captain "spoke highly of our organization and of the morality and good order which characterized us. He seemed much interested in the welfare of the passengers. He had been on board with us eight days and had not heard a single oath from us."[9] The relationship with Captain Reed was so cordial that groups of Saints would gather around him and sing their favorite hymns.[10]

While crossing the Atlantic, the Saints experienced the joys of marriage and birth—and the heartache of death. Four couples were married on the ship. Four babies were born, including one girl and one boy who were given *Horizon* as a middle name. Five people died, including two of the babies who were born at sea.

Edward Martin was unwearying in looking after the needs of the passengers. "I make it my business to visit every part of the ship six or seven times a day," he wrote during the first week.[11] Beginning these visits at first light, he would go throughout all three of the ship's decks, inquiring about the welfare of more than 850 people.

The Wind, the Waves, and the Slop Pail

At least five passengers on the *Horizon* kept journals of the voyage. Almost always they wrote about the wind and the sea—whether the breeze was favorable or contrary, whether the water was calm or rough. Some days the ship made only two miles an hour, a slow walking pace. Such days seemed especially tedious when a steam-powered ship passed the *Horizon* at what John Jaques described as a "tearing pace."[12]

On June 4, Samuel Openshaw wrote, "Low breeze and calm sea. . . . Made little or no progress."[13] John Jaques likewise expressed frustration at being entirely dependent on the whims of the wind: "The idle wind . . . makes one feel like getting out and pushing behind."[14] On such days, a literary man such as he must have recalled the words of Coleridge's *Rime of the Ancient Mariner:*

> *Day after day, day after day,*
> *We stuck, nor breath nor motion;*
> *As idle as a painted ship*
> *Upon a painted ocean.*[15]

But then the wind would begin to whip with a vengeance, often from the front or the side, sometimes even tearing sails. On those occasions, wrote John Jaques, "the willing ship dashes through the waters like a mad thing, at the rate of a dozen miles or more an hour. We tack to the right and tack to the left, and after sailing so heartily for 200 or 300 miles, the captain takes an observation and finds that we are 20 miles worse for all our trouble, or perhaps we are in about the same place as when becalmed."[16]

At the end of the third week, the ship's second mate said they had not sailed on due course for even six hours since leaving Liverpool and estimated the journey would take six weeks.[17]

Seasickness was the biggest problem for most of the Saints. One day they would be singing songs of joy. The beauties of the ocean would be sublime, with reflections that John Jaques described as "a band of burnished silver" and "a galaxy of glittering gems."[18] But the next day a contrary wind would arise, causing the ship to pitch and rock. Songs were forsaken as countenances were changed to "a pitiful, pallid hue."[19]

As the misery persisted, Samuel Openshaw wrote, "I began to think that I should never get accustomed to rocking, as I was almost always sick. Mother also, and she was very low in spirits."[20] John Jaques was more sensory in his description of the seasickness: "Such a worshipping of buckets and tins, and unmentionable pans, I shall not attempt to describe. For my part I paid the most devoted attention to the slop-pail about every half hour."[21] Even a month after he left the ship, this particular challenge of life on the sea quickened his pen:

"Who can possibly like to be continually rocked about, as though he were having a child's ride in an English swing boat? Who has any taste for a dizzy head at every breeze? Who wishes to be forced into a gait as unsteady, staggering, and uncertain as the drunkard's? Who admires treading on a platform that seems the plaything of an everlasting earthquake? I have no great taste for these things."[22]

Seasickness was expected to subside after a few days, but for many passengers it continued throughout the voyage. Most of them did not fully regain their strength and vigor until they landed in Boston.

Spiritual Outpouring

The journey was not all slop pails and contrary winds, however. There were also times of rich spiritual outpouring, with singing and prayers, meetings and miracles. Reporting on the first few days, John Jaques told President Richards, "The brethren and sisters congregated upon the deck [and] made the air vocal with their songs of praise and joy to the Lord their God for the deliverance . . . from Babylon."[23]

Throughout the voyage, George Waugh, the elderly second counselor to Edward Martin, went through the ship comforting and blessing the sick.[24] Other leaders were also called on to bless the sick. Jesse Haven wrote: "Just as I was going to bed last night, a young sister was taken with a fit. I administered to her. It made her some better. She soon was better and went to bed."[25]

Fourteen-year-old Mary Barton recalled the following experience of being healed after receiving a priesthood blessing: "One day while on the ship, I was up in the cooking room cooking dinner. It was so crowded there was hardly standing room. The people were all cooking their dinner. One man was boiling soup in a milk can. When he took the soup from the stove, he lifted it over my head in order to carry it through the crowd. While doing so, somebody knocked him and it fell out of his hand onto my back. . . . I ran out to [my father] and he said, 'Come downstairs and let's get some oil.' So we ran down the steps and got one of the Elders to administer to me. It was better in a few minutes. The pain had entirely gone and I never felt any more of it."[26]

The ship was organized into nine wards, which met often. In addition to Sunday meetings, the Saints held prayer meetings each morning and evening, as well as testimony and fellowshipping meetings during the week. John Jaques recorded that these meetings "tended to comfort and cheer the Saints, build them up in their holy faith, and establish them in the practice of the principles of eternal life."[27] After one meeting, Joseph Beecroft wrote, "Elder Broderick preached to us and unfolded our past, present, and future estates, and his remarks were truly grand."[28] In another meeting, Jesse Haven addressed the young men about being too noisy, exhorting them "to set patterns to all, because [the] eyes of many were upon them, and the young were the persons who must build up this kingdom and bear it off triumphantly."[29]

Playing and Working Together

The Saints also had fun during the voyage. When the waters were calm, they danced to a fiddle and tambourine. Children played marbles and skipped rope both above and below deck. "So merrily we live together," wrote John Jaques. "We want but the stalls and gingerbread to give our deck the appearance of an English country fair, barring the drunkenness, quarreling, profanity, and obscenity."[30]

The Saints' industry and cooperation during the voyage were exemplary. At 5:00 each morning they were called from their beds by cornet. Every day they would air and disinfect their bedding and then scrub the ship from bow to stern. They also worked hard to prepare for the handcart portion of the journey, finishing 45 tents.

Captain Reed was especially impressed by the cooperation in cooking meals. This was no trifling matter for a company of more than 850. The ship had only one galley, and each family had its own pot—a recipe for strife. Instead, most of the time they got along favorably. John Jaques reported, "[The captain] contrasted our deportment with that of the Irish emigrants, stating how they would quarrel and fight among one another over their cooking, and that his chief reliance to procure order among them was by turning the hose on them while the crew were at the pump."[31]

Joseph Beecroft seemed equally impressed that the people were so cooperative in living conditions that allowed little peace or personal space. Describing the scene below deck, he wrote:

"In looking down the gangway or passage on either side of our berths, it looks like a long bazaar. Some [are] eating, some preparing food, some reading, others passing to and fro, one making a bed. It is one continued scene of bustle from morn to night, but amidst all this bustle and jostling together, we do not hear one cross word but all move on like clockwork."[32]

ARRIVAL IN BOSTON

After a month at sea, on June 26 the Saints began to see driftwood and other encouraging signs that land was near. That night at least one of the wards celebrated these signs with a tea party. The following day several boats were sighted, including a Boston fishing boat. The next day, June 28, the *Horizon* finally skimmed into Massachusetts Bay. Describing that day, John Jaques wrote:

"Beautiful calm morning. Many small vessels seen. A thin sandy broken black streak was pronounced land, which proves to be true, being Cape Cod. Great rejoicing at this. . . . It was truly refreshing to see the houses, trees, and the green landscape after being deprived of the privilege for some time. We cast anchor at 6 P.M. within a mile or two of Boston."[33]

Joseph Beecroft was exultant when he arrived in America: "I feel grateful to my Father in Heaven for his goodness in sparing our lives to see the land of Zion, the land of the free, . . . the land of Joseph, choice above all lands. Glory to God in the highest and good will to men. [It is] one of the most important days that ever dawned in my history."[34]

After being so far away from home for so long, Jesse Haven also recorded feelings of joy on arriving in Boston: "Towards night I went ashore [and] rejoiced. I had the privilege of setting my feet once more on my native land after being absent nearly 4 years."[35]

The next afternoon the Saints gathered on the main deck for a final meeting on the *Horizon*. They sang and prayed, heard from Elder Martin and other leaders, and gave three cheers to Captain Reed and his crew. The captain spoke for a few minutes and said "that this company of emigrants was the best he had brought across the sea. He complimented them on their good behavior and said that we sung, 'We'll Marry None But Mormons,' and he said he would say that he should 'Carry None But Mormons.' "[36]

On June 30, two days after arriving in Massachusetts Bay, the *Horizon* was towed to Constitution Wharf, where the emigrants first set foot on American soil. They had been on the ship for 37 days. Though at times the voyage had seemed interminable, their pace turned out to be a little faster than average for a westbound sailing vessel.

Seventeen years later Captain Reed traveled to Salt Lake City by rail and visited some of the people he had carried across the Atlantic. "Very much pleased was the old gentleman to see them," wrote John Jaques.[37]

CHAPTER 22

FROM BOSTON TO IOWA CITY

Some of the Saints who sailed on the *Horizon* stayed in Boston or went to Philadelphia, New York, or other cities to wait until the next year to complete the journey to Zion.[1] Most of them—about 700—left Boston within two days, destined for the handcart outfitting site in Iowa City. Traveling by train, they made an eight-day journey through Albany and Buffalo, New York; Cleveland and Toledo, Ohio; and Chicago and Rock Island, Illinois. They began the rail journey in cattle cars, using their luggage for seats.[2] Their second train was a slight improvement, having what Joseph Beecroft described as "a convenience on one end."[3] Eventually they got on a train that had seats with padded backs.

During the journey by rail, Joseph Beecroft reflected on how the gospel bonded people from different economic classes. For part of the way he rode next to a wealthy convert named Thomas Tennant. Joseph wrote about him with admiration and awe:

"We had among others Squire Tennant for a carriage passenger before we changed carriages, and when we got into the other carriages we had Mr. Tennant for our nearest neighbor. He had his wife, her mother, and his child. What has Mormonism done? Such a spectacle was scarcely ever witnessed as to see one who has been so rich [and] so high in life come [to] be huddled together with the poorest of the poor. [To] see how patiently he endures all things is truly wonderful."[4]

Before leaving England, Thomas Tennant paid $25,000 to buy a home that Brigham Young offered for sale to help replenish the Perpetual

Emigration Fund.[5] *This purchase provided the greatest single contribution to financing the 1856 emigration.*[6] *Thomas Tennant would never see the home, however, as he would die in October near Scotts Bluff, Nebraska.*

These Saints faced many challenges during their first days in America. Two young children died while the company was in Boston, likely of the measles. Another child died between Albany and Buffalo, another between Cleveland and Toledo, and another near Chicago. A middle-aged woman and an elderly woman also died. Rushed funerals and burials were held, the final amen still lingering as loved ones hurried to the next train, never to visit the graves again. Brief journal entries recording these deaths belie the anguish: "Brother Palmer's child died this evening."[7] "Buried an old sister and a child at Chicago."[8]

The journey by rail had plenty to commend itself as well. Samuel Openshaw was favorably impressed by his new country. The land, the people, and the level of civilization seemed to dispel some of the British stereotypes:

"We passed through a most delightful country, fruit trees and vines all along the side of the railway. . . . They gave a most agreeable smell. There was, here and there, a house, and then a group of houses, but not those miserable huts which are built in the midst of a howling wilderness, which one might imagine are in the back settlements of America, but beautiful homes, as if they had a taste for finery."[9]

Though preferring the pastoral, Samuel Openshaw was also impressed by the city of Buffalo. The Saints passed through on July 4, and he was among 40 men who stayed with the luggage until late in the evening while the rest of the company continued to Cleveland. Afforded an opportunity to explore, he described the city as "a very healthy place, streets very wide and the telegraphic wires running to every part of the city."[10] He enjoyed the Fourth of July festivities, noting the flags on the houses and across the streets, as well as the shooting and fireworks.

John Jaques recalled that for most of the journey by rail, the Saints were treated "with civility and more or less courtesy."[11] However, they had difficulties in Cleveland, Toledo, and Chicago on July 5, 6, and 7. In Cleveland they secured a barn for the night, but John Southwell recalled that there was little opportunity for sleep:

"After [we] had retired for the night, a mob of bullies, including some females, gathered around the barn and kept up for hours . . . a howling and bombarding with stones and bats. . . . Finally the presidency of the company found a person who it seemed had some authority, who persuaded the mob to desist and go to their homes. . . . Not a person closed an eye that night in sleep."[12]

At Toledo the next day some of the railroad employees hurled "vulgar salutations" at the Saints as soon as they arrived at the depot. John Jaques viewed such coarse behavior as a consequence of some Americans' intoxication with personal freedom. These employees, he said, "must have belonged to that peculiar class of people who are never tired of boasting that they live not in a despotic empire nor in an effete monarchy, but in a democratic republic, a free country, a land of liberty, where one man is as good as another, and a great deal better if he has more cheek and impudence and less principle. . . . I might safely wager that in no effete monarchy nor despotic empire in Europe would any kind of railway passengers be so rudely treated."[13]

Difficulties continued the next day in Chicago. The railroad company provided a warehouse for the Saints to sleep in, but again it provided little respite. William Binder wrote that some of the men had to stand guard all night to keep the "roughs" away from the building, "their motives being anything but pure."[14] By morning another crowd had gathered and tried to create a different kind of disturbance. William Binder said they "were very liberal in circulating lies respecting the life and character of the Prophet Joseph Smith, and used their efforts to influence the weak and inexperienced."[15]

The Saints left Chicago on July 7 and spent the day crossing Illinois. Most of them reached Rock Island, on the state's western border, by 10:00 P.M. The next day they crossed the Mississippi River and boarded one last train for the end of the rail in Iowa City, 50 miles away.

ARRIVAL AND ORGANIZATION IN IOWA CITY

The Saints from the *Horizon* began arriving in Iowa City on July 8, just 12 days after the Willie group arrived. The last of them arrived on July 9.[16] The Willie and Martin groups were in Iowa City at the same time for a few days until the Willie company left on July 15. Although these two groups are often spoken of as a unit, this was the only time they would be in the same place at the same time.

Jesse Haven records that on July 12, Daniel Spencer, who supervised the emigration in Iowa City, "organized [the camp] for traveling. The Saints that came with me and Brother Martin were divided into two companies. Brother Martin was appointed President of one and I the other."[17] Edward Martin's group was known as the fifth handcart company, and Jesse Haven referred to his group as the "6th company of handcarts."[18] Because the groups would be combined after the journey across Iowa, however, historical records recognize them as one company—the fifth, or Martin, handcart company.

Some of those who came on the *Horizon* joined the Hunt and Hodgetts wagon companies. These were independent companies composed of Church-owned wagons and of people who were financially able to buy their own wagons and teams. The wagon companies would leave Iowa City at about the same time as the Haven and Martin groups and travel closely with them for most of the journey.

Because of the central roles of Edward Martin and Jesse Haven in the handcart story, it is helpful to know more about their lives to that point.

EDWARD MARTIN

Edward Martin was born in Preston, England, in 1818. He was among the earliest English converts when he was baptized by Elder

Orson Hyde in the River Ribble in 1837. He married Alice Clayton in 1840, and early the next year they left for America. After steaming up the Mississippi River from New Orleans, they arrived in Nauvoo in April 1841 and were greeted by the Prophet Joseph Smith.

Edward Martin

Edward and Alice Martin settled in Nauvoo for five years, living in a small home they built down the hill from the temple. Having been apprenticed as a painter in England, Edward helped paint the Nauvoo Temple and the interior of Joseph Smith's store. Edward also played the violin and was an original member of the Nauvoo band. The highlight of the Martins' time in Nauvoo came during the last few months, when they were endowed and sealed in the Nauvoo Temple.

The Martins also knew grief and tragedy in Nauvoo. First came the martyrdom of Joseph Smith in 1844. Then came the death of their oldest child, Lucy Ann, in 1845. Then came the expulsion from the city in 1846. Edward and Alice and their two surviving children, Mary Ellen and Edward, were among the thousands who left nearly everything behind and crossed the Mississippi River in February 1846.

The Martins headed west across Iowa with the other exiled Saints. Describing this trek, Edward wrote to his friend John Melling in England: "We had a very wet spring. There was something like 500 families all out of doors through frost and snow and mud and rain, day after day and week after week, in consequence of which we made very little progress."[19]

Service in the Mormon Battalion

After being driven out of Nauvoo, the Martins toiled for five months to cross Iowa, a distance of 300 miles. In July they finally arrived at Iowa's western border in the area of Council Bluffs, where difficulties continued to multiply. On July 14 their youngest child died. Six days later, Edward left his grieving wife, who was pregnant again, to serve in the Mormon Battalion. "The United States sent a messenger after us with a requisition for 500 men to march to California," he wrote. "We were all out of doors with our families, and whilst in this situation we were called to leave [them] and enlist into the United States service. We accordingly left our families in this situation, committing them into the hands of God for support and preservation."[20]

Edward Martin was gone from his family for nearly 18 months. In his letter to John Melling, the miles accumulate relentlessly: 180 to Fort Leavenworth, 1,000 to Santa Fe, 1,500 to San Diego, 300 within California. During all this time, Alice and Mary Ellen stayed at Winter Quarters, a temporary community the Saints established across the river from Council Bluffs. There Alice gave birth to the Martins' fourth child, a son who lived only five months. Edward Martin never saw him.

Edward completed his service with the battalion in July 1847 and started for Salt Lake City. After another long march, he arrived there in October, less than three months after the first pioneer company. He immediately began inquiring about his wife and learned that she was still at Winter Quarters. Although it was late in the season, a week later he began the 1,000-mile journey eastward, and on December 10, 1847, he was finally reunited with Alice and Mary Ellen. He estimated that since being driven from Nauvoo less than two years earlier, he had traveled 6,120 miles, most of it on foot, all of it—even the military march for his new country—motivated by his testimony of the restored gospel. "The suffering and privations we had to pass through I say nothing about," he wrote, "but suffice it to say we did it for Christ and the Gospel's sake."[21]

Settling in the Salt Lake Valley

Edward Martin still had another thousand miles to travel before he could settle down again. In June 1848, he, Alice, and Mary Ellen started for Utah in a company of 300 wagons. They finally arrived in Salt Lake City on September 25. The Martins' fifth child was born on the Wyoming plains, but she died two weeks after the family arrived in Utah. Despite all the hardships the Martins had endured the previous few years, their faith remained strong, as Edward expressed toward the end of his letter to John Melling:

"I and my family are now in the Salt Lake Valley in the midst of the mountains, and I thank my Heavenly Father for it. Thus far, his hand has been over us for good. . . . As in respects to the Church, I am as well satisfied as I ever was, and the more I see into its doctrine and order the better I am satisfied, and once more bear testimony to the truth of the same, and I also give my invitation to all men to embrace the truth and obey the everlasting gospel. . . . Our God is a merciful God, and he will hear the cries of his children."[22]

In Salt Lake City, Edward resumed his trade of painting. Alice gave birth to another daughter, who lived only one year, and another son, the second to be named after his father.

Mission to England: "My Whole Heart Is Engaged in This Work"

After three years in Salt Lake City, in August 1852 Edward Martin was again called to leave his family, this time to return to his homeland as a missionary. A change in the salutation in his letters reveals yet another tragedy for his family. As late as December 1852 he wrote, "Dear wife and children." Later letters are addressed, "Dearly beloved wife and child."[23] The Martins' youngest child, one-year-old Edward, had died in October, just a month after his father left for the mission field. Of the seven children born to Edward and Alice Martin, only one, Mary Ellen, still survived.

Edward Martin arrived in England in February 1853. He visited his mother and stepfather in Preston and then went to Scotland, where he labored more than two years. His letters to Alice are invariably positive about his mission. "My whole heart is engaged in this work," he wrote soon after arriving in Scotland, "and I feel determined by the help of Almighty God to do right. I am busily engaged all the time travelling from branch to branch and doing business in the capacity that I am called to act in."[24] The next year he wrote: "It is more to me than my meat and my drink to labour for the building up of this kingdom. I never enjoyed myself better in my life than I do preaching the Gospel. Although I have a great many trying scenes to pass through, yet I find the grace of God sufficient for them all."[25]

In contrast, Edward Martin's letters are decidedly pessimistic about the condition of the world, sometimes reading like a doomsday sermon: "The world is full of calamity and woe; poverty is staring the poor in the face; pestilence is stalking amongst both rich and poor, and laying its thousands cold in the arms of death. . . . Tens of thousands are slain in war and lying as dung on the ground. Every invention imaginable is entered into, to destroy the inhabitants from the face of the earth. . . . The world of slaughter is increasing every day. The hearts of men are getting hardened against their neighbors, [and some] even go so far as to shed the blood of a man for a little filthy lucre."[26]

Correspondence with Mary Ellen

The correspondence between Edward Martin and his only surviving child, eight-year-old Mary Ellen, is of special interest. At some point in most of his letters, he shifts from addressing Alice to addressing Mary Ellen. He encourages her in her writing, asks what kind of musical instrument she would like him to bring home, and admonishes her to obey her mother's teachings. In response, Mary Ellen adds notes in a youthful cursive at the end of her mother's letters. Much is revealed in a letter she wrote three months after her father left and two months after her little brother died:

"I miss you much, though I must miss you more before I have the privilege of seeing you again. . . . I should be as happy as anyone if I had my dear little brother to play with, and I think Mother would not look so solemn if he was alive. I am going to the ward school according to your request. . . . We go to meeting every Sunday and hear good teachings from Brother Brigham and others. O father, I wish you could hear him but this cannot be till the due time of the Lord."[27]

After her father had been gone for three years, 11-year-old Mary Ellen wrote: "It would be pleasing to me if I see you once more, but as the time has not come I must be contented. It seems as if I never had a father."[28]

Service in the Emigration Department

In April 1855, President Franklin D. Richards asked Edward Martin to come to Liverpool to work in the Emigration Department of the mission office. Edward stayed there for a month and then returned to Scotland. "We were kept very busy in the office," he wrote in his journal. "Indeed we were engaged half the night the greater part of the time."[29] His service must have been commendable because the next year he was asked to return to the office for most of the emigration season.[30] During these last few months of his mission, he helped oversee the emigration of more than 4,400 converts, the largest number to that time. When that season's emigration work was finished—and the time away from his family was approaching four years—Edward Martin boarded the *Horizon* for home.[31]

JESSE HAVEN

Jesse Haven was a younger cousin of Brigham Young, their mothers being sisters. He was born in Massachusetts in 1814 and was baptized in 1838 at age 24. Immediately after his baptism he left home to gather with the Saints in Far West, Missouri. He arrived in time for the worst of the Missouri persecutions, which culminated in the Saints being driven from the state.

Soon after Church members went to Illinois, Jesse Haven was

called to serve a mission in the eastern states. He then married Martha Hall in 1842. In 1844 he was ordained a seventy, and in 1845 he was appointed one of the presidents of the 14th quorum of seventy in Nauvoo. Like most of the Saints there, he and Martha were forced to leave in 1846 and spent the following winter in Winter Quarters. They stayed in that area until 1848, when Jesse was called to serve another mission. Jesse returned in 1849, and he and Martha finally journeyed to Salt Lake City in 1850. Soon afterward, Jesse married Abby Cram. For the next two years he taught school, clerked, and farmed.

Like Edward Martin, Jesse Haven was among the group of 106 men who were called as missionaries during a conference held in August 1852. As was customary at the time, they were called from the pulpit without any notice. Within a month, they left Salt Lake City for many parts of the world, including some of the most remote. Jesse Haven's assignment was among the most challenging. Rather than going to England, where the Church was well established, he, Leonard Smith, and William Walker were called to be the first Latter-day Saint missionaries to South Africa.

"I left my family with tears in my eyes," Jesse Haven wrote in his journal on September 18, 1852, the day he left for South Africa. "I felt bad when I left, prayed to God to sustain me on my journey and bless my family in my absence." Part of his anxiety was that he was 38 years old, had been unable to establish himself financially, and was leaving his two wives nearly destitute. This worry and the associated concern about the love of his wives would continue to trouble him throughout his mission.

Departure for South Africa

Getting to South Africa first required crossing the pioneer trail in the western United States. Jesse Haven camped in places that would look much different when he returned four years later. After the missionaries passed the frontier and reached the eastern part of the country, they met with the Saints in cities such as St. Louis,

Cincinnati, and Philadelphia. Jesse Haven had the following remarkable experience after their meeting in Philadelphia:

"A brother . . . came to me and wanted me to lay hands on him and rebuke a pain he had in his breast, which pain he had had for some time. He told me of a vision he had nearly a year ago. He said, 'I saw the heavens open. . . . A man came out . . . and laid his hands on me. When I saw you, Brother Haven, my heart rejoiced, . . . for you are the man [who] laid hands on me. I told the Presiding Elder some time ago that something is going to happen that will be a blessing to the Saints in Philadelphia. There will be a man here of a stern countenance but a kind heart who will be a comfort to the Saints.'

"This vision," Jesse Haven continued, "made my heart to rejoice. I felt, perhaps I shall yet do some good in the world."[32]

Jesse Haven and his companions departed for Liverpool and landed there on January 3, 1853. On the first day of the new year, he wrote the following resolutions. Similar sentiments, in both prose and poetry, would fill his journals in the coming years:

"I now commence a new year, and I pray [to] my Heavenly Father that I may commence a new life. I feel determined and resolved to walk more humbly and by the help of God to set a better example before the world and before the Saints. I am also determined to make a better improvement of my time, and seek continually by fasting and prayer to know the will of God in all things. Help me, O Lord, to fulfill these resolves that I have made. Assist me to live to Thy glory, that I may do honor to Thy name, wherever I go."[33]

These missionaries were in England for five weeks before leaving for South Africa. Wherever they went, they were taken in and cared for by the Saints. Because they had almost no means to support themselves, the Saints also helped them financially. Jesse Haven gratefully recorded in his journal every shilling they received. Some of his new English friends became so dear to him that he wrote poems for them and nearly wept when he had to leave them for South Africa.

"It Has Weaned Me from the World"

Departing from London on February 11, the missionaries were nine weeks on the sea to South Africa. Jesse Haven spent much of this time studying the scriptures and the writings of Orson Pratt. "I have a great desire to learn truth," he wrote. "I ask my Heavenly Father, in the name of His Son Jesus, to guide me into all truth, that when I read His holy word, I may enjoy the gift of the Holy Spirit, that it may rest down upon me, . . . so that I shall get the true meaning of every passage I read, even so, Amen."[34]

Jesse Haven also wrote lengthy letters during the voyage and copied them into his journal. One was to his brother, a Congregationalist minister in Massachusetts. On the day the ship passed the equator, he wrote a letter to a family he had stayed with in London. One part of the letter reveals much about his life and his perspective toward it:

"Trials are hard to bear, but they will work for the good of those that love and fear the Lord. For the last three or four years, I have known sorrow; I have been called to drink a bitter cup. If I had buried every relative I have on the earth, it would have been a sweet beverage compared to the cup whose very dregs I have been required to drink. Though it was bitter, yet it prepared me for the mission which I am now called to fill. It has weaned me from the world. I have now [a] desire . . . only to do good. If my work is done, I can lay my bones in a foreign land, and rejoice that my time is come."[35]

The hint of melancholy in this letter comes into full bloom in his poetry two days later and recurs in cycles throughout his mission:

Is there a soul that cares for me,
In the fair land of Deseret?
Is there one that is bound to be
A friend whatever may beset?

If I am called to lose my life
While preaching in a foreign land;

Have I got a friend or a wife
To weep, and, for me, a tear lend?[36]

By the next week, Jesse Haven had cycled back to a more hopeful mood. The power of the scriptures is evident in helping him do so. He wrote:

"Enjoyed today a good degree of the Spirit of God. Taken much pleasure in reading the word of God. Sanctify me, O Lord, through truth. Thy word is truth."[37]

"Feel more and more every day to persevere in the ways of holiness and virtue. May the Lord assist me to do all things right, is my prayer, even so, Amen."[38]

The next week Jesse was discouraged again, beset by frustrations over human weakness and sorrows:

"Mind rather sober. . . . I am constrained to cry, O Lord, when shall I be free from sin, sorrow, and trials? When will this warfare be over? How long shall I covenant before God to live free from sin, and go on as though I had made no covenant? O Lord, be merciful to all my weaknesses, succor me in the hour of temptation, and deliver me from all evil."[39]

Beginning the Work in South Africa

Elder Jesse Haven and his companions arrived in Cape Town, South Africa, on April 18, 1853. Opening the work in an unknown land among unknown people without any money, contacts, or support was a daunting challenge, but they faced it with faith. The three elders went to a mountain and sustained Jesse Haven as president of what they called the Cape of Good Hope Mission. As they went to work, Jesse Haven's melancholy became less frequent even though adversity intensified.

The first week in South Africa, the elders scheduled the town hall for meetings on six consecutive nights and placed advertisements in the newspaper. The first meeting started well, but the people soon created such a disturbance that it was broken up. The next evening the elders found that the town hall was locked against them—for good. Unfazed, they found another place to meet, but a mob soon assembled, shouting insults and throwing stones. The elders tried to meet the next night, but again the meeting was broken up. Opposition grew until mobs of up to 500 people would gather wherever the missionaries tried to meet. When the mobs were not using sticks and stones, they pelted the elders with eggs.

Hoping to build understanding, Jesse Haven wrote some material for the newspaper, but the editors refused to print it. In a further attempt to shut out the missionaries, the ministers in Cape Town went from door to door telling the people not to admit them or give them anything to eat. "[They are] using all their influence and power to starve us and drive us out of the country," wrote Elder William Walker.[40] For six weeks these missionaries had only one meal a day, usually a little graham bread and some pears.[41]

Compounding these difficulties, the missionaries also had some problems among themselves. Jesse Haven wrote in his journal:

May 14, 1853: "Gave some counsel to Bro. Smith also Bro. Walker, but I find that I have got to be very careful how I give counsel or I shall give offense. O Lord give me wisdom, knowledge, and understanding that I may conduct this mission to thy glory."

May 16, 1853: "This evening Bro. Walker and myself talked over some difficulties that have occurred. Bro. Walker appears distant and cold in his feelings. O Lord may he be led by Thy Spirit to unite . . . his feelings with me and Bro. Smith, and may we all be united."

Despite all these problems, Jesse Haven, who openly reveals his vulnerabilities in his journal, gave no hint of backing down, giving up, or wanting to return home. Rather, with almost all forces against them, these missionaries turned to the only sure source of help. William Walker wrote, "[We] fasted and prayed that the Lord would open the hearts of the people that they might receive the truth and minister to our wants. No one invites us to eat, and we have no money to hire our board."[42]

Perhaps as a result of their fasting and prayer, Elders Smith and Walker began proselyting in rural areas and found the people more receptive. Elder Haven stayed in Cape Town, where opposition continued to be strong.

Jesse Haven the Writer

The missionaries soon distributed all the tracts they had brought, and additional tracts were slow in coming from England. To remedy the problem, Jesse Haven began writing his own. Using and expanding on the Articles of Faith—even retaining their format—his first pamphlet was titled *Some of the Principal Doctrines or Belief[s] of The Church of Jesus Christ of Latter-day Saints.*[43] Jesse Haven was denied when he tried to borrow money to print the pamphlets, so he went begging and eventually raised the 60 shillings he needed. During the next two years he published 10 more pamphlets, becoming one of the most prolific tract writers of the time.

Today, Jesse Haven's journals are perhaps even more important than his pamphlets. The journals of his mission provide valuable insight into the early history of the Church in South Africa. And his journal of 1856 is one of the three or four most reliable sources documenting the experiences of the Martin and Hodgetts companies, because official journals for these companies do not exist.

Success and Emigration

In June 1853, two months after the missionaries arrived in South Africa, they baptized the first convert. In August they organized the first branch, and in September they organized another. The work grew slowly but steadily, and by late 1855 there were 175 members and six branches in South Africa.

Some of the converts were eager to emigrate to Zion. For six months the missionaries tried unsuccessfully to arrange for their passage. Elder Walker explained the problem: "All of the ship owners and agents had colleagued together and agreed not to allow any Mormons to emigrate from the country."[44] Eventually one of the converts bought a ship—the *Unity*—so they could emigrate. "This was a stumper to everybody," wrote Elder Walker, "that those . . .

ignorant Mormon elders, in less than two years after their arrival in this country, without money or friends, had succeeded in exercising such a powerful influence over all classes of people, especially some of the most wealthy and respectable citizens, and have grown to such a power as to purchase a ship."[45]

The *Unity* left South Africa on November 28, 1855, with Elders Walker and Smith leading a company of 15 Saints. After arriving in England, they sailed from Liverpool on the *Caravan,* leaving in February 1856.

Jesse Haven left South Africa in December 1855. He arrived in England in February and was sent to labor in Scotland until May, when he returned to Liverpool and boarded the *Horizon* for home. The *Millennial Star* included the following brief résumé of Jesse Haven in announcing his appointment to serve as a counselor to Edward Martin on the ship:

"Elder Haven has been labouring with Elders Walker and Smith in South Africa, where, under Elder Haven's presidency, they have established a mission of the Church, which will yield its fruits in all time to come. [These] elders have laboured faithfully in their callings, and they go home to Zion with our blessing."[46]

CHAPTER 23

AN ENTHUSIASTIC RESPONSE

The power that moved our gospel forebears was the power of faith in God. It was the same power which made possible the exodus from Egypt, the passage through the Red Sea, the long journey through the wilderness, and the establishment of Israel in the Promised Land.

—PRESIDENT GORDON B. HINCKLEY

As the Saints from the *Horizon* streamed into the handcart camp outside Iowa City, emigration leaders must have been troubled not only by their large number and late arrival but also by their lack of able-bodied men. The demographics of this group made them seem even less likely than the Willie company to succeed in one of the most demanding journeys in the western migration of the United States. Three-fourths of them were women, children, and elderly.[1] One member of the company wrote that it "contained the most aged and infirm, the cleanings up of that season's emigration."[2] Even Franklin D. Richards later observed of them, "They have a great proportion of cripples and old gray-headed men."[3]

Why did Church leaders in England assemble such a company? Why did they allow them to leave England so late? John Jaques explains the dilemma these leaders faced:

"The handcart project became very popular with the Saints in Europe. . . . Many of these, carried away with the idea of gathering to Zion that season, left their various employments in their native lands before proper arrangements had been completed for their transportation. The result was that they were left to choose between the alternative of remaining at home to starve, or go to the poor house, or else

243

run the risk of a late journey across the plains. They chose the latter course, in which the presidency of the British Mission, seeing no better way out of the difficulty, acquiesced."[4]

Despite problems with demographics and a late departure from England, these Saints were undeterred in their enthusiasm to gather to Zion. Most of them became part of the Martin handcart company. Others joined the wagon companies that traveled closely with the Martin company and shared in their experiences. The stories of a few of them are introduced in this chapter and developed within the chronology of their westward trek. Summaries of their lives after they reached the Salt Lake Valley, along with some of their reflections on the handcart experience, are included in a later chapter.

Even if these stories had not originated as the result of a great spiritual cause, they would be compelling for their human interest. They are even more compelling when viewed in their spiritual context—a people who had Zion in their hearts and would pay any price to help build it, not just during these few trying months, but throughout their lives. In either context, most of these stories are inspiring, and all are instructive.

JOHN AND ZILPAH JAQUES FAMILY

John Jaques was the Martin company's most prolific writer and reliable observer.[5] He had been the company's historian while on the ship from England, and he kept a daily journal of their journey through October 18—the last day before the onslaught of winter storms. Twenty-two years later he wrote an eight-part series of reminiscences on the handcart experience for the *Salt Lake Daily Herald*. These add valuable insights that were developed through years of reflection.

Opposition from Family; Service as a Missionary

John Jaques was baptized in 1845 at age 18. He first heard the gospel from Thomas Ward, a man he worked with while apprenticing as a cabinet maker. "There seemed to be good scriptural reason for the faith that was in him and the doctrines he taught," John recalled. "I was earnestly seeking the true religion. . . . Finally I became convinced that 'Mormonism' was true."[6]

The master to whom John Jaques was apprenticed was unhappy with John's decision to join the Church, and he made it known. "He sent word to my father as a deplorable matter that I had be-

John Jaques

come a Mormon," John wrote.[7] John's father raged with disapproval in two letters. He faulted his son for allowing himself to "be led away in this manner" and for disobeying "one of the great commands in Scripture—honor and obey your parents."[8] He also sent his son a publication criticizing the Church, accompanied by the following message:

"I [have] sent you a book to read and hope you will give up the idea of belonging to such a party. Join some other. I am quite of the same opinion as [the minister] that it is fiction. . . . I hope your eyes will be opened to see different than to go with such a set of deluded people. If I had common sense, I would use it different than that."[9]

John wrote a lengthy reply to his father—11 single-spaced pages when typed—refuting the contents of the publication.[10] In the letter John also bore testimony of how the gospel had blessed his life:

"Since I have obeyed the gospel of Jesus Christ, my eyes have been opened, and I have been able to understand the truth. I can bear testimony to the truth and beauty of the doctrines advanced and believed in the Church of Jesus Christ of Latter-day Saints. . . . I have been surprised at the beauty, order, glory, light, and intelligence of the principles held forth, even by unlettered men, and indeed they are so gloriously simple in themselves, that I have oft wondered how it is that men should have so blindly gone past the mark."[11]

John Jaques was ordained an elder in 1848 and was called to serve a mission in his native land from 1850 to 1852. During his mission he visited his parents, who were still displeased with him. "Went to visit my father's house, found all pretty well," he wrote. "My father and mother were very vexed at my having left my trade to go preach the Gospel. They said I was idle and [had] done so that I might live without working by subsisting upon other people. . . . My father ranted at me [and] would not bid me goodbye, told me I need not write to, nor visit him until I began to work at my trade again."[12]

That was the last time John Jaques saw his father.

"A Joy and Blessing . . . in the Use of His Pen"

John Jaques began writing articles and poetry for the *Millennial Star* in 1849, when he was 22 years old. His first poem was set to music and included in Church hymnals as "Softly Beams the Sacred Dawning." The next year he published two articles and four poems. One of the poems, written in Shakespeare's garden at Stratford-upon-Avon, was included in hymnals as "Oh Say, What Is Truth?"[13] The music was written by a convert from John's mission.[14]

Recognizing John's literary talents, President Franklin D. Richards appointed him assistant editor of the *Millennial Star* at the end of his mission in 1852. The *Millennial Star* was the official Church periodical in England. As mission president, Franklin D. Richards was the editor, but with all his other responsibilities he determined that he needed assistance. In announcing John Jaques's appointment, he explained:

"Finding the duties of presiding, publishing, and emigration are so numerous and arduous, we have concluded to call to our aid Elder John Jaques, who is favourably known as the writer of many interesting and valuable articles. He entertains much of the Spirit in his calling, and will be a joy and blessing to the Saints by his services in the use of his pen."[15]

John Jaques continued editing the *Millennial Star* until he emigrated four years later. During this time he edited other publications as well, including a book of Eliza R. Snow's poetry and parts of the *Journal of Discourses*.[16] He also continued to write prolifically, publishing some 55 articles and poems.[17] One of his best-known works was a course of religious study called *Catechism for Children*.[18] At the end of John's service, President Richards paid him the following tribute: "By his labours with the pen, he has done much to instruct and bless the Saints, and preach the Gospel in these lands."[19]

Marriage and Emigration

During his mission, John Jaques met James and Amy Loader in Oxfordshire. The year after he was released, he married one of their daughters, Zilpah. His marriage inspired him to write eloquently on the subject:

"Marriage is a wonderful thing, the wonder of wonders. It is a veritable garden of delights, of felicities unspeakable, a perennial fountain of the most exquisite sweetness, happiness, pleasures imaginable, a land of enchantment. The riches and honors of the world are nothing in comparison with it."[20]

By 1855 the talents of John Jaques came to the attention of Brigham Young, who wrote to Franklin D. Richards, asking that "[Brother] Jaques might come to the Valley [in] the ensuing season."[21] Working so closely with President Richards and emigrating at the request of Brigham Young did not gain John Jaques any privileges in the mode of travel. Three months before leaving England he wrote in his journal:

"Had an interview with President Richards concerning my emigration. It appeared to be in his mind that I should go in a handcart company, with my wife's father and family. I obtained 5 pounds from him to prepare for my emigration."[22]

John Jaques did not want any privileges in his mode of travel. In a letter to his wife's family, who were initially opposed to pulling handcarts, he described the handcart plan as a "holy ordinance of the

Lord, revealed through His Prophet Brigham."[23] Later this zeal about the plan would be tempered, however. John and Zilpah Jaques would pay a premium price to emigrate by handcart.

Revealing both the commitment and the poverty of the Jaques family, John sold most of their furniture nine days after his interview with President Richards—for only three pounds.[24] Two days later he sold his "four fowls" to his landlord.[25] In future weeks he recorded every detail of preparation for the journey to Zion. A little at a time he bought nine yards of blue striped shirting, four yards of flannel, some waterproof felt, a pair of Puritan trousers, nightgowns for his daughter, socks, shoes, handkerchiefs, hats, and gloves.

When the Jaques family left their homeland in May 1856, John was 29, Zilpah 25, and their only child, Flora, nearly 2. John left behind his parents, four brothers, and four sisters. Even 11 years after he had joined the Church, most members of his family were still embittered by his affiliation with it. Only one brother visited John before he left.

John Jaques was given many responsibilities during the emigration. In addition to being historian on the *Horizon,* he presided over one of the ship's nine wards.[26] When the Martin company arrived in Iowa City, John was made captain of the camp guard and captain of the second hundred.[27] He carried out these responsibilities while also caring for Zilpah, who was pregnant when she left England, and for Flora, who suffered poor health throughout the journey.

In Iowa City, John and Zilpah met up with Zilpah's family, the Loaders. James and Amy Loader and six of their children had left England in December 1855 and stayed in New York before going on to Iowa City. Traveling together, the Jaques and Loader families would suffer terrible losses—but would also bless and support each other in essential ways. Somewhat balancing their losses, Zilpah would give birth to a son in Nebraska, and he would become the longest surviving member of the Martin company.

James and Amy Loader Family

For 35 years James Loader worked as a gardener for Sir Henry Lambert, a wealthy English nobleman who owned a large estate in Oxfordshire. During most of that time James was foreman of the gardeners and was provided a comfortable home on the estate. There he and his family were treated well and lived in a setting that one of his daughters described as enchanting—a thatched-roof home, a veranda covered with roses and honeysuckles, beautiful gardens, red-brick walkways, and a playground full of amusements.[28] Most of the Loaders' 13 children—nine daughters and four sons—were born on the estate.

The Loader family met the missionaries in 1848. Amy was baptized that year, but James hesitated because Sir Lambert said he would lose his position if he joined the Church. Despite this threat, James was baptized in 1851. Hoping James would reconsider this decision, Sir Lambert gave him one year to give up his new faith. When James declined to comply, his furnishings were moved out of the home, and he was dismissed. James left the estate with great regret, having loved his work, his home, and the people he worked for.

Nine of the Loaders' 13 children were eventually baptized. One of their adult daughters, Patience, had been away from home for six years and was working in London when she heard that some members of her family had joined the Church. The woman who conveyed this news told Patience she felt sorry for her family. Patience wrote to her parents, hoping they would refute this report, but to her dismay they soon confirmed it. Patience vented strong feelings of disapproval:

"I wrote back and told them that they must think themselves better than anyone else to be so conceited as to call themselves saints, and I did not feel very good over it either, and I asked mother if she thought that to be baptized by a man was going to wash her sins away and told her I did not believe any such nonsense as that. [I] said I believed there were other churches just as good as theirs, and I said that

Patience Loader

I had found out [from] my brother that there were none but poor folks that joined their church."[29]

When Patience went home for visits during the next two or three years, she learned more about her family's new religion. For a time she continued to reject it and resented efforts to convert her, but eventually she had a change of heart. She recalled: "Before I left my father's home again, [the] Spirit worked upon me and opened my eyes and my understanding and showed me the necessity of baptism for the remission of sins and true repentance and [that] obedience to the gospel of Jesus Christ would bring everlasting joy and happiness, but the pleasures of this world [were] only for a short time."[30]

Patience was baptized in 1853, when she was nearly 26. Two days later she returned to London "rejoicing," she said, "but in a different way to which I had intended to rejoice when I left London two weeks previous to my going home. The hand of God was with me and his Spirit was around me to teach me the way to real happiness, and I am thankful I accepted it just at the right time. It was a safeguard to me at a time when I was young and full of life and needed a guardian angel around me in the midst of worldly pleasures."[31]

"A Terrible, Severe Voyage"

After the Loaders were forced to leave their home on the Lambert estate, they lived for a few years in a small house that one of their adult sons rented for them. Then in December 1855 they went to Liverpool and sailed for America on the *John J. Boyd.*

James Loader was 56 years old when he left England, Amy 53.

Traveling with them were their daughters Patience (age 28), Maria (18), Jane (14), and Sarah (11); their sons John (34) and Robert (9); and John's wife and two children. One daughter had emigrated the previous year, and two others, Zilpah and Tamar, would come six months later. Zilpah was married to John Jaques and had a baby daughter.

Leaving England had its sorrows for the Loaders. The four children who had not joined the Church stayed behind. And 22-year-old Tamar had to leave a young man whom she had hoped would join the Church and come with her.[32] She would have to endure not only a heavy heart but also physical infirmity during the handcart trek; however, she would be blessed in a remarkable, revelatory way for her sacrifice.

Compared to the *Horizon* six months later, the *John J. Boyd* had what Patience Loader called "a terrible, severe voyage."[33] The Saints on the *Horizon* thought their five-week voyage was long, but the *Boyd* took nine weeks, crossing the Atlantic during the stormy winter months. Whereas only five people died on the *Horizon,* Patience reported that 62 died on the *Boyd.*[34] Among them was John Loader's one-year-old daughter. "It did indeed seem very hard to roll her in a blanket and lay her in the big waves and see the little dear go floating away out of sight," wrote Patience, the girl's aunt.[35]

Also differing from the *Horizon,* the captain and crew on the *John J. Boyd* were antagonistic toward the Saints. Patience recalled: "At one time the captain told us if we did not stop our d——d preaching and praying we would never land in New York. I told the mate that was the only thing that saved his vessel, for he was such a wicked, drinking man and neglected his duty."[36]

The storms were so bad that the passengers on the *Boyd* feared for their lives. During the worst storm, Patience had an experience that helped her realize she was remembered of the Lord. She wrote:

"It really seemed sometimes that we would never see land again. One night when we had a bad storm, we could not sleep as we had to hold on to the berths to keep from being thrown out. We were all in the dark. My poor mother was fretting and thought we would all be lost and drowned in the sea. . . . Just when the ship was tossing and rolling the worst, I opened my eyes. We were in darkness, but in a moment . . . a beautiful, lovely figure stood there. . . . The light was so bright around him that I could see the colour of his eyes and hair. . . . As I looked at him, he said, 'Fear not. You shall be taken there all safe.'"[37]

The ship reached New York a few days later.[38]

"Father and Mother Think This Cannot Be Done"

The *John J. Boyd* left England three months before the first ship carrying handcart Saints—and six months before the ship that carried most of the Martin company. The story of how the Loaders eventually joined the Martin company takes many unexpected turns that could have broken the family apart but were finally resolved through a declaration of faith.

The Loaders expected to travel the first part of the overland journey by train and the last part by wagon. After arriving in New York, they rented rooms and began working so they could save enough money to buy a wagon outfit. James worked as a gardener, some of the daughters sewed in a cloak factory, and some did housekeeping and tended children.

After a few weeks in New York, the family received distressing news. Their son-in-law, John Jaques, wrote from England, saying they would be expected to travel by handcart rather than wagon. Patience immediately sent her brother-in-law a letter expressing the family's objections. She felt that pulling a handcart like draft animals would be humiliating. Being limited to only 17 pounds of luggage on the handcart was also objectionable, because it would require the family to leave behind most of their clothes and other possessions. Finally, Patience was emphatic that it would be physically impossible for the family to travel by handcart:

"Father and mother think this cannot be done, and I am sure I think the same, for mother cannot walk day after day, and I do not think that any of us will ever be able to continue walking every day.

. . . If we girls were strong boys, then I think it might be done, but father is the only man in our family. I don't feel myself that I can go like this. . . . Mother, I am sure, can never go that way. She says herself that she cannot do it."[39]

At a later time Patience explained further why her mother thought the journey would be impossible for her: "My poor mother [was] in delicate health. She had not walked a mile for years."[40] How, then, could Amy Loader not only walk 1,300 miles but pull a handcart? Joining a wagon company seemed the only possible way to complete the journey to Zion.

When John Jaques received the letter from Patience, he wrote an indignant reply to his father-in-law, James Loader (see pages 31–35). President Franklin D. Richards published both letters in the *Millennial Star*, feeling that the reply could serve as "an excellent and pertinent rebuke" to others who had reservations about the handcart plan.[41] Word got back to the Loaders that some people who read the letters thought the family was apostatizing. Recalling her father's reaction to this news, Patience wrote:

"One day T. B. H. Stenhouse came from President [John] Taylor's office [in New York]. He said, 'Did you know that your name is in the *Millennial Star*, Brother Loader? You are thought to be apostatizing from the Church. It says that Father Loader has brought his family out of one part of Babylon and now wants to settle down in another part of Babylon.' This hurt my poor dear father's feelings very much. He said to mother, 'I cannot stand to be accused of apostasy. I will show them better. Mother, I am going to Utah. I will pull the handcart if I die on the road.'"[42]

Within a few days, all family members quit their jobs in New York and started for Iowa City. Soon after the Loaders arrived in Iowa, the large group of Saints who sailed on the *Horizon* with Edward Martin arrived. Among them were the Loaders' daughters Zilpah and Tamar, as well as Zilpah's husband, John Jaques. The Loader and Jaques families would travel to Utah together as part of the Martin company; however, the Loaders' oldest son, who had already lost a baby daughter at sea, remained in Iowa City because his wife was due to have another baby. It would be another 10 years before his family completed the journey to Utah.

The concerns that Patience expressed about her family pulling a handcart would be well founded. Within the first 270 miles, two members of the family would become incapacitated—with more than 1,000 miles still to travel. Other family members, who had been so certain they could not even walk that distance, would have to see if they could pull the handcart on their own for hundreds of miles through heat and cold, sand and snow.

FRANCIS AND ANN ELIZABETH (BETSY) WEBSTER

Francis Webster joined the Church in 1848 when he was 18 and then almost immediately went to Australia. After working there for a year, he heard of the Gold Rush in California and started for America. He prospected on the Calaveras River until February 1852, accumulating $1,500 in gold.

After being gone from England for nearly four years, Francis returned home for a visit. There he found that his standing in the Church was in question because he had been away for so long without the counsel of Church leaders. Six weeks later he left again for America, this time making a point to take some Church literature. He returned to the Calaveras River, where he prospected and operated a provision store. After three years of fair success, he returned to England again and began to chart a new course for his life. First he was rebaptized, and then in December 1855 he married Ann Elizabeth (Betsy) Parsons. Just six months later, Frances and Betsy left England on the *Horizon.*

With the money Francis saved from prospecting, he planned to buy a wagon outfit for the journey from Iowa City, allowing him and Betsy to travel in relative comfort and security. Why, then, did they end up pulling a handcart? Without elaborating, Francis explained, "[I paid] the fare for nine persons besides myself and wife to Salt Lake City."[43] A man who knew Francis provided more detail about this change in plans and the sacrifice it required:

"With sixteen hundred dollars cash in hand, the Websters would be able to outfit themselves in luxury for a trip from London to Great Salt Lake City. Francis placed five hundred dollars with a Church agent to purchase for him a good wagon with full camp equipment and two yoke of good cattle . . . to be ready for him at the point in America where Mormon emigrants started across the Plains.

"Soon after this order was placed, advice came from Brigham Young to the Saints in England for the well-to-do to share with and give assistance to the poor members of the Church so that they also might come to Zion. Francis Webster heard that advice and was ready to obey counsel. The price of that good outfit he had ordered would pay the passage of nine additional persons to Utah. So . . . the Websters cancelled the wagon order and elected to travel by hand-cart [so] their money might bring nine more souls to Zion. They would obey counsel and trust themselves to the providences of God."[44]

Giving up the security of a wagon outfit must have been especially difficult because Betsy Webster was expecting a baby who would be born during the journey. Even further sacrifices would be required of this couple. Francis would suffer with dysentery and severely frozen feet, and he would finish the journey with only a little clothing to his name. Nevertheless, this one-time prospector who had traveled the world seeking his fortune would later testify that through these experiences he became acquainted with God and that the price he paid for that blessing was a privilege to pay.

SAMUEL AND MARGARET PUCELL FAMILY

On the day the *Horizon* left Liverpool, President Franklin D. Richards and a few other mission leaders went on board to address the Saints. One of these leaders, Elder Cyrus Wheelock, told the group that among them were some of England's first converts, Samuel and Margaret Pucell.[45] When the first missionaries came to England 19 years earlier, Margaret Pucell attended their first meeting.

She was baptized a few days later in the River Ribble, the second woman in England to receive the ordinance. Samuel was baptized a month later. Although the Pucells were poor, they gave the first sixpence to the missionaries and continued to support them, sometimes pawning clothes or going hungry to provide them food.

The Pucells had sacrificed and saved for nearly 20 years before they were able to emigrate. Five of their ten children had died before the family left England. The rest of the family traveled together as far as Boston, where the three oldest children decided to stay and work until the next year. Samuel and Margaret took their two youngest children, Margaret (14) and Ellen (9), on to Iowa City. A daughter-in-law and baby grandson traveled with them. Before the trek was finished, Margaret and Ellen would be orphans. One of them would suffer severe consequences from frozen flesh. Despite these setbacks, Margaret and Ellen would still realize the fulfillment of many of their hopes and dreams in Zion.

WILLIAM AND MARY ANN BARTON FAMILY

William and Mary Ann Barton were emigrating with the youngest daughter from William's first marriage, 14-year-old Mary, and their daughters Francis (nearly 4) and Elizabeth (1). William Barton's first wife had died in 1842, shortly after Mary was born. William then married Mary Ann Taylor in 1850. The six oldest children from William's first marriage did not emigrate.

During the voyage across the Atlantic, 14-year-old Mary Barton had been healed after being burned (see pages 223–24). The outcome was not so fortunate for 1-year-old Elizabeth, who became ill and died near Chicago. Her life was not the only loss this family would suffer.

JOHN AND JANE BAILEY FAMILY

"Why go to America where there are savage Indians and wild beasts?" So inquired John Bailey's father when John announced his plans to emigrate. William Bailey was not antagonistic toward his son's religion—he just felt a parent's regret at having a child move so far away. "Grandfather said he was very sorry to part with him," wrote one of John's sons, for he had always "behaved like a dutiful son."[46]

John and Jane Bailey joined the Church in 1844 and were anxious to finally be gathering to Zion. Their four sons, ages 5 though 18, accompanied them. Their only daughter had died as an infant.

Before leaving England, John Bailey hired an auctioneer to sell the family's furniture. To spread word of the auction, the town crier walked through the streets ringing a bell and exclaiming, "Oh yes, oh yes, Brother and Sister Bailey are leaving for Zion. Come one, come all, and buy their goods." This public display embarrassed the Baileys' oldest son, Langley, who asked his father to stop the man. His father declined, his mother explaining that they "were not ashamed to let people know that we . . . are Latter-day Saints."[47]

These words of Jane Bailey foreshadow her unfaltering faith and conviction that would pull her family through many trials, not only during the handcart trek but also after arriving in Zion. When two members of this family, one of them Langley, would so deeply despair that they wanted to give up and die, Jane Bailey would keep them going.

WILLIAM AND SARAH ANN ASHTON FAMILY

The story of the William Ashton family is one of the most tragic in the handcart annals, but its ending is uniquely redemptive. William and Sarah Ann were baptized in 1841 and married in 1844. William worked in the mills as a spinner.

The Ashtons were parents of six daughters. The oldest was 11, and the youngest would be born soon after the family left Florence. Their second daughter had died as an infant before leaving England, and their fifth daughter, 1-year-old Elizabeth, died in Boston. Only three members of this family would survive the journey, and only two would make it to Utah that year. The third would finally complete the journey more than 30 years later.

JAMES AND MARY ANN MELLOR FAMILY

James and Mary Ann Mellor were faithful, long-time members of the Church who had been too poor to emigrate until assistance was provided through the Perpetual Emigration Fund. They were the parents of nine children, seven still living, ages 2 to 16. Mary Ann was about seven months pregnant when they arrived in Liverpool to begin their journey.

James Mellor had grown up in a very poor family with a father who was nearly deaf and a mother who was nearly blind. Of necessity, he began working as a yarn winder to help support the family when he was only six years old. He continued working various jobs in the fabric industry for most of his life in England.

During his early life, James had many narrow escapes with death. Once he was run over by a mail coach. Another time he was nearly burned to death. Yet another time he fell headfirst into a cistern. Soon after he was married, he had a serious factory accident. "The machine that I was working at . . . flew all to pieces," he wrote, "and the spikes caught me in many parts of my body. . . . I was lying all covered with blood as though torn all to pieces. . . . They took me off to the infirmary or hospital. . . . Their patients and all that saw me said, 'That poor fellow will not trouble [us] long.' For three days and nights I lay and heard the clock strike its rounds and tell the hour, for I could not close my eyes to sleep for pain."[48]

Concerning these brushes with death, James later wrote, "[It] seems as though . . . the Devil was trying to destroy me, but that God in His mercy was determined to save me for some other purpose."[49] That purpose began to make itself clear in 1844, when James was 25 years old. He had moved from Leicester to Yorkshire the previous year to work at wool combing, and there he first heard the elders preach the gospel. He investigated earnestly:

"I read the Bible through from Genesis to Revelations, and the more I read the more I was convinced of the truth of the things they preached. . . . I went regular on Sunday to hear the Elders and came home and told my wife the things they preached. [I] read to her out of the New Testament . . . to show her it was the same as was preached by the Apostles of Jesus Christ."[50]

Both James and Mary Ann Mellor were baptized in April 1844. They soon moved back home to Leicester, where James thought his friends would eagerly receive the gospel because, in his words, "it [was] so plain and scriptural." To his great surprise, most of them disapproved. "Many of my friends began to oppose me and looked shy at me as if I were something to be shunned," he recalled.[51]

For a few years the Mellors went back and forth between Yorkshire and Leicester as James searched for employment. While in Yorkshire, he was appointed to watch over the Saints in the Bradford area. After returning to Leicester in 1850, he was ordained an elder and set apart to preside over the nearby Blaby Branch. Two years later he was released and appointed president of the Leicester Branch, a position he held until he emigrated. While serving in these callings, he said, "I preached in and around all the villages," walking many miles each Sunday to do so.[52] Some he baptized, and many more, in his words, he "reclaimed."

When the family was finally preparing to emigrate in 1856, Mary Ann grieved because of concern for her widowed father. Her oldest daughter, 16-year-old Louisa, recalled: "The hardest [part] was to leave my poor grandfather. . . . He was a good man. He wept and offered money to his daughter, my dear mother, but relief was offered too late, for the gospel was more than anything else."[53]

Mary Ann became ill after arriving in Liverpool and gave premature birth to conjoined twin daughters. They lived only seven hours, and Mary Ann was so near death herself that she could not board the ship. She told her husband to leave her and take the children to America, saying she would go later. When the ship still had not departed two days later, James Mellor returned to the hospital and carried Mary Ann out on a stretcher. The family sailed to Zion together after all.

WILLIAM AND MARY GOBLE FAMILY

William and Mary Goble, future great-grandparents of Marjorie Pay Hinckley, joined the Church in November 1855 and immediately began preparing to emigrate. Six months later they sailed for Zion with their six children, ages 2 through 13. A seventh child would be born on the trail.

The Gobles were among the Saints on the *Horizon* who joined the Hunt wagon company, which traveled near the Martin company for most of the journey. The Gobles's oldest child, 13-year-old Mary, explained: "We had orders not to pass the handcart companies. We had to keep close to them to help them if we could."[54]

Mary's account of the journey includes this tragic event in Iowa City: "My sister Fanny broke out with the measles on the ship, and when we were in the Iowa campground, there came up a thunderstorm that blew down our shelter, made with handcarts and some quilts. . . . We sat there in the rain, thunder, and lightning. My sister got wet and died the 19th of July 1856. She would have been two years old on the 23rd. The day we started our journey, we visited her grave. We felt very bad to leave our little sister there."[55]

Sadly, other tragedies would soon follow for this faithful family.

WILLIAM AND ALICE WALSH FAMILY

William and Alice Walsh left England with three small children ages 6 months to 5 years. Living near Preston, Alice had joined the Church in 1845, when she was 16. She married William Walsh sometime between 1847 and 1850. Alice was the only member of her parents' family to join the Church. Telling of her conversion and emigration—and the associated sacrifices—she wrote:

"We find in the New Testament that Jesus said [that] unless we forsake fathers and mothers, brothers and sisters, houses and lands, for His and the Gospel's sake, we cannot be worthy of Him or to enter into the Kingdom of Heaven. This I have done for Him, because I am the only one of my Father's or Mother's family that ever have joined the Church, and I in doing so left my houses and lands in England."[56]

For the Walsh family, the handcart trek would require even greater sacrifices than leaving loved ones, houses, and lands. Their losses would be so terrible that after the trek, Alice's mother would offer her daughter money if she would return home.

Alice Walsh

SARAH FRANKS AND GEORGE PADLEY

Sarah Franks and George Padley were engaged to be married when they left England. Four other couples were married on the ship, but Sarah and George wanted to wait until they reached Zion.

Sarah joined the Church in April 1848, when she was 16. Because her parents objected, she had to leave home. She began working in a lace factory, saving money to emigrate. When her father died in 1853, she returned to her family. Eventually Sarah helped bring her mother and sisters into the Church, though she was the only member of her family to emigrate in 1856.[57]

Sarah and George were known as the sweethearts of the Martin company.[58] They talked frequently of the home and family they would have in Zion. Years later, President James E. Faust would call their story one of the great love stories of the western migration.

AARON AND ELIZABETH JACKSON FAMILY

Elizabeth Jackson

Elizabeth Jackson was the oldest of 11 children. Her family joined the Church in 1841, when she was 15. In 1848 she married Aaron Jackson, and eight years later she and Aaron were finally emigrating with their three children, ages 2, 4, and 7. One of Elizabeth's brothers had emigrated earlier, and one of her sisters traveled with her. Elizabeth's mother had died a few months earlier, but her father would emigrate the next year with other family members.[59]

In the memoirs that Elizabeth later wrote of the handcart journey, she began, "I have a desire to leave a record of those scenes and events, through which I have passed, that my children, down to my latest posterity, may read what their ancestors were willing to suffer, and did suffer, patiently for the Gospel's sake."[60] The events she alludes to would include some of the most distressing—and faith promoting—that anyone would experience on the trek.

MARY JOHNSON

Seven-year-old Mary Johnson (known then as Maren Johansen) joined the westward trek of 1856 in an unusual way and place. She had emigrated from Denmark the previous year with her parents and five siblings. They went to Mormon Grove in eastern Kansas, one of the main outfitting sites for Saints who were going west in 1855.

Plans for Mary's family to continue to Utah soon changed drastically. Her father and baby brother died at Mormon Grove—likely from cholera, which claimed 50 lives in the camp that season—and her mother became gravely ill. Camp leaders were concerned that if

Mary's mother died, the children would be left alone for the winter. Accordingly, they suggested she let some of them go to the Salt Lake Valley with other families. The family that took in Mary's oldest sister went to Utah that year (1855), but Mary's guardians went to Omaha and waited until 1856 to continue the journey west. Mary's other sister stayed to care for their mother, and her two brothers stayed in the area to work. In November 1855, after Mary left Mormon Grove, her mother passed away.

Not only was Mary a 7-year-old orphan but she was in an unknown land, unable to speak the language, and separated from her brothers and sisters. Making matters worse, her guardians were an older English couple who seemed to resent having to care for her. Mary later wrote, "My lot fell with unloving guardians."[61] When the last handcart and wagon companies came through Florence in August 1856, Mary and her guardians joined the Hunt wagon company.

Mary's parents had sacrificed everything to come to Zion. When they died, Mary and her siblings must have wondered how the decision to leave Denmark could ever result in more good than bad. But these children would ensure that their parents' sacrifices were not in vain. Because Mary had so much going against her—and because she would experience even more life-altering adversity during the journey—she would be especially remarkable in fulfilling the hopes that her parents were unable to realize for themselves.

Mary was christened Maren Kjirstine Larsen. The children of this family later followed the Scandinavian custom of adding "son" to their father's name, Johan. Thus, they began using the last name Johansen *and later* Johnson. *All of these children eventually reached Utah.*

Mormon Grove was located near Atchison, Kansas, a Missouri River town. European converts traveled by ship to New Orleans, up the Mississippi River to St. Louis, and up the Missouri River to Kansas. In 1855 more than 2,000 Saints began their trek west from Mormon Grove.

The Church largely abandoned Mormon Grove after 1855. One reason was that Iowa City became the major point of outfitting because of the advance of the railroad and the introduction of the handcart plan.

Another reason was that Brigham Young wanted the emigrants to try a more northerly route, thinking there would be fewer problems with cholera and other diseases. A Kansas State Historical Society marker near Mormon Grove was dedicated on May 17, 1986. The marker is located along Highway 73 about four miles west of Atchison.

JOSEPH AND ELIZABETH SERMON FAMILY

Joseph and Elizabeth Sermon were some of the most unlikely members of the Martin company, and their story is one of the most compelling. Elizabeth joined the Church in 1852 and wanted her family to gather to Zion, even though it meant leaving their comfortable home near London. Joseph did not join the Church and did not want to leave. Nevertheless, seeing that Elizabeth was determined to emigrate, and not wanting her to go alone, Joseph reluctantly agreed to accompany her. Their four youngest children, ages 3 through 8, went with them. Their oldest son remained in England with a grandparent to finish an apprenticeship. "I never saw him again," Elizabeth later wrote.[62]

The Sermons sold their home and went to Liverpool. They left England three months earlier than most members of the Martin company, sailing on the *Caravan* in February 1856.

After arriving in New York on March 27, the Sermon family traveled to Iowa City. Because they planned to be part of an independent wagon company, they bought a wagon and team. However, as Elizabeth recalled, "after much discussion and counsel from the Elders, we were convinced (at least I was) that it was God's will that the [wagon] be sold and we buy handcarts so that more Saints could make the journey to Zion."[63]

The Sermon family was in Iowa City at least a month before the first handcart emigrants. If they had joined any of the first three companies, they probably would have experienced minimal troubles. But Joseph Sermon was "full of misgivings" about pulling a handcart, feeling that it was demeaning, so he decided not to go any farther.[64] As a result, his family remained in Iowa City for several weeks as each of the handcart companies was organized and then departed. Eventually, knowing that the Martin company provided the last opportunity to finish their journey that season, Elizabeth persuaded Joseph to proceed. "I was faithful, and willing to draw a handcart," Elizabeth wrote. "I hungered for the gospel of Christ."[65]

They bought a handcart, paid their ration money, and started across Iowa with the Martin company. Elizabeth recalled: "My heart was happy, and I rejoiced in singing the songs of Zion. My only hope and desire was to reach the Valley, where my children could be raised in the true gospel."[66]

ROBERT AND MARGARET MCBRIDE FAMILY

When 13-year-old Heber McBride boarded the *Horizon,* he eagerly anticipated the adventure of a lifetime. The oldest son of Robert and Margaret McBride, Heber had always loved the ocean. His grandfather McBride was a sailor who had "landed in every port where a ship could stick its hull," and Heber had similar aspirations.[67] When he was six years old, Heber used to run away from school with some friends and sail out on the bay near his home in Rothesay, Scotland. His mother worried that he would drown, and his father disapproved of his desire to grow up and be a sailor.

Punishments didn't stop Heber from sneaking down to the bay, so Robert McBride tried a different deterrent. Hoping to frighten his six-year-old son away from sailing, Robert put him on a boat for a two-week voyage to Ireland. However, this experience failed to produce the result Robert hoped for. "We had a very rough trip," Heber later wrote, "but [it] made me want to be a sailor more than ever."[68] After returning home, Heber cried when the ship left and his parents refused to let him go with it.

Robert and Margaret McBride had joined the Church in Preston, England, six years before Heber was born. When the first missionaries arrived in England in July 1837, they began their work in Preston. The first converts were baptized on July 30 in the River Ribble, and Robert McBride was baptized two days later. Margaret hesitated because of opposition from her family and then was baptized in January 1838 by Elder Heber C. Kimball.

The McBrides moved to Scotland in 1844, when Heber was one year old, and then moved back to the Preston area when he was eight or nine. Wherever the family lived, they welcomed the missionaries. Heber's younger brother Peter recalled: "Our home was open to the elders. . . . Services were held, the sacrament administered, and many missionaries found a haven of rest. Mother held open house [and] always had something ready to serve hungry elders and a good bed for them to rest in."[69]

Missionaries had been encouraging the McBrides to emigrate since 1840. When the opportunity finally came in 1856, Robert and Margaret had five children, ages 3 through 16. None of them was more excited than their 13-year-old sailor, Heber. He later recalled: "I was delighted at the thought of being on the water in such a big ship. It was all fun and pleasure for me. I was in and out of everything and kept my parents in hot water."[70] Heber was perhaps the only person on the ship who felt sorry when land was finally sighted.

Heber McBride was a carefree boy when he left England, prone to the typical mischief for his age, perpetually seeking fun and adventure. The journey to Zion would soon require this boy to mature into a man almost overnight.

THE LONDON BRANCH PRESIDENTS

The Martin company included six branch presidents and their families from the London Conference of the Church. According to Lynne Jorgensen, these "were respectable, middle-class families" who were emigrating both because of their own desires and to set an example for branch members.[71] The age and experience of these branch presidents varied greatly, but all of them shared a deep commitment to the gospel and had served diligently in building up the Church. For three of them, the cost of going to Zion would be life itself.

John and Margaret (Elizabeth) Griffiths Family

John Griffiths was the longest tenured of the London branch presidents to emigrate with the Martin company, having served for 15 years. He and his wife, Margaret, joined the Church in 1840 while living in Liverpool. Later that year they moved to London so John could work in the Woolwich Dock Yards, a ship-building center on the Thames. He was a boilermaker by trade.

In February 1841, only a year after John was baptized, Elders Wilford Woodruff and Heber C. Kimball called him to be the first president of the Woolwich Branch. The branch was small at first, with only six members, so John devoted himself to building it up. His daughter Margaret recalled:

"He would work all day from six in the morning until six at night, and then he would eat his supper and then go preaching at night. Sometimes it would be eleven [or] twelve o'clock before he would get home, as he had to walk. . . . Father raised up Woolwich Branch, Welling, Elton, Greenwich, Deptford, and lots of other places."[72]

John and Margaret Griffiths had 10 children, 5 of whom died in infancy. While giving birth to her last child in 1853, Margaret also died. In February 1856, three months before he left England, John Griffiths married Elizabeth Webb. John's oldest son, Thomas (21), had emigrated in 1853. His other four surviving children emigrated with him and Elizabeth in 1856: Margaret (16), John (12), Jane (8), and Herbert (6).

This family would pay the utmost price to come to Zion. Half of them—all the males—would die. Other separations would follow. John Griffiths's two young daughters had trusted their father to lead them to a better life in Zion. Despite all this tragedy, they would find such a life.

Henry and Sarah Squires Family

Henry Squires served as president of the St. Albans Branch in the London Conference. He and his wife, Sarah, joined the Church in

1847. When they left England nine years later, they had five daughters, ages 1 through 8. Sarah was also pregnant with another child. She would carry this baby throughout the entire six-month journey from England to Utah, somehow surviving starvation rations and frigid exposure to give birth to a sixth daughter four days before arriving in Salt Lake City. This child would be given a unique name in honor of the place of her nativity.

The story of the Squires family has many unusual turns. Before Henry Squires joined the Church, he was a Baptist minister. Before he died, he would be a Baptist minister again. And when the light of Zion had dimmed for many in this family, the daughter who was born on the handcart trek would seek it out again as a teenager and walk in it for the rest of her life.

William and Eliza Binder

William Binder was called to preside over the Lambeth Branch in the London Conference when he was not quite 23 years old. Born in 1832, he joined the Church in 1849, having heard the gospel during his apprenticeship as a bread and biscuit maker. He later wrote of his conversion:

"My ears were saluted with the glorious latter-day work, being invited by a fellowservant to read some tracts and some copies of the Latter-day Saints' *Millennial Star,* after which I was induced to attend the Saints' meetings, all of which created in my mind a thirst for knowledge and an earnest desire to obtain the promised blessings which are the result of obedience."[73]

During the next few years, William was active in building the Church in London. In 1852 he was ordained an elder and called to serve as a local missionary. "The Lord abundantly blessed our labors," he wrote, "and directed [us to] the honest in heart, . . . who gladly received our testimony and the message of life which we had to declare unto them. In the course of about 6 months [the branch] numbered 28 members."[74] The next year, 14 of these members emigrated to Utah.

On Christmas Day 1853, William married Eliza Camp. Fifteen months later he was called as president of the Lambeth Branch. After serving a little more than a year, William was released so he and Eliza could emigrate. "In answer to my earnest and unceasing prayers, the Lord opened my way to gather with His people to Utah," William wrote.[75] On the eve of his departure for Liverpool, members of the branch held a tea meeting to express gratitude to William for his service. They also presented him a certificate that included the following "testimonial":

"It is with feelings of real pleasure that we the officers and members of the Lambeth Branch avail ourselves of the present opportunity of expressing our satisfaction with the manner which you have conducted the business of the Branch. Your councils have been dictated by the Spirit of God, and the counsel of them that were over you has been strictly observed by you. We therefore with all confidence recommend you to the fellowship and confidence of the Saints and the priesthood in any portion of the Earth wherever your lot may be cast."[76]

William and Eliza Binder were both 24 years old when they emigrated. They had no children.

Robert and Mary Clifton Family

Little information is available about Robert and Mary Clifton. They joined the Church in 1844, when Robert was 38 and Mary was 34. Before emigrating, Robert had served as president of the Hackney, Tottenham, and Haggestone Branches.[77] He and Mary were parents of eight children, three of whom emigrated with them: Rebecca (20), Sophia (12), and Ann (6). Four of their children had died, and one stayed in England.

David and Deborah Blair Family

Information about David Blair and his family is even more sparse than about Robert Clifton. David was a professional soldier who was a member of Queen Victoria's elite Life Guard. He and his wife, Deborah, joined the Church in 1842. David was appointed president of the Windsor Branch in 1851 and continued this service until he emigrated in 1856. He and Deborah had three children: Deborah (7), Elizabeth (5), and David (6 months). David Blair was 46 when he emigrated, Deborah 37.

James and Elizabeth Bleak Family

As a boy, James Bleak (pronounced *Blake*) suffered nearly every loss a person could experience. Four of his five siblings died as infants. Then in 1844, when James was 14, his father passed away. Two years later his mother also died. Orphaned, James and his only living brother, 7-year-old John, went to live with an aunt. Within two years, John died. James was 18 years old and alone.

From this lowest point, James's life almost immediately began to improve. In 1849 he married Elizabeth Moore, and in 1851 he was baptized. Within a few months he was ordained an elder, and the next year he was called as a counselor in the Whitechapel Branch, the largest in London. In 1854, when James was only 24, he was called to preside over the branch.

James Bleak's journal during his years as branch president reveals a man who tended his flock with great care. He made frequent visits to the sick; he helped settle differences among members to maintain a unity of faith; and he officiated in many baptisms and ordinations, including the rebaptism of Francis Webster after he returned from the California gold fields.

"For some days past I have been asking the Lord to open my way to go home to Zion," James wrote in his journal in 1855.[78] When the opportunity to emigrate came in 1856, he sent money to the mission office in Liverpool so the missionaries who were leaving to assist with the emigration could buy a wagon and ox team for his family. However, the handcart plan was announced soon after James sent the money, and it was, as he recalled, "accompanied by the suggestion that those able to emigrate that season by ox or horse teams would be blessed if they had faith to go by handcart, costing so much less than teams and wagons." The savings would be used "to emigrate other faithful Saints who did not have means to gather to Utah that year."[79]

At first James decided not to give up his wagon because his wife was not used to traveling and his four children were "of tender years," ranging from 11 months to 6 years. He changed his mind, however, when other branch members who were emigrating began to use his example to justify traveling by wagon rather than handcart. James explained:

"[I] had always striven to set a becoming example in temporal and spiritual matters to the brethren and sisters entrusted to [my] care, [so I] hesitated no longer, but at once wrote to President Franklin D. Richards, asking to be numbered on the handcart list. . . . After receiving the approval of President Richards, this change was announced in public meeting; and, to the credit of those who emigrated from that branch that season, all adopted the same method of gathering."[80]

President Richards soon published an editorial in the *Millennial Star* in which he praised presidents such as James Bleak "who have been blessed with means to purchase teams [but] have concluded to cast their lot with the Lord's poor, and share with their brethren in the handcart companies."[81]

Usually when a person experiences as much loss as James Bleak did as a youth, he instinctively does all he can to protect against further loss. He might even become obsessively cautious. But in choosing to give up his wagon for a handcart, James Bleak responded to an even deeper desire than self-preservation. He was committed to setting the right example regardless of the sacrifice it might require. On the handcart trek, this sacrifice would require him to give up far more than comfort,

James Bleak

convenience, and security. After James Bleak reached the Salt Lake Valley, such willingness to sacrifice would almost immediately make an impression on Brigham Young. This willingness would be called on again and again—and would be rewarded with rich blessings.

CHAPTER 24

FROM IOWA CITY TO
FLORENCE, NEBRASKA

The experiences of the *Horizon* Saints in Iowa City were similar to those of the previous handcart companies. They struggled with the Iowa heat and thunderstorms. They worked feverishly to get ready for the trail, building handcarts and making other preparations. And they had to make difficult decisions about what to leave behind. "The members of the company were told that the 100 pounds of luggage and personal belongings allowed each person on the sea voyage would be reduced to 17 pounds for each cart," John Jaques wrote 10 days after arriving in Iowa City. "This caused many heartaches, for many of the cherished articles brought from the old country were disposed of at great sacrifice."[1] His regret over the sacrifice of these belongings was still evident in the reminiscence he wrote 22 years later:

"As only a very limited amount of baggage could be taken with the handcarts, during the long stay in the Iowa City camping ground there was a general lightening of such things as could best be done without. Many things were sold cheaply to residents of that vicinity, and many more things were left on the camping ground for anybody to take or leave at his pleasure. It was grievous to see the heaps of books and other articles thus left in the sun and rain and dust, representing a respectable amount of money spent therefore in England, but thenceforth a waste and a dead loss to the owners."[2]

LEAVING IOWA CITY

Jesse Haven's handcart company left the camp in Iowa City on July 22, two weeks after arriving—and just one week after the Willie company left. They traveled only three miles in the first four days, and Jesse Haven and others were still going back to the main camp during that time to finish preparations, so their real departure was not until July 26. They began slowly, traveling only eight miles in the next three days. They finally began to make better progress on July 29, when they traveled 15 miles.

Edward Martin's handcart company moved a quarter mile from camp on July 25 and also got a slow start. They didn't travel the next day, went only a short distance the next, and then were stalled for three days while searching for cattle. They finally left the vicinity of Iowa City on July 31, when they traveled seven miles. By then, they were 38 miles behind the Haven company.

The earliest official count of these companies was made after they were combined in Nebraska a few weeks later, when they had 576 members. Their number when they left Iowa City was probably about 650, since some people left the companies in Iowa, a few died, and some stayed behind in Florence. Together these companies also had 146 handcarts, 7 supply wagons, 6 mules and horses, and 50 cows and beef cattle.[3]

The Hodgetts and Hunt wagon companies, which were assigned to travel closely with the handcarts, left Iowa City on July 30 and August 1. The Hodgetts company had 185 people, 33 wagons, 84 yoke of oxen, and 250 heifers and other loose cattle.[4] The Hunt company had 240 people, 50 wagons, 297 oxen and cows, and 7 horses and mules.[5] Before leaving Iowa City, these wagon companies had been combined under the direction of Dan Jones, who was returning from his second mission to Wales (see page 380). The company divided when one of the subcaptains, Benjamin Hodgetts, led a group of wagons out of camp on July 30. Less than two weeks later, Dan Jones would relinquish his position as captain of the other 50 wagons to the other subcaptain, John Hunt.

THE JOURNEY ACROSS IOWA

After having more stops than starts during their first few days of pulling handcarts, both the Haven and Martin companies made better progress on their 270-mile trek from Iowa City to Florence. Both of them traveled this distance a little more quickly than the first three handcart companies and at about the same pace as the Willie company.

They maintained this pace despite a multitude of challenges. A sampling of the delays experienced by the Martin company is helpful in understanding what it took—both physically and spiritually—to bear the setbacks that occurred almost daily on the journey. Soon after being stalled for three days because of missing cattle, the company was delayed until noon because of a thunderstorm. Two days later they were held up because a wheel came off a handcart. The next day they were again delayed until noon because of a thunderstorm. A few days later they had to wait while a coffin was made. The next day they had to search for two mules that ran away. Two days later they had to wait while another coffin was made, this time for a child.[6]

Such delays must have tested the patience of many people. Moving forward, though toilsome, was much preferable to being stalled for hours or days in the oppressive Iowa heat. The delays also must have heightened the anxiety about the late start.

Jesse Haven's company had similar challenges. Worse, there was apparently more conflict and criticism in his group. Five days after leaving the main camp, Jesse Haven had trouble with some unruly cattle and left behind the wagon that carried the tents. Late in the day he sent some men to retrieve it, but by then it was dark and raining, so they could not get it back. The next day he recorded in his journal:

"[The Saints were in a] rather bad predicament. Being without tents, all their things got wet. . . . Last night and this morning [they] found much fault [and] grumbled much about me. [They] blamed me because the tents were left behind. In the evening [we] had a meeting. . . . I told them if they did not cease their grumbling, that sickness would get into their midst and they would die off like rotten sheep, but if they would be humble and keep united, the blessings of the Lord should attend them."[7]

Ten days later Jesse Haven recorded more problems. "So many leaving," he wrote with obvious discouragement on August 6. "Saints traveled badly today. Much scattered. After we got into camp, 11 left us," he wrote on August 9. In all, his journal tells of at least 20 people who turned back after leaving Iowa City.

While some people murmured as they left the companies, a few left in good faith. After the Martin company had traveled only 100 miles, Joseph Beecroft was too ill to continue. Excerpts from his journal show an anguishing decline:

August 6: "I felt much fatigued, feverish, and pained."

August 7: "[I was] so near finished I could not fetch water. . . . My misery was traveling. I could not help with the tent."

August 8: "I could get no further. . . . I felt finished when I got into camp. . . . I was cheered to hear my lad singing a little before reaching camp."

August 9: "My poor wife and boy were nearly finished with fatigue and poor feet."

August 10: "I . . . endured horrid pain in my limbs, particularly below my hips."

August 11: "My handcart was tied to a wagon, and after walking the whole distance I rode into camp and felt better than usual but by no means good."

August 12: "[We] came up to the long wished-for sight—the city of Fort Des Moines. [I] then resolved I would not leave this city till [I was] better. . . . I could bear to stand no longer. . . . My wife and John sought lodgings, being directed by a kind-hearted man . . . who told me I must save what money I had and he would bear our expenses."

August 13: "Yesterday morn some brethren came from camp

with a handcart [and] left our goods. . . . My wife told them I could not be moved. They left their blessing and departed."

The Beecrofts stayed in Des Moines for three years before they were able to finish the journey to Utah. During this time, two of their older children joined them from England.

For many in the Haven and Martin companies, one compensation for their difficulties was the beauty of the Iowa countryside. The open prairies and fresh air prompted Samuel Openshaw to express strong opinions about the problems of crowding together in cities:

"We . . . traveled through a beautiful country where we could stand and gaze upon the prairies as far as the eye could carry, even until the prairies themselves seemed to meet the sky on all sides, without being able to see a house. [I] thought how many thousands of people are there in England who have scarce room to breathe and not enough to eat. Yet all this good land [is] lying dormant, except for the prairie grass, to grow and decay, which if men would spread themselves and obey the commandment of God to replenish the earth, instead of thronging together in cities and towns and causing the air to be tainted with stinks and giving rise to disease, what a blessing it would be."[8]

Meeting Opposition with Kindness

Like the earlier handcart companies, the Martin and Haven companies faced some opposition as they traveled across Iowa. John Southwell recalled that "the usual mobocratic spirit . . . filled the souls of the people, and they felt to vie with each other in uttering oaths and curses upon us."[9] One day the Haven company's animals were put out to feed where there was a nice stream and good grass. Apparently the land was privately owned, and two men immediately came charging toward the group, vowing to kill all of them. In relating how this conflict was resolved, John Southwell also recorded the accompanying lessons learned:

"Captain Haven met [the men] and in his gentlemanly way apologized and offered them pay in order to secure a night's feed for the poor, hungry brutes. This kind act on his part took them by surprise, and they consented to leave them there without further trouble.

"The singing of the young ladies at [the] evening service drew the attention of the kinder disposed people, and in the morning they brought butter and milk into camp and expressed themselves as being pleased with the way we conducted ourselves traveling through the country. At their request, on breaking up camp we sang the handcart song, which pleased them. They bid us success on our journey.

"This circumstance is one that a kind word turneth away wrath, and as Jesus said to his disciples, do good to them that hate you, [was] truly exemplified in this case."[10]

Heat, Thunderstorms, and Signs of Wonder

The heat that prostrated many of the emigrants in Iowa City became an even greater problem when they had to pull handcarts in it. "It seemed like pulling the very pluck out of one, the pluck physical and corporeal," recalled John Jaques.[11]

Coming mostly from England, members of the Haven and Martin companies were accustomed to rain, but they were not accustomed to being jolted and deluged by violent thunderstorms while living outdoors, as occurred frequently in Iowa. John Southwell's description of one of these storms illustrates the problems they typically caused:

"When [we were] a half mile from camp, one of the most horrible electric storms I ever saw fell upon us, accompanied by hail and rain. It proved a perfect deluge. . . . In the space of ten minutes the roads became almost impassable, and oh, what a scene to behold. . . . Here was no sign of shelter. Our tents were rolled up in the wagons. After everyone was drenched and many were unable to move out of their tracks, the captain gave orders to pitch camp and set up the tents the best [we] could in the mud. [We] were protected from the rain but . . . were still ankle deep in the mud."[12]

An even greater spectacle than these displays of thunder and lightning occurred on August 3, a few days after the Martin company left Iowa City. Joseph Beecroft recorded, "Just as we had left camp, a meteor fell at a short distance."[13] The other diarists in the company described this event with such wonder that they seemed to feel it was more than a chance phenomenon.

From William Binder: "Soon after we had started from camp we saw a bright luminary descend very rapidly and when within about 50 feet of the surface of the earth it suddenly disappeared. The object was seen by all the camp."[14]

From John Jaques: "After traveling half a mile [we] saw a ball of fire before us shooting down from the sky; when near the ground, it changed into the likeness of a spear and then vanished."[15]

From Samuel Openshaw: "When we had traveled about a quarter of a mile we beheld a ball of fire brighter than the sun before us in the air. [It] came within about three yards of the ground and then drew out in the form of a spear and vanished out of our sight."[16]

Before these Saints left England, President Franklin D. Richards had drawn parallels between them and ancient Israel, even seeing similarities in their mode of travel.[17] Knowing that the Lord had gone before the children of Israel in a cloud by day and a pillar of fire by night, did the handcart Saints see a parallel in this event? Their tone of wonder and awe suggests that they may have seen it as some kind of heavenly manifestation.

Service and "Service"

Most members of the Haven and Martin companies looked out for each other and served generously. John Jaques reflected with wry humor on an incident in Iowa when a man offered to carry a woman across a slough:

"[He] took pity on a woman (she was a few pounds heavier than a woman at that time) and essayed to carry her over a slough, but in his impulsive kindness he had overestimated his own strength, or underestimated her specific gravity, and he soon found that he had undertaken a more difficult task than he at first supposed. However, he accomplished the feat at three times trying—first, he carried her into the slough and set her down in the mud; second, he picked her up again and carried her out of [it], but minus her shoes, which were left sticking in the mud; third, he went back . . . and fetched out her shoes."[18]

Progress of the Wagon Companies

Ideally, the Hodgetts and Hunt wagon companies were to travel closely enough to the handcart companies to assist them when needed; however, none of the handcart diaries mentions any interaction with the wagons while crossing Iowa, probably because the wagon companies were traveling even more slowly than the handcarts. The Hunt company journal shows that they struggled with their own share of difficulties and delays—straying cattle, capsized wagons, slippery roads, bad bridges, and a death. In addition, some members of the company were at least occasionally uncooperative. The journal gives the following report for August 11, when the captain addressed this problem:

"[He] show[ed] their several duties and wherein they had lacked in fulfilling them, and their want of union and unwillingness to perform what is required of them. Several of the Captains of Tens also spoke, and all agreed . . . that something must be done. A good spirit prevailed, and those present appeared willing to answer the calls made upon them in the future."[19]

Several days later some members of the Hunt company were still not heeding their captains. On August 20 the matter was addressed again, this time with penalties specified:

"At the prayer meeting held at 7:30 P.M., instructions [were] given by Captains Hunt and Davis . . . that any man, woman, or child who has come to years of accountability, [who was] found disobeying the commands or instructions of their Captain, [should] be compelled to leave the company. [It was] also proposed . . . that any man found taking out a gun for the purpose of shooting before the corral is formed, or shooting within 1/2 mile of the camp, [should] forfeit the said gun."[20]

This meeting apparently resolved the problems because the company journal does not mention them again during the last week of the journey to Florence.

CHAPTER 25

DIFFICULT DECISIONS
IN FLORENCE

Jesse Haven's handcart company pulled into Florence, Nebraska, on August 19, two days after the last part of the Willie company left. Like the Willie company, they had taken nearly four weeks to travel the 270 miles from Iowa City. Edward Martin's handcart company arrived three days later, on August 22. The Hodgetts wagon company arrived sometime after the Martin company but before the Hunt company, which arrived on August 28.

After Iowa City, Florence was the most important stop for the handcart pioneers. It was the last Church-operated site for resupply, repairs, and other assistance. From there the companies had to travel the remaining thousand miles of the journey without substantial assistance except potential resupply from Salt Lake City. The forts that were scattered over those thousand miles could provide only modest amounts of supplies and other help—and usually at high prices.

The first two handcart companies had been delayed in Florence for two weeks, the third company nearly as long.[1] The Willie company had hurried through Florence in five days, concerned by the lateness of the season. The Haven and Martin companies would be ready to move out even more quickly.

ARRIVAL OF PRESIDENT FRANKLIN D. RICHARDS

Jesse Haven's company spent August 20 and 21 repairing handcarts and "making all things ready to pursue our journey."[2] At the

282

close of August 21, Jesse Haven told his company to be ready to leave Florence by noon the next day.

Edward Martin's company was just nearing Florence on August 21. They passed through Council Bluffs and camped about four miles from the site where they would ferry across the Missouri River to Florence. Soon after they made camp, a small company led by President Franklin D. Richards caught up with them.[3] President Richards had

Franklin D. Richards

overseen the departure of most of these Saints from England. He had bidden them farewell in May and then left Liverpool in July with a few returning missionaries and emigrants. His group had journeyed by steamship across the ocean, by express train to St. Louis, by riverboat up the Missouri to St. Joseph, and by stagecoach to Florence, taking only 26 days to travel the same distance that had taken the handcart emigrants three months.[4]

President Richards stayed only briefly with the Martin company that evening before continuing forward a few miles to Florence. There his group was greeted joyfully by emigration leaders and by members of Jesse Haven's handcart company.

The next morning Jesse Haven was preparing to break camp and get back on the trail when Cyrus Wheelock, a returning missionary in President Richards's company, told him to "tarry till tomorrow."[5] That day the Martin company spent six hours ferrying across the Missouri River and pulled into Florence. That evening, with both the Haven and Martin companies in camp, President Richards called them together. During this meeting he reorganized them into one company under the direction of Edward Martin. Although this could have felt like a slight to Jesse Haven, he reported it without emotion in his journal:

"In the evening, Brother Martin's and my company were called together, and both companies were put into one under the presidency of Brother Martin by F. D. Richards."[6]

Why did President Richards combine the companies? Jesse Haven did not record the reason. The only diarist who gave a reason was William Binder of the Martin company, who wrote that the action was taken because "Captain Haven . . . refused to conduct the emigrants any further without [being] issued a certain amount of provisions which he deemed necessary for the journey."[7] One problem with this explanation is that it does not reconcile with Jesse Haven's actions in preparing his company to leave Florence so quickly. Perhaps William Binder's explanation was based on rumor. Or maybe Jesse Haven had indeed objected to being given insufficient rations—the journey across Iowa had shown him the problems that short rations caused—but planned to proceed anyway. If that was the case, perhaps all William Binder heard about was the objection.

Years later two other men who had traveled across Iowa with Jesse Haven gave different explanations for why the companies were combined. Benjamin Platt wrote, "We . . . joined the two companies together on account of hostile Indians on the plains."[8] John Southwell had yet another understanding: "To our sorrow, Captain Haven was needed in another direction. There was a wagon company without a competent man to guide the people on their trip, so Jesse was called to officiate in that capacity."[9]

Indeed, Jesse Haven traveled with the Hodgetts wagon company for most of the rest of the journey, and he says he was appointed president.[10] However, Benjamin Hodgetts continued to lead the company. It appears to be more accurate to say that Jesse Haven was given charge of five wagons.

President Richards may have had some unstated reasons for consolidating the handcart companies. Perhaps he had more confidence in Edward Martin, whom he knew well. Perhaps he was concerned by the number of people who had left Jesse Haven's company in Iowa. Or perhaps he thought the groups would be stronger if they were together for the last thousand miles.

The wagons that Jesse Haven took charge of belonged to Thomas Tennant, the wealthy convert from England who had bought a home from Brigham Young.[11] Thomas Tennant was traveling with the Hodgetts wagon company and had earlier offered to let Jesse Haven use a wagon and oxen.[12]

DISCUSSION ABOUT STOPPING OR CONTINUING ONWARD

Florence was the main switch point for the late handcart and wagon companies of 1856. The tragedies these companies would soon face can be blamed on many factors—their late departure from England, their demographics, their delays in Iowa City, their poorly constructed handcarts, the lack of sufficient rations, the lack of resupply, and the severe winter storms. But when Brigham Young later addressed the cause of the tragedy, he focused almost exclusively on the decisions that emigration leaders made in Florence.[13] For that reason, the actions of these leaders during the Martin company's three-day stay in Florence merit careful examination.

In addition to being a repair and resupply stop, Florence was also a potential site for spending the winter. The Church had established Winter Quarters there after the exodus from Nauvoo 10 years earlier. More than 3,500 stayed there that winter, and some 400 died from cold, hunger, and disease.[14] Winter Quarters then became the staging ground for the first pioneer companies that traveled west in 1847.

Like the Willie company several days earlier, the Martin company discussed whether they should stay in Florence for the winter or proceed to the Salt Lake Valley. Josiah Rogerson recalled that this subject "was the main and nearly the only one of daily discussion by President Franklin D. Richards and a score of returning missionaries, including members of the Mormon Battalion, who had crossed the plains several times before."[15]

Church leaders had not specified a definite cutoff date for leaving Florence, but emigration officials knew that leaving in late August was risky. Several Church "epistles" during the previous few years had encouraged early departures from the Midwest. A few months later, in response to the handcart tragedy, Brigham Young would issue an edict that companies were not to leave Florence later than August 1, with May or June being preferable. The penalty for noncompliance would be excommunication.[16]

The Willie company's earlier discussion of whether to proceed or to stay in Florence is well documented. Details of the dramatic meeting in which Levi Savage tearfully pleaded with the company to stop for the winter are included in his own journal and other contemporaneous sources (see pages 79–84). The Martin company's discussion of this subject a few days later is not as well documented. The sources that are typically most reliable—the members of the company whose daily diaries are available—all mention the meetings in Florence but provide few details about them.

From John Jaques: "Met Elder Richards, Spencer, Linforth, Grant, Kimball, Ferguson, and McAllister, who welcomed us. In the evening we were addressed."[17]

From Jesse Haven: "Meeting today. A number of the brethren spoke."[18]

From James Bleak: "We had two meetings and partook of the sacrament."[19]

From Samuel Openshaw: "A meeting at eleven o'clock and four o'clock. Elder [Wheelock] and others addressed us."[20]

The account of a fifth diarist, William Binder, provides the most helpful information about the intent of emigration leaders. Although he does not state it explicitly, William Binder implies that leaders planned to move the companies forward that season:

"Pres. F. D. Richards called a meeting of the Saints and addressed them upon subjects of importance to the children of God. Bro. Wheelock and Spencer also delivered addresses, and many blessings were promised the Saints upon conditions of implicit obedience to the servants of God who would take charge of the company across the plains."[21]

In addition to the diarists, many years later at least four members of these companies wrote about the discussion in Florence. Although these recollections are less credible than the diaries, they provide other perspectives that are helpful in the absence of more detailed contemporaneous accounts.

Recollection of John Jaques

The lengthy reminiscence that John Jaques wrote 22 years after the handcart trek is probably the most reliable of all such accounts. He was a careful observer who could base his recollections on his own daily journal. Although he lamented the decision to proceed, he did not explicitly address the role of any individuals in it:

"Owing to the lateness of the season, the important question was debated, whether the emigrants should winter in that vicinity or continue the long and wearisome journey to Salt Lake. Unfortunately, warm enthusiasm prevailed over sound judgment and cool common sense, and it was determined to finish the journey the same season. . . . The results of the determination to proceed were fraught with disaster and death."[22]

The most intriguing part of John Jaques's account is the recollection that "one prominent sanguine gentleman proffered to eat all the snow the emigrants would find between [Florence] and Salt Lake, an offer of the hasty and impulsive nature of Jephthath's rash vow."[23] When the Willie company had been in Florence several days earlier, William Kimball, one of the emigration leaders, had made such an offer. Apparently he repeated it to the Martin company.

Recollection of John Bond

One difference between the Martin company's stop in Florence and the Willie company's was the presence of President Franklin D. Richards. He had not been a factor in the Willie company's decision to proceed because he did not arrive in Florence until they had left. What was his role in the Martin company's decision? According to John Bond of the Hodgetts wagon company, he encouraged the people forward:

"A council was called, urging the Saints not to fear the lateness of the time. . . . Franklin D. Richards spoke with great passion and feeling. He told the Saints that they had come this far on their faith and had arrived safely. . . . He told them he believed they would arrive at the valley safely. [He] told them that as they had the faith to travel this far, they had better journey on to the end, and he prophesied in the name of Israel's God that the Saints would arrive safely in the valley in spite of the inclement weather and storms from all directions, that God would keep them safe."[24]

How reliable is John Bond's account? One concern is that he was only 12 years old when this meeting was held. A second is that he may not have been an eyewitness to the meeting. Another problem is that he mixes the meetings of the Martin and Willie companies, at one point mentioning Levi Savage in the Martin company's meeting even though Savage had already left Florence with the Willie company.

Although these problems compromise the reliability of John Bond's account, three factors argue in favor of at least moderate credibility. First, his 47-page account of the journey is more accurate than many other recollections when compared to the daily diaries. Second, to compensate for his young age at the time, and perhaps his absence from the meeting, he consulted with other members of the companies in writing his account. Finally, his recollection of President Richards's encouragement to proceed is consistent with nearly every other record of President Richards's words about the handcart companies.

Recollections of Josiah Rogerson and Benjamin Platt

Josiah Rogerson provides the most detail about the meetings in Florence. Contradicting John Bond on essential points, he later wrote:

"I can hear, even now, the voice of President Richards, as he stood there and reasoned with us in his fatherly and gentlemanly manner, as to the lateness of the season, as to the possibility of the storms coming on earlier than usual, that no doubt many of the infants and aged might fall by the way, and some others through disease and from the impurities of the water in the streams, fatigue, and exhaustion; and that it was left for us now to decide, whether we would go on and take the risks and chances of these possible and probable fatalities, or remain there and around Florence, Council Bluffs, and other villages in the vicinity till an earlier date for starting the next year.

"[He said] that if we chose and decided to stay, we could have what provisions and supplies were in the store or warehouses there and ready for loading into our wagons, . . . that he would purchase for us what more he could with means still in his hands, and assist us in every other way for our remaining there till next spring.

"About the only encouraging words we remember as to our not staying and going ahead were when he said that as it had been one of the largest season's emigrations that had ever been shipped from the British Isles, [and since] it contained hundreds of the first converts of Mormonism from 1837 to 1850, . . . [and since] they were this far on their way to Zion, he would be gratified by the help and favor of God to see all reach there in safety that season. . . .

"[Before the vote was taken,] Elder John D. T. McAllister, the author of the handcart song, spoke . . . for going on, and Cyrus H. Wheelock, General George D. Grant, and others; but Brother [Chauncey] Webb urged that we should not start, but stay there for the winter. His remarks were Webb's alone. Some others spoke and then President Franklin D. Richards, arising at last, advised all to vote with their free agency and responsibility.

"The vote was called, and with uncovered heads and uplifted hands to heaven and an almost unanimous vote, it was decided to go on. If Webb or any others voted to the contrary, I do not remember it, nor the number.

"Now who was responsible or to blame for the fatalities or the results of the journey—President Franklin D. Richards or the members of the companies and the missionaries? This has been in question for fifty-one years."[25]

How reliable is Josiah Rogerson's account? Like John Bond, he was young when this meeting was held—only 15 years old. Another concern is that he wrote his recollection of this meeting more than half a century later. Another is that his account has undertones of hindsight. A final concern is that some of the language attributed to President Richards seems inconsistent with everything else he is recorded as saying about the handcart plan.

Despite these compromising factors, Josiah Rogerson should not be dismissed as unreliable. In trying to prepare a book on the Martin company, he went to great lengths to contact survivors and solicit their recollections. He likely had a much larger store of information from which to write than John Bond had. Moreover, his account of President Richards issuing a warning and then calling for a vote is corroborated by one other source. Benjamin Platt of the Martin company recalled:

"Apostle F. D. Richards called a meeting and advised us to stop at Florence until the next season, but . . . we declared we would go through or die trying and we prevailed, and seeing we were determined he consented but he said he did not want anyone to try [who] could not walk every foot of the way. . . . He told us that President Young had promised to send out teams to meet us and that we might have ten weeks of Indian summer and we might get within reach of the teams before the cold weather set in."[26]

Recollection of Franklin D. Richards; Conclusions

Six weeks after this meeting in Florence, President Franklin D. Richards arrived in Salt Lake City and reported on it in general conference. The date was October 5—two weeks before any winter storms or any expectation of disaster. His own account strongly implies that although the decision to proceed was made by a vote of the people, their leaders, presided over by President Richards, had encouraged them forward:

"When we had a meeting at Florence, we called upon the Saints to express their faith to the people, and requested to know of them, even if they knew that they should be swallowed up in storms, whether they would stop or turn back. They voted, with loud acclamations, that they would go on. Such confidence and joyful performance of so arduous labors to accomplish their gathering will bring the choice blessings of God upon them."[27]

In the final analysis, what was President Richards's role in the Martin company's decision to proceed from Florence? He appears to have given at least moderate or implicit encouragement to finish the journey that year. However, this encouragement may not have been the primary factor that pushed the company forward, because all indications suggest they planned to proceed even before he arrived. Jesse Haven, for example, was so determined to keep going that he was ready to get back on the trail in three days, much faster than the companies before him.

Although President Richards probably was not the determining factor in the Martin company's decision to proceed from Florence, he could have been the determining factor in stopping the company. Ordering them to stop was within his authority—and that is what Brigham Young would later say he expected. In a public reprimand of emigration leaders, Brigham Young would criticize them not so much for *encouraging* the companies to go forward, but rather for *permitting* them to go. He would suggest that this decision should not have been left to a vote of inexperienced emigrants, regardless of their unity and enthusiasm. Rather, this was a time for leaders to give counsel based on sound judgment—and to exercise their authority, if necessary, to ensure that the counsel was heeded. In Brigham Young's own words:

"If, while at the Missouri river [Florence], they had received a hint from any person on this earth, or if even a bird had chirped it in the ears of Brothers Richards and Spencer, they would have known better than to rush men, women, and children on to the prairie in the autumn months . . . to travel over a thousand miles. [If] they would have stopped and considered for one moment, they would have stopped those men, women, and children there until another year."[28]

Staying in Florence for the winter would have been very difficult, however. A few months later a correspondent wrote that the weather that winter had been "of unprecedented severity in Nebraska. For several days at a time the thermometer has stood at 12 or 15 degrees below zero. The third and fifteenth of this month it stood respectively at 32 and 26 degrees below. Much suffering has ensued from the excessive cold and storms. Nearly every week we receive the intelligence that some person or persons have frozen to death. . . . The snow is now about three feet deep, on the average."[29] Given these conditions, it is possible that if the handcart Saints had stayed in Florence in 1856, they might have suffered as badly as the Saints who had stayed there in 1846.

PREPARING TO MOVE FORWARD

President Richards's group remained in Florence for nearly two weeks, helping the Martin, Hodgetts, and Hunt companies prepare for the last 1,031 miles of their journey. Describing this experience, President Richards wrote to his associates in the mission office in Liverpool:

"It certainly would warm your heart with melting kindness to pass the line of camp going by handcarts, and receive the cordial shakes of the hand, with a fervent 'God bless you,' as I did when I visited Captain Edward Martin's train, several of whom expressed their thanks in a particular manner for being permitted to come out this year."[30]

One of President Richards's traveling companions, Cyrus Wheelock, also marveled at the spirit of the handcart pioneers:

"In less than an hour after our arrival [we] engaged in practical 'Mormonism,' in assisting to complete the organization of the handcart and wagon companies for their journey over the Plains. [Our presence] among them seemed like the magic of heaven. Their spirits and bodies seemed almost instantly refreshed, and when we passed up and down the lines we were met with those hearty greetings that none but Saints know how to give and appreciate.

"All were in good spirits, and generally in good health, and full of confidence that they should reach the mountains in season to escape the severe storms. . . . I have never seen more union among the Saints anywhere than is manifested in the handcart companies. And hundreds bear record of the truth of the words of President Young, wherein he promised them increasing strength by the way."[31]

During part of his mission, Cyrus Wheelock served as second counselor to President Richards in the mission presidency.[32] He wrote the words of the hymn "Ye Elders of Israel."

STRUGGLES OF LANGLEY BAILEY

Eighteen-year-old Langley Bailey was the oldest of four sons of John and Jane Bailey. While crossing Iowa, he had become too ill to walk. "I was taken down with hemorrhage of the bowels," he later wrote. "I was unable to walk [and] had to be hauled on Brother Isaac J. Wardle and my brother John's cart."[33]

When the Baileys got to Florence, they consulted a doctor about Langley's illness. "[He] said I must not go another step or I would die and be buried on the roadside," Langley recalled. An elder in the company was asked to give him a blessing, but according to Langley he "said he did not have faith enough to raise the dead." Langley's mother then asked Franklin D. Richards and Cyrus Wheelock to administer to him. Although Langley was unconscious at the time, they promised that he would live to see the Salt Lake Valley.[34]

Miraculously, Langley was able to resume the journey, but he still had great difficulties. When he got discouraged, his mother would remind him of the promise given in his blessing and tell him, in effect, that he had to do his part for it to be fulfilled. One morning when Langley was particularly discouraged, he started out early so he could "get away, lay down under a sagebrush, and die." While stretched out to die, he saw his parents pass by with their cart. He later recalled:

"Just then, a voice said, 'Your mother is hunting you, jump up.' I saw mother in haste coming towards me, wanting to know what had gone wrong with me. I told her I had planned to lay down and die. I felt it was too much to pull me on the cart [when they] had as much luggage as they could manage. [She] scolded me a little. She reminded [me] what I was promised by Apostle F. D. Richards. I rode on the cart until the teams from the Valley met us."[35]

Margaret Nadauld, who served as Young Women general president and is a descendant of the Baileys, feels gratitude for the perseverance of both Langley and his mother:

"Jane Allgood Bailey wasn't about to give up the light of her new religion. She would not be defeated by the cold, starvation, and sickness on the plains of Wyoming. . . . On the trek, her 18-year-old son, Langley, became ill and was so weak that he had to be pushed on the handcart much of the way. One morning he rose from his bed on the cart [and] went ahead of the company and lay down under a sagebrush to die, feeling that he was too much of a burden. When his faithful mother found him, she scolded him and told him: 'Get on the cart. I'll help you, but you're not giving up!' . . .

"Upon arrival in the Salt Lake Valley, Langley was still alive! He was 18 years old and he weighed only 60 pounds. That 18-year-old boy was my great-grandfather. I'm grateful for the preservation of his young life and for the fortitude and stamina of his noble, courageous mother, who was a light to her family and kept her son going in spite of deathly odds."[36]

Margaret Nadauld saw in her great-grandfather's experience a modern-day application for young women:

"You probably will not have to push a handcart in a blizzard over the plains, sisters, or run away from a mob, but you may have to walk away from friends and fashions and invitations which would compromise your standards of goodness. And that takes courage. Soon you will be Relief Society sisters and one day mothers who must lend strength and testimony to future generations. Now in your preparing years, you can't afford to say: 'I'm going to give up. The Church standards are too high. It's too hard to live the standards of personal purity with exactness. I'm too weak.' You can do it! For the sake of your future, you must do it!"[37]

CHAPTER 26

FROM FLORENCE TO
FORT LARAMIE

The Martin company left Florence on August 25, after three days of repairing handcarts and resupplying. The Hodgetts wagon company began moving out on August 28, and the Hunt wagon company began leaving on August 31. A few members of the Hunt company decided to stay in Florence,[1] and the same is likely true for the other groups.

During the 522-mile journey from Florence to Fort Laramie, the Martin and Hodgetts companies stayed close to each other, often camping in the same area.[2] The Hunt company was usually about three days behind. Nathan Porter of the Hodgetts company observed: "The handcart company was in our rear, [and] Captain Hunt's company was in their rear. Thus the handcart company was between the independent companies, having as it were a front and rear guard."[3]

After concluding the season's emigration business in Florence, President Richards and his group left on September 3.[4] They would catch up with the handcart and wagon companies partway across Nebraska and meet with them briefly before continuing homeward in their carriages and light wagons at a pace of about 35 miles a day.

THE JOURNEY ACROSS NEBRASKA

For the Martin company, September's journey across Nebraska was more difficult than August's across Iowa. One reason is that the handcarts were heavier, each loaded with 100 pounds of flour and some carrying tents. Another reason is that water was sometimes scarce. At one point the company went two days without fresh water, getting by on occasional "mud water."[5] They were so desperate that they traveled until 10:00 one night and 11:00 the next night before reaching fresh water at Prairie Creek. These Saints from water-rich England had to worry and wonder about what might lie ahead as the climate became more arid. Contrasting the two lands, Samuel Openshaw wrote:

"It would truly be an amusing and interesting scene if the people of the old country could have a bird's-eye view of us when in camp; to see everyone busy—some fetching water, others gathering buffalo chips, some cooking and so forth upon these wild prairies where the air is not tainted with the smoke of cities and factories, but is quiet here. One may see a creek at a distance and start and travel one hour towards it, yet seem no nigher than you did when you started."[6]

Another difference between the old country and the new was the concern about Indians. The Martin company heard terrifying stories about them. "The Indians are very hostile about here," wrote Samuel Openshaw. "They have attacked some of the immigrants who have passed through this season, and rumor says that some have been murdered."[7] Ten days later the Martin company began to see evidence that these rumors were true. After seeing one scene of hostility, Samuel Openshaw wrote with a sense of foreboding, "[The Indians] are committing depredations behind and before [us]."[8] William Binder was equally shaken by this scene. "We could not help a feeling of horror passing through us," he wrote.[9] That night the company had no cooking fires, and every man was placed on guard duty.[10]

Despite these worries, the Martin company saw Indians only occasionally and had no troubles with them. One day they were visited by some Cheyenne Indians, whom William Binder said "appeared friendly and kind."[11] Peter McBride, who was six years old and wrote his account much later, recalled meeting 3,000 Sioux, all in war paint. Although this number is likely exaggerated, the account accurately reflects the company's anxiety and explains one reason the Indians did not bother them:

"Our people were much frightened. Fear held the whole camp

in its grip as they all expected to be annihilated. But [our] fears were groundless. They told our interpreters they were going to fight the Pawnee tribes. They wouldn't hurt us because we were mostly squaws and papooses. It would be cowardly to fight us, so they gave us the road."[12]

George Waugh and the "Aged Advance Guard"

Sixty-eight-year-old George Waugh had served as second counselor to Edward Martin on the *Horizon*. During the voyage across the Atlantic, Father Waugh, as the Saints called him, had walked the ship administering to the sick and afflicted. "On shipboard [he was] lively as a cricket," recalled John Jaques.[13] During the handcart journey, George Waugh continued to look after the disadvantaged, taking charge of the "aged advance guard." John Southwell recalled his daily routine with the company's oldest and most infirm members:

"There were the invalids to be looked after and cared for. An old gentleman 70 years old was elected to this office. He would muster them together, make an early start, and travel them so far as they were able to walk. Those who tired out would fall back to be taken up by some young man and carried to camp on his handcart. . . .

"In his company was one of the worst cripples I ever saw to be a traveler. His lower limbs were paralyzed and his body badly deformed, but he was strong in the faith. He was able to propel himself with surprising speed with the use of crutches."[14]

Josiah Rogerson paints a heroic picture of George Waugh leading his fellow elderly Saints across Nebraska:

"Father George P. Waugh, then between 65 and 70 years of age, would be seen and heard calling between tents for his company to muster between 7 and 7:30 A.M. These consisted of all the aged who [were] not required to pull at the carts. . . .

"Away they would start ahead of [us], singing and talking and cheering each other with the hallowed reminiscences of the early days of the gospel in the British Isles. . . . The oldest and most feeble of this advance guard would be picked up by the wagons as often as possible. . . .

"[After] an hour or two for our noon rest, . . . we were going again. The same aged advance guard [was] ahead of us, with Father Waugh . . . , one of the most devoted Scottish worthies that ever came to Utah."[15]

After caring for so many people for more than six months and 5,000 miles, George Waugh would eventually wear down. John Jaques recalled, "In the latter part of the journey he failed gradually and [then] rapidly until he died on Canyon Creek."[16] Canyon Creek is near Big Mountain, within one or two days of the Salt Lake Valley. George Waugh's body would be carried into Zion in a wagon.

THE CURSE OF THE CORNET

John Jaques called it a cornet. John Southwell called it a bugle. But they were united in their feelings about it. This instrument sounded many times each day, beginning at 5:00 A.M. to call the company to arise and cook breakfast. At 6:00 it sounded again to call everyone to public prayers. At 7:00 it blew to signal the time to take down tents, break camp, and start on the trail. Toward the middle of the day it blew for lunch and then again an hour or so later to resume traveling. Toward the end of the day it blew to halt and make camp. At 8:00 it sounded again for public prayers, and at 10:00 it sounded a final time for the fires to be put out and everyone except the guards to go to bed.

"Oh, that bugle, that awful bugle," recalled John Southwell, as if he could still hear it when he wrote 56 years later in American Falls, Idaho. "How disgusting it was to the poor, weary souls who needed rest. . . . Tired and weary as they were, some of the older people would lie down on their hard beds and almost instantly be in the land of dreams. Then that accursed bugle would blow the call for prayers. Which, I ask, did the poor souls need the most?"[17]

Recollections of the bugle also provoked a blast from John Jaques's normally even-tempered pen:

"The undeviating regularity of all this for so long a time grew to be wearyingly . . . monotonous. How some of the emigrants did long for the time to come when they could be freed from the odious and relentless tyranny of those unfailing cornet calls, and be left to enjoy a little rest and quiet! . . .

"Each cornet call was some well-known air or tune. How hateful those tunes did become! I verily believe . . . that eventually they were abhorrent to every ear in camp. It was a shame to use good and innocent tunes in that way and render them forever after repulsive. . . . There are different ways of murdering music. Those unfortunate tunes are hateful to this day."[18]

GUARDING: "THAT MOST LABORIOUS AND HARASSING DUTY"

"Monday 21st. I went on Guard tonight.

"Tuesday 22nd. I went to guard cattle from 12 midnight till 8 A.M.

"Wednesday 23rd. I went on Guard from 6 P.M. till 12 P.M.

"Thursday 24th. I went on Guard at 6 P.M.

"Friday 25th. I was relieved at 7 this morning.

"Saturday 26th. . . . I went on Guard at 8½ o'clock P.M.

"Sunday 27th. I was relieved at 8½ o'clock A.M. We had Sacrament meeting today.

"Monday 28th. . . . I went on Guard at 9 o'clock.

"Tuesday 29th. Came off Guard at 6 o'clock this morning."[19]

Such were the journal entries for James Bleak for nine consecutive days in Iowa. Three times he was on guard all night. The cumulative effects of the men standing guard at night and then pulling handcarts all day became even more evident as the company crossed Nebraska.

For several months before the first handcart was built, President Franklin D. Richards had frequently explained how traveling by handcart would be preferable to traveling by wagon (see pages 27–29).

One of the main advantages, he said, was less need for guarding at night:

"There being but few animals in a handcart company, there will be less to tempt the cupidity of the Indians. A large share of that most laborious and harassing duty—guarding—can be dispensed with, and the time occupied with sleep and refreshment—with songs of rejoicing and prayer."[20]

Although handcart companies required less guarding than wagon companies, several men still had to watch over the people and their small group of cattle—their milk and meat—every night. And for part of the journey the Martin company was driving an additional herd of young stock, increasing the number of men needed for guarding and nullifying one of the promised benefits of handcart travel.[21] Some of these cattle belonged to Thomas Tennant, the wealthy Englishman who was emigrating with the Hodgetts company.[22] Emigration leaders were apparently trying to take as many cattle as possible to Utah because thousands of animals had died during the previous winter due to severe cold and heavy snow.[23]

Guarding was usually divided into two shifts, the first going until midnight and the second from midnight to 6:00 A.M. The weariness the men experienced from a night on guard was still heavy in the recollection of Josiah Rogerson 50 years later:

"Our night guarding began . . . not later than 6 to 7 P.M. The moment we dropped our cart we had to spring to this arduous duty every other night for six hours. [When assigned the second shift, we were] roused from our quilts by midnight and on guard until 6 A.M., when the oxen and mules were ordered to be brought for yoking and harnessing.

"One of the most trying [problems] that [even] the most hardy and sound of body [had to] endure was six whole nights, straight ahead, guarding one week, [then] pulling the cart every day twenty to twenty-four miles a day, between Kearney and Laramie. The only 'winks' the writer got in this service was from 6 to 7 A.M. while his mother was cooking him a little breakfast."[24]

Guard duty also stood out for John Southwell many years later, who said that after "pushing the horrible cart all day," the necessity of guarding cattle at night "by those poor, weary souls [deprived] us of our much needed rest."[25]

Some have wondered why the mortality rate was higher for the men of the Martin company than for the women. Benjamin Platt, a member of the company who once helped bury nine men in one morning, explained that the burdens of guard duty were a key contributor. "We had to herd at nights and pull handcarts all day," he wrote, "and many times I have been kept up until midnight and then stood guard until morning and then started again [on the trail], and it was this everlasting guarding that killed the people."[26]

Another Tragedy for the Ashton Family

Perhaps the best indication of the Martin company's difficulties between Florence and Fort Laramie was the number of deaths. The Willie company suffered 6 deaths during this 522-mile march. The Martin company suffered 20.[27] The first death occurred on August 26, the day after the company left Florence. It was the second loss for the family of William Ashton.

William and Sarah Ann Ashton had left England with their four daughters, ages 1 through 11, and were expecting another child. Their one-year-old daughter had died in Boston. The day after leaving Florence, Sarah Ann died while giving birth to another daughter.[28] She was buried in an old wagon box, wearing a dark red cashmere dress and wrapped in a white bedspread.[29] Two weeks later, the baby also died.

In less than two months, William Ashton had lost his wife and two of his daughters. He was so despondent that he would soon leave the company at Fort Laramie, enlist in the army, and then return to England. His other three daughters, ages 5, 7, and 11, would continue the journey west without a parent. Members of the Martin company would do their best to care for these girls, but death would strike again before the end of the journey.

TRAGEDY FOR THE LOADER FAMILY

"I cannot stand to be accused of apostasy. I will show them better. . . . I will pull the handcart if I die on the road." These were the words that James Loader spoke to his wife, Amy, when he heard that people thought he was apostatizing because of his family's objections to pulling a handcart.[30]

Those objections seemed reasonable. Because of poor health, Amy Loader had not been able to walk even a mile for years.[31] James Loader was the only man in the family, and at 57 years old he was past his prime physically. He was also a small man, standing only five-foot-three, and not very robust.[32] Nevertheless, when accusations of apostasy reached his ears, he set aside any such worries and chose to prove his faith by pulling a handcart, whatever the cost.

"Father, You Are Not Able to Pull the Cart"

The Loaders were right about the problems they would face. After 100 miles, 22-year-old Tamar became so ill she could no longer walk. Her brother-in-law, John Jaques, pulled her in his handcart the rest of the way to Florence, a distance of 170 miles.[33] By the time the company arrived in Florence, James Loader was also getting weaker and could hardly walk. His daughter Patience recalled:

"My poor dear father's health began to fail him, and before we got to Florence he became very weak and sick. His legs and feet began to swell. Some days he was not able to pull the cart, and when we arrived at Florence we put up the tent, made the bed, and he went to bed. We did not think he could live. [He] said he wished to be administered to, and Brother Richards and three other brethren administered to him . . . and told him that he should get better and continue his journey and get to Salt Lake City. This seemed to give him new strength and courage."[34]

When the company left Florence one or two days after this blessing, James Loader tried to help his daughters pull the handcart. Patience recalled the following exchange:

"I said, 'Father, you are not able to pull this cart today.' He said, 'Yes I am, my dear. I am better. The brethren blessed me and said I should get well and go to the Valley, and I have faith that I shall.' . . .

"That afternoon we had not traveled far when my poor sick father fell down and we had to stop to get him up on his feet. I said, 'Father, you are not able to pull the cart. You had better not try to pull. We girls can do it this afternoon.' He said, 'I can do it. I will try it again. I must not give up. The brethren said I shall be better, and I want to go to the Valley to shake hands with Brigham Young.' So we started on again. We had not traveled far before he fell down again. He was weak and worn down. We got him up again, but we told him he could not pull the cart again that day. So my sister Maria came and worked with me inside the shafts, and Jane and Sarah pulled on the rope until we got into camp."[35]

Early the next morning Zilpah Jaques, the Loaders' daughter who was married to John Jaques, gave birth to a son. Soon after sunrise, Captain Martin came to tell the family to prepare to leave with the rest of the company. Zilpah and her baby lay on quilts on one side of the tent, and Tamar lay on the other, neither of them able to move. "Put them up on the wagon," Captain Martin said, referring to the wagon that carried the sick. Patience asked if one of the sisters could ride with them to help, but Captain Martin denied the request. "[Then] we will stay here for a day or two and take care of our two sick sisters," Patience told him.[36]

Left Behind

The Martin company moved out, leaving the Loader and Jaques families behind. That evening James Loader and John Jaques built a big fire and kept it going all night to keep the wolves away. "I never heard such terrible howling of wolves in my life," Patience recalled.[37] The next morning these families, still weak, packed their handcarts to try to catch up with the company. John Jaques could no longer carry Tamar on his cart because his wife and two small children needed to ride. So Tamar rode on the cart that Patience and her sisters pulled. These women who had been so sure they could not walk across the plains, much less pull a handcart, were learning more each day about what they could really do.

They would have some unexpected help that day in catching up with their company. The fire that had kept the wolves away was so bright that emigration leaders could see it as a nightglow on the sky from the vicinity of Florence. Some of these leaders went to investigate, and one of them was moved by compassion when he saw the condition of this beleaguered family. Historian Wallace Stegner relates:

"William Cluff . . . was so troubled to see the frail father and the women pulling the two sick [women] and two small children that he hitched on with his lariat and gave each of the two handcarts a long boost along the road before he had to ride back. Twenty-two miles from [Florence], at two in the morning, after being threatened by five Indians and frightened by coarse squatters and by the wolves that howled all that moonlit night, this family of the ill and the incompetent caught up with the rest of the company, went to bed on a supper of water gruel, and rose after two or three hours of sleep to tug their carts through another day of Platte valley sand."[38]

"You Know I Love My Children"

James Loader's health improved slightly for the next two or three weeks, but then it began to fail again. On September 23 he walked 17 miles. At camp that night he couldn't even raise himself to go into the tent. The next morning while Patience was preparing him some gruel, she heard an urgent call from the tent:

"My sister Zilpah called, 'Patience, come quick! Our father is dying.' When I got into the tent, my poor mother and all our family [were] kneeling on the ground around him. Poor, dear father, realizing he had to leave us, [was] too weak to talk to us. He looked at us all with tears in his eyes, then he said to mother with great difficulty, 'You know I love my children.' Then he closed his eyes. These were the last words he ever said."[39]

James Loader fell unconscious. A leader in the company said to put him on a sick wagon, but again the family's request to ride on the wagon to care for a loved one was denied. Instead of separating themselves from him, the Loaders carried him on their handcart that day. Patience recalled:

"That was a terrible day never to be forgotten by us, and poor father dying on the handcart. He did not seem to suffer much pain. He never opened his eyes after he closed them in the morning. It was a great comfort to us all that we had him with us on the cart. . . .

"The brethren came to administer to Father in the afternoon. They . . . knew he was dying. They said, 'We will seal Father Loader up to the Lord, for He alone is worthy of him. He has done his work, been a faithful servant in the Church, and we the servants of God seal him unto God, our Father.' To our surprise, my dear father said 'Amen' so plain that we could understand him."[40]

At 11:15 that night, September 24, James Loader passed away, fulfilling his vow that he would pull a handcart even if he died on the road. He had traveled 381 miles—a full month—since those unsteady steps from Florence.

James Loader was buried the next morning. Without time or materials to make a coffin, the family wrapped his body in a quilt. After the Saints sang "The Resurrection Day," the grave was dedicated and the company moved on. Patience recalled the family's grief and hope:

"I will never forget the sound of that dirt being shoveled onto my poor father's body. . . . It did indeed seem a great trial to have to leave our dear father behind that morning, knowing we had looked upon that sweet smiling face for the last time on earth, but not without hope of meeting him again on the morning of the resurrection. . . .

"Brother Daniel Tyler came to us and tried to comfort us by telling us that our father was a faithful, true servant of God. . . . He said father had laid down his life for the gospel's sake. He had died a martyr to the truth. . . . Of course, this was all very comforting to us, but it did not bring our dear father back to us."[41]

James Loader's Tent Pins

As long as James Loader had strength, he would come into camp at night and begin making tent pins. This may seem a small matter, but it reveals much about James Loader. He made the pins because he anticipated the winter storms. Not certain he would live long enough to help his family through them, he did what he could while he was alive. Thus, when he gave his daughters a full bag of tent pins shortly before he died, they knew they were holding evidence of his love—and a good-bye gift. His daughter Patience recalled:

"He said to us girls, 'I have made you lots of tent pins because when the cold weather comes you will not be able to make [them], your hands will be so cold.' By this we knew that he would not live the journey through, and he also grieved to know that mother and we girls would not have anyone to help us make a home or help us to make a living. . . . He had always been a good, kind husband and father."[42]

John Jaques on James Loader

John Jaques, the ever-reliable record keeper, did not record his feelings about his father-in-law's death. He surely loved his father-in-law and mourned his loss, but he records his death in the same documentary tone he used for others in the company: "James Loader, age 57, Aston Rowant Branch, Warwickshire Conference, died of diarrhea at 11 P.M., buried west side of sandhill, 13 miles east of Ash Hollow."[43]

In the reminiscence he wrote 22 years later, John Jaques paid tribute to his father-in-law: "He was confident almost to the last that he should reach 'the valley,' and his chief solicitude was for his wife, who, he feared, would not be able to endure the journey. But she . . . endured it bravely, although it made her a sorrowing widow. She [is] still a widow, for she could never believe there was a man left in the world equal to her husband."[44]

Tragedy for the Barton Family

William Barton had left England with his youngest child from his first marriage, 14-year-old Mary; with his second wife, Mary Ann; and with their two children, Francis (4) and Elizabeth (1). Elizabeth had died near Chicago. Then while crossing Nebraska, both William and Francis became very ill, leaving only Mary Ann and Mary to pull the handcart. Francis rode in the cart, and William hung onto the back for support as he plodded forward. Mary's historical sketch relates her father's decline:

"After dragging on the rear of the handcart for days and nights, one night came when he could only creep. A captain came along and gave him a push with his foot, telling him to get up, not to give up, and to be brave. That night, late in September, just as the guard was calling out the twelve o'clock shift, [father] died."[45]

It was a pathetic scene in the Bartons' tent that night near Chimney Rock, Nebraska, 472 miles from Florence. Mary was doing her best to care for her father as he was dying. Nearby her stepmother was caring for little Francis, who also lay near death. How alone Mary must have felt on that vast prairie. Her mother had died when

Chimney Rock

Mary was a baby, her father was dying beside her, her six older siblings had turned against her when she joined the Church, and she was far from home with so much unknown still ahead. Before the journey's end, the other three men in her tent would die. More trials were to come for this grieving young girl, her stepmother, and her only little sister.

TRIALS FOR THE McBRIDE FAMILY

During the long pull across Nebraska and into Wyoming, both Robert and Margaret McBride became so weak that they had to rely heavily on their two oldest children, Jenetta (16) and Heber (13). The three younger children also looked to their older brother and sister for help. Heber felt overwhelmed as he and Jenetta were suddenly thrust into the role of the family's caretakers:

"Mother being sick and nothing for her comfort, she failed very fast. She would start out in the morning and walk as far as she could. Then she would give out and lie down and wait until we came along. . . . Father [also] began to fail very rapidly and got so reduced that he could not pull any more at the handcart. . . . No tongue or pen could tell what my sister and I passed through, our parents both sick and us so young. . . .

"Sometimes we would find Mother lying by the side of the road first. Then we would get her on the cart and haul her along until we would find Father lying as if he was dead. Then Mother would be rested a little and she would try and walk and Father would get on and ride."[46]

MORE TRIALS FOR THE SERMON FAMILY

"I think I pulled first rate for a new beginner in shafts and harness," Elizabeth Sermon wrote.[47] Not only did she have to pull the handcart but she continued to have to pull along her husband's attitude. When the extra flour was put in the carts at Florence, the children had to walk, which greatly annoyed Joseph and even caused

Elizabeth to wonder. She did not murmur, though, knowing it would only increase her husband's complaints. "I told you how it would be," he said many times.[48]

During the journey across Nebraska, Joseph's health began to fail. "His heart was almost broken," Elizabeth wrote, and "he would say, 'What have you brought us to, you, yourself in the shafts, drawing like a beast of burden, your children hungry and almost naked, myself will soon be gone, and . . . what will become of you and the children? You will find out how true all I have told you is, when it is too late.'"[49]

His words finally began to affect Elizabeth. She began to think about how hungry her family was, a hunger made even more acute by looking all day at the bag of flour in the handcart. She was troubled that her children had to walk while others were riding. Feeling that her first duty was to look after her family, she stopped the cart at noon that day, threw the bag of flour on the ground, and told Captain Martin she would not carry it any farther unless her family could have some.[50]

The family's trials continued to worsen, and Elizabeth continued to bear most of the burden. For a while, when her eight-year-old son and husband were ill, she pulled both of them, her two youngest sons, and the family's belongings, assisted only by a young man and later a young woman. Despite this physical burden, the lack of support from her husband, and other challenges, Elizabeth maintained her hopes of a better life in Zion.

MORE TRIALS FOR THE MELLOR FAMILY

Mary Ann Mellor had been carried onto the ship in Liverpool two days after giving birth to her second consecutive set of twins—conjoined daughters who died within hours. Mary Ann regained some of her strength, but during the handcart journey she often felt like quitting. Her 16-year-old daughter Louisa recalled the following experience that gave her mother both the physical and spiritual strength to continue another day:

"My mother, still being weak, finally gave up and said she could go no further. The company could not wait for her, so she bade my father goodbye and kissed each one of the children Godspeed. Then my mother sat down on a boulder and wept. I told my [14-year-old] sister Elizabeth to take good care of the twins and the rest of the family, and that I would stay with mother.

"I went a few yards away and prayed with faith that God would help us, that He would protect us from devouring wolves, and asked that He would let us reach camp. As I was going back to where Mother was sitting, I found a pie in the road. I picked it up and gave it to mother to eat. After resting awhile we started on our journey, thanking God for the blessings.

"A few miles before we reached camp, we met my father coming out to meet us. We arrived in camp at 10:00 P.M. Many times after that, Mother felt like giving up and quitting, but then she would remember how wonderful the Lord had been to spare her so many times, and offered a prayer of gratitude instead."[51]

PRESIDENT RICHARDS'S REPORT; THE RESCUE BEGINS

While the Martin company was toiling across Nebraska, the first three handcart companies were arriving in Salt Lake City. The Ellsworth and McArthur companies arrived on September 26, the Bunker company on October 2. At that point, the handcart plan was being celebrated as a great success; however, the excitement about the plan was muted just two days later.

On October 4 the Martin company passed Scotts Bluff, a prominent landmark in western Nebraska. They had walked 472 miles from Florence but were still 559 miles from their destination. That same day, President Franklin D. Richards and his group reached Salt Lake City. President Richards immediately reported to Brigham Young that there were some 1,300 people still on the trail, hundreds of miles from the Salt Lake Valley.

This report greatly surprised and concerned Brigham Young. According to his own writings, he thought the Bunker company was

Brigham Young

the last on the trail.[52] As a result, no substantial effort had been made
to resupply any other companies. After hearing this report, he knew
the people would need more food to survive the journey. He also
knew they would need warm clothing and bedding to protect them
from the elements.

Brigham Young responded to this problem with great urgency.
When general conference convened the next day, he made the rescue
of the handcart companies the theme. Using his most powerful rhetoric, he called for immediate action. He asked bishops to assemble
mule teams and wagons—that day. On the next day of the conference, he called for volunteers to come to the stand during the meeting and be on their way the next morning, not "next week, or in ten
days, or in a fortnight hence."[53]

On October 7, the first team of rescuers left the Salt Lake Valley.
Led by Captain George D. Grant, this group consisted of 27 men
and 16 wagons.[54] Six of the men, including Captain Grant and
Brigham Young's son Joseph, had been home for only three days
since returning from their missions with President Franklin D.
Richards.[55]

CHAPTER 27

From Fort Laramie to the Last Crossing of the Platte River

The Martin company arrived at Fort Laramie on October 8, having walked 522 miles in 45 days from Florence, an average of 11.6 miles a day. Like the Willie company, they had brought a 60-day supply of flour from Florence.[1] By the time they reached Fort Laramie, the halfway point between Florence and Salt Lake City, they had consumed three-fourths of their rations.

Like the Willie company, the Martin company hoped to find resupply wagons at Fort Laramie. However, because no substantial resupply effort was initiated until President Richards reported to Brigham Young four days earlier, the only supplies headed toward them were on the wagons of the first rescue team. This team was only one day into the journey from Salt Lake City—and still 500 miles away.[2]

Departure from Fort Laramie; Food Rations Reduced

Running out of food, members of the Martin company sold their watches and anything else of value to buy what they could at Fort Laramie. The prices were high, so they obtained only small amounts. They left Fort Laramie on October 10. Describing that day, John Jaques wrote:

"Laramie Peak, in the distance, gave the first adequate idea of the Rocky Mountains—grand, gloomy, and mysterious. . . .

"Up to this time the daily pound of flour ration had been regularly served out, but it was never enough to stay the stomachs of the emigrants, and the longer they were on the plains and in the mountains the hungrier they grew. . . . It [was] an appetite that could not be satisfied. . . . You feel as if you could almost eat a rusty nail or gnaw a file. You are ten times as hungry as a hunter, yes, as ten hunters, all the day long and every time you wake in the night. . . . Eating is the grand passion of the pedestrian on the plains, an insatiable passion, for he never gets enough to eat. . . .

"Soon after Fort Laramie was passed, it was deemed advisable to curtail the rations in order to make them hold out as long as possible. The pound of flour fell to three-fourths of a pound, then to a half pound, and subsequently yet lower. . . . As the necessities of man and beast increased, their daily food diminished."

"Near Fort Laramie one of [the company], after having eaten his supper one night, took a stroll through the camp of one of the wagon companies nearby, where an acquaintance and friend kindly asked him to have some supper. With thanks he thought he would. So he sat down with the wagon people and did full justice to some fried beef and bacon, with biscuit, which he thought was as savory a dish as he had tasted for many a day. After eating as long as he could put on a face to do so, he finished his second supper, but without feeling much more satisfied than when he first sat down. If anybody else had kindly extended to him another invitation to supper that night, I have no doubt he would have accepted gladly and done full justice to the supper."[3]

Like John Jaques, 12-year-old John Bond of the Hodgetts wagon company saw ominous signs, especially for the ill-equipped Martin company, as he looked toward Laramie Peak:

"The wind is blowing hard and snow is seen on the Laramie Peak in the distance, giving every indication that a storm is near at hand. The wolves are following [us], making their monotonous howling, a hideous sound to the ears from all directions. These snow-capped peaks bring much alarm for fear of the suffering of the [Martin company]. Their bed clothing is badly worn from lying on the campground, and it is now getting damp and cold to lie on. Their wearing apparel is in very bad condition, and their toes are protruding from worn out shoes. It is a shocking and heart-aching sight to see them with their skeleton-like and emaciated forms, the tears rolling down their sunburned cheeks. God pity them; he knows of their wounded and aching hearts."[4]

John Bond was moved by the compassion that members of the Martin company showed for each other. After pulling into camp, they would be ready to drop from exhaustion, too weary to raise their tents. But even in that condition, when they discovered that members of their company were missing, they would go back and search for them. Often they would find them sitting "by the roadside where the large gray wolves were howling," too worn down to walk another step. The friends would "tenderly lift them on their carts and carry them back to camp, as none but tender-hearted brothers and sisters could do in their dark trial. Such devotion is beyond my comprehension."[5] Sometimes these searchers would have to backtrack many miles before finding those who were left behind, returning to camp at midnight or later.[6]

There was not enough help to go around for everyone, however. A sense of abandonment is evident in the recollection of 13-year-old Heber McBride. Both of his parents were so weak that they had to trade off riding in the handcart, pulled only by Heber and his 16-year-old sister, Jenetta. Three younger siblings also needed caring for, including a 3-year-old sister who rode in the cart. The weight of this responsibility often brought Heber and Jenetta to tears. "We used to cry and feel so bad," Heber recalled. "We did not know what to do. We would never get into camp until way after dark, and then we would have to hunt something to make a fire."[7]

MORE WEAKNESS AND EXHAUSTION

Already weak before their rations were reduced, members of the Martin company began to fail more rapidly after leaving Fort Laramie. Describing their condition, John Bond wrote: "The handcart Saints lie down on the way, getting more exhausted. . . . All ambition and life seems to be leaving them as it was not possible to pull and tug at their carts day after day with the food allowance they had. They were continually asking and begging their captains for more bread to keep their children and themselves from death."[8]

On October 14, four days after leaving Fort Laramie and halfway to the last crossing of the Platte, John Jaques finally began to break down. He had pulled his sister-in-law in his handcart for 170 miles in Iowa. After his wife had a baby in August, he had pulled her on the cart for more than 100 miles in Nebraska. He was exhausted from caring for his wife; his sick two-year-old daughter; his baby son; his wife's family, who had been without a man since his father-in-law died three weeks earlier; and the hundred members of the handcart company over whom he was subcaptain.

The company traveled a hilly, heavy road that day. John's legs swelled, he was short of breath, and he could hardly walk. Where would help come from? His wife, Zilpah, seemed an unlikely source. Not only had she recently given birth but her health had always been frail. Moreover, she was nursing her baby while she herself had scarcely enough to eat. "It seemed to her that [her baby] was taking her own life from her," wrote her sister Patience Loader.[9] Yet that day, Zilpah stepped inside the shafts of the handcart and pulled beside her husband. That night John wrote in his journal with appreciation and perhaps some feeling of personal failure, "Zilpah pulled the cart with me nearly all day."[10]

In this precarious condition the Jaques family would face the first winter storm, only five days away.

CHAPTER 28

LAST CROSSING OF
THE PLATTE RIVER

When thou passest through the waters, I will be with thee; and through the rivers, they shall not overflow thee.

—ISAIAH 43:2

On October 17, a week after leaving Fort Laramie, the Martin company arrived at Deer Creek (present-day Glenrock, Wyoming). The company traveled 98 miles that week, and the people and teams were getting weaker due to lack of food. To make the carts easier to pull, baggage was reduced from 17 to 10 pounds for each adult and 5 pounds for children under 8. John Jaques wrote that "good blankets and other clothing were burned as they could not be carried further, though [they were later] needed more badly than ever, for there was yet 400 miles of winter to go through."[1] William Binder's journal entry for the day shows how much these Saints depended on and deferred to their leaders, obeying them even when they disagreed:

"This action of the Elders in charge seemed to us a terrible hardship, as we were only very scantily provided with clothes and bedding, and to stand by and see our bits of clothing and bedding burned on the spot caused anything but a good feeling to exist in our hearts towards our leaders."[2]

During the western migration, travelers had to make a final crossing of the Platte River in the area of present-day Casper, Wyoming. There were several places in a distance of about 16 miles where the crossing could be made. At various times, bridges were built and ferries were established to assist with the crossing. When the companies of 1856 came through, however, ferries were no longer operating. The only bridge was located about five miles east of Casper, in present-day Evansville. It had been built by a French-Canadian named Jean Baptiste Richard (pronounced *Reshaw*) and was called Reshaw's Bridge, Richard's Bridge, or the Platte Bridge.

The bridge was the easiest way for the companies of 1856 to cross the river, but few had the money to pay the toll. As a result, most of them had to ford the river on foot. Even in the best of circumstances, river crossings could be difficult. Captain Edmund Ellsworth of the first handcart company, which had crossed the Platte weeks earlier when the weather was good, reported:

"When we came to the large streams that had to be crossed, such as the Platte, it seemed almost too much for human nature, . . . and some would tremble at it."[3]

The Martin and Hodgetts companies faced the last crossing of the Platte on October 19. They selected a place a few miles west of the bridge and plunged into the river. What would have been difficult in good weather became deadly as the first winter storm arrived partway through the day. President Gordon B. Hinckley described the scene:

The Platte River near the area of the last crossing

"The river was wide, the current strong. . . . Bravely they waded through [it]. A terrible storm arose with fierce winds bringing drifting sand, hail, and snow. When they climbed the far bank of the river, their wet clothing froze to their bodies. Exhausted, freezing, and without strength to go on, some quietly sat down, and while they sat, they died."[4]

Josiah Rogerson later wrote, "The crossing of the North Platte was fraught with more fatalities than any other incident of the entire journey."[5] Fourteen people died that night and the next day.[6]

Some of the people who died had used the last of their strength carrying others across the river. Many in the company were too old, too weak, or too small to cross on their own. Some of them were taken across in wagons, but most had to be carried. Although Robert McBride was one of the people needing help, his son Peter recalled that he "worked all day pulling, pushing, wading through the icy river, and he made about twenty-five trips across the river helping to get all the carts across."[7] Robert collapsed soon afterward.

Young John Bond especially noticed the service of John Latey, George Haines, and George Dove (age 14) of the Hodgetts company and Thomas Franklin of the Martin company. He admired these men not only for their courage in helping others across the river but also for their devotion to "giving them every care."[8] Some of the women also helped. Nineteen-year-old Sarah Ann Haigh reportedly carried 16 people across the river.[9]

These sacrifices made at the last crossing of the Platte River are not as well chronicled as those that would be made by the rescuers at the Sweetwater two weeks later, but they were just as heroic. The Platte was wider and swifter, and the elements that day were severe. Having been on short rations, those who assisted at the Platte were generally weaker than those who would assist at the Sweetwater.

After crossing the river, many were wet from head to foot. With the wind beating snow onto their tattered clothing, they could not get dry or warm. Everyone looked "quite wretched," John Bond recalled. "Their clothing was like icicles."[10]

This early winter storm of October 19, the first of several successive storms, is the same one that was afflicting the Willie company between the Fifth and Sixth Crossings of the Sweetwater, approximately 100 miles to the west. The express members of the rescue team met the Willie company on this day; it would be another nine deadly, miserable days before they reached the Martin company.

After being a little behind the Martin and Hodgetts companies since leaving Iowa City, the Hunt wagon company caught up with them just as the Hodgetts company finished crossing the Platte. The Hunt company crossed three days later, traveled one mile, and established the camp where they would later be found by the rescuers.[11]

JOHN JAQUES'S ACCOUNT OF THE LAST CROSSING OF THE PLATTE

John Jaques had been struggling for some time before the last crossing of the Platte. Five days earlier his legs had been so swollen that he could hardly walk. But his description of the last crossing does not make any reference to his own problems:

"That was a bitter cold day. Winter came on all at once, and that was the first day of it. The river was wide, the current strong, the water exceedingly cold and up to the wagon beds in the deepest parts, and the bed of the river was covered with cobble stones. Some of the men carried some of the women over on their backs or in their arms, but others of the women tied up their skirts and waded through, like heroines as they were, and as they had done through many other rivers and creeks. The company was barely over when snow, hail, and sleet began to fall, accompanied by a piercing north wind. . . . That was a stinging night, and it told its tale on the oxen as well as the people."[12]

TRIALS OF THE JACKSONS AT THE LAST CROSSING

"How the Dreary Hours Drew Their Tedious Length Along"

Aaron and Elizabeth Jackson were emigrating with their three children ages 2, 4, and 7. Aaron became seriously ill during the trek, and the last crossing of the Platte brought on tragedy for this young family. Elizabeth recalled:

"My husband attempted to ford the stream. He had only gone a short distance when he reached a sand bar in the river, on which he sank down through weakness and exhaustion. My sister, Mary Horrocks Leavitt, waded through the water to his assistance. She raised him up to his feet. Shortly afterward, a man came along on horseback and conveyed him to the other side of the river, placed him on the bank, and left him there. My sister then helped me to pull my cart with my three children and other matters on it. We had scarcely crossed the river when we were visited with a tremendous storm of snow, hail, sand, and fierce winds."[13]

After the crossing, Aaron Jackson was carried to camp because he was unable to walk. Soon afterward he was "still sinking." His wife continues:

"His condition now became more serious. . . . I prepared a little of such scant articles of food as we then had. He tried to eat but failed. He had not the strength to swallow. I put him to bed as quickly as I could. He seemed to rest easy and fell asleep. About nine o'clock I retired. Bedding had become very scarce, so I did not disrobe. I slept until, as it appeared to me, about midnight. I was extremely cold. The weather was bitter. I listened to hear if my husband breathed—he lay so still. I could not hear him. I became alarmed. I put my hand on his body, when to my horror I discovered that my worst fears were confirmed. My husband was *dead*. He was cold and stiff—rigid in the arms of death. It was a bitter freezing night, and the elements had sealed up his mortal frame.

"I called for help to the other inmates of the tent. They could render me no aid; and there was no alternative but to remain alone by the side of the corpse till morning. . . . Of course I could not sleep. I could only watch, wait, and pray for dawn. But oh, how the dreary hours drew their tedious length along.

"When daylight came, some of the male part of the company prepared the body for burial. And oh, such a burial and funeral service. They did not remove his clothing—he had but little. They wrapped him in a blanket and placed him in a pile with thirteen others who had died, and then covered him up in the snow. The ground was frozen so hard that they could not dig a grave. He was left there to sleep in peace until the trump of God shall sound, and the dead in Christ shall awake and come forth in the morning of the first resurrection. We shall then again unite our hearts and lives, and eternity will furnish us with life forever more.

"I will not attempt to describe my feelings at finding myself thus left a widow with three children, under such excruciating circumstances. I cannot do it. But I believe the Recording Angel has inscribed in the archives above, and that my sufferings for the Gospel's sake will be sanctified unto me for my good."[14]

Josiah Rogerson's Account of Aaron Jackson's Death

Josiah Rogerson, who as a 15-year-old was assigned guard duty on that bitter night, described the painful events that attended the Jackson family at the last crossing and the night afterward:

"Aaron Jackson . . . was found so weak and exhausted when he came to the crossing of the North Platte, October 19, that he could not make it, and after he was carried across the ford in a wagon [I] was again detailed to wheel the dying Aaron on an empty cart, with his feet dangling over the end bar, to camp. After putting up his tent, I assisted his wife in laying him in his blankets.

"It was one of the bitter cold, blackfrost nights, . . . and notwithstanding the hard journey the day before, I was awakened at midnight to go on guard again till 6 or 7 in the morning.

"Putting jacket or coat on (for both sexes had for weeks past lain down at night in the clothing we had traveled in during the day), and passing out through the middle of the tent, my feet struck those of poor Aaron. They were stiff and rebounded at my accidental stumbling. Reaching my hand to his face, I found that he was dead, with his exhausted wife and little ones by his side, all sound asleep. The faithful and good man Aaron had pulled his last cart. . . .

"Returning to my tent from the night's guarding, I found there one of the most touching pictures of grief and bereavement in the annals of our journey. Mrs. Jackson, apparently just awakened from her slumber, was sitting by the side of her dead husband. Her face was suffused in tears, and between her bursts of grief and wails of sorrow, she would wring her hands and tear her hair. Her children blended their cries of 'Father' with that of the mother. This was love; this was affection—grief of the heart and bereavement of the soul— the like of which I have never seen since."[15]

PATIENCE LOADER'S ACCOUNT OF THE LAST CROSSING

James Loader had died nearly a month before the last crossing of the Platte, leaving his wife, five daughters, and 10-year-old son to endure the most difficult part of the trek on their own. Telling of the family's trials on October 19, his daughter Patience wrote:

"We came to the last crossing of the Platte River. [We] had orders from Captain Edward Martin to cross the river that afternoon and evening. . . . We started to cross the river and pull our own cart. The water was deep and very cold, and we were drifted out of the regular crossing and we came near to being drowned. The water came up to our armpits. Poor mother was standing on the bank screaming. As we got near the bank I heard [her] say, 'For God's sake, some of you men help my poor girls.' Mother said she had been watching us and could see we were drifting down the stream. Several of the brethren came down the bank of the river and pulled our cart up for us, and we got up the best way we could. . . .

"When we were in the middle of the river, I saw a poor man carrying his child on his back. He fell down in the water. I never knew if he was drowned or not. I felt sorry that we could not help him, but we had all we could do to save ourselves from drowning. . . .

"We had to travel in our wet clothes until we got to camp. Our clothing was frozen on us, and when we got to camp we had but very little dry clothing to put on. We had to make the best of our poor circumstances and put our trust in God our Father that we may take no harm from our wet clothes. It was too late to go for wood and water. The wood was too far away. That night the ground was frozen so hard we were unable to drive any tent pins and the tent was wet. When we [had taken] it down in the morning it was somewhat frozen, so we stretched it open the best we could and got in under it until morning."[16]

TRIALS OF THE SERMON FAMILY AT THE LAST CROSSING

After leading her family through countless adversities, Elizabeth Sermon had to dig even deeper into her spiritual reserves as the weather turned colder and the Platte had to be crossed one last time:

"Our food was giving out, our bodies growing weak. Cold weather chilled the body. . . . The dead and dying [were] all around us. [The] poor souls would sit down by the roadside. It was not often they moved again until carried into camp by handcarts or by some kind-hearted person. . . . It was a miracle any of us lived."[17]

Continuing her recollections of the journey in a letter to her children, Elizabeth wrote:

"It was after wading a very wide river [that] the freezing commenced. We had no wood, only sagebrush. I went out and cut the sage to keep the fire all night, covering you all with your feet to the fire and [your] heads covered over, and then I went out and cut more sagebrush and kept the fire as well as I could—my clothes frozen stiff like starched clothing. Well, we got through that night.

"Next day we moved on our way again, painful and slow. Your father could hardly walk now. . . . [He] would take my arm, walk a little distance, fall on his knees with weakness, then try again."[18]

TRIALS OF THE PUCELL FAMILY AT THE LAST CROSSING

Samuel and Margaret Pucell were some of the earliest converts in England and were finally emigrating after 19 years. Of the five children they brought to America, the three oldest stayed in Boston. Only their two youngest daughters, ages 14 and 9, made the trek with them. President Gordon B. Hinckley described what happened as this family approached and then crossed the Platte for the last time:

"Margaret became sick. Her husband lifted her onto the cart. They were now climbing in elevation toward the Continental Divide, and it was uphill all the way. Can you see this family in your imagination?—the mother too sick and weak to walk, the father thin and emaciated, struggling to pull the cart, as the two little girls push from behind with swirling, cold winds about them, and around them are hundreds of others similarly struggling.

"They came to a stream of freezing water. The father, while crossing, slipped on a rock and fell. Struggling to his feet, he reached the shore, wet and chilled. Sometime later he sat down to rest. He quietly died, his senses numbed by the cold. His wife died five days later. I do not know how or where their frozen bodies were buried in that desolate, white wilderness. I do know that the ground was frozen and that the snow was piled in drifts and that the two little girls were now orphans."[19]

MORE DIFFICULTIES FOR THE MELLOR FAMILY

Despite illness, discouragement, and homesickness, Mary Ann Mellor continued the journey, often riding in the handcart. She was sustained by her husband and strong teenage daughters, Louisa and Charlotte Elizabeth. Describing the physical condition of the family, Louisa wrote:

"We were so fatigued and hungry that we would sometimes stop and get rawhide to chew on, as our food was diminished. We tried to keep a little flour as long as we could to make porridge for the children; at first it was biscuits; then pancakes; then porridge. Often we would cook a hide, or a piece of it, to get a little strength; it being winter, we could not find weeds to help out."[20]

Mary Ann's 14-year-old daughter Charlotte Elizabeth described the last crossing of the Platte as follows:

"On entering the water, our first impulse was to turn back and not wade across. The water was so cold that it sent pains right to the bone and the muscles cramped. We steadied ourselves as we held on to the cart and pushed. Father pulled. By the time we got across, our limbs were so numb that we could hardly keep from falling as we trudged along. The north wind cut like a sharp knife."[21]

TRIALS OF THE GOBLE FAMILY: "THAT WAS THE LAST WALK I EVER HAD WITH MY MOTHER"

William and Mary Goble were traveling with the Hunt wagon company, which arrived at the last crossing right after the Martin and Hodgetts companies. Their 2-year-old daughter had died in Iowa City, and another daughter had been born during the journey across Nebraska. Their oldest daughter, 13-year-old Mary, had the following recollection of crossing the Platte for the last time:

"We traveled on till we got to the Platte River. That was the last walk I ever had with my mother. We caught up with the handcart compan[y] that day. We watched them cross the river. . . . It was bitter cold. The next morning there were fourteen dead in camp through the cold. We went back to camp and went to prayers. We sang the song 'Come, Come, Ye Saints, No Toil Nor Labor Fear.' "[22]

Although Mary's mother did not die that day, she apparently became so ill that she was unable to walk again. Mary did all she could to attend to her mother's needs:

"We had been without [fresh] water for several days, just drinking snow water. The captain said there was a spring of fresh water just a few miles away. It was snowing hard, but my mother begged me to go and get her a drink. Another lady went with me.

"We were about halfway to the spring when we found an old

man who had fallen in the snow. He was frozen so stiff we could not lift him, so the lady told me where to go and she would go back to camp for help, for we knew he would soon be frozen if we left him.

"When she had gone, I began to think of the Indians and looking in all directions. I became confused and forgot the way I should go. I waded around in the snow up to my knees and I became lost. Later when I did not return to camp, the men started out after me. It was 11:00 o'clock before they found me. My feet and legs were frozen. They carried me to camp and rubbed me with snow. They put my feet in a bucket of water. The pain was so terrible. The frost came out of my legs and feet but not out of my toes."[23]

CHAPTER 29

SNOWBOUND AT RED BUTTES

As a boy of 16 . . . , my experience cannot be compared with fathers of families, whose heart strings were fretted and jarred when perchance a boy of six years with his big blue eyes filled with tears asked for bread.

—ALBERT JONES

The first storm raged for three days. Fighting through it, the Hodgetts wagon company traveled 10 miles to Red Buttes on October 20, the day after the last crossing of the Platte. Slowed by weather, weakness, and burials, the Martin company took four days to travel those 10 miles, finally arriving on October 23.[1] Recalling the difficulty of pulling their handcarts through the storm, William Binder wrote, "The whole of our day's march [we faced] a bitterly keen wind and drifting snow."[2]

After following the Platte River for hundreds of miles, the trail leaves it soon after the last crossing. One strand of the trail leaves the river almost immediately after the crossing, and another strand—the one the Martin company was following—leaves it near Red Buttes. From there, companies had to make a 40-mile overland drive to the next reliable water source, the Sweetwater River. These 40 miles were some of the most difficult of the trail, crossing arduous, barren terrain with only occasional water. Too weak to face this prospect, the Martin company would be mired in the Red Buttes camp for six days, the Hodgetts company for nine.

Tragedy for the Martin company did not start at Martin's Cove. In many ways the 11 days from the last crossing of the Platte to the end of the Red Buttes camp on October 29 were even more trying than the camp at Martin's Cove from November 4 to 9. Physical assistance from the rescuers was not available at Red Buttes but was at Martin's Cove. Hope was perhaps more tenuous at the Red Buttes camp because not even the express rescuers arrived until the end of it. Daily flour rations fell to four ounces during most or all of the Red Buttes camp—a longer period than at Martin's Cove. And at least 56 people died during these 11 days, more than are estimated to have died at Martin's Cove. William Binder described the march of death at Red Buttes:

"During our sojourn at this camp . . . it became our painful duty to bury very many of our friends and traveling companions, also to see our cattle vanish from our view through starvation every day."[3]

The Red Buttes camp was located below some distinctive red bluffs on a bend of the Platte River. Today this area is also known as Bessemer Bend. A park and a historical marker are located at Bessemer Bend, about 10 miles east of Casper on Highway 220. The park and marker are about two miles from the highway.

On October 21, two days after the Martin company's last crossing of the Platte, the first rescue team reached the Willie company on the

Platte River near the Red Buttes camp

Sweetwater River, 100 miles to the west. By the time the Martin company left Red Buttes on October 29, the rescuers who stayed with the Willie company had helped them cross Rocky Ridge, bury 15 people at Rock Creek, and continue on to the Big Sandy crossing, putting them 175 miles ahead of the Martin company.

Trials of the McBride Family

Robert and Margaret McBride both became so sick after leaving Florence that their two oldest children, Jenetta (16) and Heber (13), carried most of the responsibility for the family. Often they pulled one of their parents in the handcart. At the last crossing of the Platte River, when Robert McBride needed to receive help himself, he made some 25 trips across the river to give help.[4] This service cost Robert McBride his life. His son Heber recalled the events of the next two days, climaxing with the heartbreak of finding his father's body covered with snow:

"There were about 6 inches of snow on the ground, and then what we had to suffer can never be told. Father was very bad [the] morning [after the last crossing] and could hardly sit up in the tent, but we had to travel that day through the snow. I managed to get Father into one of the wagons that morning, and that was the last we saw of him alive. We only made one drive, as it began snowing very hard. When we camped, the snow was getting very deep. My sister and I had to pitch our tent and get some wood. . . .

"After we had made Mother as comfortable as we could, we went to try and find Father. The wind was blowing the snow so bad that we could not see anything, and the wagons had not [yet come] into camp. It was then after dark, so we did not find him that night.

"The next morning the snow was about 18 inches deep and awfully cold. While my sister was preparing our little bite of breakfast, I went to look for Father. At last I found him under a wagon with snow all over him. He was stiff and dead. I felt as though my heart would burst. I sat down beside him on the snow and took hold of one of his hands and cried, 'Oh, Father, Father!' There we were, away out on the plains, with hardly anything to eat, Father dead, and Mother sick and a widow with five small children, and not hardly able to live from one day to another."[5]

After finding his father's body, Heber, the 13-year-old boy who was suddenly the man of the family, had to break the news to his mother and siblings:

"After I had my cry out, I went back to the tent and told Mother. To try to write the feelings of Mother and the other children is out of the question. Now, we were not [the only] family that was called upon to mourn the loss of a Father this morning, for there were 13 men dead in camp."[6]

Robert McBride was buried in a common grave with the others who had died. Writing of the burial, Heber McBride recalled:

"The men who were able to do anything cleaned off the snow and made a fire and thawed out the ground and dug a big hole and buried them all in one grave, some side by side and on top of one another—any way to get them covered—for I can assure you that the men had no heart to do any more than they had to.

"We never knew how Father died—whether he died in the wagon and was lifted out or he got out himself and fell down exhausted and froze to death."[7]

Because Margaret McBride continued to suffer poor health after her husband died, her children Jenetta and Heber continued to be the family's main caretakers. The sacrifices of 16-year-old Jenetta were burned into the memory of her 6-year-old brother, Peter, who later wrote:

"My mother was sick all the way over, and my sister Jenetta had the worry of us children. She carried water from the river to do the cooking. Her shoes gave out, and she walked through the snow barefoot, actually leaving bloody tracks in the snow."[8]

Peter McBride had the following additional recollections of the camp at Red Buttes:

"We camped at the [Platte] River. A meeting was held. It was decided that we could go no further, the snow so deep and no food. We were doomed to starvation. They gave me a bone of an ox that had died. I cut off the skin and put the bone in the fire to roast. And when it was done some big boys came and ran away with it. Then I took the skin and boiled it, drank the soup, and ate the skin, and it was a good supper.

"The next day we had nothing to eat but some bark from trees. Later we had a terrible cold spell [and] I knew I would die. The wind blew the tent down. They all crawled out but me. The snow fell on it. I went to sleep and slept warm all night. In the morning I heard someone say, 'How many are dead in this tent?' My sister said, 'Well, my little brother must be frozen to death in that tent.' So they jerked the tent loose, sent it scurrying over the snow. My hair was frozen to the tent. I picked myself up and came out quite alive, to their surprise."[9]

Like Peter, Heber McBride recalled the desperate efforts to satisfy their hunger when flour was reduced to four ounces at Red Buttes: "I don't know how many days we had to lay over. The snow was so deep that we could not pull our handcarts through, and there we were in a starving condition, and the oxen that pulled the wagons began dying. [The oxen] that died were devoured very quickly, and us little boys would get strips of rawhide and try and eat it all. The [only] way we could do anything with it was to crisp it in the fire and then draw a string of it through our teeth and get some of the burnt scales off that way and then crisp it again and repeat the operation until we would get tired."[10]

PATIENCE LOADER'S ACCOUNT

Unable to set up their tent after the last crossing of the Platte River, the Loader family had stretched it out on top of themselves for the night. Patience Loader tells of the difficulties the family faced during the next day or two and of their loving efforts to care for a dying man:

"It snowed and drifted and the wind blew all day. . . . After we got to camp, we found we had to go a long way . . . for wood, so my sister Maria and myself went with the brethren to get the wood. We had to travel in the snow knee deep for nearly a mile to the cedars. We found nothing but green cedar, as all the dry wood on the ground was covered with snow. I asked one of the brethren to cut me down a shoulder stick, so he kindly gave us quite a large, heavy log. My sister took one end on her shoulder, and I raised the other end onto my shoulder and started back to camp. We had not gone very far when we both fell down with our load. The snow being so deep made it very hard work for us to get back to camp with our load, but after much hard work we got there. My mother and sisters were anxiously waiting our return, for they were both hungry and cold. . . .

"As soon as I could get some wood chopped, I tried to make a fire to make a little broth, as I had an old beef head. I was always on the lookout for anything I could get to eat, not only for myself but for the rest of the family. We got off the skin from the beef head, chopped it in pieces the best I could, put it into the pot with some snow, and boiled [it] for a long time. About four o'clock in the afternoon we were able to have some of this fine made broth. I cannot say that it tasted very good. It was flavored both with sagebrush and from the smoky fire from our green cedar fire. [But] after it was cooked we all enjoyed it and felt very thankful to have that much. . . .

"We [girls] had drunk our broth, [and] mother was still drinking hers [when] the captain of the company came with two other brethren and fetched poor Brother John Laurey to our tent. Since our father died, this brother had stayed in our tent as he had no friends with him. . . . Brother Toone said to mother, 'Give him something warm.' Mother said, 'I have a little hot soup Patience made for us. I will share with him.' . . . We tried to give him a little [soup] with a teaspoon, but could not get the spoon between his teeth. Poor dear man, he looked at us but could not speak a word. He was nearly dead frozen. [When] it got dark, we wrapped him up the best we could to try to get him warm, but he was too far gone.

"We all laid down to try to get warm in our quilts the best we could. . . . Poor man, he had only one old blanket to wrap himself in, and we had a burlap robe [which we put] over him. After we were in bed, it was a dark and lonesome night. He commenced to talk to himself. He called for his wife and children. He had told me previously that he had a wife and nine children in London and that they would come out as soon as he could make enough money to send for them. . . .

"In the night we could not hear him talking any more. I said to Mother, 'I think poor brother is dead. I have not heard him for the last hour.' Mother asked me to get up and go to him. I got up, but everything seemed so silent and . . . dark and drear that I said to Mother, 'I cannot go to him.' She said, 'Well, get back in bed and try to get warm and wait until daylight.' Of course, we did not sleep. [As soon as there] was a little light, I got up and went to the poor man and found him dead, frozen to the tent. As I turned him over to look in his face, never can I forget that sight.

"Poor man, I told mother that he was dead. She said, 'Go tell Brother Toone.' I went to his tent and told him. . . . He told me we would have to wrap him in a quilt. I said he has no quilts; he has only one small thin blanket, and we cannot spare any of our quilts as we had already used one to wrap my dear father in when he died. So we wrapped him in his own little blanket, and the brethren came and took him away to bury him with [others who] died during the night. What a deplorable condition we were in."[11]

John Jaques's Account of the Red Buttes Camp

Describing the camp at Red Buttes, John Jaques wrote:

"The company . . . camped again near the Platte at the point where the road left it for the Sweetwater. It snowed three days, and the teams and many of the people were so far given out that it was deemed advisable not to proceed further for a few days. . . . It was hoped that the snow and cold would prove only a foretaste of winter and would soon pass away and the weather would moderate, but that hope proved delusive. . . . In this camp the company stayed, resting and recruiting as well as could be under the circumstances, the snow remaining on the ground and the frost being very keen at nights.

"Here the flour ration fell to four ounces per day. . . . In addition to the flour ration, considerable beef was killed and served to the company, as had been the case most of the journey. But the cattle had now grown so poor that there was little flesh left on them, and that little was as lean as lean could be. The problem was how to cook it to advantage. Stewed meat and soups were found to be bad for diarrhea and dysentery, . . . of which there was considerable in the company."[12]

Four ounces of flour provide 450 calories. A person needs an estimated 4,000 calories per day to pull a handcart. It is no wonder, then, that the Martin company did not move from Red Buttes.

JOHN BOND'S ACCOUNT OF THE RED BUTTES CAMP

Twelve-year-old John Bond and the Hodgetts wagon company were stalled beside the Martin company at Red Buttes. Like the Martin company, the Hodgetts company was low on food and had their rations greatly reduced. John Bond's parents had seven children to feed. John recalled that even before this camp, when the children were "given the short allowances, they beg[ged] for more. It nearly [broke] my parents' hearts to hear their piteous pleadings."[13] John Bond's account of the dark days at Red Buttes includes the following confession as he tried to relieve the grip of his relentless hunger:

"Day after day passes and still no tidings of help coming from the westward. The bugle is sounded again . . . to call all the Saints together for prayers and to ask the infinite Father to bring food, medicines, and other things necessary for the sick and needy. After prayers, all are ordered to bed. I had been to many of the meetings previously, but this time I saw Sister Scott cooking a nice pot of dumplings just before the bugle sounded. She hid the dumplings under the wagon, being a zealous woman, and went to prayer meeting, but I did not go this time. I stood back and looked for the dumplings, found them, and being so hungry I could not resist the temptation, sat down and ate them all. I admit that those dumplings did me more good than all the prayers that could have been offered, but I felt I had done a great wrong in that act, and I regret it and ask God to forgive me for that temptation that overcame me in a time of hunger."[14]

John Bond's account of the Red Buttes camp also includes moving observations of how people died and were laid to rest. Some died "lying side by side with hands entwined, showing the last agonies and suffering of life with a gasp of love and affection, facing each other in death's embrace. . . . In other cases, they were found as if they had just offered a fervent prayer and their spirit had taken flight while in the act. . . . Some died sitting by the fire; some were singing hymns or eating crusts of bread."[15]

Describing the burials, John Bond recalled that after shallow graves were dug, a bugle would sound and men would slowly carry the dead and lay them in the earth. After a hymn and dedicatory prayer, all would "go to their several tents and wagons, tenderly leading the bereft ones to their tents, giving them words of comfort and consolation."[16] Often these services were punctuated by gunshots from Captain Martin, who "stood over the grave of the departed ones with shotgun in hand, firing at intervals to keep the crows and buzzards away from hovering around in mid-air, waiting for the services to close."[17]

ELIZABETH JACKSON'S ACCOUNT OF THE RED BUTTES CAMP

Elizabeth Jackson's husband, Aaron, had died the night after the last crossing of the Platte. The following recollection from Elizabeth was written about the time between the death of her husband and the arrival of the express members of the rescue team, which was when the Martin company was camped at Red Buttes:

"A few days after the death of my husband, the male members of the company had become reduced in number by death; and those who remained were so weak and emaciated by sickness that on reaching the camping place at night, there were not sufficient men with strength enough to raise the poles and pitch the tents. The result was that we camped out with nothing but the vault of Heaven for a roof and the stars for companions. The snow lay several inches deep upon the ground. The night was bitterly cold. I sat down on a rock with one child in my lap and one on each side of me. In that condition I remained until morning."[18]

Widowed, camped in miserable conditions, and unable to protect or provide for her three young children, Elizabeth was at the point of despair. Then at her time of greatest need, she received divine help. She wrote:

"It will be readily perceived that under such adverse circumstances I had become despondent. I was six or seven thousand miles from my native land, in a wild, rocky, mountain country, in a destitute condition, the ground covered with snow, the waters covered with ice, and I with three fatherless children with scarcely nothing to protect them from the merciless storms. When I retired to bed that night, being the 27th of October, I had a stunning revelation. In my dream, my husband stood by me and said—'Cheer up, Elizabeth, deliverance is at hand.'"[19]

CHAPTER 30

THE RESCUERS ARRIVE

There is no more heroic episode in all of our history.

—PRESIDENT GORDON B. HINCKLEY

The first rescue team of 27 men and 16 wagons had left Salt Lake City on October 7 and received small reinforcements along the way. Four express rescuers from this team found the Willie company near the Ice Slough on October 19, the day of the first winter storm. Captain George D. Grant and the rest of the rescue team met up with the Willie company late on October 21.

The express rescuers had stayed only briefly with the Willie company on the 19th, leaving them with the hopeful word that the rest of their team would arrive in a day or two with supplies. The express riders then hurried forward to find the Martin, Hodgetts, and Hunt companies. Traveling through the storm, they needed three days to cover the 45 miles to Devil's Gate, arriving on October 22. Franklin D. Richards had thought the Martin company would be at least as far as Devil's Gate, but the rescuers found no sign of them. Rather than continue eastward, they stopped and waited for the rest of their team, as Captain Grant had instructed them to do.[1]

Five miles west of Independence Rock, Devil's Gate is a well-known landmark of the trail. Here the Sweetwater River flows between rock walls nearly 400 feet high.

Devil's Gate was the site of an abandoned trading post known as Fort Seminoe (not Seminole). At the time it consisted of a few cabins and

Devil's Gate

a small stockade. Because the fort was unoccupied in 1856, the rescuers used it as their headquarters.

Fort Seminoe was originally built in 1852 by two French-Canadian brothers, Charles and Basil Lajuenesse. One of these brothers had the nickname of Seminoe; hence, the fort's name. It was quite successful for a couple of years, being located on the trail where thousands of people came through. In 1853 the military closed down the trading business and took possession of the fort, saying it could no longer guarantee safety from Indian uprisings. The original fort burned in about 1857. Latter-day Saint missionary couples have constructed a replica of the fort near the original site.

The area around Devil's Gate was settled by Tom Sun in 1872 and was called the Sun Ranch. The ranch remained in the Sun family for several generations, and during that time it was necessary to cross ranch property to reach Martin's Cove. In 1996 the Church purchased part of the ranch, including the portion that would allow access to Martin's Cove. The ranch house has been converted into a visitors' center, with Devil's Gate rising dramatically in the background. The Martin's Cove pioneer trek reenactments begin here.

The express rescuers waited at Devil's Gate for four days before Captain Grant and the rest of their team arrived on October 26.[2] Because some of Captain Grant's team had stayed to help the Willie company and some had stayed with Reddick Allred near South Pass, there were perhaps as few as 16 to 20 men and 8 to 10 wagons at Devil's Gate. These rescuers had been on the trail for four weeks— longer than expected—and were running short of feed for their animals. They were traveling blindly, with no knowledge of the location or condition of the Martin, Hodgetts, and Hunt companies. Perhaps these groups had decided to spend the winter at Fort Laramie; perhaps they had already perished.

Daniel W. Jones of the rescue team recalled that when they were back together at Devil's Gate, "at first we were at a loss what to do, for we did not expect to have to go further."[3] He said that after seeing the condition of the Willie company, the rescue team "more fully realized the danger the others were in."[4] The rescuers who had recently returned from missions to England were especially troubled because they had many friends in the Martin company. Those rescuers, Dan Jones recalled, "suffered great anxiety, some of them feeling more or less the responsibility resting upon them for allowing these people to start so late in the season across the plains."[5]

On October 27, the morning after Captain Grant arrived at Devil's Gate, he decided to send another express team to find the missing companies. This time he told them "not to return until they were found."[6] This could mean they would have to travel all the way to Fort Laramie, another 180 miles. This second express team consisted of Joseph Young, Abel Garr, and Dan Jones.[7] The rest of the rescuers remained at Devil's Gate.

EXPRESS RESCUERS FIND THE MARTIN AND HODGETTS COMPANIES

The express rescuers rode their horses at full gallop wherever the trail permitted, and by the next day, October 28, they had traveled nearly 50 miles. As they approached the bend of the Platte River at

Red Buttes, Joseph Young saw a "white man's shoe track."[8] Dan Jones recalled, "We put our animals to their utmost speed and soon came in sight of the camp at Red Bluff."[9] As members of the Martin and Hodgetts companies saw the rescuers approach, despair thawed into hope. "It is impossible to describe the joy and gratitude that filled every heart upon the arrival of such messengers of Salvation," wrote William Binder.[10] "More welcome messengers never came from the courts of glory," wrote John Kirkman.[11]

John Bond's Account: "As Angels from Heaven"

Young John Bond of the Hodgetts wagon company was one of the first to see the rescuers in the distance. Recalling their arrival, he wrote:

"All came to the conclusion that they must die, far away from the civilized world, all for the reason and sake of truth. Along in the afternoon, I was playing in front of Sister Scott's . . . wagon with her son Joseph. . . . His mother was looking to the westward. All at once, Sister Scott sprang to her feet in the wagon and screamed out at the top of her voice, 'I see them coming! I see them coming! Surely they are as angels from heaven!'

"At such a thing being said, I looked the way she was looking, that I may see what she saw in the distance. Then she called out, 'I can see them plainer! plainer! plainer!' I still looked the way she was looking but could not see anything.

"By this time more of the brethren and sisters came from their tents and wagons from all over the camp, anxious to see what she saw in the distance. All kept looking to the westward for the moving objects, when all commenced to see in the distance at the curve of the hill, what Sister Scott saw, appearing to be three men on horses, driving another slowly in the deep crusted snow, as the wolves howled from all directions. . . .

"As the moving objects could be seen distinctly, a general cry rent the air. Hurrah! Hurrah! Some of the voices choked with laughter and falling tears, [knowing] that they would be saved and delivered from the fears of death. . . .

"Joseph A. Young, Daniel W. Jones, and [Abel] Garr came into camp with a small dun-colored pack mule packed with supplies. The broken-hearted mothers ran, clasping their emaciated arms around the necks of the relief party, kissing them time and time again as [did] the brethren also, rushing up in groups to fall on their necks, the tears falling from their eyes in profusion. . . . 'God bless Brigham Young and the rescuing parties . . . ' was heard all over camp."[12]

Like Mary Scott, a 39-year-old widow, many members of the Martin and Hodgetts companies must have been looking frequently "to the westward" during the long days at Red Buttes.

Patience Loader's Account

Patience Loader recorded that when the express rescuers arrived on the 28th, "Brother Young asked, 'How many are dead and how many are alive?' I told him I could not tell. With tears streaming down his face he asked, 'Where is your Captain's tent?' He called for the bugler to call everybody out of their tents. He then [asked] Captain Edward Martin if he had flour enough to give us all one pound of flour each and said if there were any cattle, to kill [them and] give us one pound of beef each, saying there were plenty of provisions and clothing coming for us on the road, but tomorrow morning we must make a move from there. . . . Then he said he would have to leave us [to go find the Hunt company]. He would have liked to travel with us the next morning, but we must cheer up and God would bless us and give us strength. He said, 'We have made a trail for you to follow.' . . .

"After the brethren had left us, we felt quite encouraged and we got our flour and beef before night came on and we were all busy cooking and we felt to thank God and our kind brothers that had come to help us in our great distress and misery, for we were suffering greatly with cold and hunger."[13]

Respite for the Sermon Family

The arrival of the express rescuers provided hope for the Sermon family. Even Joseph seemed to have a change of heart. His wife, Elizabeth, wrote:

"After our food had given out, . . . we went to our tents, a great many to die. Myself, I always thought I should get through to Salt Lake, and tried so hard to encourage [Joseph], but he was starving. He had always lived good at home and could not stand the severe hardships. [One day] there was a shout in camp. Joseph Young and [others] had come on pack mules and brought us some flour, meat, and onions."[14]

As soon as Elizabeth received her ration of food, she prepared a meal for her family. "I took the fat off from the meat, chopped it fine, minced the meat and onions, and made dumplings," she said. "We had no salt, but we had a good meal and blessed Brother Joseph [Young] from the depths of our hearts. Whenever I think of them since, my heart is full of gratitude.

"They told us we had 70 miles [actually 50] to travel to get to the wagons that had been sent from Salt Lake with food and clothing."[15]

The hope brought by the express rescuers seemed to revive Joseph Sermon. Elizabeth recalled: "He said to me, 'God bless you, Eliza,' that being the name he called me. 'You have saved my life this time. I will try hard [to] hold out now and get to the wagons.'"[16]

Louisa Mellor's Account: "The Lord Sent Us Deliverance"

Recalling the arrival of the express rescuers at the Red Buttes camp, 16-year-old Louisa Mellor wrote:

"At last, some of the company gave up and decided they could go no further. We all gathered around and held a meeting, praying [for] God to help us, as we knew it was He alone who could deliver us from death. We were happy and willing to die for a just cause. The Lord knew our desperate condition and sent us deliverance. A 'hurrah!' burst from the camp as three messengers came riding in. . . .

They told us to cheer up as there were ten wagons loaded with provisions [nearby]."[17]

Albert Jones's Account: "A Blue-Winged Angel Flying to Our Rescue"

Albert Jones (age 16) gave the following vivid account of the arrival of the express rescuers:

"It was at this place [Red Buttes] that Joseph A. Young arrived as the leader of the relief party sent from the valleys by President Brigham Young. He rode a white mule down a snow-covered hill or dugway. The white mule was lost sight of on the white background of snow, and Joseph A. with his big blue soldiers' overcoat, its large cape . . . rising and falling with the motion of the mule, gave the appearance of a big blue-winged angel flying to our rescue.

"The scene that presented itself on his arrival I shall never forget: women and men surrounded him, weeping, and crying aloud; on their knees, holding to the skirts of his coat, as though afraid he would escape from their grasp and fly away. Joseph stood in their midst drawn up to his full height and gazed upon their upturned faces, his eyes full of tears. I, boy as I was, prayed 'God bless him.' "[18]

"Better Than Angels for This Occasion"

Daniel W. Jones recalled that when he and the other two express rescuers rode into camp, they found that "this company was in almost as bad a condition as the first one [Willie company]. They had nearly given up hope. . . . Many declared that we were angels from heaven. I told them I thought we were better than angels for *this* occasion, as we were good strong men come to help them into the valley, and that our company, and wagons loaded with provisions, were not far away."[19]

The Blue Angel—Joseph Angell Young, *by Julie Rogers*

DEPLORABLE CONDITION OF THE MARTIN COMPANY

Mixed with the joy of the rescuers finding the Martin company were problems. Those who were dying were not just the old, the young, and the sick. Many of the middle-aged men—husbands and fathers with families to care for—were also failing. Members of the express team "were aghast at the shattered spirit of some of the men," who seemed to be experiencing "not merely broken pride but shock resulting from physical and emotional trauma."[20] John Jaques described how this trauma was affecting even the strongest in the company:

"Worn down by the labors and fatigues of the journey, and pinched by hunger and cold, the manliness of tall, healthy, strong men would gradually disappear, until they would grow fretful, peevish, childish, and puerile, acting sometimes as if they were scarcely accountable beings.

"In the progress of the journey it was not difficult to tell who was going to die within two or three weeks. The gaunt form, hollow eyes, and sunken countenance, discolored to a weather-beaten sallow, with the gradual weakening of the mental faculties, plainly foreboded the coming and not far distant dissolution."[21]

The express rescuers later reported: "We found the Martin Company in a deplorable condition, they having lost fifty-six of their number since crossing the North Platte, nine days before. Their provisions were nearly gone, and their clothing almost worn out. Most of their bedding had been left behind, as they were unable to haul it, on account of their weakened condition."[22]

As had happened when the express rescuers met the Willie company, they were traveling light and were unable to provide much material assistance to the Martin company. The best they could offer was the promise of assistance nearby, though 50 miles must have seemed an impossible distance in those conditions.

How to make up that distance was a difficult question. The express rescuers could not immediately return to summon the rest of the team because they had to continue eastward until they found the

Hunt company. So they advised the Martin company to start moving again. Dan Jones recalled:

"Brother Young told the people to gather 'up' and move on at once as the only salvation was to travel a little every day. This was right and no doubt saved many lives for we, among so many, . . . could do but little, and there was danger of starvation before help could arrive unless the people made some headway toward the valley."[23]

EXPRESS RESCUERS FIND THE HUNT COMPANY

After finding the Martin and Hodgetts companies on October 28, the express rescuers stayed only briefly and pushed on until they found the Hunt company several miles farther east near the last crossing of the Platte. Dan Jones said they were not in such a bad condition as the earlier companies—that they "were just on the eve of suffering."[24] However, another report from these rescuers paints a bleaker picture:

"We rode over to the Hunt camp . . . and found them almost out of provisions, and their cattle dying for want of food. The majority of them had become so discouraged that they knew not what to do. We explained to them how impossible it was for us to give them substantial aid. . . . We urged them to move on towards the Valley, every day, no matter what the sacrifice might be. We gave them to understand that the authorities at Salt Lake City had no idea that they were so far from home, and had made no arrangements to meet such conditions."[25]

The express rescuers stayed with the Hunt company that night and tried to get them started again the next morning. Dan Jones reported the following problems in getting the company to break camp: "There was a spirit of apathy among the people, [and] instead of going for their teams at once, several began to quarrel about who should go. This made us feel like leaving them to take care of themselves."[26] Soon Abel Garr gave them a warning, and the company moved out and traveled three miles.

MARTIN COMPANY ON THE MOVE
AGAIN—IN DISTRESS

On October 29 all the companies were finally moving westward again. Somehow rallying their strength, the Martin and Hodgetts companies broke camp that morning and began the 50-mile trek toward Devil's Gate. Samuel Openshaw recalled the difficulty of moving forward again: "Our strength being very much reduced, the snow, cold, and the blasting winds, it seemed impossible for us to travel."[27]

After leaving the Hunt camp, the express rescuers rode hard toward Devil's Gate to report to Captain Grant. They soon overtook the Martin company, which was struggling up a long, muddy hill. Dan Jones described the scene:

"A condition of distress here met my eyes that I never saw before or since. The train was strung out for three or four miles. There were old men pulling and tugging their carts, sometimes loaded with a sick wife or children—women pulling along sick husbands—little children six to eight years old struggling through the mud and snow.

"As night came on, the mud would freeze on their clothes and feet. There were two of us and hundreds needing help. What could we do? We gathered on to some of the most helpless with our [lariats] tied to the carts, and helped as many as we could into camp on Avenue Hill. This was a bitter, cold night and we had no fuel except very small sagebrush. Several died that night. Next morning . . . we three started for our camp near Devil's Gate."[28]

Patience Loader was glad to leave Red Buttes because so many had died there, but the effort required to travel seemed almost too much for some. Patience told the following story about the experiences of David Blair and his family that day:

"I remember well poor Brother Blair. He was a fine, tall man, had been one of Queen Victoria's lifeguards in London. . . . He made a cover for his cart and put his [three] children on the cart [ages infant to 7]. He pulled his cart alone; his wife helped by pushing behind the cart. [The] poor man . . . was so weak and worn down that he fell down several times that day, but still he kept his dear little children on the cart all day. This poor man had so much love for his wife and children that instead of eating his morsel of food himself, he would give it to his children."[29]

John Bond, ever observant for a 12-year-old, had the following recollection of the Sermon family at this time: "As we slowly go ahead, Sister Sermon is tugging and pulling her cart with the help of her sons, John and Robert. Her husband had been an invalid for some distance of the way, yet she was so faithful to her husband that she gave every care that none but a true-hearted wife could give. She was quite weak herself, but had such faith that she believed her dear ones would arrive in Zion, though her sons' feet were badly frostbitten with the appearance that both would have to be amputated."[30]

RESCUE WAGONS MEET THE MARTIN COMPANY AT GREASEWOOD CREEK

On October 30 the three express rescuers arrived back at Devil's Gate and reported the desperate plight of the companies. Immediately Captain Grant and most of his men hitched up six wagons and moved eastward. Meanwhile, in the two days since being found by the express, the Martin company had traveled about 30 miles toward Devil's Gate.

On October 31, after the Martin company had endured nearly two weeks of freezing temperatures and scanty food rations, Captain Grant's rescue team met the Martin company at Greasewood Creek (also called Horse Creek), 17 miles east of Devil's Gate. John Jaques recollected meeting the rescuers and their provision wagons: "This was [a] time of rejoicing. Some of the relief party had met the emigrants a mile or two away from camp and had helped pull some of the carts along. Here some stockings, boots, and other clothing were distributed, . . . also a few onions, which were highly prized, and a pound of flour ration was served out. . . . This was the beginning of better days as to food and assistance, but the cold grew more severe and was intense much of the way."[31]

Greasewood Creek—Martin company rescue site

Patience Loader recalled that when the Martin company struggled into Greasewood Creek, the rescuers had already gathered wood and made about a dozen big fires. She also said the rescuers had "plenty of lovely spring water," which was a treat because she'd had "nothing but snow water and that did not taste good as we had to melt it over the campfire and it tasted of sagebrush [and] sometimes of cedar wood smoke." Continuing, she said:

"We felt very thankful to our brethren for making us these good fires and supplying us with wood so abundantly. I really must say I was very thankful, for since our dear father died, it had fallen on me and my sister Maria to get most of our wood, and I thought it was so good that we did not have to get wood that night after such hard pulling all day through the snow."[32]

Patience was also grateful to receive a quilted hood and a pair of slippers, "as I was nearly barefoot."[33]

THE GROUND TOO FROZEN FOR TENT PEGS

The next morning, November 1, the rescuers gave every possible assistance in helping the Martin and Hodgetts companies move toward Devil's Gate. Because there were only six rescue wagons, most of the people still had to pull their handcarts. They traveled about 10 miles and camped at the first crossing of the Sweetwater River, near Independence Rock. John Jaques recalled the difficulties of making camp that night:

"On the evening of November 1st, the handcart company camped at the Sweetwater bridge, . . . about five miles [east] of Devil's Gate, arriving there about dark. There was a foot or eighteen inches of snow on the ground. As there were but one or two spades in camp, the emigrants had to shovel it away with their frying pans, or tin plates, or anything they could use for that purpose, before they could pitch their tents, and then the ground was frozen so hard that it was almost impossible to drive the tent pegs into it. Some of the men were so weak that it took them an hour or two to clear the places for their tents and set them up."[34]

Independence Rock is a smooth, rounded mass of granite at the eastern end of the Sweetwater valley, about 50 miles southwest of Casper and five miles east of Devil's Gate. It was one of the most prominent landmarks on the trail.

The headwaters of the Sweetwater River are in the Wind River Mountains in western Wyoming. The trail crosses this river nine times in the 100 miles between Independence Rock and South Pass. The Sweetwater flows into the North Platte River, now going through Pathfinder Reservoir.

TRIALS OF THE GRIFFITHS FAMILY

At Independence Rock the family of John Griffiths, a former branch president in the London Conference, experienced their second loss and seemed to be on the verge of more. John's 12-year-old son had died the previous week at Red Buttes. Then at Independence Rock his only other son on the trek, 6-year-old Herbert, froze to death. John's health was also failing, and the fingers and feet of his two daughters were frostbitten.

John Griffiths may have also felt broken in spirit. Earlier he had ridden in one of the provision wagons because he was too sick to walk. After regaining some of his strength, he tried to walk again. However, his rheumatism was so bad that he could not keep up and began holding onto the back of the wagon to help support himself. When the teamster noticed, he struck John on the legs with a whip. John fell to the ground and could not get up.

Whipping a person was not common in the pioneer companies, but an occasional lash—not a scourging—was not forbidden. Nothing can justify the practice to modern sensibilities, but it is important to understand that it was not typically done with malice or anger. One author has suggested that the teamster "may have been trying to keep Griffiths moving rather than driving him away."[35] Even one of the emigrants, a young girl named Nicholas Gourley, seemed to accept that the whip had its place: "Often the people would get so tired they would lie down under a bush or tree and then they would be very hard to get up. The leaders had to take a whip to them and lash them back to consciousness, when they would beg to be left to die."[36]

When John Griffiths went down, he was left to his own resources. His family was unaware of his predicament because they were ahead pulling the handcart. No one would be coming along to help him because he was traveling with the last wagon. And uncharacteristically for the handcart companies, where brother so often helped brother, the teamster kept rolling forward while John lay crumpled in the snow. Perhaps the teamster thought this would motivate John to catch up, but John was unable to stand. Knowing his survival depended on getting to camp, John began to crawl. Soon he came to some tracks that led to the camp of the Hodgetts wagon company. He inched forward on his hands and knees until he reached the camp, badly frozen.

Meanwhile, as the Martin company made their camp, John's family feared the worst when the last wagon arrived without him. His oldest daughter, 16-year-old Margaret, rushed back three miles looking for him but was unsuccessful. "I was nearly wild. I thought the wolves might have him," she wrote.[37] Worries were finally calmed at 11:00 that night, when two men from the Hodgetts company brought John back to his own camp. Although John Griffiths survived this ordeal, he would never be well again.

Progress of the Hunt Company

After traveling three miles on October 29, the day after the express rescuers found them, the Hunt company traveled only seven miles on the 30th and did not move at all on the 31st. The next day they were met by Cyrus Wheelock and two other rescuers who came from Devil's Gate. The following day, November 2, the company traveled only four miles, slowed by weather conditions and by having to search for strayed cattle. Apparently there was still some dissension in the camp, as suggested by the company journal's account of a meeting held that night:

"Meeting in the evening addressed by Elders Wheelock, Webb, and Broomhead, and a unanimous vote was taken, that all would be willing to do as they were bidden, [even if they were] required to leave all they have behind and . . . be glad to get into the Valley with their lives only, and they would cease to complain at coming so late in the season, [since] everything possible [had been] done to start the company early."[38]

The next day the Hunt company made better progress.

CHAPTER 31

At Devil's Gate

On November 2, the second day after the rescue wagons met up with the Martin and Hodgetts companies, the group arrived at Devil's Gate. Samuel Openshaw of the Martin company described the arrival:

"The brethren who came out to meet us did administer every comfort and help that was within their power to the sick and the infirm. [At Devil's Gate] we were obliged to stop, the snow being about fourteen inches deep on the level, and notwithstanding the teams that had come out to help us, there was not sufficient help to move the aged, sick, and the women and children along, so that we again stopped several days."[1]

The Hunt company was still three days behind at the time. On the morning of November 3, they left "fourteen or fifteen oxen on the road."[2] That night they camped at Greasewood Creek, scraping away snow by the creek to uncover some meager grass for their cattle. On November 4 they made only five miles. Finally, at 8:00 P.M. on November 5, the Hunt company reached Devil's Gate.

Tragedy for Alice Walsh

The number of widows in the camp was growing each day. Alice Walsh had already lost her oldest child, 5-year-old Robert, in September. Now her husband was failing. She recalled the arrival, and personal tragedy, at Devil's Gate:

"On account of the nightly fatalities of the male members of our company for two or three weeks previously, there were many widows in our company, and the women had to pitch and put up the tents, shoveling the snow away with tin plates, etc. . . .

"One night I dropped to the ground in a dead faint with my baby in my arms. I had some pepper pods with me, and recovering from my stupor I took some of them . . . to recover my strength. During these times we had only a little thin flour gruel two or three times a day, and this was meager nourishment for a mother with a nursing baby.

"My husband died and was buried at or near Devil's Gate, and the ground was frozen so hard that the men had a difficult task in digging the grave deep enough in which to inter him and nine others that morning, and it is more than probable that several were only covered with snow. Here I was left a widow with two young children."[3]

GATHERING WOOD

Patience Loader said the company arrived at night in "snow which was deep and freezing." What would be the most welcome sight in such a circumstance? To Patience it was a fire. Just as she had seemed most grateful for the fires the rescuers had built at Greasewood Creek two days earlier, the need for warmth dominated her recollections of arriving at Devil's Gate:

"When we got to camp we found several big fires. . . . We were all so hungry and cold; many ran to the fire to [get] warm, but the brethren asked for all to be as patient as possible and we should have some wood to make us a fire so we could get warm."[4]

Gathering wood had been a constant, draining task for Patience and others in the company, often requiring them to go a considerable distance from camp and grub through the snow. The desperate desire to avoid this duty is vivid in the following recollection from Patience:

"Brother George Grant [Captain Grant's son] . . . told us all to stand back, for he was going to knock down one of those log huts to make fires for us. He said, 'You are not going to freeze tonight.' . . . He raised his ax and with one blow knocked in the whole front of the building, took each log and split it in four pieces, and gave each family one piece. Oh, such crowding for wood. Some would have taken more than one piece, but Bro. Grant told them to hold on and not to be greedy. There were some that had not got any yet."[5]

Patience was one of those who had not received any wood, and George Grant made sure she got some. "I was very thankful to get wood," she wrote. "I had waited so long that my clothing [was] stiff and my old stockings and shoes seemed frozen on my feet and legs. My poor mother was sitting down waiting until we got back with wood to make a fire. . . . [Then] we had to wait some time before we got our flour for supper."[6]

DIFFICULT DECISIONS FOR THE RESCUERS

On November 3 the rescuers held a council to discuss whether to stay at Devil's Gate for the winter or continue on to the Salt Lake Valley. Because so many people needed medical help, and because there was not adequate food or shelter, the council decided to press on as soon as the weather improved. That day, though, another winter storm arrived, adding more than a foot of snow and dropping the temperature below zero. To inform Brigham Young of the situation, Captain Grant sent Joseph Young and Abel Garr on an express journey to Salt Lake City.

These two men, the tireless couriers, had already been on all of the rescue team's express missions. By this time they had been traveling express nearly nonstop for more than three weeks. On October 14 they had left from Black's Fork (west of the Green River crossing) to find the Willie company. After finding them, they had continued their express journey some 100 miles eastward before finding the Martin, Hodgetts, and Hunt companies. Then they had retraced the 60 miles from the last crossing of the Platte back to Devil's Gate to notify their team. Finally, they had hurried back with the rescue wagons to meet the Martin company at Greasewood Creek.

In the message Captain Grant sent with these men to Brigham Young, he wrote:

"It is not of much use for me to attempt to give a description of the situation of these people, for this you will learn from your son Joseph A. and Br. Garr, who are the bearers of this express; but you can imagine between 500 and 600 men, women, and children, worn down by drawing handcarts through snow and mud; fainting by the wayside; falling, chilled by the cold; children crying, their limbs stiffened by cold, their feet bleeding and some of them bare to snow and frost. The sight is almost too much for the stoutest of us; but we go on doing all we can, not doubting nor despairing.

"Our company is too small to help much; it is only a drop in the bucket, as it were, in comparison to what is needed. I think that not over one-third of Martin's company is able to walk. This you may think is extravagant, but it is nevertheless true. Some of them have good courage and are in good spirits, but a great many are like children and do not help themselves much more, nor realize what is before them.

"I never felt so much interest in any mission that I have been sent on, and all the brethren who came out with me feel the same. We have prayed without ceasing, and the blessing of God has been with us.

"Br. Charles Decker has now traveled this road the 49th time, and he says he has never before seen so much snow on the Sweetwater at any season of the year. . . .

"We will move every day toward the valley, if we shovel snow to do it, the Lord helping us."[7]

Joseph Young and Abel Garr traveled the 327 miles to Salt Lake City in 10 days, arriving on November 13.[8] On their way, they overtook and turned around many rescue wagons that had given up the search and started for home.[9] With their news that the last companies had been found and were perishing, even more teams and provisions were sent immediately.[10]

Like Captain Grant, Daniel W. Jones was also concerned about the inadequacy of one small rescue team for some 900 people: "The winter storms had now set in, in all their severity. The provisions we took amounted to almost nothing among so many people, many of them now on very short rations, some almost starving. Many were dying daily from exposure and want of food."[11]

How serious were the rescuers' shortages? The food supply was shrinking, and the shoes, clothes, and bedding they brought were also in short supply. Captain Burton kept a count of items distributed:

> 102 pairs of boots and shoes
> 157 pairs of socks and stockings
> 100 coats and jackets
> 27 women's undergarments
> 24 petticoats
> 8 pairs of mittens
> 36 hoods
> 18 shawls
> 27 handkerchiefs
> 14 neckties[12]

All together, there were just over 500 articles of clothing, as well as a few quilts and blankets. Only about half of the people at Devil's Gate received something to supplement what was left of their own shoes and ragged clothing.

CHAPTER 32

Taking Shelter in Martin's Cove

We camped in a little cove in the mountains where the wind would not get such a sweep at us. . . . Then was the time to hear the children crying for something to eat. Nearly all of them would cry themselves to sleep every night. My two little brothers would get the sack that had flour in it and turn it inside out and suck and lick the flour dust off it.

—Heber McBride, age 13

The Martin company camped at Devil's Gate on the nights of November 2 and 3. The rescuers then decided to move them to an area that would provide better protection from the elements and more plentiful firewood. This is the place that came to be known as Martin's Cove—also known, less evocatively, as Martin's Ravine or Martin's Hole.[1]

Today Martin's Cove is on public land that is managed by the U.S. Bureau of Land Management and leased to the Church.

Crossing the Sweetwater

The Martin company moved to Martin's Cove on November 4. To get to there, they had to trudge two and a half miles through the snow. Worse, they had to cross another river in wintry conditions. The pioneer trail's nine crossings of the Sweetwater River did not normally include this one, but Martin's Cove was off the trail, and the extra crossing was necessary to get there.

Although the Sweetwater was not as wide or deep as the Platte,

John Jaques wrote that "the passage of the Sweetwater at this point was a severe operation to many of the company. . . . It was the worst river crossing of the expedition."[2] In one of his many allusions to Napoleon's retreat from Moscow 44 years earlier, John Jaques compared this river crossing to Napoleon's desperate and disastrous crossing of the Beresina River. One significant difference from Napoleon, though, was that "this handcart expedition was an *advance,* not a *retreat.* The handcart company never retreated one day nor one yard, never thought of retreating."[3]

Recalling the last crossing of the Platte River two weeks earlier, many felt that they could not face a similar ordeal at the Sweetwater. Men and women shrank back and wept. Patience Loader said that when she saw the river, "I could not keep my tears back. I felt ashamed to let those brethren see me shedding tears. I pulled my old bonnet over my face so they should not see my tears."[4] John Jaques provides the following account of a man who had a similar reaction:

"When [we] arrived at the bank of the river, one [man], who was much worn down, asked in a plaintive tone, 'Have we got to go across there?' On being answered yes, he was so much affected that he was completely overcome. That was the last straw. His fortitude and manhood gave way. He exclaimed, 'Oh, dear! I can't go through that,' and burst into tears. His wife, who was by his side, had the stouter heart of the two at that juncture, and she said soothingly, 'Don't cry, Jimmy. I'll pull the handcart for you.'"[5] As it turned out, rescuers carried both of them across. Jimmy might have been better off pulling the handcart, however, because the rescuer who carried him slipped, tumbling both of them into the river.

This family's handcart still had to be pulled across the river and at least a mile to the cove, so another man began pulling it by himself. The man was likely John Jaques, who tells the story in third person but supplies enough detail to allow a reasonably sure identification:

"While in the river the sharp cakes of floating ice below the surface of the water struck against the bare shins of the emigrant, inflicting wounds which never healed until he arrived at Salt Lake and the dark scars of which he bears to this day."[6]

John was stalled in the river until two rescuers came to help him. After they got the cart across, John was on his own again. He described the scene: "The way to camp was over rising ground, covered with sagebrush, and with about a foot of snow on the surface. All alone he pulled his heavy laden cart over the snow and clumps of brush, for road there was none, till he reached the camp."

After John was in camp, he found that all the wood the rescuers had gathered had been apportioned. In his weakened state he headed into the hills with a little hatchet. "Nothing but dry cedar was really serviceable for fuel," John wrote, "and the dry cedar was almost as hard as iron. . . . I will leave you to imagine how long he was that night before he succeeded in getting fuel for those depending on him."[7]

This crossing of the Sweetwater was the site of great heroism by some of the rescuers. Seeing how traumatized the people were by the prospect of wading through another freezing river, the rescuers carried many of them across. John Jaques identified four of these rescuers as David P. Kimball (17; son of Heber C. Kimball and brother of William Kimball), George W. Grant (17; son of Captain Grant), C. Allen Huntington (25), and Stephen W. Taylor (22).[8] By the time everyone was across, darkness was beginning to fall and these men had spent hours in the river. Recalling this service, Patience Loader wrote:

"Those poor brethren [were] in the water nearly all day. We wanted to thank them, but they would not listen to [us]." Patience also reported that David Kimball "stayed so long in the water that he had to be taken out and packed to camp, and he was a long time before he recovered, as he was chilled through and [afterward] was always afflicted with rheumatism."[9]

The sacrifice of these rescuers was later brought to the attention of Brigham Young. According to one account, President Young wept when he heard the story and declared, "That act alone will ensure C. Allen Huntington, George W. Grant, and David P. Kimball an everlasting salvation in the Celestial Kingdom of God, worlds without end.' "[10] There is a question about whether Brigham Young spoke these actual words, however. Six years before this statement was published, the same author reported Brigham Young's words somewhat differently: "When President Brigham Young heard of this heroic act, he wept like a child, and declared that this act alone would immortalize them."[11] Perhaps one explanation for the difference in these accounts is that they were written in 1908 and 1914, more than 50 years after the rescue and 30 years after Brigham Young's death. Regardless of the differences in these statements, what is most important remains undisputed: the heroic service of these rescuers and Brigham Young's feelings of gratitude toward them.

Another commonly quoted statement that merits examination is that "the strain was so terrible, and the exposure so great, that in later years all the boys died from the effects of it."[12] The death dates of these men raise questions about the accuracy of this statement. Although they suffered varying degrees of long-term effects from this experience, it seems unlikely that they all died as a direct result of it. Stephen W. Taylor lived another 63 years (died at age 85), Allen Huntington lived another 40 years (died at age 65), David P. Kimball lived another 27 years (died at age 44), and George W. Grant lived another 17 years (died at age 34).

"Like an Overcrowded Tomb"

The company remained in Martin's Cove for five miserable days. The temperature reached 11 degrees below zero on November 6, and people continued to die.[13] John Kirkman, who was eight years old at the time, later described the relentless march of death in the cove: "Death had taken a heavy toll; the ravine was like an overcrowded tomb; no mortal pen could describe the suffering."[14]

Elizabeth Jackson's Description of Martin's Cove

After Elizabeth Jackson's husband died at the last crossing of the Platte, she alone had the care of her three young children. It is

Martin's Cove

heart-rending to picture her trying to protect these children as the storm raged and the temperature dropped. Although God did not use his power to turn away the storm, Elizabeth felt his power in helping them survive:

"We camped for several days in a deep gulch called 'Martin's Ravine.' It was a fearful time and place. It was so cold that some of the company came near freezing to death. The sufferings of the people were fearful, and nothing but the power of a merciful God kept them from perishing. The storms continued unabated for some days. . . . When the snow at length ceased falling, it lay thick on the ground, and so deep that for many days it was impossible to move the wagons through. I and my children with hundreds of others were locked up in those fearful weather-bound mountains."[15]

TRAGEDY FOR THE SERMON FAMILY

Joseph Sermon's health revived only briefly at Red Buttes before failing again. "The friend death would soon end his sufferings," his wife wrote. He made it to Devil's Gate and then to Martin's Cove, being carried over the Sweetwater by David Kimball. "My poor husband blessed him for so doing," Elizabeth recalled.[16]

Sensing the end was near, Joseph Sermon called his children together and told them to be good and to do all they could for their mother. Then at about 3:00 he went to bed. "He put his arm around me," Elizabeth wrote, "and said, 'I am done,' and breathed his last."[17]

Joseph Sermon was buried the next morning in a common grave with several others. Recalling the burial, Elizabeth wrote: "I stood like a statue, bewildered, in tears. The cold chills, even now as I write, creep over my body, and it seems I can still hear and see the wolves watching for their bodies, as they would come down to camp before we were very far away."[18]

JOHN BAILEY: "HE THEN GAVE UP DYING"

For most of the handcart trek, Jane Bailey had struggled to keep her 18-year-old son, Langley, alive. He was so ill that he had to be pulled in a cart and wanted to die. At Martin's Cove, Jane also had to persuade her husband to keep going when he felt that death would be a welcome relief. Langley recalled:

"My father went to gather some brush, willows, etc., there being no wood, to keep me warm. His hands became very benumbed. He laid down by my side [and] told mother he was going to die (it was not any trouble to die). Mother took hold of him and gave him a shaking up, and told him she was going on to the Valley. He then gave up dying."[19]

MARY BARTON: "I WONDER IF SHE'S DEAD"

Mary Barton, whose father and baby sister had already died, related the following experience about the first night in Martin's Cove. This account reveals much about the conditions there:

"After pitching our tents, we lay down on the ground to get some sleep and rest. In the night the tents all blew over. It was all ice and snow where I was laying, and when the tent blew off from me,

I didn't wake up, I was so tired. One man came and looked at me. He called some more men over, saying, 'I wonder if she's dead.' He patted me on the head, and just then I opened my eyes. He jumped back, thinking I was dead. I tried to raise my head but found that my hair was frozen to the ground. They chopped the ice all around my hair, and I went over to the fire and melted the large piece of ice which was clinging to my hair. The men laughed to think that I could lie there all night with my hair frozen in the ice, but were very glad that I wasn't dead."[20]

JAMES BLEAK: "WE FELT AS CONTENTED"

The increased food rations from the rescuers lasted for only a few days. In Martin's Cove, rations were again reduced to four ounces of flour because the rescuers' supplies were insufficient to feed 900 people. The second day in the cove, James Bleak, one of the London branch presidents, wrote in his journal:

"No travelling. Weather very severe. Sister Mary Harper died aged 64. Our ration of flour was reduced to 4 oz. and 2 oz. for the children, making 1 lb. a day for the 6 of us."

James concludes this journal entry with one of the most extraordinary sentences in all the handcart writings. His feet were frozen, his wife and four children were suffering, the weather showed no signs of moderating, and now rations were being reduced again. Yet he wrote, "Through the blessing of our Father, we felt as contented as when we had 1 lb. per head."[21]

SAMUEL S. JONES: "LET THE CURTAIN FALL GENTLY"

Nineteen-year-old Samuel S. Jones later wrote the following recollection of the time in Martin's Cove:

"We stayed in the ravine five or six days on reduced rations. One night a windstorm blew down almost every tent. Many perished of cold and hunger at this place. . . . I remember the pinched, hungry faces, the stolid, absent stare, that foretold the end was near, the wide and shallow open grave, awaiting its numerous consignments.

"[I remember] the start from that place in the wagons when the camp broke up, the looks of the living freight, the long cold rides, the longer nights, the pitiless sky, the lack of sleep, many dozing down by the fire and turning at intervals all through the night. . . . Let the curtain fall gently!

"This is not written in any spirit of complaint. I cannot recall a rebellious spirit or feeling on the trip. We started for Zion, and to help build up the same in the valleys of the mountains, and thank God we are here."[22]

AMY LOADER'S DANCE

For many years before emigrating, Amy Loader had been in delicate health and was unable to walk even a mile.[23] When she learned that she was expected to walk 1,300 miles—and to pull a handcart as well—she was understandably distressed. As a result, her voice against pulling a handcart is one of the strongest on record. Once she began the journey, however, she became a stalwart example of strength.

Amy Loader

After Amy Loader had walked more than 600 miles, her husband died. Looking ahead, Amy saw another 700 miles without a man to help pull the cart. The miles would be the most sandy, the most rocky, the most hilly—the most difficult even in favorable weather. They would include at least a dozen dreaded river crossings. Although Amy had already far exceeded what she thought she could do, she knew she would have to do even more. Besides bearing an increased burden of physical labor, she would be the sole parent in caring for her six children—all while grieving the loss of her husband. That three of her daughters were adults did not make their illnesses and struggles any less taxing for a loving mother.

Amy Loader could have murmured or despaired. She could have told her adult daughters and even her younger daughters and 10-year-old son that they would have to pull her through. Instead, as conditions deteriorated, this 54-year-old woman of delicate health was one of the most resilient, resourceful, and hopeful people in the company. Patience Loader tells of her mother finding ways to keep extra socks and underskirts dry while crossing the rivers so her daughters could have some dry clothing afterward. Patience also tells of her mother finding creative ways to feed her children. But the depth of Amy Loader's love and influence is best revealed in the story of her dance at Martin's Cove. Patience recalled:

"That night was a terrible cold night. The wind was blowing, and the snow drifted into the tent onto our quilts. That morning we had nothing to eat . . . until we could get our small quantity of flour. Poor mother called to me, 'Come, Patience, get up and make us a fire.' I told her that I did not feel like getting up, it was so cold and I was not feeling very well. So she asked my sister Tamar to get up, and she said she was not well and she could not get up. Then she said, 'Come, Maria, you get up,' and she was feeling bad and said that she could not get up."[24]

At that point Amy Loader would have been justified in raising her voice and desperately asking her daughters, "Do you want to die? Do you want *me* to die? Are you just going to lie there and freeze to death? Are you going to get up and do your part?" But there was no anger, no impatience, no frustration, no imposing of guilt—only this remarkable incident:

"Mother said, 'Come, girls. This will not do. I believe I will have to dance [for] you and try to make you feel better.' Poor, dear mother, she started to sing and dance [for] us, and she slipped down as the snow was frozen. In a moment we were all up to help [her,] for we were afraid she was hurt. She laughed and said, 'I thought I could soon make you all jump up if I danced [for] you.' Then we found that she fell down purposely, for she knew we would all get up to see if she was hurt. She said that she was afraid her girls were going to give out and get discouraged, and she said that would never do. . . . We [had never] felt so weak as we did that morning. My dear mother had kept up wonderfully all through the journey."[25]

STORY OF SARAH FRANKS AND GEORGE PADLEY

Four couples who were emigrating together had gotten married during the voyage on the *Horizon*. Another couple, Sarah Franks and George Padley, were waiting to be married in Salt Lake City so they could be sealed. By the time they got to Martin's Cove, both were failing due to hunger and exposure. Sarah was taken into one of the sick wagons. George tried to care for her, but his strength waned. According to one account, he had "overexerted himself in trying to help other members of the handcart company. He had gotten wet and chilled from the winter wind."[26] Suffering from a combination of pneumonia and hypothermia, he died in the cove. Sarah mourned not only the loss of her fiancé but also the inevitable work of the wolves on his body. Her family history relates:

"Sarah took her long-fringed shawl from her almost freezing body and had the brethren wrap her sweetheart's body in it. She couldn't bear to think of his being buried with nothing to protect him."[27] Some men then reportedly placed George's body in a tree to protect it from the wolves.

During one of President James E. Faust's visits to Martin's Cove, President Kim W. McKinnon of the Riverton Wyoming Stake told the story of Sarah Franks and George Padley. President Faust "was very moved by the story. With a tear in his eye he said it had to be one of the great love stories of the western migration."[28]

For Sarah Franks, the future seemed desolate without George. Their dream of raising a family together in Zion was over. Already close to death herself, with no family to look after her, with her hopes disappointed, she could have easily lost the will to live. Nevertheless, she persevered and would yet live a life of fulfillment.

DOUBLE TRAGEDY FOR THE GOBLE FAMILY

During the first week of November, tragedy twice struck the family of William and Mary Goble of the Hunt company. Their two-year-old daughter had died six weeks earlier in Iowa City. Then on November 3 their infant daughter Edith, who was born in Nebraska, died "for the want of nourishment."[29] Edith's oldest sister, 13-year-old Mary, recalled her feelings at the grave:

"I felt like I couldn't leave her, for I had seen so many graves opened by the wolves. The rest of the company had got quite a ways when my father came back for me. I told him I could not leave her to be eaten by the wolves. It seem[ed] too terrible. But he talked to me and we hurried on."[30]

That same week the Gobles' four-year-old son also died. His sister Mary recalled:

"When we arrived at Devil's Gate, it was bitter cold. We left lots of our things there. . . . While there an ox fell on the ice and the brethren killed it and the beef was given out to the camp. My brother James ate a hearty supper [and] was as well as he ever was when he went to bed. In the morning he was dead.

"My feet were frozen, also my brother Edwin and my sister Caroline had their feet frozen. It was nothing but snow. We could not drive the pegs in our tents. Father would clean a place for our tents and put snow around to keep it down. We were short of flour, but Father was a good shot. They called him the hunter of the camp, so that helped us out. We could not get enough flour for bread as we got only a quarter of a pound per head a day, so we would make it like thin gruel. We called it skilly."[31]

This family that had started the journey with six children and expecting a seventh had now lost the three youngest children, including the one born on the trail. This would not be the end of their losses.

CHAPTER 33

LEAVING MARTIN'S COVE AND DEVIL'S GATE

During the council that Captain George D. Grant held at Devil's Gate on November 3, the rescuers discussed how to move the Martin company to the Salt Lake Valley. Most members of the company seemed unable to pull their handcarts, and many were unable to walk. With only a few wagons, the rescuers could not accommodate everyone who needed to ride. At one point Captain Grant asked Joseph Young, "What would your father do now if he were here?" Joseph answered, "If my father was here, he would take all the books and heavy material and cache them in order to save the lives of the people."[1]

That is what Captain Grant decided to do: empty some of the wagons of the Hodgetts and Hunt companies, store the freight in the cabins at Devil's Gate, and use those wagons to carry the sick and incapacitated members of the Martin company to Salt Lake City. He informed the members of the Hunt wagon company of this plan the same night they arrived in camp. The company journal reports:

"Brother Grant told [the wagon companies] that they would have to leave their goods here till they could be sent for, such as stoves, boxes of tools, [and] clothing, and only take just sufficient to keep them warm with their bedding. . . . All present appeared willing to do what was expected of them."[2]

This news may have been unwelcome to those in the wagon companies. They had invested considerable money to purchase wagons and teams so they could take needed or treasured possessions from home. Now they would have to leave these possessions behind with some uncertainty about ever getting them back.

For the next few days, the men at Devil's Gate emptied the goods from about 40 wagons into the log buildings.[3] The cold is tangible in the journal of Robert T. Burton, one of the leaders of the rescue team:

"November 6: Colder than ever. Thermometer 11 degrees below zero. Stowed away the goods of Capt. Hunt's train. None of the companies moved; so cold the people could not travel.

"November 7: Remained very cold. Could not travel. Stowing away the goods, trying to save the people, stock, etc."[4]

On November 8 the weather began to improve, and preparations were made to proceed to the Salt Lake Valley. On Sunday, November 9, the wagons moved to Martin's Cove to pick up the handcart company. As many people as possible were crowded into the wagons. The meager loads from the handcarts were also put into the wagons, and most or all of the carts were left behind.

There were only enough wagons to accommodate those most in need. John Jaques recalled the difficulty of determining who could ride and who should walk:

"It was a trying time that day in leaving the ravine. One perplexing difficulty was to determine who should ride, for many must still walk, though . . . for most of the company the cart operation was gone. There was considerable crying of [those] whom the wagons could not accommodate with a ride. One of the relief party remarked that in all the mobbings and drivings of the 'Mormons,' he had seen nothing like it. Cyrus H. Wheelock could scarcely refrain from shedding tears, and he declared that he would willingly give his own life if that would save the lives of the emigrants."[5]

Alice Walsh faced uncertainty about whether she would ride or walk until almost every wagon was gone. Her 5-year old son had died in September, and her husband had died the previous week. Most of the wagons were full—and no one seemed to be taking notice of her. Would they expect her to walk with children ages 4 years and 11 months? The first part of her recollection paints a picture of quiet desperation:

"When the relief help reached us and nearly all of us had been assigned to some wagon, I was sitting in the snow with my children on my lap, and it seemed that there was no chance for me to ride, but before the last teams had left the camp I was assigned to ride in the commissary wagon, and did so until our arrival in Salt Lake City."[6]

Patience Loader was happy that her widowed mother was able to ride in a wagon: "The morning we had orders to leave there, we were told to leave our handcarts. We were all very glad to leave the cart, but we had to walk for several days before we could all ride in the wagons. It seemed good [not to] have a load to pull through the snow. We got dear mother in the wagon to ride, and we girls were young and we were willing to walk until such time as it was convenient for us to ride."[7]

Eighteen-year-old Langley Bailey, who had been seriously ill since Iowa, wrote the following description of leaving Martin's Cove:

"On leaving this morning, my brother John saw the wolves devouring the bodies he had helped to bury the day before. He tried to drive them away, [but] he had to run for his life.

"That morning in starting I was placed in a wagon on top of frozen tents. . . . [We] made about 4 miles. When the company stopped that evening, mother came around the wagons calling 'Langley.' I could hear her calling, [but] she could not hear me answer. When she found me [and] lifted me out of the wagon, my legs and arms [were] stiff like a frozen shirt. An ox was about to die. He was killed, [and] mother got some of the meat, boiled it, and gave me some of the broth. It ran through me like going through a funnel."[8]

On the same day the Martin company left Martin's Cove, the Willie company arrived in the Salt Lake Valley. Ahead of the Martin, Hodgetts, and Hunt companies stretched another 325 miles of desolation and mountains deep with snow.

Although many people lost their lives at Martin's Cove, there is no consensus on the number. One estimate is 17 deaths; other estimates are higher.[9] Some accounts say that 56 died there, but that is the number who died earlier during the nine days between the last crossing of the Platte and the departure from Red Buttes.

DANIEL W. JONES AND OTHERS ASSIGNED TO STAY AT DEVIL'S GATE

The freight from the Hunt and Hodgetts wagons could not be left unattended for the winter, so a delegation was chosen to remain behind to guard it. This would be perhaps the most unenviable assignment of the entire operation. According to Daniel W. Jones, Captain Grant thought it would be asking too much for anyone to stay, and he was not sure anyone would accept even if called upon. The assignment would be fraught with risk and misery. Whoever stayed would almost certainly have to fend off attempts to steal the goods that were left behind. Whoever stayed would have little to eat, because there were almost no provisions to leave. They would also have to endure winter in a very inhospitable place and be away from family and friends for several months longer than expected.

When Captain Grant asked who would accept such an assignment, Dan Jones said that any of them would. "I had no idea I would be selected," he wrote, "as it was acknowledged I was the best cook in camp and Capt. Grant had often spoken as though he could not spare me."[10] But Dan Jones was apparently just as well known for his willingness to obey and sacrifice as for his frontier cuisine, and George Grant asked if he would take this assignment. Dan later recalled:

"There was not money enough on earth to have hired me to stay. I had left home for only a few days and was not prepared to remain so long away; but I remembered my assertion that any of us would stay if called upon."[11]

Those who were about to leave Devil's Gate could hardly conceive of anyone staying there. They especially felt bad that one of the express rescuers, who meant so much to them, would be left in such a situation. John Bond recalled, "When this order was announced, many of the Saints shed tears as they had met Brother Jones at Red

Buttes when the first relief party came from Utah, and they hated to see him stay in such a bleak, cold place."[12]

Daniel W. Jones's Background

Daniel W. Jones was a Missourian who had been orphaned at a young age. Historian Wallace Stegner described him as "a harder Huckleberry Finn who from the age of eleven had made his tough way on a tough frontier."[13] Dan Jones described himself as "probably as willful a boy as ever lived. No one could control me by any other means than kindness, and this I did not often meet with."[14]

In 1847 Dan Jones went to the Southwest as a member of the Missouri volunteers to fight in the Mexican War. After the war he stayed in Mexico until 1850, living what he described as a "wild, reckless life . . . of gambling, swearing, fighting, and other rough conduct."[15] How did such a man come to the point that he would willingly make perhaps the greatest sacrifice of any of the rescuers?

In the summer of 1850, Dan Jones came through Utah as part of a company that was driving 8,000 sheep from Santa Fe. One day while camped at the Green River, he accidentally shot himself. Describing the injury, he wrote: "The ball ranged downward, entering the groin and thigh, passing through some fourteen inches of flesh. . . . Almost everyone in the company expressed the belief that I would die."[16]

The company's guide advised Dan to try to "get to the Mormon settlements, telling me about their goodness, and that if I could reach them, they would care for me."[17] Dan was surprised, having heard the usual stories about why the Mormons had been driven from Missouri and other states. Nevertheless, he accepted his guide's advice and was carried for 15 days to Spanish Fork, where he convalesced in the home of Bishop Isaac Higbee. Wallace Stegner described how the experience with this family changed Dan Jones's life:

"The kindness with which he was treated smote his orphan heart; he found himself hankering after the security of the Mormon confidence in the Lord. Before long he joined the Church, married a

Mormon girl, and settled down. It was proper that when Brigham Young . . . said that men were needed to rescue the handcart emigrants . . . , Dan Jones should volunteer. Kindness for kindness. He was a man who honored his obligations."[18]

The Ordeal Begins

For Dan Jones, honoring his obligations in this case meant spending six months in miserable conditions to guard freight on which he had no personal claim. Captain Grant said he could select any two men from the rescue team to stay with him. "I had a . . . mind to [select] Captains Grant and Burton," he said.[19] Instead he selected Thomas Alexander and Ben Hampton, men who would prove faithful through the most trying hardships. Seventeen members of the Hunt and Hodgetts wagon companies stayed behind to assist them.

Captain George Grant addressed these men before he left with the handcart company. He emphasized that a great trust was being placed in them and that they must be men of integrity, men of God. He did not want any fault-finding or grumbling, nor did he want "one of the company to be the butt of the others because he may not be so smart."[20] They were to "sleep with one eye open and one leg out of bed" to guard against any troublemakers who might prowl around. They were to be industrious physically and spiritually, repairing the "old shanties" and keeping water in their vessels. They were to be obedient to Dan Jones, who was counseled to "maintain the dignity of his calling and not joke too much or suffer himself to be joked with" so he would not lose his influence.[21] In addition to protecting the freight in the buildings, the men were to protect some 75 cattle that were being left behind because they were too weak to continue. Besides protecting the cattle, they were requested not to use them for such services as hauling wood.

Although several months of winter lay ahead, Dan Jones and his men were given only 20 days of rations. Their nearest potential sources of supply were 50 miles to the east at the Platte Bridge and

215 miles to the west at Fort Bridger, though neither was a real possibility. At one point Dan Jones would beat a 50-mile path through the snow to the Platte Bridge only to find that the mountaineers there were out of flour and living on meat alone.

The Rawhide Diet

Within the first week, wolves killed at least 25 of the cattle and were becoming increasingly bold. At risk of losing all the cattle to the wolves, Dan Jones's men killed the other 50 and dressed and hung what little meat remained on them. Before long, the flour was gone and the men had nothing to eat but beef. By January the beef was gone, so they resorted to eating the hides, which provided a gluey mix that made them sick. "They knelt in meeting and prayed for the Lord to direct them," Stegner writes, and "he directed them back to the hides. These lay stacked outside the cabins, half snowed-over, frozen as still as crumpled sheet metal. Reluctantly they scalded and scraped the hair off another one and cut it up and boiled it until it was soft enough to be chewed. It still had a lot of unpleasant glue in it, but they got it down this time."[22]

This probably was not the answer to prayer the men were hoping for, but they accepted it nevertheless. Soon Dan Jones called upon his culinary expertise to evolve a recipe to make the hides more palatable:

"Scorch and scrape the hair off; this had a tendency to kill and purify the bad taste that scalding gave it. After scraping, boil one hour in plenty of water, throwing the water away which had extracted all the glue, then wash and scrape the hide thoroughly . . . in cold water, then boil to a jelly and let it get cold, and then eat with a little sugar sprinkled on it. This was considerable trouble, but we had little else to do and it was better than starving.

"We asked the Lord to bless our stomachs and adapt them to this food. We hadn't the faith to ask him to bless the rawhide."[23]

Acts of Faith; the Lord Provides

The men at Devil's Gate subsisted on this rawhide diet for six weeks. Toward the end of this time, Dan Jones learned that some of the men had become so desperate that they were secretly "cutting steaks" from the carcasses of cattle that had died months earlier.[24] Some men were even being tempted by the frozen offal from the butchered cattle. Dan Jones saw this as the start of something ugly. He believed that the Lord would provide if they would purify their hearts, so on their monthly fast day he had the men dispose of all the old carcasses and offal so they would no longer be tempted. They washed out the storehouse they had used for butchering and presented it clean—but empty—before the Lord. After this demonstration of faith, it was, as Wallace Stegner said, the "Lord's move."

Would wild game be the answer this time? Dan Jones had shot a buffalo several weeks earlier, but game had become scarce since then. Attempts to hunt were also hindered by deep snow, which slowed the men and allowed the occasional animal to see them and move out of range.

Again the Lord provided in an unexpected way. Later that day an Indian came by the fort. At first the men thought he might be the answer to their prayers, but he was as hungry as they were. They found a small piece of rawhide for him to eat and then all waited together, fully expecting to receive the most unlikely of suppers. Toward 9:00 P.M. they heard voices outside. "Here comes supper!" one of the men exclaimed. The voices came from some mail carriers who were seeking shelter.

"I am glad to get here," said Jesse Jones, the leader of the group.

"I am as glad to see you," Dan Jones answered.

"Why are you so glad to see us?" Jesse asked.

"We were waiting for you to bring our supper," Dan told him.[25]

The mail carriers put everything they had in the pot. The men at Devil's Gate—and their Indian friend—finally had a meal, but the windfall did not last long. The next day the cupboard was bare again, even for the mail carriers. What next? "Nothing in such a basic western plot as this is wasted," Stegner writes.[26] One of the mail carriers could speak to the Indian, who said "his band was camped a day upriver, out of meat and hungry, but that he thought he could find game if some of them would come along to protect him from the Crows. The mail outfit, now without provisions to go on, had no choice but to . . . see if the Indian could prove his brag. He did. He took ten men out and brought them back after dark with their mules laden with buffalo meat."[27]

The Man That Ate the Pack Saddle

By early March, Dan Jones and his men were again out of food. This time they had consumed every scrap of cowhide, every moccasin, all the rawhide ties off the handcarts and wagon tongues, and even an old doormat made of buffalo hide. "They took inventory and found nothing edible in the whole place," Stegner says, "except a set of harness (dubious) and a rawhide pack saddle (sporting)."[28] Just as the men were soaking the pack saddle to cook, the Lord intervened again. An express mail team led by Bill Hickman arrived, and the mules were carrying buffalo meat. The saddle was removed from the pot and replaced with the meat, and the men had another providential meal. Stegner concludes:

"Hickman and the other express men were a long time getting over that dinner they saw on the fire. For years they called Dan Jones the man that ate the pack saddle. He always denied it, but admitted that if they hadn't arrived just when they did, he might have been talked into taking a wing or a leg."[29]

Protecting the Goods from Attack

Captain Grant's departing words several months earlier suggest that he thought Dan Jones and his men might have to fend off frequent attacks from marauders and Indians who wanted to steal the goods at the fort.[30] Instead, the only real attack came from a group of apostate Church members.

In early May a group of reinforcements from Salt Lake City

arrived and told Dan Jones that 40 to 50 apostates were headed toward the fort to demand the freight that was stored there. When the apostates arrived, Dan Jones released the goods to those who presented receipts, but he declined to release anything to the others. His refusal brought on a confrontation as the apostates took cover behind the cabins and threatened a gunfight. Dan Jones not only stood his ground but seemed to welcome the fight, telling them:

"We have been here all winter eating poor beef and rawhide to take care of these goods. We have had but little fun, and would just as soon have some now as not; in fact would like a little row [fight]. If you think you can take the fort, just try it. But I don't think you can take me to commence with; and the first one that offers any violence to me is a dead man. Now I dare you to get past me towards the fort."[31]

The men backed down, though not without a taunt: "For your family's sake I will spare you," one of them said, "for I think you [are a] d——d fool enough to die before you would give up the goods."[32]

False Accusations

Dan Jones returned to Salt Lake City in the early summer of 1857. Unfortunately, some of the people whose belongings he had been guarding were "unable to tell a Lone Ranger from a rustler," and they began to accuse him of stealing from them.[33] One person even searched Dan Jones's house for missing items.

When some of the accusers filed a formal complaint, Brigham Young asked Dan Jones if he would come to a hearing to discuss the allegations. Dan Jones agreed, but he was so hurt—and so concerned that Brigham Young would believe his accusers—that he considered leaving the country. He stayed only because the Spirit whispered to him that Brigham Young would discern the truth because he was a prophet.

The hearing was held in Brigham Young's office. When Dan Jones arrived, he worried because he didn't see any witnesses on his behalf. "When we need them we will send for them," Brigham

Young said. Dan Jones was then asked to give an account of all the expenditures for keeping his men at Devil's Gate through the winter. When he finished, his accusers again questioned his honesty, not because the expenses were too high but because they were suspiciously low—only 75 cents a week for each man. Brigham Young asked Dan Jones to explain why the amount was so low. Dan's itemization made his defense better than any collection of witnesses could have done:

- Forty head of cattle that were already dying: no charge
- Occasional wild game: no charge
- Two weeks of thistle roots: no charge
- One week of wild garlic bulbs: no charge
- Three days of minnows caught in a dip net: no charge
- Several meals of roasted prickly pear cactus: no charge
- Quite a few days of nothing but water: no charge

What did the 75 cents a week cover? Dan Jones reported: "All meats bought of Indians or anyone else. All groceries, soap, candles, in fact everything used belonging to the companies, including some leather owned by F. D. Richards, who remarked to me that he was glad it was there for us to use."[34]

After Dan Jones finished his statements, Brigham Young gave the accusers a chance to respond. No one spoke. Brigham Young then stood and chastised the men for making false accusations. As his tone became more condemning, Dan Jones interrupted and asked him to stop. "I . . . told him I could bear [the men's] accusations better than they could bear his curse," he reported.[35]

On June 11, 1857, Brigham Young sent a letter to the bishops in Utah exonerating Dan Jones and making an offer to any others who felt inclined to accuse or criticize him:

"Beloved Brethren:

"Inasmuch as there are some persons disposed to find fault with the management of Brother Daniel W. Jones while at Devil's Gate, we feel desirous to express ourselves perfectly satisfied with his labors while there, and with the care that he has taken of the property intrusted to him. He has our confidence, and we say, God bless him for what he has done. The men who find fault with the labors of Brother Jones the past winter, we wish their names sent to this office, and when the Lord presents an opportunity we will try them and see if they will do any better."[36]

One common point of confusion is that two men by the name of Dan Jones were prominent in the emigration of 1856. Before the rescuer Daniel W. Jones came into the story, the returning missionary Dan Jones had a leadership role.

Elder Dan Jones was a native of Wales who was returning from his second mission to his homeland. Under his direction, a handful of missionaries baptized some 4,000 converts during his first mission and thousands more during his second. Like James Willie and Edward Martin, Elder Dan Jones was assigned to preside over an emigrant ship when he was released from his mission in 1856. His ship, the S. Curling, *carried mostly Welsh converts and left Liverpool five weeks before Edward Martin's* Horizon.

Nearly half of the Saints on the S. Curling *were organized into the third handcart company when they reached Iowa City. Instead of leading this handcart company, Elder Dan Jones was made captain of the wagon company that was assigned to travel closely with the Martin handcarts. He was not captain for long, however. The company divided when Benjamin Hodgetts led an advance group of wagons out of Iowa City. Less than two weeks later, Elder Jones relinquished his position as captain of the other 50 wagons to John Hunt.*

After leaving the wagon company, Elder Jones went ahead to Florence. When the season's emigration work was finished there, he traveled with Franklin D. Richards's group to the Platte Bridge (modern-day Casper, Wyoming). He finished the journey to Salt Lake City with the Smoot wagon train.

CHAPTER 34

HELP FROM EPHRAIM HANKS

One reason the men at Devil's Gate had not been left with much food is that the rescuers' food supply was dangerously low. The few wagons of the first rescue team had been on the trail for more than a month, and the provisions were quickly exhausted in trying to feed some 900 people. Additional relief wagons were supposed to be coming, but there was no way to know when they might arrive. So even with the help of the rescuers and improvement in the weather, the outlook still seemed bleak for the Martin company. The weight of what lay ahead is heavy in the following description of the group after leaving Martin's Cove with the rescuers:

"The company moved slowly—not all together as they had at

Ephraim Hanks

first, but strung out in a long line that made a needle and a trailing black line in the snow. No one sang, no one talked. Folks just pushed along at their own pace and tried not to think of how the days might stretch into weeks and months before the last of them found a long sleep in a trench of snow."[1]

Just before sunset on November 10, the day after leaving Martin's Cove, "a strange quiver like a thrill of hopefulness was communicated down the wavering line. . . . Coming toward the train was a lone man leading two horses with great pieces of buffalo hung on each side of the animals."[2] The lone man was Ephraim Hanks, one of the premier frontiersmen of the day. He provided most timely assistance. He also provided hope, being the first person to bring word that additional rescuers were coming.[3]

"I AM READY NOW!"

The story of how Ephraim Hanks came to help the Martin company shows great spiritual sensitivity, courage, and determination. After the first rescue team left Salt Lake City, Ephraim heard a voice in the night calling him to help the handcart companies. The next day he went to the city, where he heard a call for more rescuers. Eph said, "When some of the brethren responded by explaining that they could get ready to start in a few days, I spoke at once saying, 'I am ready now!'"[4] The next day he began the journey east with one light wagon.

When Ephraim reached South Pass, he was stopped by storms for three days. He said, "In all my travels in the Rocky Mountains both before and afterwards, I have seen no worse." He stayed at South Pass with Reddick Allred, unable to move his wagon. Then, "being deeply concerned about the possible fate of the immigrants, . . . I determined to start out on horseback to meet them."[5]

Soon after leaving South Pass, Ephraim Hanks was preparing his camp in the snow. "I thought how comfortable a buffalo robe would be on such an occasion," he wrote, "and also how I could relish a little buffalo meat for supper, and before lying down for the night I was instinctively led to ask the Lord to send me a buffalo."[6] Eph then looked around and saw a buffalo within 50 yards. He killed it with his first shot and then skinned and dressed it, ate some of the meat, and went to bed.

MEETING UP WITH THE MARTIN COMPANY

The next morning Ephraim Hanks killed another buffalo at Ice Springs Bench. He loaded the meat on his horses and resumed his journey. Later that day he finally found the Martin company. Recalling this experience, he wrote:

"I think the sun was about an hour high in the west when I spied something in the distance that looked like a black streak in the snow. As I got near to it, I perceived it moved; then I was satisfied that this was the long looked for handcart company led by Captain Edward Martin.

"I reached the ill-fated train just as the immigrants were camping for the night. The sight that met my gaze as I entered their camp can never be erased from my memory. The starved forms and haggard countenances of the poor sufferers, as they moved about slowly, shivering with cold, to prepare their scanty evening meal was enough to touch the stoutest heart. When they saw me coming, they hailed me with joy inexpressible, and when they further beheld the supply of fresh meat I brought into camp, their gratitude knew no bounds. Flocking around me, one would say, 'Oh, please, give me a small piece of meat'; another would exclaim, 'My poor children are starving, do give me a little'; and children with tears in their eyes would call out, 'Give me some, give me some.'

"At first I tried to wait on them and handed out the meat as they called for it; but finally I told them to help themselves. Five minutes later both my horses had been released of their extra burden—the meat was all gone, and the next few hours found the people in camp busily engaged in cooking and eating it, with thankful hearts."[7]

CARING FOR THE SICK AND FROZEN

Ephraim Hanks tried to lift the people's drooping spirits. He gave special care to those who were most sick and frozen. On the night he met the Martin company, David Blair, the London branch president who had been a member of Queen Victoria's Life Guard, was at the point of death. In tears his wife went to Daniel Tyler, a subcaptain, and asked him to administer to her husband. When Daniel Tyler saw him, he said, "I cannot administer to a dead man" and asked Eph Hanks to prepare the body for burial. Instead,

Eph anointed David Blair with oil and administered to him, "command[ing] him in the name of Jesus Christ to breathe and live."[8] David Blair was soon much better, and his wife ran through camp expressing her joy. Although he would die within the next two weeks, this brief respite provided a few more days with his family.

A constant flow of people sought blessings from Ephraim Hanks. As he administered to them, he witnessed many manifestations of God's power and love. Describing this experience, he later wrote:

"The greater portion of my time was devoted to waiting on the sick. 'Come to me,' 'help me,' 'please administer to my sick wife,' or 'my dying child,' were some of the requests that were being made of me almost hourly. . . . I spent days going from tent to tent administering to the sick. Truly the Lord was with me and others of His servants who labored faithfully together with me in that day of trial and suffering."[9]

To those whose limbs were severely frozen, Eph Hanks provided a harder service. He explained:

"Many of the immigrants whose extremities were frozen lost their limbs, either whole or in part. Many such I washed with water and castile soap, until the frozen parts would fall off, after which I would sever the shreds of flesh from the remaining portions of the limbs with my scissors. Some of the emigrants lost toes, others fingers, and again others whole hands and feet; one woman . . . lost both her legs below the knees, and quite a number who survived became cripples for life."[10]

Eph Hanks's son Sidney explained in more detail how his father helped those with frozen limbs:

"The next morning everyone in camp was talking about Brother Hanks, about his prayers for the sick, but even more the operations he had performed with his hunting knife. Many of the Saints were carrying frozen limbs which were endangering their lives. Brother Hanks amputated toes and feet. . . . First [he] anointed these folks and prayed that the amputation could be done without pain. Then . . . he took out his great hunting knife, held it to the fire to cleanse it, and took off the dying limb with its keen blade; many with tears in their eyes said they hadn't 'felt a thing.' "[11]

"HE ALWAYS COUNTS ON HUMAN FOLKS TO HELP HIM OUT"

Ephraim Hanks's son Sidney also recounted the following words from his father to those he assisted in the Martin company. Although Sidney was not there to hear these words, he likely heard them when his father told the story:

"The Lord does do strange things," Eph said, "but I notice He always counts on human folks to help Him out. Now I've traveled this road time and again, and at this time of year I wouldn't ever have expected to meet a buffalo. But you folks needed meat, and he was put in my way."[12]

Ephraim Hanks remained with the Martin company, serving those in need all the way to the Salt Lake Valley. Six years later he married Thisbe Read of the Martin company.

ARZA HINCKLEY'S ACCOUNT

Although few accounts mention it, Ephraim Hanks apparently had a companion as he assisted the Martin company. The man was Arza Hinckley, who had served with Eph in the Mormon Battalion 10 years earlier. Arza's handwritten account of meeting and assisting the handcart company is only three modest sentences:

"We met the handcart folks at Ice Springs on the Sweetwater River, from there in to Salt Lake City. Eph Hanks, one of my battalion chums, spent much of our time while in camp administering to the sick. Ephraim was a man of great faith."[13]

A more detailed account of Arza's experiences is given by a daughter, Luna Ardell Hinckley Paul. It has some significant differences from the account given by Ephraim Hanks, but it seems plausible enough to justify including in the record.

At the time of the rescue, Arza Hinckley was Brigham Young's personal teamster. A week after the first rescuers left, Brigham Young asked Arza to drive him toward the handcart companies. When they got to Big Canyon Creek, Brigham Young became too ill to continue, so they returned home.[14] Several days later, Daniel Wells asked Brigham Young if he could spare Arza to go help with the rescue. Brigham Young assented and offered the use of his mules. Arza and a friend, Dan Johnson, each left Salt Lake City with a four-mule wagon loaded with supplies.

When Arza and Dan reached Fort Bridger, they were delayed for a few days by a blizzard. Soon after they got back on the trail, they met two companies of rescuers who were returning home. These men explained that they felt the rescue was futile because they had gone all the way to Pacific Springs and had not received any word of the handcart company. Although Arza does not mention these men in his account, his daughter identifies one of them as Ephraim Hanks.

After listening to the men's explanation for returning home, Arza said, "I will make a proposition with you. There is a good place to camp just a short distance from here. You go on and camp and wait until you hear about the carts, and Dan and I will go and find the handcarts."

"What makes you think you can find them when we couldn't?" one of the men asked.

"Brigham Young sent me to find the handcart folks, and I will find them or give my life trying to find them," Arza answered.[15]

According to this account, Eph Hanks was troubled when Arza Hinckley left. He kept thinking about the voice in the night that had called him to help the handcart companies. He was also stirred by Arza's determination to press forward. He soon told his friends that he was leaving to catch up with Arza and Dan. Riding one horse and leading another, he met them at the Green River crossing. "I hoped you would follow us," Arza told him.

One of Brigham Young's mules had died, and the others were struggling, so the men decided that Dan Johnson should take them back to Fort Bridger for shelter.[16] Eph Hanks hitched his horses to one of the wagons, and he and Arza continued forward on their own.

They went more than 100 miles—50 miles past Pacific Springs—before meeting up with the Martin company.

On November 10, Eph and Arza made camp in the afternoon because their mules needed to rest. Arza stayed with the mules while Eph went hunting buffalo. After hunting for a long time, Eph killed a large cow buffalo. By the time he packed the meat on his horses, it was almost dark. Eph was preparing to ride back to camp when he noticed a flicker of firelight in the opposite direction. Thinking the light must be from the Martin company, he rode toward it. As he got closer, he saw more lights, and his heart began to pound. Shouts of joy rang through the air as he rode into camp.

After Eph distributed the meat from his horses, he returned to his camp with Arza, who was so elated he couldn't sleep. Early the next morning, Arza and Eph drove their provision wagons into the handcart camp. Both men then proceeded to care for the sick and help the company all the way to the Salt Lake Valley.[17]

James Bleak was so grateful to Arza Hinckley that whenever he saw him, he put his arms around him and said, "My savior."[18]

CHAPTER 35

SOME OF THE RESCUERS TURN BACK

Ephraim Hanks and Arza Hinckley were the first rescuers to meet the Martin company after the first rescue team had found them nearly two weeks earlier. Daniel W. Jones said the rescuers were at a loss to know why others had not come to help. "When we left Salt Lake it was understood that other teams would follow until all the help needed would be on the road," he wrote.[1]

What had happened to all the other rescuers? Many of them did the same as those whom Arza Hinckley met: they turned back. In a sympathetic analysis of these rescuers, Rebecca Bartholomew and Leonard J. Arrington wrote:

"First, without hard facts as to where they were going and what was needed, it was difficult to know how much to risk. Second, the roads in places were nearly impassable by late October. . . . These later rescuers were in as much danger of frozen limbs and starvation if they pushed too far too fast as were the immigrants. Crossing Big Mountain, [some] had encountered snow 'up to the tops of our wagon bows.' Some . . . had their feet badly frozen and had to be left on the Weber, Bear, and Yellow rivers to recuperate. . . .

"The hardier teams had reached Fort Bridger. There they congregated with other wagons originally sent out to help [the] Willie [company] but who had been commandeered into heading east toward Martin's camp. At Fort Bridger there had been no word on what to do next. . . . [Some of the rescuers concluded] that the Martin company must have either wintered or perished along with Captain Grant's relief teams. They were the ones who had started back toward the valley, causing . . . all 77 teams which had arrived at Bridger to return with them."[2]

An express courier was sent from Fort Bridger to inform Brigham Young that these rescuers were returning home. On November 11, two days after the Martin company left Martin's Cove, this courier arrived in Salt Lake City and reported on the return of these wagons. Brigham Young immediately sent a four-man express to intercept the rescuers, turn them back around, and tell them to keep going until they met the Martin, Hunt, and Hodgetts companies.[3] According to one account, Brigham Young told these men "that he did not care if [they] turned some so quick that it would snap their necks."[4]

The men in this express were William Kimball, Hosea Stout, Joseph Simmons, and James Ferguson.[5] William Kimball's participation is especially noteworthy. He had been working tirelessly on behalf of the emigrants since concluding his mission in England earlier in the year. From England he had gone to the Midwest to help outfit the companies. After working for several months to complete that assignment, he left Florence in September with President Richards's group and traveled to Salt Lake City. Three days after returning home, he left Salt Lake City with the first rescue team, led by George D. Grant. After finding the Willie company, he was put in charge of leading them back to Salt Lake City. He completed that assignment on November 9. Just two days later, Brigham Young sent him east again.

That night the express sent by Brigham Young camped five miles east of Salt Lake City. The next morning they met John Van Cott and his wagons near Big Mountain. Hosea Stout recorded:

"Van Cott justified himself for returning and abandoning the handcart company as he could get no information of them and had concluded they had returned to the states, or stopped at Laramie, [or] been killed by the Indians . . . , and for him to have gone further was only to lose his team and starve to death himself and do no good after all. As for G. D. Grant and those with him who had gone to meet them, they had probably stopped at Fort Laramie. So on these vague conclusions he had not only turned back but had caused all the rest of the teams to return and thus leave the poor suffering handcarters to their fate."[6]

However reasonable John Van Cott's explanation may have seemed, William Kimball was unmoved by it. Hosea Stout wrote that "Br. Kimball reprimanded him severely for his course." He then presented a letter from Brigham Young, and John Van Cott turned around and started eastward again.[7] Whether John Van Cott turned his wagons around out of obligation or altruism, doing so must have been difficult when he was so close to home. Like others who made errors, John Van Cott should be commended for his efforts to make amends.

Later that day this group received their first word about the Martin company. As they neared the Weber River, they met Joseph Young and Abel Garr, the express that Captain Grant had sent from Devil's Gate on November 3. After hearing their report, William Kimball pushed the group forward with even greater urgency, averaging over 30 miles a day. Each day they overtook other wagon teams, some of which Joseph Young and Abel Garr had already turned around.[8] By November 17 this rescue train numbered 30 wagons.[9] Finally, after losing precious days and perhaps weeks, most of the rescuers who had turned back were again headed in the right direction.[10]

John Van Cott had been president of the Scandinavian Mission from 1853 to 1856. Earlier in the year he had returned to the United States with George D. Grant to help outfit the handcart companies. He then returned to Salt Lake City as part of President Franklin D. Richards's group.

The difference between George D. Grant's approach to the rescue and the approach of those who turned back is striking. George Grant did not wait for instructions before continuing past the point where he thought he would find the companies. He apparently did not calculate the risks to himself or his teams. And he did not make assumptions about the fate of the companies that caused him to stop pressing forward.

CHAPTER 36

FROM THE PLAINS OF WYOMING TO THE MOUNTAINS OF UTAH

Assisted by Ephraim Hanks and Arza Hinckley, Captain George Grant's rescue team steadily moved the Martin company westward. They crossed Rocky Ridge on November 16, six days after Eph Hanks rode into camp. It was a "bitterly cold day," John Jaques recalled, as the "snow fell fast and the wind blew piercingly from the north."[1] Because many members of the Martin company were in wagons and none were pulling handcarts, they did not experience the terrible ordeal that the Willie company had suffered on Rocky Ridge nearly four weeks earlier.

On the day the Martin company crossed Rocky Ridge, the first substantial reinforcement of rescuers arrived with 10 wagons from Salt Lake City.[2] This assistance must have been especially welcome to Captain Grant and his small team of rescuers. By November 16, Captain Grant's men, already divided in strength when some of them stayed to help the Willie company, had been caring for the 900 members of the Martin, Hunt, and Hodgetts companies for 17 days without substantial assistance. Having expected additional help in the first few days, they must have begun to wonder if it would ever come.

The rescuers who met the Martin company on Rocky Ridge were led by Anson Call.[3] He had returned from a colonizing mission about a week after Brigham Young issued the initial call to rescue. Soon after returning home, he was asked to leave again to lead a group of rescuers from Bountiful. It is significant that this group did not turn back despite what could be considered good reasons to do so.

Anson Call's rescue team met the Willie company at Fort Bridger on November 3. Some of them felt that they had fulfilled their duty when they met the Willie company, but Anson encouraged them to keep moving forward. "This company [Willie] with a little help . . . will reach the Valley," he told them. "Those following never can. We must push on. My teams, start now!"[4]

Soon after leaving Fort Bridger, these rescuers became stalled at the Green River for a few days due to snow and cold. Again, rather than turning back, they proceeded forward as soon as they could move. Their timeliness in meeting the Martin company on Rocky Ridge is clear from Anson Call's own words: "We found them starving and freezing and dying, and the most suffering that I ever saw among human beings."[5]

Anson Call later married Emma Summers of the Willie company and Margaretta Clark of the Martin company.

Two days after crossing Rocky Ridge, the Martin company reached Reddick Allred's station on the Sweetwater near South Pass.[6] When the first rescue team had crossed South Pass a month earlier, Captain Grant assigned Reddick Allred and a few other men to stay in the area with some provision wagons and be ready to assist the handcart companies as he brought them through. This was an unenviable assignment, requiring weeks of waiting while enduring the severe storms at one of the highest elevations on the trail. At least two men returned home and tried to persuade Reddick to do likewise (see pages 159–62). However, he stayed true to this assignment, showing the tenacity of his nickname, Bulldog, even though he was suffering with pleurisy.

More than three weeks earlier Reddick Allred had provided life-sustaining aid to the Willie company. Now he provided assistance to the Martin company. Captain Grant was so happy to see him that he greeted him with a cheer: "Hurrah for the Bulldog. Good for hanging on."[7]

There was also other good news at Reddick Allred's station.

Waiting for the Martin company were William Kimball, Hosea Stout, and many of the rescue wagons they had turned around—enough that everyone would be able to ride. Reddick Allred wrote:

"Nov. 18th. The teams having all arrived we were organized into companies of tens by wagons, each ten taking up a company of 100 as they were organized in the handcarts. . . . All could ride, although much crowded. We then set out for the City with this half starved, half frozen, almost entirely exhausted company of about 500 Saints. But from that time on they did not suffer with hunger or fatigue but all suffered more or less with cold. As well as I was provided I even lost my toenails from frost."[8]

Recalling this day when all could ride, young Peter McBride wrote: "We got word that some teams were coming to meet us from the Valley. . . . No one but a person having gone through what we had suffered can imagine what a happy moment it was for this 'belated handcart company.' Men, women, and children knelt down and thanked the Almighty God for our delivery from certain death. It put new life into all the Saints. The next day several more teams arrived, and there was room for all to ride."[9]

FURTHER TRIALS OF ELIZABETH SERMON AND HER SONS

After her husband died at Martin's Cove, Elizabeth Sermon had much to do to care for her four children. Each night she would clear away the snow with a tin plate, gather wood, make a fire, carry her children to the fire, and make their beds. "We went to bed without supper," she wrote, "so that we could have more for breakfast. I found it some help to toast the rawhide on the coals and chew it. It kind of kept the terrible hunger away."[10]

Three of Elizabeth's children had severely frostbitten feet. What Elizabeth had to do for those children was unimaginable for a loving mother:

"I had to take a portion of poor Robert's feet off, which pierced my very soul. I had to sever the leaders with a pair of scissors. Little did I think when I bought them in old England that they would be used for such a purpose. Every day some portion was decaying until the poor boy's feet were all gone. Then John's began to freeze; then after a while my own. . . .

"I was terribly put to for clothes to wrap my poor boy's legs in, his feet all gone. I got all I could from the camp, then I used my underclothing until I had but two skirts left on my body, and as such I finished my journey."[11]

After all that Elizabeth had endured, after pulling her family through so many trials, after remaining strong through her husband's misgivings, illness, and death, she for the first time yearned for the relief that death would bring:

"At last the old handcart was laid by without a regret; we got to the wagons, were taken in, and some days we rode all day and got a little more food. A severe storm came up. . . . My eldest boy John's feet decaying, my boys both of them losing their limbs, their father dead, my own feet very painful, I thought, 'Why can't I die?' My first thought of death."[12]

TO THE END OF THE TRAIL

The Martin company made faster progress once they were all in wagons, traveling an average of 22 miles a day. Although they were more adequately fed and clothed, it was still hard to get relief from the cold. Some felt that riding in the wagons was actually colder than walking because they were not generating any body heat. And some felt that sleeping in the wagons was colder than sleeping on the frozen ground. On the ground, John Jaques wrote, "if the biting, frosty air got the upper hand of you, it could not get the underside of you as well, but it could do both in a wagon."[13] Patience Loader, John's sister-in-law, also wrote about this unexpected problem:

"The good brother [who owned] the wagon told us that we could sleep in [it] and he would make a hole in the snow and make his bed there. He thought we would be warmer in the wagon. We made our bed there, but we only had one old quilt to lie on, and in the night I woke up and called to mother, 'I am freezing.' The side I had laid on was so benumbed with cold. Mother got up and helped me out of the wagon. There were some big fires burning in several places in the camp, and lots of the sisters [were] sitting and sleeping near the fire to keep warm. So I went to the fire and stayed there the remainder of the night."[14]

These emigrants, most of whom had never pitched a tent or built a campfire, were not only learning how to live in the outdoors but were also learning winter survival skills. "The way to have a warm sleeping place," John Jaques discovered, was to "sweep away the ashes of the campfire and lay your bed on the spot where the fire was built."[15] But sleeping in such a spot may have been unsettling when its next intended use was known. "In the morning," John Jaques continued, "the same spot was found to be the most available for a graver use—it was the easiest place in which to dig a grave to bury the night's dead. No pun is here intended. The subject is too serious. Besides, the punning propensity is detestable. Thus, in this severe winter traveling and camping economy, the earth served three separate, distinct, and important purposes."[16]

Patience Loader later figured out how to stay warmer in the wagon: "After we baked our bread, we put the hot coals in our bake kettle and took it in the wagon and that made it quite comfortable and warm for us to sleep."[17] She also continued to appreciate the kindness of the rescuers:

"I can well remember how kind the brethren were to us poor, distressed-looking creatures. I think we must have looked a very deplorable set of human beings to them when they first met us camped in the snow. . . . What brave men they must have been to start out from Salt Lake City in the middle of winter in search of us poor folks. . . . They did not know how far they would have to travel in the snow before they would find us."[18]

The wagons carrying the Martin company reached the Little Sandy on the 19th and the Big Sandy on the 20th. That day, Captain Grant, William Kimball, and Hosea Stout started an express journey to Salt Lake City, leaving Robert T. Burton in charge of the companies. Their main purpose in going ahead was to give a report to Brigham Young. Their pace was so intense that by the time they reached Fort Bridger, Hosea Stout said he could "scarcely stand alone or keep awake."[19]

The Big Sandy Crossing was near the intersection of Highways 191 and 28 in present-day Farson, Wyoming.

The Martin company camped at the Green River crossing on the 21st, Black's Fork on the 22nd, and Fort Bridger on the 23rd. All the trials that John and Zilpah Jaques had endured for the previous six months did not compare with what occurred on November 23. Their two-year-old daughter, Flora, who had contracted the measles on the ship and never recovered her health, died that day. Her father cited multiple causes of death, the last one the most heartbreaking: "The poor little thing died . . . of dysentery, cold, insufficient nourishment, and unavoidable lack of needed attention."[20]

On November 23 the Martin company camped at Muddy Creek, and the next night they camped at the Bear River crossing, a few miles south of modern-day Evanston. John Jaques described the continuing cold in his usual sensory way: "In passing along, how the wagon tires did grind the hard frozen snow. . . . The wheels fairly whistled as they rolled through the elevated Bear River country."[21]

On November 26 the company camped in Echo Canyon. There the final birth of the journey occurred when a little girl was born to Sarah Squires. "The mother did quite as well as could have been expected," John Jaques recalled. "The little newcomer also did well, and was named Echo in honor of the place of her nativity."[22] When Echo was born, Henry and Sarah Squires were so destitute that they had nothing to dress or wrap her in. To remedy this problem, Henry ran around camp until he solicited a piece of underclothing from one of the rescuers and a pin to fasten it.[23]

What is left unmentioned in the accounts of Echo Squires's birth is how Sarah Squires managed the last horrific month of the journey in the last month of her pregnancy.

On November 27 the company camped on the Weber River, near modern-day Henefer. They camped in East Canyon the next night and by the head of Emigration Canyon the next. Four feet of fresh snow had fallen in the mountains, drifting much deeper in places. Joseph Young, Brigham Young Jr., and others were there packing the snow with their teams to keep the road open.

CHAPTER 37

ARRIVAL IN SALT LAKE CITY

As these poor people, many of them with badly frozen hands and feet, some of them nearer death than life, arrived in the valley, the women who were here opened their homes to them, nurtured them, dressed their wounds, fed them, and encouraged and blessed them through that long, bitter winter.

—PRESIDENT GORDON B. HINCKLEY

The Martin company finally reached the Salt Lake Valley on Sunday, November 30. They passed by the Temple block at about noon, just as the congregation was leaving a worship service in the old Tabernacle, and stopped at the tithing yard. According to John Jaques, the joy that should have accompanied the company's arrival was tempered because of the sobering condition of the people:

"The meeting of the emigrants with relatives, acquaintances, and friends was not very joyous. Indeed it was very solemnly impressive. Some were so affected that they could scarcely speak, but would look at each other until the sympathetic tears would force their unforbidden way."[1]

Although 18-year-old Langley Bailey was among those in precarious health, he described the thrill of finally seeing their destination: "We arrived in Salt Lake City Sunday noon, coming out of Emigration Canyon. I was lifted up in the wagon [and] could see houses in the distance. It was like the Israelites of old in beholding the promised land."[2]

"RECEIVE THEM AS YOUR OWN CHILDREN"

When Brigham Young learned of the Martin company's imminent arrival, he canceled the afternoon worship service so the people could go prepare to help them. He said:

"When those persons arrive, I do not want to see them put into houses by themselves. I want to have them distributed in the city among the families that have good and comfortable houses; and I wish all the sisters now before me, and all who know how and can, to nurse and wait upon the new comers and prudently administer medicine and food to them. To speak upon these things is a part of my religion, for it pertains to taking care of the Saints.

"As soon as this meeting is dismissed I want the brethren and sisters to repair to their homes, where their Bishops will call on them to take in some of this company; the Bishops will distribute them as the people can receive them. . . .

"The afternoon meeting will be omitted, for I wish the sisters to go home and prepare to give those who have just arrived a mouthful of something to eat, and to wash them and nurse them up. You know that I would give more for a dish of pudding and milk, or a baked potato and salt, were I in the situation of those persons who have just come in, than I would for all your prayers, though you were to stay here all the afternoon and pray. Prayer is good, but when baked potatoes and pudding and milk are needed, prayer will not supply their place on this occasion; give every duty its proper time and place. . . .

"Some you will find with their feet frozen to their ankles; some are frozen to their knees and some have their hands frosted. . . . We want you to receive them as your own children, and to have the same feeling for them. We are their temporal saviors, for we have saved them from death. . . . Now that most of them are here, we will continue our labors of love until they are able to take care of themselves."[3]

The Saints of Salt Lake City were moved by compassion for their frozen, ragged brothers and sisters. They immediately took them into their homes, where they cared for them and made them as comfortable as possible. Alice Walsh recalled, "The bishops of the wards of Salt Lake were on hand at the minute of our arrival and did all they possibly could for us, allotting so many to each ward."[4]

Brigham Young did not insulate himself from the tragedy. "I have sent word to Bishop Hunter that I will take in all that others will not take," he said from the pulpit. "I am willing to take my proportion."[5] Among those who were cared for by Brigham Young's family were some who had the greatest challenges—Emily Wall and Henrietta McPhail of the Willie company and Mary Johnson of the Martin company. Henrietta McPhail's mother died before the family emigrated, and her father died on the journey. Seven-year-old Mary Johnson's legs had to be amputated at the knees. Mary would go live with her sister after a few months in Brigham Young's home, but the prophet would continue to care about her. Several years later he would help her buy a sewing machine and make it possible for her to pay for the machine by learning to sew for others (see page 447).

Among those who finally made it to the Salt Lake Valley that day was Reddick Allred, the member of Captain Grant's rescue team who had faithfully stayed at his post near South Pass. "Thus ended one of the hardest and most successful missions I have ever performed," he wrote. While this assignment had not been as long as his earlier service in the Mormon Battalion, he seemed to feel it was just as difficult, describing it as "sharp in the extreme."[6] His faithfulness was later publicly recognized by President Heber C. Kimball:

"President Kimball blessed me from the stand with a multiplicity of blessings for my integrity and labors in not leaving my post, but sticking to the last under trying circumstances and influences."[7]

ARRIVAL OF THE HODGETTS AND HUNT COMPANIES

Soon after leaving Martin's Cove, the Hodgetts and Hunt wagon companies began to fall behind the Martin company. As more rescuers arrived, they primarily assisted the handcart Saints. Placing them in wagons pulled by fresh horses and mules, they stretched one to two weeks ahead of the wagon companies, which for a time were still pulled by lumbering, emaciated oxen.

On December 2, two days after the Martin company arrived in the Salt Lake Valley, another 60 rescue teams started east to help the Hodgetts and Hunt companies. The first wagons from these companies arrived in Salt Lake City in early December, and most of the rest of them arrived by December 15, having dug through several feet of snow in the mountains. Jesse Haven, who left his wagons at Fort Bridger and rode the rest of the way home with the rescuers, recorded the following feelings after being away more than four years:

"Glad to see my family and they [were] glad to see me. My wives and my little son whom I had never seen met me at the door. He was 3 years and 6 months old. I felt to thank my Heavenly Father that I had been permitted to see my family once more, also the City of the Saints. . . . I felt that I had been blessed while absent from the Saints, though I had passed through many hardships. . . . When I came out of Emigration Canyon, I shed tears of joy to [be] so near home."[8]

DEATH TOLL

A precise death count for the Martin company will probably never be determined. Josiah Rogerson, a member of the company, says that between 135 and 150 lost their lives on the trek, a figure that may be high.[9] Another member of the company, John Jaques, made a similar estimate, while acknowledging estimates as low as 100.[10] One modern study has documented 103 deaths—a figure that may be low because the sketchy records that exist likely exclude some deaths.[11]

These estimates would give the Martin company a mortality rate of between 18 and 26 percent. The mortality rate of the Willie company was about 15 percent (74 deaths). Mortality rates in the wagon companies were considerably lower, the Hodgetts company suffering 9 deaths (5 percent) and the Hunt company 21 deaths (8 percent).[12]

The most remarkable aspect of these figures is not how high they were but that they were not much higher, given the handcart companies' demographics and the deadly combination of starvation and exposure. On the matter of the mortality rate, Josiah Rogerson concluded:

"Taking into consideration that we were the last company of that season and that we had three veterans of Waterloo, between 75 and 80 years of age, . . . and considering that more than half of our . . . members were from 35 to 55 years of age, it is hardly to be wondered at that our loss was so great."[13]

CHAPTER 38

AFTER THE TREK:
DIFFICULTIES AND BLESSINGS

Legion are the stories of those who were there and who suffered almost unto death and who carried all of their lives the scars of that dreadful experience. It was a tragedy without parallel in the western migration of our people. When all is said and done, no one can imagine, no one can appreciate or understand how desperate were their circumstances.

—PRESIDENT GORDON B. HINCKLEY

The Martin company had taken six months to travel from England to Salt Lake City. They had pushed and pulled handcarts for more than three of those months. Rarely in the history of the Church has there been such tragedy and suffering. But rarely have the experiences of such a compressed time had such a lasting, far-reaching impact for good. Most members of the company began the journey with strong faith. Forged in the fires of affliction, this faith became unbending.

These Saints would need such faith, for their hardships would continue. Many would lose limbs and suffer other physical effects from the journey for the rest of their lives. Perhaps even more difficult, many would be sent to colonize the most remote, inhospitable areas of the West. Some women who left comfortable homes in England would begin their lives in Zion in crude dugouts with dirt roofs that leaked water onto them as they gave birth.

What is the eternal impact of those few months? While this question cannot be answered definitively, the following postscripts of those whose stories have been included in this account provide at least some vision of the handcart legacy that transcends time and place.

EDWARD MARTIN: "HE SHALL LEAD THOUSANDS TO ZION"

Edward Martin was 38 years old when he finished the handcart trek. In the 15 years since coming to America, he had personally known more adversity than most families experience in generations. He had endured the exodus from Nauvoo. Six of his first seven children had died. During six of those 15 years he had been away from his family in arduous military and Church service. But none of this compared to what he had just experienced with his handcart company. Raw horrors he could not have imagined were permanently etched in his mind. Even worse than seeing the suffering was being unable to provide any relief to the constant appeals for help.

As Edward Martin entered the Salt Lake Valley for the first time in more than four years, he must have wondered how much more he would be called upon—and be able—to bear. As it turned out, tragedy would continue to stalk him. Two wives and eight more children would precede him in death.

Leadership during the Trek

What kind of leader was Edward Martin? During the voyage across the Atlantic, he had looked after the welfare of more than 850 people by visiting every part of the ship six or seven times a day. One of the people under his care, Josiah Rogerson, recalled, "Every deck and its division received his daily surveillance, not as a spy or Boss, but as a brother and friend charged with keeping their safety and welfare."[1]

While overseeing nearly 600 people on the handcart trek, Edward Martin was equally vigilant. Josiah Rogerson recalled: "If he ever gave any thought as to his health or fatigue, we fail to remember it. . . . To the end of our fearful journey . . . he was everywhere [that] he was needed and responded to every call of sickness and death. When our company was traveling, he was in the front, in the center, and in the rear, aiding, assisting, and cheering in every instance needed."[2]

Young Peter McBride also praised Edward Martin's leadership, acknowledging some of the challenges he faced:

"We had to burn buffalo chips for wood, not a tree in sight, no wood to be found anywhere. . . . A great many handcarts broke down [and] oxen strayed away, which made traveling rather slow. [It was] quite an undertaking to get nearly [600] persons who had never had any camping experience to travel, eat, and cook over campfires. It took much patience from the captain to get them used to settling down at night and to get started in the morning."[3]

An incident that is perhaps most revealing about Edward Martin's leadership is his showing of empathy toward Elizabeth Sermon. During one of the most bleak, bitter days in Wyoming, she had shivered out a question to him. Her husband was near death, and her sons' feet were so frozen they would have to be amputated. Her question was one that hundreds must have wearied him with: Is help coming? Edward Martin's answer reveals his anguish, his compassion, and the hope that he somehow kept alive:

"It makes me very sorrowful to see such sickness and distress that the Saints are enduring," he began. "There are a great many frosted feet from lack of shoes, and from six to ten are dying daily. I almost wish God would close my eyes to the enormity of the sickness, hunger, and death among the Saints." But then he continued, "I am as confident as I live that [President Young] has dispatched the relief valley boys to us, and I believe they are making all the haste they can. . . . God bless you, sister, for the dutiful kindness to your husband and sons in this dark hour of trial."[4]

Family Life

When Edward Martin returned to Salt Lake City, Alice and their only surviving child, 12-year-old Mary Ellen, were waiting for him. In 1859, Alice gave birth to their eighth child. Three months later,

Alice died, only 43 years old. Six of her eight children had preceded her in death.

Edward Martin married another wife in February 1857, two and a half months after returning home. Originally from Scotland, Jane Gray had been a member of the second handcart company. Between 1858 and 1863, Edward and Jane had four children, only one of whom lived past age three. They named their last child Edward—the third of Edward Martin's sons to be given his name. Eight days after giving birth to Edward, Jane died at age 31. Four days later, like his older brothers with the same name, baby Edward died.

In 1863, Edward Martin and Eliza Salmon were sealed in the Endowment House. Eliza had emigrated on the *Horizon* and is listed on the ship's manifest as a 24-year-old "spinster." By some accounts, however, she and Edward Martin were married before coming to America.[5] According to these accounts, Eliza was also expecting a baby when she emigrated. For unknown reasons, she is not included on most rosters of the Martin handcart company. If she did not travel with the Martin company, perhaps she stayed in the Midwest to have the baby and then came to Utah the next year.[6]

Between 1864 and 1874, Edward and Eliza had seven children, four of whom died before they were six months old. Showing an eclectic taste for names, they named one of their children Joseph Hyrum, another Napoleon Bonaparte, and another Edward, the fourth of Edward Martin's sons to receive his name—and finally the one who would live to adulthood.

In 1869, Edward Martin married Rachel Brimley, his fourth wife. They had two sons, one of whom died as an infant.

Daily Life in Salt Lake City

Much less is known about Edward Martin's daily life after the handcart trek than before. With no diaries or letters available, details are sketchy. He stayed in Salt Lake City and resumed his painting business for a time. Soon he started a photography business, locating his studio on Main Street in the block immediately south of

Temple Square. Eventually he turned to real estate and other related businesses.

Edward Martin died in Salt Lake City on August 18, 1882, at age 64. Of his 21 children (or possibly 24), 14 or 15 had preceded him in death. He was survived by his wives Eliza and Rachel, who both remained widows for more than 30 years. In his patriarchal blessing, Edward Martin had been told that he would lead thousands to Zion.[7] In the midst of adversity that would have broken most men, he dedicated many years of his life to fulfilling this promise.

JESSE HAVEN

"I have been in this Church 19 years, [and] I saw more suffering last fall than I ever saw before among the Saints," wrote Jesse Haven after he returned home. "I was in Missouri when the Church was driven from there, and I believe what the Saints suffered there with the exception of those that were taken prisoners was nothing more than a drop to a bucket compared to what those Saints suffered that came in last fall. Many had their hands and feet frozen so that they had to be taken off after they got in."[8]

Jesse Haven was soon appointed chaplain of the Utah legislature. He was also appointed to be a "home missionary" to labor in the Salt Lake 8th Ward. His duties included meeting with ward members to go through a catechism, or series of questions. This catechism was part of the Reformation, a movement intended to help the Saints become more committed in their religious observance.

After his mission, Jesse Haven was reunited with his two wives, Martha and Abby. Three months later he also married Sarah Taylor. Like him, she had been a member of the Hodgetts wagon company. This marriage lasted only briefly, as Sarah sought a divorce in 1859. When Jesse reluctantly signed the bill of divorcement, he wrote to Sarah: "I have no reflections to cast. I have no hard feelings towards you. Wherein you have injured me, it is all forgiven in my bosom. If I have erred in my conduct towards you, it has been the error of the head and not of the heart."[9] Sarah remarried within two months of the divorce.

In about 1862, Jesse Haven moved to Morgan County, where he lived the last 43 years of his life. For many years he served as a probate judge in Morgan County and a circuit judge for Weber, Davis, and Morgan Counties.[10] He also continued to dedicate his life to service in the Church. He was the presiding elder in Enterprise, Morgan County, for 10 years. When the Morgan Stake was organized in 1877, he was called as a member of the high council.

Jesse Haven's journal writings were widely spaced after he returned from his mission, with lapses as long as 17 years. The angst and melancholy so prevalent in his earlier writings are almost entirely absent, except during 1860 when he wrote about his divorce. During the 1880s he typically wrote only on Sundays and told of his travels to speak to different Church congregations.

Jesse Haven's journals tell of only one child—his son Jesse, born while he was serving a mission—and two grandchildren. His wife Martha died in 1861, and his son also preceded him in death. A poignant journal entry in 1888 tells of Jesse taking his two grandchildren to Salt Lake City to visit the graves. His last journal entries, made in 1892, tell of the deaths of a brother in Massachusetts and a sister in Bountiful. Jesse died in Peterson, Morgan County, in 1905 at age 81. He was buried in Salt Lake City.

JOHN AND ZILPAH JAQUES FAMILY

Before leaving England, John Jaques labored behind the scenes to help promote the handcart plan. As assistant editor of the *Millennial Star,* he had worked with President Franklin D. Richards to produce much of the official printed word about it. In his unbounded enthusiasm for the plan, he had called it a "holy ordinance of the Lord, revealed through His Prophet Brigham."[11] However, the harsh realities of the actual journey took their toll, and by the end John Jaques almost lost his will to live. He later wrote of this time:

"I, who for weeks together stood face to face with death . . . , who witnessed [its] victories daily under heart-rending circumstances, who saw those near and dear to me succumb to [its] attacks under such circumstances and fall helpless victims of [its] all-conquering power, . . . at that time would scarcely have cared the toss of a button to avoid a decisive wrestle with the grim monster myself."[12]

The deaths that most directly affected John Jaques and his wife, Zilpah, were those of Zilpah's father, James Loader, and of their only daughter, two-year-old Flora. When Flora died near Fort Bridger, her grieving parents wrapped her body in a blanket and carried it in a wagon the last week of the journey so she could be buried in Salt Lake City. One of her aunts described her appearance: "[The] dear little . . . girl, robed in a quilt, frozen stiff, looked like a piece of marble."[13]

An old friend and mentor met John and Zilpah Jaques and their three-month-old son when they arrived in Salt Lake City. President Franklin D. Richards, who had assigned the Jaques family to the Martin company earlier in the year, welcomed them into his home and helped nurture them back to health. Flora was buried on his lot.[14]

Building Zion with the Pen

Brigham Young had asked for John Jaques to come to Utah, ostensibly for his literary talents. During the next 44 years, John used those talents in many ways for the benefit of Zion. In 1858 Brigham Young called him to work as a clerk in the Church historian's office, a position he held for five years. Soon after this appointment, John wrote: "Since my arrival in Utah, I have been employed literally in building up Zion with the axe, saw, plane, hammer, etc. I am now at work with the pen in the Historian's office."[15]

In 1864 John Jaques became the primary editor of a new daily newspaper in Salt Lake City, *The Daily Telegraph.* Five years later, in 1869, he returned to England on a mission to work again in the office of the *Millennial Star.* He wrote 122 articles and poems during that time.[16] Immediately after returning to Salt Lake City from his mission, he began working for the *Deseret News* as an assistant editor. He later returned to the Church historian's office for 20 years.

He also served as President Wilford Woodruff's personal secretary and as librarian and secretary of the Utah Genealogical Society.

Family Matters

After arriving in Utah, John and Zilpah Jaques had seven more children, making nine in total. Their five sons all lived relatively long lives, ranging from 61 to 89 years. Alpha, the son who was born on the handcart trek, became the longest surviving member of the Martin company, living until 1945.[17]

John and Zilpah Jaques were not so fortunate with their four daughters. After Flora died on the trail, the family was elated when a second daughter was finally born seven years later. The next year, though, her health began to fail. A feeling of helplessness over her lack of appetite is evident in her father's journal entry for August 30, 1864: "Rose has been very sick for nearly a week, continually getting weaker and wasting away. She eats very little."[18] Rose held on for several more weeks before passing away on October 17. That day her father lamented:

"At about 8 o'clock in the morning our poor little darling died. This was a heavy blow to us, as she was a lovely and sensible child, and we had fondly hoped that she would live to be a help and comfort and companion to her mother. We both felt that were it not for our boys, we could cheerfully have gone down to the grave with our dear little daughter. When will the resurrection come, that we may have our darling back again?"[19]

After Rose was buried two days later, her father felt that all of life's beauties had gone with her. "How desolate the house seemed," he wrote, "and the garden and the trees and vines. All their charms seemed to have gone into the grave with our poor darling."[20] The next year the family had Flora's body moved from Franklin D. Richards's lot and reburied next to her little sister.[21]

The Jaques's third daughter was the only one to live to adulthood, and even she was outlived by her mother. Like their first two daughters, their fourth daughter died at a very young age.

Tensions had broiled between John Jaques and his parents and siblings ever since he joined the Church in 1845. After leaving England, John received no letters from his family for seven years.[22] The first letter he received came from a brother who informed him that his estranged father had suffered a stroke. Three years later John received a letter from another brother informing him of his father's death and "berating me soundly for not sending help to my father and mother."[23]

When John returned to England in 1869 for his mission, he reconciled with most of his family. He was able to see his mother before she died in 1870, and he learned that she had often spoken kindly of him.[24] All the siblings who were present in his mother's home during her final illness "were very glad to see me," he wrote.[25] He even began a warm correspondence with some of them.

Afterthoughts about the Handcart Plan

The handcart plan that John Jaques had so zealously supported exacted a heavy price of him and his wife. His tone 22 years after the journey is decidedly different from before:

"The affair was one of those disagreeable things, like some hateful dream, or dreadful vision, or horrible nightmare, that people seem indisposed to refer to but rather tacitly agree to forget."[26]

"To all, the journey, with its great and incessant toils, its wearing hardships and wasting privations, was a hard and bitter experience, wholly unanticipated. But to many, and especially to women and children who had been delicately brought up and tenderly cared for, and who had never known want nor been subject to hardships previously, as well as to the weakly and elderly of both sexes, it was cruel to a degree far beyond the power of language to express, and the more so for the reason that the worst parts of the experience were entirely unnecessary, [being] avoidable by timely measures and more [wise] management."[27]

Despite the hardships of the journey, John Jaques did not retract his original feeling that the handcart plan was inspired. Therein is perhaps an important lesson from the handcart experience: just because an idea is inspired does not mean the Lord will automatically ensure its success. Even inspired ideas usually depend on wise human judgment, often refined through counsel, to succeed.

One of the most extraordinary characteristics of John Jaques and most other handcart pioneers is that despite all they suffered, and despite knowing that they suffered largely as a result of human error, they rarely gave even a hint of blaming or finding fault with their leaders. The words of John Jaques are representative:

"The question may be asked, whom do I blame for the misadventures herein related? I blame nobody. I am not anxious to blame anybody. I am not writing for the purpose of blaming anybody. . . . I may say that notwithstanding the serious misfortunes of this company, I have no doubt that those who had to do with its management meant well, and tried to do the best they could under the circumstances. Captain Martin and his assistant, D. [Daniel] Tyler, were very active, careful, and vigilant all the way and especially where the exercise of those qualities was most required of them . . . before any relief was obtained."[28]

Forty years after the handcart trek, and three years before his death, John Jaques wrote these final words about the experience: "Although suffering so much privation, [the emigrants] felt nothing like the discouragement which many people feel now-a-days when they go to our grand City and County Building to pay their burdensome taxes."[29]

"I Intend to Stick to the Old Ship Zion"

After all he had suffered and sacrificed for the gospel's sake, John Jaques prepared an informal balance sheet to show that it had been worth it:

"I intend to stick to the old ship Zion. . . . I see nothing in the beggarly elements of the world worth going back for. Amid the Gentiles I might obtain a little better clothing and more of it, a few more creature comforts, and enjoy more of the luxuries of life, and then again I might not. I hope that I have too high an appreciation of the light, intelligence, and certainty which I have received in the Gospel, and too vivid a recollection of the fogginess, darkness, doubt, and uncertainty in which I groped as a blind man for the wall, previous to my acquaintance with the grand and glorious principles set forth by the Latter-day Saints, to turn my back to the cause of Zion."[30]

John Jaques died in 1900 at age 73. Speakers at his funeral included Joseph F. Smith and George Q. Cannon of the First Presidency, as well as future Apostle Charles W. Penrose. Joseph F. Smith's eulogy "teemed with feeling and love," describing John as "one of God's noblemen" who could be trusted with even the most sacred things.[31] George Q. Cannon described him as "a humble, unobtrusive man, a silent man in many respects," and a man of "much integrity and valor in fighting against evil."[32] Charles W. Penrose said he "was indefatigable, laboring continually and untiringly in his chosen work. . . . His soul was great, and it was expressed in the poetry and prose which came from his pen. . . . Though a modest man here, [he] will shine in the next world."[33]

The *Deseret News* paid tribute to one of its former editors, recognizing John as modest, hard working, and trustworthy:

"John Jaques was no common mortal. He did not shine among his fellows with that glitter that is sometimes taken for brilliant mentality. He was retiring in manner and not forward in speech. He made no special effort at oratory. Even in conversation his words were few. . . .

"John Jaques was for many years a great worker. For full half a century he labored incessantly in that which he firmly believed was the cause of human redemption. . . . In poetry and in prose he reflected the light of truth for the benefit of his fellows. . . .

"[As assistant editor of the *Deseret News* for many years,] he was a safe man. The editors-in-chief under whom he served could trust him implicitly. They were not afraid to leave him in charge when necessary. His judgment was good and his heart in the right place, and he was always at his post."[34]

After John died, Zilpah remained in Salt Lake City until 1906, when she moved to Rexburg, Idaho. Her sister Tamar lived there, and her son Alpha also lived in the area. She died in Rexburg in 1919 at age 88. Her obituary described her as "a true and noble woman and a kind and loving wife and mother [who was] highly esteemed by all who knew her."[35] Her body was returned to Salt Lake City to be buried next to her husband.

JAMES AND AMY LOADER FAMILY

After being accused of apostasy for his family's objections to traveling by handcart, James Loader had declared his faith by vowing to pull a handcart even if he died on the road doing so. He ended up paying that price, dying near Ash Hollow, Nebraska.

After thinking she could not walk even one mile, much less pull a handcart, Amy Loader walked nearly a thousand miles, riding in a wagon for only a brief time after her husband died and again after leaving Martin's Cove. James Loader's death left Amy with five daughters and a 10-year-old son to finish the most difficult part of the journey on their own. Amy could have become paralyzed by grief or bitter with resentment. After all, she had known better than to try this. Instead, she led and cheered even her adult daughters through times of starvation and frozen stupor. Largely through her faith and determination, she and all her children survived.

The day after the Loaders arrived in Salt Lake City, all of them except Patience and Tamar went to Pleasant Grove to be with Amy's oldest daughter, who had emigrated the previous year. Amy Loader lived the rest of her life in Pleasant Grove, as did many of her children.

Soon after the journey's end, Amy wrote to her children in England to inform them of their father's fate and to send them a remembrance of him. Her son Marshall responded with tender words of comfort: "Dear Mother, I was sorry to hear that Father is dead. I could not help dropping a tear when I saw the lock of hair. Dear Mother, I hope you will not fret about him, for I think you will see him again."[36]

Amy Loader died in 1885 when she was 83 years old. She never remarried during her nearly 30 years in Zion. Her son-in-law John Jaques explained, "She [remained] a widow, for she could never believe there was a man left in the world equal to her husband."[37]

Patience Loader (Rozsa Archer)

Patience Loader was 29 years old when she entered the Salt Lake Valley for the first time. She had lived in London for more than a decade and enjoyed its lively pace, its shops and parks, its elegant architecture, and its theater and other amusements. By comparison, she found the fledgling Salt Lake City wanting:

"When first we arrived in the city, to us everything looked dreary and cold. The streets were all covered with snow, but the people were kind and tried to encourage us and make us feel as good as they could. . . .

"At that time the city was not built up very much. The houses were scattered. . . . I had been living eleven years in the city of London before I left England, and to me [Salt Lake City] seemed a very lonesome place."[38]

When most of her family went to Pleasant Grove the next day, Patience decided to stay in Salt Lake City. She told one of her friends, "If this is Salt Lake City, what must it be like to live in the country? I don't think I will go to Pleasant Grove."[39]

Patience would soon find herself in an even more remote place than Pleasant Grove. In 1858, at age 31, she married Sergeant John Rozsa. On the surface this was an unlikely match because John had come to Utah the previous year as part of a consignment of federal troops known as Johnston's Army. The U.S. government had ordered these troops to march on Utah in response to false reports of a Mormon rebellion. The crisis was resolved without bloodshed, but the army remained until 1861. During a furlough in December 1858, John Rozsa joined the Church and married Patience. Two days after their wedding he returned to Camp Floyd, a military base in the desert west of Utah Lake. He readied his rooms and returned the next week for Patience. They made their first home together in this isolated outpost where Patience had no other family or friends. Camp Floyd was not quite like home for John Rozsa either. Born in Hungary, he had received a university education, learned to speak seven languages, and served 14 years in the Hungarian army before emigrating to America in 1853.

Patience Loader could be strong-willed and outspoken, but she should also be known for adapting to conditions that at first seemed unwelcome. Her adjustments in attitude toward the Church, toward the handcart plan, toward rural living, and even toward doing the laundry for all the soldiers in her husband's company were only the beginning. When the Civil War broke out in 1861, John Rozsa was ordered to Washington, D.C. Although family and friends told Patience she should stay in Utah, she had promised John she would go with him as far as she was permitted to travel. So she left her home and once again made the laborious journey across the country, this time with an infant son.

Soon after arriving in Washington, John left Patience for his first Civil War battle. On leaving, he said, "My dear Patience, I have been in battle before many times, but then I did not have this trial to go through. I had no wife and child to leave behind. Now I go with a heavy heart. We don't know if we will meet each other again or not. We will not all escape. We don't know who will be killed in battle."

Patience recalled her response to her husband's departure—and the outcome: "I told him I would pray to God for him that his life should be spared for him to return again to me and his child. He told me after he came home that when he was in the greatest danger, he thanked God that he had a faithful, good wife who was continually praying unto God for the safety of his life."[40]

Patience and John made their home in Washington for four or five years. They both endured difficult and dangerous circumstances in which they felt the protecting hand of God. They had two more sons during this time.

In 1866 the family started back to Utah. On the way they went through Iowa City and picked up Patience's older brother, John, and his wife and son. When the Martin company left Iowa City in 1856, John and his family had stayed behind. With encouragement from Patience, they finally finished the journey to Zion (see page 421).

Patience and her husband often talked about the time when he would be discharged from the army and they would be free to do as they pleased; however, their hope of enjoying civilian life together in Zion was not to be. Once again Patience faced tragedy in Nebraska. Her father had died there 10 years earlier, and on the way back to Utah her husband died near Fort Kearny. He was only 45 years old. "To part with my husband was almost more than I could endure," wrote Patience, who was five months pregnant at the time. "To be left alone with my three baby boys to care for and raise without the help of their dear kind father, this seemed too much for me in my condition, but thank God, he blessed me and gave me strength day by day to endure my severe trials."[41]

Two months after her husband's death, Patience finished crossing the pioneer trail for the third time and arrived at her mother's home in Pleasant Grove. Two months later she gave birth to a daughter. Just before John Rozsa had died, he told Patience, "If God gives you a daughter, you must name her after your mother and my mother."[42] Patience named her Amy Rosalie.

John Rozsa's death was especially hard on his second son, four-year-old Frank. "He grieved and pined away," Patience wrote. "He said, 'Where is my papa?' . . . I had to tell him his Papa died and God took him to heaven. He then said, 'I want to go to my Papa. I don't like this home. I don't want to stay here.' I said to him, 'Oh, Frank, you don't want to leave Mama, do you?' 'Yes, I want to go to my papa's home. I don't like this home.' I tried in every way to console him."

Sometimes son would console mother. Patience recalled: "Whenever [Frank] would see me grieve or cry, he would come and wipe away my tears and he would do some little kind act for me. Then he would put his dear little arms around me and say, 'Don't cry any more for my Papa. I will take care of you, Mama.'" Once when Frank noticed his mother's sadness, he put some peaches in a small bucket and said, "Mama, I brought you some nice peaches. Take this large one. Now you will not cry any more for my papa, will you? Oh, don't cry, Mama. I will get you lots of nice peaches."[43]

Four-year-old Frank's separation from his father did not last long. A month after his baby sister was born, Frank became ill with a sore throat. Within three days he could not maintain his body temperature. Until then, Patience had no idea she was about to lose him. She handed baby Amy to her mother and pulled Frank into the bed beside her, as he wished. As soon as they lay down, Frank put his arm around her neck and went to sleep. He passed away within an hour, the family's second death in five months. When Patience's mother came back into the room, Patience cried, "Surely God is not going to take all away from me that is so near and dear to me." Her mother reassured her, "God will be merciful unto you, I hope, and spare your other children."[44] These words would prove to be true.

As happened frequently in her life, Patience had a change of heart about Pleasant Grove. She had an adobe house built and lived there for more than 50 years. For many of those years, while her three surviving children were young and finances were tight, the house had only one room. Patience and her children worked together to support themselves by growing fruit and sewing carpet rags. One year Patience took her children up American Fork Canyon to cook for 60 men in a mining camp, working 17 hours a day. The next year they went to Deer Creek to cook for 30 men.

In 1876, when Patience was nearly 50 years old and had been widowed for 10 years, she married John Archer. They were together for more than 30 years before John died in 1909. Patience lived another 12 years, dying in Pleasant Grove in 1921 at age 93. Her only daughter, Amy, paid her the following tribute:

"Mother had a strong social nature, was noted for her hospitality, and had many friends, young and old. Many times the officers of the Mutual, Primary, Sunday School, and Deacons brought their classes to our home to hear her relate experiences and teach them the Gospel. She was a teacher in the Relief Society for many years and later the president for a few years. . . .

Patience Loader Rozsa Archer

"She loved to do charity work among the sick and unfortunate and used to say to us that by helping others we will be blessed and find it a great pleasure. Mother was always cheerful and looked on the bright side of life. She learned to play the organ after she was 80. She was by nature spiritually minded and was always valiant in teaching the Gospel of Christ."[45]

Although Patience Loader got a reluctant start in both joining the Church and pulling a handcart, once she got on the path she was a faithful, courageous traveler. Choosing the right path never meant an easy journey for Patience, but she lived for a higher purpose than a life of ease. She described the handcart trek as terrible and her trials as severe, and yet she wrote, "I can testify that our Heavenly Father heard and answered our prayers."[46] Such faith that God loved her and heard her while still calling upon her to bear the horrific trials of that experience was needed again and again in her life. That faith helped her see the temporary, tutoring nature of mortality's tests, enabling her to persevere with purpose and hope.

Tamar Loader (Ricks)

Twenty-two-year-old Tamar Loader left England with a heavy heart because a young man she loved had decided not to join the Church and emigrate with her. When she was only 100 miles into the 1,300-mile handcart trek, she became so ill that she had to be carried on a cart for the remaining 170 miles to Florence, Nebraska. There she received a blessing from President Franklin D. Richards that she would walk again before the journey's end, which she did.[47]

While crossing the plains, Tamar became discouraged both because of poor health and because she missed the young man she had left in England. At her lowest point, she had a dream that forecast a remarkable event, as recounted in the family's history:

"One . . . morning [Tamar] told her mother that she had dreamed that her sweetheart came and stood beside her and he seemed so real. But he was not alone. Another man was with him. . . . In the dream the sweetheart finally faded away but the other man remained. When [Tamar] first saw Thomas E. Ricks in the rescue party, she took her mother by the arm and said, 'Mother, that's the man.' "[48]

This was a dream that came true. After arriving in the Salt Lake Valley, Thomas Ricks invited Tamar to stay at his home in Farmington while she recovered her strength. They were married the next year, Tamar becoming his second wife. Their marriage of 44 years was happy, but Tamar enjoyed relatively few of the comforts, charms, and enchantments of her English home. Thomas Ricks was a leader in pioneering new settlements, moving to these areas even before they were named. While building these settlements from bare ground with few resources, the family endured many hardships.

The Ricks family moved to Logan just two years after Thomas and Tamar were married. They stayed there 25 years, helping build it into a thriving community. Six of their seven children were born there. Only three lived to adulthood.

Tamar would have been content to stay in Logan, but in 1882 Thomas Ricks was called to lead a colony in settling the Upper Snake River Valley in Idaho. He and a few others moved there in 1883 and founded Rexburg, which was named in his honor. Tamar, who by then was 50 years old, moved there the next year with the youngest of her surviving children. Her married children also moved to the area either that year or soon afterward.

Compared to Logan, Rexburg at the time was a remote wilderness, and adjusting to a new home there was difficult. One of Tamar's descendants wrote, "It was a homesick family that Tamar had the task to help adjust themselves to their new surroundings, [but] in a short time the wilderness was subdued."[49]

Thomas and Tamar Ricks lived the rest of their lives in the Rexburg area, as did most of their children. Soon after Thomas Ricks died in 1901, the academy he helped form in 1888 was renamed Ricks Academy. It later became Ricks College and eventually Brigham Young University–Idaho.

After nearly dying on the handcart trek, Tamar Loader Ricks lived to be 90 years old, spending her last 23 years as a widow. She made many sacrifices to follow the Lord's will, often going down lonely, difficult paths she would not have chosen otherwise, and the Lord blessed her richly for doing so.

John Loader

John Loader was 34 years old when he left England with his wife and two children, his parents, and several siblings. His one-year-old daughter died while crossing the Atlantic on the *John J. Boyd*. When the family reached Iowa City, his wife was nearing the time to give birth to another child. Feeling that the handcart journey would be detrimental so late in her pregnancy, John decided to postpone their journey to Utah. The postponement lasted 10 years.

In September 1856 John's wife had her baby, a daughter who lived only one month. His wife bore two more children in Iowa City, in 1858 and 1860, and they also died. Another child had died in England, so only one of the couple's six children lived to adulthood.

John worked in Iowa City until the Civil War broke out in 1861. That year he joined a volunteer regiment and served in the war until he was wounded three years later. After convalescing, he returned to Iowa City. Soon afterward, in 1866, he and his wife and son finally went on to Utah. They made the journey with John's sister Patience and her family, who went through Iowa on the way back to Utah after the war.[50] Like many of the Loader family, John settled in Pleasant Grove. He died just 10 years later at age 54.

Other Family Members

The other children of James and Amy Loader who made the handcart journey were Maria (18), Jane (14), Sarah (11), and Robert (9). Maria lived to be 86, dying in Lehi in 1924; she had six children by two husbands. Jane had the shortest life of any of these children, dying in Pleasant Grove in 1864 at age 22; she had three children. Sarah lived to be nearly 98, dying in Rexburg in 1942; she had nine children by two husbands. Robert had eight children and lived to be 89 years old, dying in 1936. The daughter who came to Utah before the rest of the family, Ann, lived to be 100 years old, dying in 1925 in Salt Lake City.

FRANCIS AND ANN ELIZABETH (BETSY) WEBSTER: "WE BECAME ACQUAINTED WITH GOD IN OUR EXTREMITIES"

As a young man, Francis Webster had gone to California and spent nearly six years prospecting during the Gold Rush. He returned to England in 1855, having been moderately successful. Soon after returning, he married Ann Elizabeth (Betsy) Parsons, and six months later they sailed for America on the *Horizon.* Francis had saved about $1,600 in gold and planned to use it to purchase a wagon for the journey and get a good start in Utah. Instead, he sacrificed it to help pay the emigration expenses of the poor.

Francis and Betsy Webster both survived the handcart trek, as did their baby daughter who was born in Nebraska. They suffered greatly, however. Describing his affliction with dysentery, Francis wrote, "[It was] so bad that I have sat down on the road and been administered to by the Elders and [then] gotten up and pulled my handcart with renewed vigor."[51]

Francis's feet were badly frozen when he arrived in Salt Lake City, but his travels were not over. Two days later the family left for Cedar City, where they would make their home. This one-time prospector who had traveled so far and spent so many years building up savings for a comfortable future—and then had given most of it away— arrived in Cedar City with only a little clothing to his name. Even then, Francis Webster found more to give. He wrote, "I paid my tithing on the little clothing I brought with me."[52]

Life in Cedar City

During his life in Cedar City, Francis Webster became a prominent civic, business, and Church leader. He served as mayor, city councilman, justice of the peace, and representative to the territorial legislature. He also served in leading positions in the Iron County Agricultural Society, the Cooperative Sheep Association, and other business organizations. In the Church he served on the high council, as president of his seventies quorum, and in many other positions.

Fewer details are known about Betsy's life after the handcart trek. As the mother of ten children, she devoted most of her time to her family. In the Church she served as Relief Society president for seven years.[53] She was also a tailor, working from home so she could care for her children. She had the ability to remake worn, shabby clothes so they looked almost new. One of her great-granddaughters wrote, "It was said at one time [that] every man in Cedar [City] was either wearing a coat or suit made by Ann Elizabeth Webster, or had worn one."[54]

"I Knew That the Angels of God Were There"

Decades after the handcart trek, William Palmer witnessed an unforgettable incident involving Francis Webster. In a Sunday School class in Cedar City, some people were discussing the handcart tragedy. Through their association with Nellie Pucell Unthank, these people had a daily reminder of the long-term physical cost of that experience. William Palmer recalled:

"Some sharp criticism of the Church and its leaders was being indulged in for permitting any company of converts to venture across the Plains with no more supplies or protection than a handcart caravan afforded.

"An old man in the corner sat silent and listened as long as he could stand it. Then he arose and said things that no person who heard him will ever forget. His face was white with emotion, yet he spoke calmly, deliberately, but with great earnestness and sincerity.

"He said in substance, 'I ask you to stop this criticism. You are discussing a matter you know nothing about. Cold historic facts mean nothing here, for they give no proper interpretation of the questions involved. [Was it a] mistake to send the handcart company out so late in the season? Yes. But I was in that company and my wife was in it and Sister Nellie Unthank, whom you have cited, was there too. We suffered beyond anything you can imagine, and many died of exposure and starvation, but did you ever hear a survivor of that company utter a word of criticism? Not one of that company ever apostatized or left the Church because every one of us came through with the absolute knowledge that God lives, for we became acquainted with him in our extremities.

"'I have pulled my handcart when I was so weak and weary from illness and lack of food that I could hardly put one foot ahead of the other. I have looked ahead and seen a patch of sand or a hill slope and I have said, I can go only that far and there I must give up, for I cannot pull the load through it. I have gone to that sand, and when I reached it, the cart began pushing me. I have looked back many times to see who was pushing my cart, but my eyes saw no one. I knew then that the angels of God were there.

"'Was I sorry that I chose to come by handcart? No. Neither then nor any minute of my life since. The price we paid to become acquainted with God was a privilege to pay, and I am thankful that I was privileged to come in the Martin handcart company.'

"The speaker was Francis Webster, and when he sat down there was not a dry eye in the room. We were a subdued and chastened lot. Charles Mabey, who later became governor of Utah, arose and voiced the sentiment of all when he said, 'I would gladly pay the same price for the same assurance of eternal verities that Brother Webster has.'"[55]

Although Francis Webster's assertion that none of the company ever apostatized is not quite accurate, all available records suggest that it is remarkably close. Like him, most of those who survived the handcart trek stand as a witness that when adversity is faced with faith, it strengthens spiritual commitment and draws a person nearer to God rather than weakening commitment and bringing alienation.

Alluding to the story of Francis Webster, President James E.

Faust said: "In the heroic effort of the handcart pioneers, we learn a great truth. All must pass through a refiner's fire, and the insignificant and unimportant in our lives can melt away like dross and make our faith bright, intact, and strong. There seems to be a full measure of anguish, sorrow, and often heartbreak for everyone, including those who earnestly seek to do right and be faithful. Yet this is part of the purging to become acquainted with God."[56]

Francis Webster died in 1906 at age 76. Betsy died the next year. Their influence continues to this day, not only on their posterity but on thousands who have been inspired by their example of faithful endurance.

SAMUEL AND MARGARET PUCELL FAMILY

After being among the first converts in England and then waiting 19 years to gather to Zion, Samuel and Margaret Pucell died five days apart in the Wyoming snows. Telling of the outcome for their two young daughters who accompanied them, President Gordon B. Hinckley said:

"The two orphan girls, Maggie and Ellen, [made it to the Salt Lake Valley but] were among those with frozen limbs. Ellen's were the most serious. The doctor in the valley, doing the best he could, amputated her legs just below the knees. The surgical tools were crude. There was no anesthesia. The stumps never healed."[57]

William Palmer, who knew Ellen personally, tells the story of her feet in more detail:

"Nothing could be done to save her feet. When they took off her shoes and stockings, the skin with pieces of flesh came off too. The doctor said her feet must be taken off to save her life. They strapped her to a board, and without an anesthetic the surgery was performed. With a butcher knife and a carpenter's saw they cut the blackened limbs off. It was poor surgery, too, for the flesh was not brought over to cushion the ends. The bones stuck out through the ends of the stumps, and in pain she waddled through the rest of her life on her knees."[58]

Nellie's Marriage and Family

Sometime after arriving in Utah, the orphaned Pucell sisters were taken to Cedar City. When Nellie was 24, she married William Unthank. Continuing with her story, President Hinckley said:

"She grew to womanhood . . . and bore and reared an honorable family of six children. Moving about on those stumps, she served her family, her neighbors, and the Church with faith and good cheer, and without complaint, though she was never without pain. Her posterity are numerous, and among them are educated and capable men and women who love the Lord whom she loved and who love the cause for which she suffered."[59]

William Palmer relates more of what Nellie endured in her daily life:

"Year in and year out she scarcely moved outside the limits of her own dooryard. Pain was the price of every step she took, and her physical world was bounded by the vision from her own humble doorstep. . . .

"Those stumps were festering, running sores as long as she lived. She never knew a moment of freedom from pain. [A doctor] offered to fix her legs by cutting the bones off farther up and bringing the flesh down over the ends so they would heal and enable her to wear artificial limbs, but the horrors of that first amputation were so vivid in her memory that she could never consent to another operation."[60]

To try to make Nellie more comfortable, her husband hollowed some pieces of aspen to fit her legs and then filled the holes with wool.[61] Toiling on these clogs, Nellie spent her life serving her family, neighbors, and church. William Palmer elaborates:

"William [Unthank] was a poor man and unable to provide fully for his family, so Nellie did all she could for herself. She took in washing. Kneeling by a tub on the floor, she scrubbed the clothes to whiteness on the washboard. She knit stockings to sell, carded wool, and crocheted table pieces. She seldom accepted gifts or charity from friends or neighbors unless she could do a bundle of darning or mending to repay the kindness.

"The bishop and the Relief Society sometimes gave a little assistance which Nellie gratefully accepted, but once a year, to even the score, she took her children and cleaned the meetinghouse. The boys carried water, the girls washed the windows, and Nellie, on her knees, scrubbed the floor. . . .

"In memory I recall her wrinkled forehead, her soft dark eyes that told of toil and pain and suffering, and the deep grooves that encircled the corners of her strong mouth. But in that face there was no trace of bitterness or railings at her fate. There was patience and serenity, for in spite of her handicap she had earned her keep and justified her existence. She had given more to family, friends, and to the world than she had received."[62]

"She Stood Tall on Her Knees"

Ellen Pucell Unthank died in 1915 at age 69. In 1991 a life-sized bronze sculpture of her was placed on the campus of Southern Utah University in Cedar City. More than 1,000 people attended the unveiling, including President Hinckley, who offered the dedicatory prayer. Honoring Nellie's faithful endurance of her crippled condition for nearly 60 years, the sculpture is titled *She Stood Tall on Her Knees;* however, it portrays Nellie as a vibrant young girl, smiling, her hair and dress flowing. What may at first appear to be a carefree pose on closer examination reveals much more about Nellie. Standing on a pedestal, she is looking far

She Stood Tall on Her Knees, *bronze sculpture of Nellie Unthank by Jerry Anderson*

ahead, as if she sees what coming to Zion would cost and knows that the sacrifice would be worth it. Not only is she looking forward, in the sculpture—as in life—she is moving forward, standing on slender bare feet, the right one poised for the next step.

Other Family Members

Nellie's older sister Margaret (Maggie) turned 15 toward the end of the handcart trek. She reportedly was able to keep her legs from freezing by walking rather than riding. Like Nellie, she married and raised her family in Cedar City. She had 11 children. She died in Cedar City in 1916 at age 75.

Apparently the only members of the Pucell family who remained in the Church were those who paid the highest price. The three oldest children had stayed in Boston to work after the ship landed, planning to come to Salt Lake City the next summer. But when they learned what had happened to their parents and youngest sister, they remained in the east.

WILLIAM AND MARY ANN BARTON FAMILY

Five members of the William Barton family began the journey, but only three survived. The youngest, 1-year-old Elizabeth, died near Chicago. William died near Chimney Rock, Nebraska. Surviving were Mary Ann (William's second wife), 14-year-old Mary (the only child from William's first marriage to make the journey), and 4-year-old Francis.

Little is known about the lives of Mary Ann and Francis after they arrived in the Salt Lake Valley. Mary Ann was 33 years old at the time and lived to be nearly 74, so it is likely that she remarried. Francis, who had nearly died on the same day as her father near Chimney Rock, eventually grew to womanhood, married, and lived another 63 years.

Mary Barton's life is well documented. As one of the emigrants without relatives in Utah, she was sent to live in the home of someone she did not know. She was unhappy there and confided the problems to a neighbor, Sarah Allen, who invited her to live with them. In March 1857, three months after finishing the handcart trek, Mary became a plural wife of John Allen. Two years later the Allens were called to help settle Parowan, and a few years later they moved several miles southwest to Summit.

Mary and John Allen had 13 children. Six of their children died as babies, and two of them lived into the 1960s.

Concerning Mary's Church activities, her daughter Alice wrote: "Mary derived a lot of pleasure from her singing, and for years led the choir in Summit. She was a teacher in the Relief Society for 15 years and served the Lord in many ways. She taught her children the gospel and saw that they attended all the Mormon gatherings."[63]

In 1885, when Mary was 43, she was left a widow with several children to care for. She lived another 29 years, dying of a stroke in 1914 in Summit. For the last years of her life, she suffered from severe rheumatism and was confined to her room. Even while she was ill, she sewed, did handiwork, and read widely.

Throughout Mary's life, one of her favorite songs was "The Handcart Song," and she sang it often. Rather than feel resentful about all she had lost on the handcart trek, she enjoyed telling her children and grandchildren about it. "She seemed proud to have lived through such harrowing experiences," her daughter Alice wrote, "and glad that she had been strong enough to surmount so many difficulties."[64]

JOHN AND JANE BAILEY FAMILY

John and Jane Bailey left England with their four sons, ages 5 through 18. The entire family survived the journey, although at various times John and his oldest son, Langley, so despaired that they wanted to give up and die. Only through the faith and determination of Jane Bailey did they keep going.

An early manifestation of Jane Bailey's strength occurred before the family left England. Langley was embarrassed by the town crier announcing the family's departure for Zion. His mother told him not to be ashamed of his religion.

Then in Florence, when Langley was unconscious and so near death that at least one person declined to administer to him, Jane in faith sought a blessing from Franklin D. Richards, who promised her son that he would live.

Some days after this blessing, when Langley lost hope and hid away from the company so he could die, his mother found him, scolded him, reminded him of the blessing's promise, and got him on a handcart.

Then in Martin's Cove, when John Bailey lost hope and was ready to give in to death, Jane literally shook him away from it.

Even after arriving in Zion, Langley and others in the family would continue to need Jane Bailey's faith and determination. Eventually they would develop these same qualities themselves.

"Mother, Is This Zion?"

Langley Bailey said that when he first saw the Salt Lake Valley, "it was like the Israelites of old in beholding the promised land."[65] Impressions soon changed, however. After a week in Salt Lake City, the Baileys were taken to Nephi. Langley describes the living conditions there:

"We [were] taken to an empty one-room house, no furniture. Some sagebrush had been placed by the door. A fire was made, [and I] watched the smoke go up the chimney. I said to my parents, 'Is this [the] Zion we have been praying and singing about?' The surrounding was very uninviting. We made our beds on the hard floor. . . . [I] was pleased to find a resting place, though very humble indeed. I looked around and saw little adobe houses, roofs made of willows covered with dirt."[66]

Indeed Zion was no gleaming city. But what about the people? Langley's first impressions of some of the young men also fell far short of his expectations of Zion:

"Opposite our window nearby [was] a corral. [It was] Sunday

morning. Some young men were roping some wild steers. The language [they] used fairly shocked me. I said to my mother, 'Is this Zion?' "[67]

These negative first impressions were reinforced the following week. What some boys thought was harmless fun instead felt like hypocrisy to Langley, who expected to join a community of the pure in heart:

"Sunday I asked the privilege to go outside the house and see what kind of people attended meeting. As some boys passed by me, they knocked me down with snowballs. I crawled back to the house. Mother helped me in. She saw how I had been treated. She got the snow out of my neck and back. I said to mother, 'Is this Zion where the pure in heart lives?' "[68]

The Baileys lived on charity that first winter. "Sometimes we had food, sometimes we were short. . . . I was always hungry," Langley wrote.[69] Having been so ill and weak that he had ridden in a handcart most of the way, Langley was fortunate to survive a winter of scant food. The next spring, when he was nearly 19 years old, he weighed only 60 pounds. As a result, he became something of a curiosity. "I was so thin people came to see me," he wrote. "Mother took off my shirt. There was nothing but skin and bones."[70]

Less than two years after arriving in Nephi, the Baileys' 14-year-old son, Thomas, froze to death when his mule team was caught in a snowstorm. According to Jane's life history, "Tom's body was returned to the sorrowing parents in Nephi and laid on the dirt floor."[71] This time it was John Bailey who asked his wife, " 'Jane, is this Zion? Is this all worthwhile?' And once again this strong woman nodded and spoke a firm 'yes.' "[72]

Zion sometimes failed to meet people's expectations, and some people never got over the disappointment. Others, like the Baileys, soon realized that Zion was not a static utopia but rather a work in progress—and went to work.

In 1859, John, Jane, and their two youngest sons moved about 20 miles away to Moroni, Sanpete County. They were some of the first settlers in that area and remained there throughout their lives.

Jane was the first schoolteacher in Moroni and also the first Relief Society president, serving for 25 years.

With the exception of 14-year-old Thomas, the Baileys all had long lives. John lived to be 83, Jane 85, Langley 91, John Jr. 88, and David 87.

Langley Bailey's Adult Life in Nephi

Langley stayed in Nephi when the rest of the family moved to Moroni. After recovering his health, he devoted his long life to building Zion in the place that at first had seemed its antithesis. He herded sheep and farmed and slowly began to prosper. In 1861 he married Sarah Andrews. Their first son was born the next year but died six months later. While anguished by this and other trials, Langley had a dream that was a turning point. He recalled:

"I owned a cow. It died. Our 6 month old child, a boy, died. I felt downcast and discouraged. I dreamed I saw a corral full of horses and cattle. A man stood nearby pointing to the animals, said [they] are all yours. Don't be so impatient. It taught me a lesson."[73]

This dream was the first of many that helped Langley Bailey during his life. Through it he learned to wait upon the Lord, gaining an assurance of the Lord's promise, given to all mortals, that if he was faithful, all that the Lord had would be his—in the Lord's own time and way.

Langley and Sarah Bailey had 11 more children. Three of them died while young, and two of them, benefiting from their paternal genes for longevity, lived into the 1970s. Langley also had five children with Sarah Emma Warner.

Langley devoted his life to service in the Church. During the 1860s he helped build the Nephi tabernacle. In 1885, when he was 47, he served a mission to England, leaving home the same day he received his call from President John Taylor. He labored in the Nottingham Conference. After returning from his mission, he served for 21 years as tithing clerk for the Juab Stake, collecting and managing the tithes. He also served as superintendent of the stake Sunday

School, overseeing 11 schools. In addition, he was a high councilor for many years. In 1921, Elder Charles W. Penrose ordained him a patriarch, and he served in this position in the Juab Stake until his death in 1929.

William and Sarah Ann Ashton Family

William and Sarah Ann Ashton were the parents of five daughters ages 1 through 11 and were expecting another child when they left England. Their second daughter had died as an infant in England, and their youngest died in Boston. The day after leaving Florence, Sarah Ann died while giving birth to the couple's sixth daughter. Two weeks later, that baby daughter also died.

Having begun the journey with a dream of raising his family in Zion, William Ashton became so despondent over the loss of his wife and two daughters that when he arrived at Fort Laramie, he left his other three daughters, enlisted in the army, and later returned to England. The oldest of these three girls, 11-year-old Betsy, died soon afterward on the frozen plains of Wyoming. Only 7-year-old Sarah Ellen and 5-year-old Mary lived to see the Salt Lake Valley. When they arrived, they wondered where they would find a home, but they were taken in and treated well.

In 1864, Sarah Ellen married Thomas Beckstead in the Endowment House, becoming his second wife. Thomas Beckstead had earlier settled in South Jordan as a farmer, and he and Sarah Ellen lived there for more than 20 years. They had 10 children, all born in South Jordan. Four of them died as babies.

After Sarah Ellen married Thomas Beckstead, her sister Mary lived with them until she married Isaac Wardle as his second wife in 1867. Isaac Wardle had been in the Martin company with Mary, but he was 21 at the time and she was 5. Two years after marrying Isaac Wardle, Mary died while giving birth to her only child. Of the six sisters, only Sarah Ellen remained.

In 1887, Thomas and Sarah Ellen Beckstead moved to Whitney, Idaho, soon to be the birthplace of President Ezra Taft Benson. There

Thomas continued farming and Sarah Ellen continued to devote herself to her family and church, living in very humble circumstances.

Soon after the family moved to Whitney, Sarah Ellen experienced one of the happiest surprises of her life. One of her granddaughters tells the story as follows:

"A man by the name of Clark came to grandmother's door with a copy of the *Millennial Star* which contained an inquiry concerning anyone who might know of relatives of William Ashton, pauper, in England, who had emigrated to America previously and left his children on the plains. Grandmother recognized this man as her father who had left when she was seven. . . . Now she was the only one of the children living. She . . . got in touch with the authorities where her father lived, sending passage money for him. He arrived with some missionaries from England and spent the rest of his years with [his daughter Sarah Ellen]."[74]

William Ashton would have been about 67 when he returned to America some 30 years after leaving midway through the handcart trek (see page 301). The time he was reunited with Sarah Ellen lasted only two or three years because he died in October 1891, but the reunion with his only living child must have been joyous for both of them.

Less than two years after Sarah Ellen's father died, her husband died, leaving her a widow at age 44. She lived another 19 years, dying in Whitney in 1912 at age 63. At the time of her death, her posterity numbered 92 by one account. Although this family had suffered so much loss on the journey, and although William Ashton had left his three daughters on the trail, this story is rich in redemptive value. Despite all these setbacks and errors, a large posterity of faithful Latter-day Saints owes much to William Ashton for his decision to accept the gospel and start his family toward Zion.

When the Becksteads moved to Whitney, all six of Thomas and Sarah Ellen's living children accompanied them. Most of these children lived in that area for the rest of their lives, and all of them were buried in Whitney along with their mother, father, and grandfather. There seems to be a kind of cosmic compensation in this after the mortal remains of Sarah Ellen's siblings and mother had been buried in England, Boston, Nebraska, Wyoming, and the Salt Lake Valley.

JAMES AND MARY ANN MELLOR FAMILY

James and Mary Ann Mellor left England with seven children. Mary Ann had almost died while giving birth to conjoined twins just before the ship's departure. Then, over a doctor's objections, James had carried her from the hospital and onto the ship. Her death looked inevitable, but she was given a blessing that promised she would reach Zion.

Mary Ann's health recovered enough that this promise was fulfilled, though not without discouragement along the way. James, Mary Ann, and all seven of their children arrived safely in Utah. Louisa (16) said that Cyrus Wheelock, the missionary who administered to Mary Ann on the ship, met the company when they arrived. Louisa recorded the following emotional scene on that occasion:

"Brother Wheelock and Brother Goddard . . . asked for James Mellor. When they saw him, they were stunned! A man 38 years of age with hair as white as the driven snow! Indeed, the trials and tribulations, the hardships and the deprivations . . . had taken [their] toll. They took him in their arms and wept."[75]

Settling Fayette; Mission to England

Most of the Mellor family spent that first winter in Provo, where they were divided up and cared for, and then moved to Springville. There in 1860, Mary Ann gave birth to their 12th and final child, John Carlos Mellor.

In 1861 the Mellors and four other families left Springville to settle the Warm Springs area of Sanpete County, later renamed Fayette. After living in a dugout, James built the first brick home there in 1870. As some of the founders of this little town, the Mellors did much to shape its destiny.

In 1875, 56-year-old James Mellor was called to serve a mission to England. His missionary journal contrasts this journey with the handcart trek 19 years earlier. That journey had taken six months. In 1875, it took only five days to travel by rail to New York and ten days to travel by steamship to Liverpool. James saw in this advancement the fulfillment of prophecy:

"In our traveling on the train I saw truly the word of the Prophets fulfilled in the Lord sending swift messengers to the nations of the earth afar off, for there were between 20 and 30 missionaries going at the speed of 40 to 50 miles per hour to many nations."[76]

James returned home in 1877, bringing with him the family of his brother John as well as Mary (Polly) Knowles. The family history records that when Mary Ann came to the door to welcome James home, he "introduced her to Polly, saying he'd brought her from England to be his polygamous wife. Mary Ann was too stunned to make any comments. She stood staring at them for a few minutes, then picked up a pan of clabbered milk and showered the contents over the surprised couple before slamming the door in their faces."[77]

Clabbered milk is made by allowing raw milk to stand at room temperature until it ferments or "sours." The fermentation causes the milk to thicken and gives it a tangy flavor. Drinking clabbered milk was common before refrigeration made it possible to keep fresh milk from spoiling. Clabbered milk is also used to make butter and cheese.

Despite Mary Ann's initial reaction, James and Polly were married, and Mary Ann and Polly established a cordial relationship. The children of the two families got along well.

After nearly dying before she left England and then again on the handcart trek, Mary Ann Mellor lived to be 76 years old. Her obituary records that shortly before her death in 1896, "she called all her children together and told them all to stand firm to the Gospel and not go astray but be faithful to it [in] all things."[78] James Mellor died in 1903 at age 84. At that time the posterity of James and Mary Ann numbered 12 children, 96 grandchildren, and 126 great-grand-children. According to their daughter Louisa, they had "reared the family in grace and truth, all of them going through the Temple."[79]

Louisa Mellor

The Mellors' two teenage daughters, Louisa and Charlotte Elizabeth, showed exceptional strength throughout their emigration, often sustaining their ill mother and caring for their five younger siblings.

In February 1857, less than three months after arriving in Utah, Louisa married Edwin Clark as his second wife. Brigham Young performed the ceremony in the Endowment House.

Louisa eventually had nine children. When her husband died in 1909, she went to live with one of her daughters in Salt Lake City. During her last years she was active in temple work. A few months before she died, she wrote to a granddaughter:

"I have been going to the Temple all winter, that is, three days a week. There are so many who come with children to be sealed to parents. That's what they have to do when they don't get married in the Temple."[80]

Louisa died at age 75 on Christmas day 1915. She was buried in Santaquin.

Charlotte Elizabeth Mellor

Charlotte Elizabeth went to the home of Susannah Roper, a widow who said she had accommodations for a girl. When Charlotte Elizabeth was brought to the front of the home, her driver said she was unable to walk because of badly frozen feet. Susannah Roper asked one of her sons, 19-year-old Henry, for assistance. The family history records:

"Mrs. Roper called, ''Enry, 'Enry, come 'elp this dear into the 'ouse.' [Henry] lifted Charlotte Elizabeth Mellor from the wagon. She was cooperative by holding her arms about his neck. Says Henry later, 'As I carried her into the house, I looked into her dark eyes, and there was a romance born. It was love at first sight.' "[81]

Henry and Charlotte Elizabeth were married on February 4, 1857, the day after Louisa's marriage. They eventually had 13 children. The family moved from Provo to Lehi to Fayette to Gunnison and finally to Lawrence, a remote area of Emery County. Charlotte Elizabeth felt very lonesome in Lawrence, though somewhat better when a ward was organized there. She died in Lawrence in 1886 when she was only 44. Her history records that "she was a devoted mother and a faithful Latter-day Saint until her death."[82] She was buried in Huntington.

WILLIAM AND MARY GOBLE FAMILY

Thirteen-year-old Mary Goble of the Hunt wagon company had already lost two younger sisters and a younger brother on the journey. As she and the rest of her family neared the Salt Lake Valley, her mother slipped away also. Mary recalled her mother's death, as well as subsequent efforts to save her own frostbitten feet:

"My mother had never got well; she lingered until the 11th of December, the day we arrived in Salt Lake City, 1856. She died between the Little and Big Mountains. She was buried in the Salt Lake City Cemetery. She was 43 years old. She and her baby lost their lives gathering to Zion in such a late season of the year. . . .

"We arrived in Salt Lake City [at] nine o'clock at night the 11th of December 1856. Three out of the four that were living were frozen. My mother was dead in the wagon.

"Bishop Hardy had us taken to a house in his ward, and the brethren and the sisters brought us plenty of food. We had to be careful and not eat too much as it might kill us we were so hungry.

"Early next morning Brother Brigham Young and a doctor came. The doctor's name was Williams. When Brigham Young came in, he shook hands with all of us. When he saw our condition, our feet frozen and our mother dead, tears rolled down his cheeks.

0

The doctor wanted to cut my feet off at the ankles, but President Young said, 'No, just cut off the toes and I promise you that you will never have to take them off any farther.' . . . The doctor amputated my toes using a saw and butcher knife. The sisters were dressing my mother for her grave. My father walked in the room where mother was, then back to us. He could not shed a tear. When my feet were fixed, they packed us in to see our mother for the last time. Oh, how did we stand it? That afternoon she was buried.

"We had been in Salt Lake a week when one afternoon a knock came at the door. It was Uncle John Wood. When he met Father, he said, 'I know it all, Bill.' Both of them cried. I was glad to see my father cry. . . .

"Instead of my feet getting better they got worse, until the following July I went to Dr. Wiseman's to live with them to pay for him to doctor my feet. But it was no use. He could do no more for me unless I would consent to have them cut off at the ankle. I told him what Brigham Young had promised me. He said. 'All right, sit there and rot, and I will do nothing more until you come to your senses.'

"One day I sat there crying, my feet were hurting so, when a little old woman knocked at the door. She said that she had felt that someone needed her there for a number of days. When she saw me crying, she came and asked what was the matter. I showed her my feet and told her the promise Brigham Young had given me. She said, 'Yes, and with the help of the Lord we will save them yet.' She made a poultice and put it on my feet, and every day she would come and change the poultice. At the end of three months my feet were well.

"One day Dr. Wiseman said, 'Well, Mary, I must say you have grit. I suppose your feet have rotted to the knees by this time.'

"I said, 'Oh, no, my feet are well.'

"He said, 'I know better, it could never be.'

"So I took off my stockings and showed him my feet. He said that it was surely a miracle."[83]

Settling in Nephi

Although William Goble's wife and three of his children died during the journey west, he still had four relatively young children when he arrived in the Salt Lake Valley in December 1856. That same month he married Susanna Patchet. The next spring William moved his family to Nephi.

Like many others, William Goble became discouraged during his first months in Zion. In his case the discouragement was so severe in the summer of 1857 that he told his children he would take them home to England as soon as he earned enough money. Those plans changed, however, through the influence of his deceased wife. One day he came home and told his children, "I have seen your mother today, and she wants us to stay here. Everything will be all right."[84]

William bought some land in Nephi and farmed it for the rest of his life. Eventually he gave part of it to the Church for the building of a meetinghouse. He died in 1898 at age 81. His descendants remember him as "a man with great faith and healing power."[85]

Mary's Marriage and Adult Life

Mary stayed in Spanish Fork when the rest of her family moved to Nephi in 1857 and then rejoined them in 1859. In June of that year she married Richard Pay. He was a 38-year-old widower who, like Mary, had sailed on the *Horizon* and joined the Hunt wagon company. His wife and baby daughter had died during the trek west. "The baby died October 4, 1856 at Chimney Rock," Mary recalled. "Bro. Pay could not get anyone to dig the grave, so he started digging it himself, when my father came and helped him."[86] Later, Richard Pay returned the favor, helping Mary's father dig a grave when Mary's baby sister Edith died at the Sweetwater.

Mary and Richard Pay started their lives together in a one-room adobe house where they used a sack to cover the only window, since they could not get glass. They made their own molasses out of squash, ate wild berries for fruit, made their own soap, made their own clothes using wool from sheep they raised, and made their own shoes. Despite their poverty and other problems, Mary described her family and friends in Nephi as "a happy band."[87]

Mary and Richard Pay had 13 children, three of whom died very young. After 22 years in Nephi, they moved to Leamington. There Mary served as president of the Primary for 12 years and also in the Relief Society.[88] Richard died in 1893, leaving Mary uncertain how she would provide for her children. "It looked pretty dark with nothing coming in," she wrote. "I had to depend on my boys, [but] they did not get much work, so I started to nurse the sick. In this I had good success."[89] Mary's oldest son had died the year before her husband, and another son died the next year, making three very trying years.

"I Think My Mother Had Her Wish"

Mary returned to Nephi and lived another 20 years as a widow. Her autobiographical account of these years covers just two pages but tells of attending three handcart reunions. One of these was the 50-year reunion—the handcart jubilee, as it was called. While in Salt Lake City for this reunion, Mary visited her mother's grave for the first time. "No one knows how I felt as we stood there by her grave," Mary wrote. "I thought of her words, 'Polly, I want to go to Zion while my children are small, so they can be raised in the Gospel of Christ. For I know this is the true Church.'"[90] Although Mary's mother did not live to raise her children in Zion herself, Mary concluded, "I think my mother had her wish."[91]

The last words of Mary's autobiography tell of another reunion in 1909. She found the experience to be bittersweet. She enjoyed meeting with old friends. She also enjoyed talking with Langley Bailey about their experiences in crossing the plains. But reliving the memories was painful as well. "It made me feel bad. It brought it all up again," Mary wrote. Although the pain of these experiences never completely healed, Mary concluded that keeping them alive had an important purpose. "It is wise for our children to see what their parents passed through for the Gospel," she wrote.[92]

"The Great Moving Faith of Our Gospel Forebears"

One of Mary Goble Pay's grandchildren was Marjorie Pay Hinckley, wife of President Gordon B. Hinckley. After telling Mary's story, President Hinckley said:

"[This] is representative of the stories of thousands. It is an expression of a marvelous but simple faith, an unquestioning conviction, that the God of Heaven in his power will make all things right and bring to pass his eternal purposes in the lives of his children.

"We need so very, very much a strong burning of that faith in the living God and in his living, resurrected Son, for this was the great moving faith of our gospel forebears. . . . With faith they sought to do his will. With faith they read and accepted divine teaching. With faith they labored until they dropped, always with a conviction that there would be an accounting to him who was their Father and their God.

"Let us look again to the power of faith in ourselves, faith in our associates, and faith in God our Eternal Father. Let us prayerfully implement such faith in our lives."[93]

WILLIAM AND ALICE WALSH FAMILY

William and Alice Walsh left England with three young children. Only Alice and her two youngest children survived. Alice's account of the journey's end aches with loneliness:

"Arriving in Salt Lake Nov. 30th 1856, with two children and the clothes I stood up in, were all of my earthly possessions in a strange land, without kin or relatives."[94]

The people in Salt Lake City took in many of those who did not have relatives or friends to stay with. Alice and her children were sent to the 10th Ward, where the bishop placed them in the home of Jacob Strong. Soon afterward, Alice and Jacob were married, and eventually they had three children. Jacob died in 1872, leaving Alice a widow for the last 52 years of her life.

When Alice's mother in England learned what Alice had

suffered, she offered to send money for Alice to return home—if she would renounce her beliefs. This offer was made with the mistaken belief that the handcart ordeal had weakened Alice's faith. Alice declined the offer, saying she had joined the Church and had gone through all the adversity of emigrating because she knew it was true.[95] Fifty-five years after the handcart trek, this testimony burned even more brightly. Alice wrote:

"I have always been proud to know that I had the individual courage to accept and embrace the faith and join the Church, to which I have ever been steadfast from that day to this.

"Though the sufferings were terrible I passed [through] in the handcart journey across the plains, [I] am still thankful that the Lord preserved my life and made it possible for me to reach Zion, in the Valley of the West. . . .

"After all that I have endured and passed through for over 55 years, my testimony is that the Gospel of Jesus Christ of Latter Day Saints is true."[96]

Alice Walsh Strong was 83 years old when she wrote this testimony. She lived to be 95, dying in 1924. At the time of her death, 14 of her children and grandchildren had served missions, further sowing the seeds of their mother's faith.[97] Her son John, who was four years old during the handcart journey, later served two missions, one of them to Great Britain when he was 70 years old. He also served as a patriarch and was one of the first mayors of Farmington. When he died in 1927 at age 75, he was in Mesa, Arizona, having been sent there by the Church to work in the new temple.[98]

While serving a mission in England, one of Alice's sons wrote the following tribute to his mother:

"She was one of the elect in deed and truth. She has passed through hardships and privations, has denied herself through love, has gone hungry and cold, and has worked hard and frugally. It made no difference how poor she was, she always had a few cents laid by in case she needed something special, which in a spirit of true love, she would give to her children.

"When we were children, she weaved and made all our clothes out of cotton, and wool that came off the sheep's backs. . . .

"Just before I left to come on my mission, she said to me at first that she did not think I should go away and leave her, as she was getting old . . . and would not stay with us long. I said, 'Mother, the prophet of the Lord has called me to give service to the Church. What shall I do?' She answered, 'Go! by all means. If I die, all is well with me; if I live it is the same. You cannot keep me here when my time comes. Go! and the Lord bless you!' "[99]

SARAH FRANKS (MACKAY) AND GEORGE PADLEY

Sarah Franks and George Padley were engaged when they left England and planned to be married when they arrived in Salt Lake City and raise their family in Zion. George died at Martin's Cove, however, and Sarah was extremely ill and weak even before the grief she felt in George's death.

Sarah survived the journey but had no relatives or friends to meet her and nurse her back to health. What followed is a powerful example of persevering and making the most of life when fervent hopes are disappointed. One of the wives of Thomas Mackay invited Sarah to come and live in their home. After a few months, in April 1857, Sarah married Thomas Mackay as his third wife. Years later when Sarah was a widow, one of her granddaughters who knew of her heartbreak at Martin's Cove asked if she had really loved Thomas Mackay. Implied in the question may have been a thought that the marriage was only for expedience. But Sarah replied, "Yes, he was a good man. He was good to us."[100]

Sarah and Thomas Mackay had five sons and four daughters. In a way Sarah never had imagined, she was able to raise a family in Zion.

Thomas Mackay died in 1880 when Sarah was 47 and their youngest child was 6. Sarah lived 31 years as a widow, dying in 1911 at age 78. During her last years, she lived with one of her daughters in Murray. "She was especially admired and loved for her thoughtfulness of little children," wrote one of her descendants. "She always had a surprise awaiting them when they called to see her. [She] would always bring us a little gift, such as a pretty little china cup and saucer, a little toy, or a box of lovely assorted cookies. . . . She was dearly loved by all."[101]

Aaron and Elizabeth Jackson Family: "My Sufferings Will Be Sanctified for My Good"

Elizabeth Jackson's husband, Aaron, died soon after the last crossing of the Platte River. With three young children to care for, Elizabeth became despondent. At her time of greatest need, her husband appeared to her in a dream. This dream may have made the difference in her ability to have hope and continue. She and her children all made it safely to Salt Lake City. She later wrote:

"I will not attempt to describe my feelings at finding myself thus left a widow with three children, under such excruciating circumstances. I cannot do it. But I believe the Recording Angel has inscribed in the archives above, and that my sufferings for the Gospel's sake will be sanctified unto me for my good. . . .

"I [appealed] to the Lord, . . . He who had promised to be a husband to the widow, and a father to the fatherless. I appealed to him and he came to my aid."[102]

Like many others, Elizabeth Jackson testified to her posterity that her sufferings and sacrifices in the handcart trek strengthened her faith rather than weakened it. She also hoped this example would strengthen her posterity:

"I have a desire to leave a record of those scenes and events, through which I have passed, that my children, down to my latest posterity may read what their ancestors were willing to suffer, and did suffer, patiently for the Gospel's sake. And I wish them to understand, too, that what I now word is the history of hundreds of others, both men, women, and children, who have passed through many like scenes for a similar cause, at the same time we did.

"I also desire them to know that it was in obedience to the commandments of the true and living God, and with the assurance of an eternal reward—an exaltation to eternal life in His kingdom—that we suffered these things. I hope, too, that it will inspire my posterity with fortitude to stand firm and faithful to the truth, and be willing to suffer, and sacrifice all things they may be required to pass through for the Kingdom of God's sake."[103]

After arriving in Utah, Elizabeth and her children were taken to her brother Samuel's home in Ogden. Elizabeth continued living in Ogden until her death in 1908 at age 81. When her father and other siblings emigrated in 1857, they also settled there.

In Ogden, Elizabeth met William Kingsford, a widower, and they were married in July 1857. When the Logan Temple was finished, Elizabeth was sealed to her first husband, Aaron, with William acting as proxy. Elizabeth felt that the blessings of the temple—the ultimate blessing of coming to Zion—more than compensated for all the suffering and despair she had endured on the handcart trek. Toward the end of her life she wrote, "The Lord has blessed me . . . with the highest blessings of a spiritual nature that can be conferred upon man or woman, in His Holy Temple, in mortality."[104]

MARY JOHNSON (PARSONS)

Seven-year-old Mary Johnson (known then as Maren Johansen) came to America from Denmark in 1855. That fall, while her family was at Mormon Grove in eastern Kansas, her parents and baby brother died. As orphans, Mary and her oldest sister were separated and placed with other families. Mary later wrote of her situation, "My guardians were careless and unfeeling.[105]

"I Would Have My Feet Again When I Got to Heaven"

Mary's feet became severely frostbitten in Wyoming. She recalled: "When we arrived at [Devil's Gate], my feet were found to be frozen very badly. While there, they were thawed out and turned black."[106] After the rescuers arrived, Mary was sent ahead to Salt Lake City in an ambulance wagon. The flesh of her feet was falling off as the wagon traveled along.

Mary was treated much better from that time forward. "The rest of the way I was taken care of by kind friends," she wrote. "All was done that was possible under the circumstances, but both my feet dropped off before we got to the city. . . . My legs were amputated above the ankles and then at the knees."[107]

In Salt Lake City, Mary was taken into the home of Brigham Young for several months. The next year she was reunited with her brothers and sisters for the first time since they were separated at Mormon Grove. Mary's brothers burst into tears when they saw her. Their joy of being together was muted by the sadness of seeing their 8-year-old little sister move around on the stumps of her knees. "How well do I remember our meeting," Mary later wrote. "I told them not to cry so, for I would have my feet again when I got to Heaven. I have walked on my knees for forty years."[108]

When Mary was about 14, Brigham Young helped her obtain a sewing machine, which she paid for by taking in sewing. With her feet and the bottom half of her legs amputated, Mary put pads on her knees to tread the machine, which Brigham Young had someone specially alter for her. Her determination, as well as her ambition to support herself, won the admiration of many people.

Mary's Marriage and Adult Life

Sometimes children are left to fulfill the hopes and dreams their parents were unable to realize. Mary's parents did everything they could to raise their family in Zion. Although their deaths in Mormon Grove prevented that, Mary and their other children sought to fulfill these dreams for future generations.

In 1869, when Mary was 19, she married Elijah Parsons in the Endowment House. A biographical sketch of Mary says "she always felt that her mission was to bring souls into the world."[109] Mary and Elijah had seven children, five of whom lived to adulthood. To this day they have a large and grateful posterity.

The Parsons family lived in Salt Lake City for a few years, then moved to Richfield, then to Cedar Grove, and then a few miles south to Koosharem, where they made their home for the rest of their lives. Elijah struggled to provide for the family, so Mary assisted by carding wool, spinning yarn, and knitting stockings, often working late into the night. Sometimes Mary would be alone with her children for extended periods while Elijah returned to Salt Lake City looking for work to support the family.

Mary tried using artificial limbs, but they were uncomfortable, so she wore the back part of men's shoes. The front part of the shoes was cut away and the open ends sewn together. The men in town saved their old boots for this purpose.

Mary's biographical sketch records that "she studied the scriptures and was well versed in the doctrines of the Church. . . . She taught her children the Gospel, which will always be remembered by them. Many times she remarked, 'I am sure I shall have my feet and legs after the resurrection.' "[110]

The suffering intensified the last 10 years of Mary's life. At times she was unable to lie down in bed because she was afflicted with asthma. She also suffered from a tumor and congestive heart failure. Nevertheless, as long as she was able to be propped up in bed, Mary continued to knit stockings, which she sold so her funeral expenses would not be a burden. She died of pneumonia in 1910 at age 61. At the time of her death, this faithful woman, who refused to be embittered by her life's buffetings, had walked on her knees for 54 years. One biographical sketch includes the following tribute:

"Mary Johansen Parsons was truly a courageous soul. Her mission [was] one of trials and tribulations, but Mary proved faithful to the end. . . . [She] endured all the hardships of pioneer life. [She] lived in poverty but was ready to share her last crust with her neighbor."[111]

Mary said the English couple who had been her guardians left the Church and returned to the east soon after arriving in Utah.

They were apparently among a very small minority who did not remain faithful after enduring the tragedies of the 1856 emigration.

Joseph and Elizabeth Sermon Family

When Elizabeth Sermon joined the Church in 1852, she was determined to gather to Zion. "My only hope and desire was to reach the Valley, where my children could be raised in the true gospel," she later explained.[112] Elizabeth's husband, Joseph, did not join the Church and did not want to leave England. He owned two homes in the London area and was comfortably established. Nevertheless, seeing that Elizabeth was determined to emigrate and not wanting her to go alone, Joseph reluctantly agreed to accompany her. Their four youngest children went with them.

The Sermons arrived in Iowa City at least a month before the season's first handcart emigrants. They could have joined any of the first three handcart companies, which left in June and got through the experience very well. But Joseph Sermon was "full of misgivings" about pulling a handcart, so he decided not to go any farther.[113] As a result, his family remained in Iowa City for several weeks as each of the handcart companies was organized and then departed. Eventually, knowing that the Martin company provided the last opportunity to finish their journey that season, Elizabeth persuaded Joseph to proceed.

The consequences for this family were catastrophic. Joseph suffered poor health most of the way and died at Martin's Cove. Although Elizabeth and her four children survived, she had to remove portions of the frostbitten feet of two of her young sons, who became crippled. Another setback occurred when Elizabeth arrived in Salt Lake City. She recalled that when people in the city came to take the handcart Saints into their homes, she was left until almost the last:

"My case was deplorable; I don't wonder no one wanted [us]. Finally, I saw a young man from my own country passing. I had been raised in childhood with him. I knew him, but he did not know me.

How could he? I looked 70 years old, worn out, shriveled, feet frozen, could not walk. My children, too, could not. Who would want us? Oh, I was crushed, but I called to him. He could not believe it was me, but he got a team and sent us to his own home. The Bishop came and provided for our wants—put my feet in tar, which I believe saved them, for the next morning I could move my toes."[114]

Soon after Elizabeth arrived in Utah, her brother learned where she was and took her to his home in Farmington. Elizabeth later wrote of this time, "Here we met with kind friends—Bishop Hess and many, many others, and I am ever grateful for their kindness to me and my children in my great trouble."[115]

In 1860, four years after her first husband's death, Elizabeth married Robert Camm. In 1868 they moved from Farmington to Cache Valley, settling in Logan. "The rest of my life . . . was not a bed of roses," Elizabeth wrote to her children. "Great trouble came to us later in Cache Valley."[116] Those troubles, among them a conflict with local Church authorities, eventually led to Elizabeth and Robert Camm leaving Cache Valley for San Francisco. Elizabeth lived there from about 1886 until her death in 1893 at age 73.

Shortly before Robert Camm left Logan, he wrote a letter resigning not only his own Church membership but also Elizabeth's. Whether Elizabeth assented—and whether this request was fulfilled—is unclear. Her feelings are perhaps most clearly indicated in the lengthy letter she wrote to her children in 1892, the year before she died. In the letter Elizabeth is occasionally bitter and critical, but her faith prevails:

"My faith [is] still in my Father in Heaven. I have never lost faith in Him. It is as sweet today to trust in Him, and my prayers are that I may always trust Him. He is a Friend and has never failed me when asked. You may perhaps say, 'Why not have asked Him to save you then, when you needed it?' I did, and He spared me through many trials to my family."[117]

Elizabeth Sermon's testimony that God had never failed her did not depend on having her trials removed. She made this declaration of faith despite a lifelong regret over her first husband's death and her sons being "made cripples" by the handcart trek.[118] She also made her declaration despite the difficulties she encountered in the Zion she had sacrificed so much to come to.

Concluding the letter to her children, Elizabeth made one final reference to the handcart trek, showing the extent to which it pervaded her life even 36 years later: "I am drawing on to the day when I shall lay my body down. Where it will be, I know not, but I don't think it will be drawing a handcart 1,300 miles again."[119]

ROBERT AND MARGARET MCBRIDE FAMILY

Heber McBride left England as a carefree 13-year-old boy who felt the ocean calling him to be a sailor. When the health of both of his parents began to fail in Nebraska, he and his older sister, Jenetta, became the family's caretakers. After the first winter storm arrived and Heber's father died, this caretaking became a desperate struggle for survival. "My sister and I had nothing to do but try and keep my mother and two little brothers and baby sister and ourselves from freezing," Heber later wrote.[120] Largely due to the efforts of Heber and Jenetta, their mother and three younger siblings all survived.

After arriving in Utah, the McBrides were sent to Ogden to live in the home of Samuel Ferrin, a widower. Soon their bishop found them a little log house that had a dirt floor and dirt roof. Six-year-old Peter McBride described the living conditions:

"When it would rain, water and mud would run down the walls and onto our beds. And we children would say . . . , 'Mother, is this Zion?' And she would answer, 'Never mind, children. The Lord will provide.' I have thought many times how mother must have felt to live in such a place after having a comfortable home all her life, but I never heard her complain."[121]

Four months after arriving in Utah, Jenetta McBride married Samuel Ferrin's son Jacob. A month later, Margaret McBride married Samuel Ferrin. Samuel was a kind husband and stepfather, but Margaret separated from him several years later. She moved to Eden, where her son Heber was living, and went back to the name of McBride. Margaret lived in Eden for the rest of her life and served as Relief Society president for 13 years.

During the winter of 1876–77, Margaret went to St. George to visit her youngest daughter, Maggie. While there, she helped sew curtains and rugs for the St. George Temple. She then attended the temple's dedication on April 6, 1877. After the dedication, she remained in St. George for a few months so she could perform the temple ordinances for her mother and other relatives. One day she was baptized for 135 people.

Margaret McBride felt that her experiences in the temple were the crowning blessing of her life in Zion. After returning to Eden, she shared her testimony of this blessing with her Relief Society sisters. "Great power was manifested," she said. "I cannot find language to convey to you the teachings we received."[122] These experiences were a sustaining strength to Margaret for the rest of her life.

During her last years in Eden, Margaret lived with her son Heber. After nearly dying on the handcart trek, she lived to be 76 years old, dying in 1891. She was buried in Eden.

Jenetta McBride (Ferrin)

Jenetta McBride and Jacob Ferrin settled in the Ogden area and had 11 children. In 1881 the family moved to Pima, Arizona, hoping the warmer climate would help Jacob's health. Loading everything they could carry into three wagons, Jenetta, Jacob, and eight of their children began a three-month journey south. Jenetta drove one of the teams while holding a six-month-old baby in her arms.

The Ferrins passed through Phoenix when it was just a village. Pima was also small, having been established only three years earlier by about 25 families. At first the Ferrins lived in a cottonwood log shack that Jenetta considered luxurious because it had two rooms. For carpet, they spread their tent on the dirt floor.

Jacob enjoyed better health in Arizona, but six months later he was killed by Apache Indians. Jenetta was left a widow for the last 41 years of her life. When she died in 1924 at age 86, she had eight surviving children, 85 grandchildren, 150 great-grandchildren, and 9 great-great-grandchildren. Despite a life of adversity, Jenetta testified that the blessings she received more than compensated for all her sorrows:

"I do not regret any moment of following the call of the prophet. Despite all the hard times, we made it to Zion. We had the gospel, and we were with the Saints. Jacob and I were married for eternity. It was what we had left England for, to obtain the blessings of the gospel. No matter what it cost, it was worth it. All my life I bore testimony of my thankfulness that I made that journey, no matter how hard it was."[123]

Heber McBride

Heber McBride's greatest sailing adventure—crossing the Atlantic when he was 13 years old—was apparently his last. He lived the last 70 years of his life landlocked in Utah and Canada. His taste for adventure never waned, however. Changing his means of conveyance from ship to horseback, Heber made many expeditions as part of a company of "minutemen" that went as far as Bear Lake to protect settlements from the Indians.

In late 1865, nine years after the rescue of the handcart companies, Heber helped rescue a wagon company that was late on the plains. When Brigham Young called for help, Heber sent a telegram volunteering. Brigham Young addressed his response to "H. R. McBride and Company," saying, "Borrow what provisions you want from the Government and I will make it good. Go till you find the immigrants, and God bless you, Bro. McBride."[124] Like the rescuers who helped the handcart companies, Heber's small company thought they would be gone for 10 to 14 days. They ended up being gone 45 days, having to travel all the way to the Platte River—nearly 400 miles—before they found the last of the company. Along the Platte, Heber found the area of his father's grave. It looked much like it had in 1856, covered with nearly a foot of snow.

When Heber finally returned home, his mother was so overcome with emotion that she nearly fainted. Not only had she worried for his life but she was stunned by his battered appearance. Heber wrote: "She had me in her arms crying, 'Oh, my rough looking boy.' [I told her,] 'Mother, don't touch me till I get a bath, for I [have had] only one change of clothing in 45 days.' "125

In the mid-1860s, Heber McBride was one of the original settlers of Eden in the mountains east of Ogden. He remained there for most of the next 38 years, raising two families. He also served in the bishopric and as president of the Mutual Improvement Association.

When Heber was 61 years old, he embarked on yet another adventure. In 1904, Church leaders asked him to move to Canada to help settle southern Alberta. Typical of this family, Heber accepted the call and left his home in Eden to start over again. He lived the last 21 years of his life in Canada, dying in 1925 when he was 82. Two years before his death, he wrote the following testimony in a letter to a granddaughter:

"I know the gospel is true. It is worth all the suffering we went through for it. Be faithful, dear granddaughter, and the Lord will guide you and bless you throughout your life."126

One of Heber McBride's daughters lived to be 103, dying in 1985.

Peter McBride

Arriving in Utah when he was six years old, Peter McBride lived with his mother in Ogden and then in Eden. During his youth, he developed an interest in music that shaped the rest of his life. Although he never had any formal musical training, he became a talented musician who could sing, compose, and play many instruments. One of his boyhood friends was Evan Stephens, who later directed the Tabernacle Choir and became a prolific hymn writer. After herding and milking cows all day, Peter and Evan would play an old pump organ that was kept in Evan's granary.

Peter married Ruth Burns in 1874. Soon afterward, Brigham

Young called them to move to Arizona, where Peter's assignment—or mission—was to teach and promote music. After a year in Arizona, the McBrides started for home. They got as far as St. George when Brigham Young met them and said they should return to Arizona. With great difficulty, Peter and Ruth turned around their wagon. A few years later they settled permanently in the Gila Valley in southeastern Arizona.

Soon after arriving in the Gila Valley, Peter married Laura Lewis. Between his two families he had 22 children, nearly half of whom died at young ages. One of his children lived to be 97, dying in 1979.

During his life in Arizona, Peter farmed 160 acres along the Gila River. He also served in the bishopric for 20 years. And he continued to share his love for music. He organized and conducted choirs in his own ward and also in other wards in the St. Joseph Stake. He taught voice, organ, piano, guitar, and banjo lessons. He even taught some vocal classes at the St. Joseph Academy in Thatcher. In his old age, Peter reflected on his lifelong efforts to bless others' lives with music: "I believe I have filled the longest mission ever required of anyone in the Church, for I have never been released from my call."[127]

When Peter McBride died in 1934, he was 84 years old—the last survivor of Robert and Margaret McBride's children. The two oldest children, Jenetta and Heber, who had tried so lovingly to keep their three younger siblings from freezing on the handcart trek, died within a few months of each other in 1924 and 1925. The three youngest children, Ether, Peter, and Maggie, died within a year of each other in 1933 and 1934. All of the children lived into their 80s. They continued in the heritage of faith established by their parents, following the call of Church leaders to leave comfort and convenience to help build Zion in its ever-expanding reaches, scattering themselves over 1,500 miles from Canada to Arizona.

THE LONDON BRANCH PRESIDENTS

The six London branch presidents in the Martin company suffered greatly during the handcart trek. Three of them died; however, all of their wives survived, as did most of their children.

John and Margaret (Elizabeth) Griffiths Family

John Griffiths was the longest tenured of the London branch presidents to emigrate with the Martin company, having served for 15 years. He survived to see the Salt Lake Valley but died the next day. Before his death, he had endured the deaths of his first wife, five children in England, and two in Wyoming. His second wife, Elizabeth, and his two daughters, Margaret and Jane, survived the handcart trek.

Death was not the only separation this family had to endure. Eight-year-old Jane explained that when they arrived in Salt Lake City, "My father and [step]mother were taken to one place, my sister and I each to another. I did not see my father again."[128] "We were pretty well scattered," wrote 16-year-old Margaret with understated resignation.[129] Margaret and Jane Griffiths also continued to be separated from their older brother, Thomas, who had emigrated three years earlier. They expected to be reunited with him when they arrived in Salt Lake City, but they learned that he had been sent with one of the Church herds to Carson Valley. From there he had gone to Sacramento, where he became sick. Margaret wrote to him and received a letter in 1858 but never heard from him after that. He died in about 1866, the location uncertain. One account says he was shot and killed in Montana over a political dispute.

Because her feet were so badly frozen, Margaret was unable to walk for nine weeks. "When I got better I lived out anywhere I could get a place," she wrote. "Finally I got to a Mr. Henry Clegg's and lived there a while and then I married him."[130] Their marriage took place in the Endowment House in August 1857. Margaret was Henry Clegg's third wife.

Soon after Margaret and Henry were married, they moved to Springville. "I had many hardships to contend with," Margaret recalled. She dug postholes, made and set fence posts, built other fences out of oak brush and willows, gleaned wheat, dug potatoes, ground bark in a tannery, and cut sugarcane, which she carried on her back to the molasses mill. To support her family, she also spun wool, made soap and candles, took in sewing, and sometimes sat up all night knitting by firelight.

In 1872 the Cleggs moved to Heber City, where they remained for the rest of their lives. Margaret lived long enough to experience every means of conveyance from handcart to airplane, with her opportunity to fly coming when she was 86. Reluctant at first, she told the pilot she would go as high as he could fly as long as she could keep one foot on the ground. Continuing her good humor, she then climbed into the plane and said, "No loop the loops." After landing, she was asked how she liked it. She replied, "It was better than pushing a handcart across the plains."[131]

Margaret and Henry Clegg had 11 children. Henry died in 1894, leaving Margaret a widow for 35 years. She died in 1929, at 89 years old. Margaret paid a high price to come to Zion, and in the short term, as she saw two of her brothers and her father die, she must have wondered how the good could ever balance the bad. Although Margaret's life was never easy, the Lord multiplied blessings to her that went far beyond balancing. One of these blessings was a large posterity that could enjoy the blessings of Zion. At the time of her death, Margaret had 49 grandchildren, 120 great-grandchildren, and several great-great-grandchildren.

Margaret's younger sister, 8-year-old Jane, had to stay in bed all winter because her feet were so badly

Margaret Ann Griffiths Clegg

frozen. Three weeks after she arrived in Salt Lake City, the family that took her in said they could no longer care for her. They contacted Jane's stepmother, Elizabeth, and said they would have to send Jane to the poor house in Provo. When Elizabeth heard this, she could not hold back the tears. Samuel Mulliner, whose family had taken Elizabeth into their home, saw her crying and asked what the trouble was. She explained the situation and said, "Little Jane is all that I have to love me." Samuel Mulliner replied, "She will never go to the poor house as long as I have a piece of bread. I will take her in." Jane recalled his compassion:

"He brought a quilt and a pillow in a wheelbarrow, set me in it, and took me to his home. At first his wife attempted to care for my feet, but they did not seem to get better. He then hired a doctor, but this doctor's treatments did not seem to help my feet. In fact, they got worse. He changed doctors, and the second doctor seemed to be able to heal my feet. I finally, in three months, felt better, although I lost the first joint on three toes of both feet."[132]

Jane married Almon Fullmer in 1864. In 1870 they moved to Cache Valley, where they lived for more than 50 years. They had eight sons and four daughters, only five of whom outlived their mother. Three of Jane's children died within four months of each other in 1918, probably from the influenza epidemic.

Jane's two brothers had died two weeks apart on the pioneer trail in 1856. Seventy-three years later, in 1929, Jane and her sister Margaret died six weeks apart. Jane was 81. Her passing occurred in Tetonia, Idaho, where she had been living the previous few months with one of her sons. Her burial was in Providence, Utah. She was survived by 77 grandchildren, 109 great-grandchildren, and 4 great-great-grandchildren. Although she was hobbled by amputations that were a lifelong reminder of the price she paid to come to Zion, Jane remained faithful to the end. A year before her death, she wrote: "I still have a testimony of the truthfulness of the gospel. I do know that my Redeemer lives and that Joseph Smith is a true prophet of God."[133]

Elizabeth Griffiths, stepmother of Margaret and Jane, married

William Keddington in September 1857. Elizabeth and William had five children, but only the youngest lived to adulthood. Elizabeth operated a small grocery store and also served as a Relief Society officer in the Salt Lake 10th Ward. She died in 1902, when she was 76, and was buried in the Salt Lake City cemetery.

Henry and Sarah Squires Family

Henry Squires had served as president of the St. Albans Branch in the London Conference before emigrating with the Martin company. He and Sarah left England with five daughters ages 1 through 8. Three days before the journey's end, Sarah gave birth to another daughter in Echo Canyon. All of the family survived.

Two of Henry Squires's brothers had emigrated earlier, and they cared for Henry and his family until they regained their strength. After living in Kaysville for two years, the Squires family moved to Salt Lake City, where Henry and a partner opened a large mercantile store. Four more daughters were born to Henry and Sarah between 1859 and 1865, making a total of 10. Henry also entered into plural marriage and had three sons and a daughter by his second wife.

In 1866, Henry Squires and most of his family did something unusual for the handcart pioneers: they returned permanently to England. Only three of the older daughters stayed in Utah. The family's reasons for returning are not known for certain, though one granddaughter said that Henry's health was failing and Brigham Young suggested he return to England to see if the change would help him.[134] That explanation is not entirely satisfactory, however, because in leaving Utah, Henry and most of his family also left the Church. In England they began attending the Baptist church again, and Henry returned to his former work as a Baptist minister.

Henry and Sarah Squires had two more children in England— their eleventh daughter and then their only son. All of their children lived to adulthood. If Henry returned to England for better health, the move was successful because he lived another 48 years.

Several years after the Squires family returned to England, Echo, the daughter who was born at the end of the handcart trek, felt stirrings to return to the land of her nativity. In 1874, when Echo was 17 years old, her mother took her and some of her siblings back to Utah for a visit. On the way, Echo prayed that she would come to know that the gospel was true. Soon after arriving in Utah, she was baptized. When Echo's mother returned to England the next year, Echo and three of her sisters stayed behind. Counting the three sisters who had stayed in Utah earlier, the Squires children were almost evenly divided between Utah and England.

Two years after returning to Utah, Echo married a young artist named Reuben Kirkham. They soon moved to Logan, where Reuben established an art business. They had five children before Reuben died in 1886, leaving Echo a widow at age 29. Because of limited financial resources, Echo learned to be almost entirely self-sufficient in feeding and clothing her children. She grew fruit, raised chickens, milked cows, sewed or knitted nearly everything they wore, and even soled their shoes. "The Lord blessed us with great blessings," she said, "and our storehouse was like the widow's cruse of oil. It never ran dry."[135]

During the six years after her husband died, Echo and her children moved from Logan to Bountiful to Idaho and back to Bountiful. Then in 1892, Echo married David DeLee, a widower who lived in Bountiful. They had four daughters, one of whom died as a baby. Much like her parents, who had 11 daughters and one son, Echo had eight daughters and one son. When she died in 1943 at age 86, Echo was survived by seven children, 20 grandchildren, and 28 great-grandchildren—all of them blessed by the yearnings Echo heeded when she was 17 years old to return to Zion.

William and Eliza Binder

William and Eliza Binder were both 24 years old when they emigrated and had been married for a little over two years. Both of them survived.

The qualities of commitment and leadership that led to William

Binder's call as a branch president at age 22 continued to be evidenced during the trek and the rest of his life. He looked out for others even if doing so was inconvenient. When one man was near death after the last crossing of the Platte River, William pulled him on his handcart to camp. When Albert Jones could not pull his cart across the icy Sweetwater, William Binder got back in the river and pulled it for him.[136]

William Binder also accepted difficult assignments—both during the trek and later in life. He stood guard on that most bitter night after the last crossing of the Platte. Another time when his guard shift was supposed to end at midnight, he stayed at his post all night because no one came to relieve him.[137] In November, after trudging to Martin's Cove in wet clothes that froze to his skin, he turned around and walked all the way back to the river because Edward Martin asked him to deliver a message to some of the men there.[138]

In 1857, the year after arriving in Utah, William accompanied troops to participate in the Echo Canyon campaign against Johnston's Army. In 1858 he was stationed in Provo Canyon, having charge of 16 men who watched the mountain passes. In both 1862 and 1863 he was called to return to Nebraska to help with the emigration. The 400 members of the company he traveled with in 1862 wrote the following letter of appreciation for his service:

"Resolved that we feel deeply indebted to brother Wm. L. Binder, the chaplain of this train, for his constant attention to our spiritual welfare, as well as to our temporal comfort in the capacity of commissary. And, that for his readiness to administer the ordinances of anointing at any time when called upon, our warmest thanks are due."[139]

The Binders made their first Utah home in Provo and then moved to Salt Lake City. There William served in many Church leadership positions, including the bishopric of the 15th Ward for 13 years. William also twice returned to England on missions. During his first mission, from 1874 to 1876, he presided over the London Conference. On his way home he led a company of 322 emigrants from Liverpool to Salt Lake City.[140] In 1898, when William was 66 years old, he served another mission to his homeland to collect genealogical data.

Eliza Binder died in 1894, four years before William's final mission to England. William died in 1902, when he was 70. They apparently never had any children, although William had a daughter by a plural wife.[141]

Robert and Mary Clifton Family

Robert and Mary Clifton left England with three daughters, ages 20, 12, and 6. The family looked very different when they arrived in Salt Lake City. The Cliftons' oldest daughter, Rebecca, remained in the Midwest. Then Robert died in November. Mary Clifton entered Zion a widow with two young daughters. Details about her life from that point are sparse. A biographical sketch written by a granddaughter sums up the rest of Mary's life in one simple but important sentence: "She raised these two little girls to be true Latter-day Saints."[142] The older of these girls, Sophia, eventually had 10 children. The younger girl, Ann, had 11 children. Although this family sustained costly losses in coming to Zion, the object of Robert Clifton's quest was fulfilled in future generations.

David and Deborah Blair Family

David Blair, the professional soldier who had been a member of Queen Victoria's Life Guard, died during the handcart trek. Ephraim Hanks had raised him from the point of death after meeting the Martin company (see pages 382–83), but David declined again and died soon afterward. His baby son also died on the trek, the date and location unknown. Deborah Blair and her two daughters survived.

Many in the Martin company had looked up to David Blair. Albert Jones, who was 16 at the time, later wrote of him:

"Brother Blair, one of the Royal Life Guards Blue of her majesty, the British queen, was with us, whose grand physique and gigantic frame [were] the admiration of us boys . . . whenever he attended meeting in his regimentals. With the lack of proper nourishment, he dwindled down to a wreck, both mind and body. . . . He died and was buried under a big tree on Quakenasp Hill."[143]

Quakenasp Hill is likely another name for Aspen Mountain in western Wyoming. If the two are the same, the most likely death date for David Blair is November 25, when the Martin company passed through that area. The help from Eph Hanks gave him a two-week reprieve from death.

Due to the lack of sources, little is known about the lives of Deborah Blair and her two daughters after the trek. Perhaps through these daughters, the hopes that their parents could not realize for themselves are being fulfilled in the lives of their posterity.

James and Elizabeth Bleak Family

Twenty-six-year-old James Bleak had already endured a lifetime of loss before he began the handcart journey. Four of his siblings had died very young, his father had died when James was 14, his mother when he was 16, and the only other member of his family, his younger brother John, when James was 18. His life began to reverse course the next year, when he married Elizabeth Moore. Two years later they both joined the Church, and the next year James was called to serve in the presidency of the Whitechapel Branch in London. He then served as branch president from 1854 until he emigrated in 1856.

It would be natural for a person who had a childhood like James Bleak's to do everything possible to protect against further loss. For that reason, a decision James made just a few weeks before leaving England is especially noteworthy. He had placed a deposit to purchase a wagon for his journey to Zion. When the handcart plan was announced soon afterward, he initially planned to retain his wagon out of consideration for his wife and four small children. He changed his mind when he realized that his example was prompting others in his branch to take exception to pulling handcarts. Wanting to set a proper example, he wrote to President Richards asking to have his name added to the handcart list. The extra money he had sent to purchase a wagon was used to help others emigrate.

James and Elizabeth Bleak and their four children all survived the handcart trek, though they suffered greatly. In September, James had been so ill that Francis Webster and others pulled him in their handcarts.[144] During the last month of the journey, James's feet became so frozen that the flesh dropped off his heels.

The Bleaks also came close to losing their 5-year-old son, Thomas. Two women in the company were helping care for him, and after a cold night they awoke to find him lifeless between them. James described how Thomas was miraculously healed after the women brought him to his parents:

"[I] began by anointing him with consecrated oil, and praying over him, calling upon the Lord to keep His promise that not one of the family should fall by the way in gathering to Zion. Tests were applied, but not a heartbeat or other sign of life was in the child. . . . After what appeared to [be] a very long time, [I] thought [I] saw a slight flutter in the child's throat. . . . Finally, by God's power and blessing, the dear child unclosed his eyes and is now a resident of Salt Lake City, father of nine children and likewise a grandfather."[145]

Despite these difficulties, James Bleak never wavered in his faith or even in his feelings of gratitude for the opportunity to come to Zion. On the day he arrived in Salt Lake City, crippled with frozen feet, he wrote, "I feel to rejoice greatly and give praise to God for my safe arrival in Zion with my wife and children."[146]

Like many others in the Martin company, James Bleak suffered physical effects of the handcart journey throughout his life. He was unable to walk for more than two months after arriving in Salt Lake City. His journal entry for February 12, 1857, records his first success: "I walked to meeting for the first time this evening and bore my testimony to the truth of the work of the Lord."

At a conference a few weeks later, James Bleak showed the same spirit of consecration he had shown when yielding his wagon for a handcart. "A collection was made to raise $125," he wrote. "As I had no cash, I gave my ring. Notice was given in the evening that three rings had been given to the collection, and as Br. Brigham had received the amount he wanted, he wished the owners of the rings to receive them back."[147]

When the conference resumed the next day, one ring still had not been claimed. James overheard Brigham Young telling the clerk, "If any person applies for the one ring remaining, send them to me." James immediately approached Brigham Young and said he wanted him to keep the ring. "He asked if it belonged to me," James wrote in his journal. "I said yes, that I had no cash and therefore gave my ring, which I wished him to accept. He blessed me in the name of the Lord and said he had as much as he wanted then and wished me to take back my ring, which I accordingly did. He asked the clerk to take my name and residence."[148]

James and Elizabeth initially settled in the Ogden area. Then at the general conference held in October 1861 they were among a large group who were called to settle southern Utah. Before leaving, James was set apart to be the clerk and historian of the Southern Utah Mission. His service in this capacity spanned nearly 50 years and culminated in his writing a lengthy history of the mission.

The Bleaks helped establish St. George and lived there for the rest of their lives. The early years in St. George were difficult, but James considered the hardships minimal compared to the blessings. His Church service included callings as a stake president's counselor, bishop's counselor, high councilor, tithing clerk, and stake patriarch. He also served in many civic positions, including city recorder, city councilman, court clerk, and postmaster. One biographer summed up his service as follows: "Wherever three people met together in St. George, they formed an organization and appointed James G. Bleak as their secretary."[149]

James Bleak returned to England to serve a mission in 1872 and 1873. His main assignment during this mission was to be the assistant editor of the Church's periodical the *Millennial Star.* While in England he went to London to visit the grave of his brother John, whose death in 1848 had left James the last surviving member of his family. James was saddened to find that the place of John's burial was occupied by a railway.

When the St. George Temple was completed in 1877, it became the focus of James Bleak's life. That year he spent 144 days in the temple. He eventually became the temple recorder and continued in that position for more than 20 years, serving with extraordinary zeal. He worked closely with Wilford Woodruff, who was the first president of the temple, and was later called to be the assistant president. In 1901 he was released from most of his temple responsibilities so he could devote his full time to writing a history of the Southern Utah Mission.

Much less is known about Elizabeth Bleak's life after she arrived in Utah. She and James had six more children, for a total of 10. Because James was frequently away from home after the family moved to St. George, Elizabeth had most of the responsibility for raising their children. Like her husband, Elizabeth loved the temple and was an ordinance worker for many years. The day she died in 1899, she worked in the temple and then returned home and passed away peacefully in her rocking chair.

James Bleak had 23 other children with three other wives. He died in 1918 at 88 years of age. At the time of his death, this man who was the sole survivor of his family when he was just 18 years old was survived by approximately 250 descendants.

CHAPTER 39

The Hearts of the Fathers

For I reckon that the sufferings of this present time are not worthy to be compared with the glory which shall be revealed in us.

—ROMANS 8:18

Standing on a crest in Martin's Cove, I look down on where the Martin company camped for five nights in November 1856. Even now, above the wind, I hear the children crying. My thoughts turn to their fathers, their providers and protectors.

John Jaques is trying to soothe little Flora while his wife tries to nurse their baby son. John thinks back to their walks in Liverpool, when Flora would hold his hand and toddle along beside him. He hopes they will walk together in Zion, but her cry is growing weaker. Each night it ceases only with complete exhaustion. Each night John Jaques wonders whether the exhaustion will bring sleep or death.

Henry Squires is finally beginning to doze when an icy canvas falls on him. He uncovers himself and looks around camp to see that the wind has flattened nearly every tent—again. He considers leaving the tent as it is, since it will probably blow down several more times in the night. But his wife is eight months pregnant, and he has five young daughters to care for. So he struggles to his feet, raises the tent poles, and tries to anchor the sides with snow.

The eyes of the fathers fill with tears as their children ask for more food. George Barnes gives his children part of his own scanty ration, as he has done for days, and then dies in the cove. James Bleak gathers his family of six around their one pound of flour—four ounces per adult, two per child—and offers a prayer of thanks and solicitation. "Through the blessing of our Father, we felt as contented as when we had 1 lb. per head," he would later write.

With the temperature below zero, John Bailey is desperately trying to keep his family from freezing. He trudges into the hills above the cove and collects some brush for a fire. He knows how quickly it will be consumed, that before long he will need to look for more. Returning to camp, he is so weak and numb that he lies down and tells his wife he is going to die. She shakes him, pleading and perhaps scolding. Soon John Bailey is back in the hills looking for wood.

Edward Martin is thinking of Mary Ellen, trying to picture what she looks like. Of his first seven children, Mary Ellen is the only one still living. She's 12 years old, and he hasn't seen her since she was 8. He realizes that between his service in the battalion and the mission field, he has been gone for half her life. Her words, written more than a year earlier, keep going through his mind: "It would be pleasing to me if I see you once more. . . . It seems as if I never had a father."[1]

Although George Padley is not a father, he keeps thinking about his future children. He has not stopped shivering since overexerting himself at the Sweetwater. Tenderly he has been caring for his fiancée, Sarah, but now he is too weak to stand. As he feels his life slipping away, he summons his most fervent hope to help him hold on—his marriage to Sarah and the children they would raise in Zion. The children are still in his thoughts when the shivering stops.

I think of the fathers who are gone—but still watching over their families. James Loader watches as his wife dances in Martin's Cove to encourage their daughters not to give up. Aaron Jackson looks on as his widow, Elizabeth, tries to wrap one blanket around herself and three little children. Samuel Pucell and his wife, Margaret, watch as someone else cares for their orphaned daughters. Robert McBride watches his two youngest sons turn a flour sack inside out so they can suck the dust out of the corners.

Where is the light in these days of darkness?

Like so many others who have come here, today our group of nearly 400 found that light as we walked silently through Martin's

Cove. Some thought of the fathers, some of the mothers, some of the children. On this warm summer day, many of us felt a chill as we thought of November 1856. And most of us came away from this sacred place with a personal message.

For some, it was a message about commitment and sacrifice.

For others, it was a message about the power of faith.

To many, it was a message about love and gratitude.

To a few, it was a message about personal rescue.

For all, it was a message of light, given as a gift from God—and from those who purchased it at such a great price.

A TRAIL OF TEARS,
A TRAIL OF HOPE

And God shall wipe away all tears from their eyes; and there shall be no more death, neither sorrow, nor crying, neither shall there be any more pain.

—REVELATION 21:4

By any temporal measure, the Willie and Martin handcart tragedy exacted a mighty price. Some 200 people paid with their lives. Many who survived suffered amputations and other physical traumas that troubled them for the rest of their lives. Many families paid the price of broken hearts and broken dreams. The price for many women was widowhood at an early age. The price for too many children was losing both of their parents.

Without minimizing these costs, it is important to examine the other side of the ledger. Besides being a costly tragedy, the Willie and Martin handcart experience was full of triumph. One of the greatest triumphs was the number who survived. Through one of the most heroic rescues ever undertaken, some 800 of the nearly 1,000 people who left Florence with these companies made it to the Salt Lake Valley.

Even among those who died, there was a kind of triumph. Most who paid with their lives "lay down with their faces Zion-ward in full faith and fellowship."[1] Speaking of them, one leader of the Martin company said, "God alone is worthy of them." From an eternal perspective, the price they paid was not in vain. Even from a mortal perspective, the price they paid often bore dividends to generations of their posterity.

Another triumph was the response of these Saints to their trials.

470

The desperate scramble for survival could have brought out the worst in them. Trail narratives of companies that did not have a spiritual purpose sometimes tell of strife that led to fighting, shootings, and breakups. "We see large companies bursting into fragments," John Edwin Banks wrote a few years earlier as he traveled along the Sweetwater.[2] In contrast, most members of these handcart companies bore their trials with dignity and faith.

Despite the high physical cost of this tragedy, another triumph was a compensating spiritual power that most of these people developed. It was a power that sustained them through every imaginable adversity that was yet to come in their lives. One of the most remarkable aspects of this power is the almost universal refusal of these pioneers to blame or find fault with their leaders for the tragedy.

A Story of Countless Miracles

President James E. Faust has not hesitated to ask the hard questions about this handcart experience. "Why were not the elements tempered to spare them from their profound agony?" he asked.[3] The storms met them head-on instead of going to the right or left, as promised. There was no figurative parting of the Red Sea, as promised. Nevertheless, this is a story of countless miracles and divine interventions.

One manifestation of divine influence was Brigham Young's prophetic foresight in the rescue. While others expected the elements to be tempered, Brigham Young seemed to foresee the severity of the weather a full two weeks before the first winter storm. The urgency with which he issued the call to rescue—an urgency that he alone felt—also seemed to result from prophetic foresight. If the rescuers had waited even one additional day, many more people would have died. A delay of a few days could have resulted in the deaths of nearly everyone.

A second way the survival of most of the handcart pioneers was miraculous has to do with the strength they drew from God in their darkest hour. Many felt that the sustaining power of God was a real force in their survival when all physical indicators say they should have died. Susanna Stone later wrote about feeling sustained by divine help:

"We traveled on, feeling that the Lord would protect his Saints, and so he did. Although we passed through many trying scenes, his protecting care was over us. . . .

"I often think of the songs we sang to encourage us on our toilsome journey. It was hard to endure, but the Lord gave us strength and courage. . . .

"We waded through the cold streams many times, but we murmured not, for our faith in God and our testimony of His work were supreme. And in the blizzards and falling snow we sat under our handcarts and sang, 'Come, come, ye Saints.' . . .

"Only once did my courage fail. One cold, dreary afternoon, my feet having been frosted, I felt I could go no further, and withdrew from the company and sat down to await the end, being somewhat in a stupor. After a time I was aroused by a voice, which seemed as audible as anything could be, and which spoke to my very soul of the promises and blessings I had received, and which should surely be fulfilled and that I had a mission to perform in Zion. I received strength, and was filled with the Spirit of the Lord and arose and traveled on with a light heart. As I reached camp, I found a search party ready to go back to find me, dead or alive. I had no relatives, but many dear and devoted friends, and we did all we could to aid and encourage each other."[4]

By choosing to see with an eye of faith, Susanna Stone felt the sustaining hand of God even at her lowest point, even when it might have been easier to feel forsaken.

Elizabeth Jackson of the Martin company was another person who testified of God's power in sustaining life. "It was so cold that some of the company came near freezing to death," she wrote. "The sufferings of the people were fearful, and nothing but the power of a merciful God kept them from perishing."[5]

Elizabeth Jackson also felt God's help in sustaining her spiritually. Her husband died after the last crossing of the Platte, leaving

Elizabeth to care for three small children during the most difficult part of the journey. In those terrible circumstances she became despondent. As she later recorded, she had only one source to draw on for strength: "I [appealed] to the Lord, . . . he who had promised to be a husband to the widow, and a father to the fatherless. I appealed to him and he came to my aid."[6]

Patience Loader of the Martin company bore a similar testimony of God's power: "I can testify that our Heavenly Father heard and answered our prayers and we were blessed with health and strength day by day to endure the severe trials we had to pass through on that terrible journey. . . . We know that if God had not been with us that our strength would have failed us and our bodies would have been left on the plains. . . . I can truthfully say that we never felt to murmur at the hardships we were passing through. I can say we put our trust in God, and he heard and answered our prayers."[7]

Millen Atwood, one of the Willie company subcaptains, also saw the people seek—and miraculously receive—divine strength:

"I have walked day by day [beside] the handcarts as they were rolling, and when the people would get weary, I have seen them by dozens on their knees by the roadside crying to the Lord for strength, and there are scores now in this city who walked from Iowa City to Fort Bridger. . . . They were filled with the Holy Spirit, and it seemed as though angels nerved them with strength."[8]

A third way the survival of most members of the handcart companies was miraculous has to do with the rescue itself. In addition to the many individual miracles associated with the rescue, there seems to be a larger miracle in its timing. The first winter storm came at the worst possible time—when the people were already weak from short rations and were facing some of the hardest parts of the trail. As if in divine response to nature's untimely fury, the rescuers arrived just in time to save most members of both companies. The express members of the first rescue team met the Willie company almost as soon as the first storm began and just hours after company leaders had issued the last ration of flour. The main body of the first rescue team met the Willie company two days later, just in time for the ascent of Rocky Ridge. The express rescuers met the Martin company nine days after the Willie company, when they were down to four-ounce-a-day rations, immobilized by weakness and cold, and nearly all at the point of death.

A fourth miracle in the survival of these companies has to do with the hearts of those in the first rescue team. These 27 men left loved ones and comfortable homes within two days of the call to rescue, not even taking time to put their affairs in order. Theirs is one of the most impressive examples of sacrifice in heeding a prophet's call in the history of the Church. When relief is administered by people who serve as instruments in the hands of God to bless his children, it is just as much a miracle as when God intervenes supernaturally to administer relief.

Many miracles, perhaps most, are like this. Although God sometimes intervenes and removes trials, whether caused by weather, natural disaster, illness, accident, bad decisions, or simply the natural course of mortality, such direct intervention seems to be the exception. Taking away all or even most of these problems would compromise the purposes of mortality, so people are often left to bear them. Nonetheless, that does not mean God is not hearing or helping. As he did with the handcart pioneers, if he does not deliver his children from adversity, he will strengthen their backs to bear it (see Mosiah 24:14–15; Alma 36:3, 27). He will also call and inspire other loving people to be instruments in his hands to minister to their relief (see Jacob 2:19; Mosiah 4:26; D&C 38:35).

AFTER MUCH TRIBULATION COME THE BLESSINGS

Throughout the scriptures, the Lord promises to bless those who faithfully endure tribulation. Many members of the handcart companies testified that the blessings they received more than compensated for the trials they endured. But the blessings were not limited to these pioneers themselves. Their posterity has also been blessed by their sacrifices. And far beyond direct posterity, generations of other people, in ever-growing numbers, have been blessed by their examples of testimony and sacrifice. The power of the handcart experience to reach through the generations and bless others is one of its most striking aspects—and shows that the impact of the experience cannot be judged only by its effects on those who went through it.

Personal Blessings to the Participants

"I have wondered why these intrepid pioneers had to pay for their faith with such a terrible price in agony and suffering," President James E. Faust said. His answer acknowledges a redemptive value in their trials:

"I believe their lives were consecrated to a higher purpose through their suffering. Their love for the Savior was burned deep in their souls and into the souls of their children and their children's children. The motivation for their lives came from a true conversion in the center of their souls."[9]

President Gordon B. Hinckley shared similar feelings about the silver lining in the storm clouds of sufferings these Saints endured. In his dedicatory prayer at Rock Creek Hollow, he said of the Willie company, "We know that they came to know Thee in a particular way in the dire circumstances in which they found themselves those early winter days in 1856."[10]

Many accounts from the handcart pioneers themselves confirm these impressions. One of the most powerful comes from Francis Webster of the Martin company, who said, "[We] came through [that experience] with the absolute knowledge that God lives, for we became acquainted with Him in our extremities! . . . The price we paid to become acquainted with God was a privilege to pay."[11]

In a strange irony, others who heard Francis Webster that day wished that they also could have gone through the handcart ordeal so they would have paid the same price that yielded the great blessing of becoming acquainted with God. Perhaps no greater blessing can come to mortals than that.

Elizabeth Jackson of the Martin company likewise kept an eternal perspective about the blessings that would come as a result of the ordeal: "I believe the Recording Angel has inscribed in the archives above, and that my suffering for the Gospel's sake will be sanctified unto me for my good."[12] Emily Hill of the Willie company similarly wrote, "I do not doubt that all my troubles have been for my good."[13] Betsey Smith expressed similar feelings: "I will not dwell upon the hardships we endured, nor the hunger and cold, but I like to tell of the goodness of God unto us."[14]

Even those who lost their limbs wrote of the compensating assurance they had received that all would be well in the eternities. Young Mary Johnson of the Hunt company, for example, tried to comfort her older brothers when they saw her walking on the stumps of her knees after her feet and part of her legs had been amputated. "I told them not to cry so," she later wrote, "for I would have my feet again when I got to Heaven."[15]

Blessings to Posterity

Beyond seeing how the handcart experience was a blessing to them individually, many handcart pioneers had the perspective to look into the future to see how it would benefit their posterity. More than compensating for their own suffering was a confidence that their descendants would be blessed by their decision to come to Zion—even if they did not arrive there themselves.

Just before John Linford died along the trail, his wife asked if he was sorry they had undertaken the journey. Taking the long-range view, he said, "No, Maria, I am glad we came. I shall not live to reach Salt Lake, but you and the boys will, and I do not regret all we have gone through if our boys can grow up and raise their families in Zion."[16]

Similarly, just before William Jones of the Hodgetts company died along the trail, he told his family, "I have pointed you

Zion-ward, and I want you never to turn back. God is in his heaven, and all is right with us whether we are in this earth or out of it. God will be with you. If you stumble and fall back, pick yourselves up and go on again."[17]

Emma James, whose father died on the journey, paid the following tribute to her mother for blessing her posterity by making the sacrifices to come to Zion: "[My mother] left a great posterity to revere her memory and give thanks that she had had the determination to come to Zion."[18]

Susanna Stone also testified that the Lord's blessings had extended far beyond herself to her posterity. "My frosted feet gave me considerable trouble for many years," she wrote, "but this was forgotten in the contemplation of the great blessings the gospel had brought to me *and mine*."[19] Some 150 years later, a descendant who bears Susanna's name is one of hundreds of Susanna's posterity who continues to receive strength from her faithful endurance.

Blessings to Others in Future Generations

Each summer, thousands of people, most of them youth, reenact handcart treks on the sites made sacred by the Willie and Martin handcart pioneers. Almost invariably at the conclusion of these treks, they say that they have been moved spiritually in ways they have never felt before. Many others who have never visited these sites are similarly moved by the accounts of these handcart companies. Through the sacrifices of these pioneers and their rescuers, the Lord continues to bless thousands of people who never knew them.

THE CONTINUANCE AND END OF HANDCART TRAVEL

Despite the severity of the Willie and Martin handcart tragedies, those companies were not the end of the handcart emigration, nor should their experience be seen as an indictment of the handcart plan. Three companies before them made the journey successfully, and five companies after them would do the same. In those five companies, totaling 1,071 people, only 12 deaths were recorded.[20] Indeed, pulling handcarts was arduous and fatiguing, but between 1856 and 1860, handcarts provided a way for many people to come to Zion who might never have been able to come otherwise.

After 1860, the handcart plan was replaced by another innovation in transporting emigrants to Utah. Until then, most people thought it was impossible for the same team of oxen to pull a wagon to the Midwest and back to Utah in the same season. After one of Brigham Young's nephews demonstrated that this could be done, the "down-and-back years" began in 1861. According to this plan, wagons typically started from Salt Lake City in the spring, cached supplies along the trail for the return trip, picked up the emigrants, and returned to Utah.[21] Although somewhat more expensive than handcarts, this system was much less expensive than buying wagons, animals, and supplies in the Midwest, so until 1868 it was adopted as the primary method for conveying emigrants to Utah. By 1869, when the transcontinental railroad was finished, most emigrants made the entire overland journey by train.

A TRAIL OF TEARS, A TRAIL OF HOPE

In many ways, the trail that the Willie and Martin handcart pioneers walked was a type, or metaphor, of mortality. Along the path to Zion, they were sometimes mocked and ridiculed. Sometimes they had to cross rivers that threatened to sweep them away. Some of those crossings were through icy waters that left them frozen and numb. Along the path there was also sand, sometimes for long distances, making progress slow and grinding. When the elements were at their worst and the Saints were at their weakest, they had to face Rocky Ridge. Toward the end, they had to go through mountains that had several feet of fresh snow. Indeed this was a trail of tears.

But the experiences of the Willie and Martin handcart pioneers show that faith and hope will triumph over the worst days on the trail. Faith and hope kept these Saints stepping forward when their strength was gone. Heaven-sent rescuers helped sustain their hope when despair began to take them off the path. And when they felt alone, when they felt that they could bear no more, a divine hand was stretched out to steady them and guide them home.

Come unto me, all ye that labour and are heavy laden,
and I will give you rest.

Take my yoke upon you, and learn of me;
for I am meek and lowly in heart:
and ye shall find rest unto your souls.

For my yoke is easy, and my burden is light.
Matthew 11:28–30

NOTES

INTRODUCTION
ONWARD TO ZION

1. In Amy L. Van Cott, *Generations of Websters* (n.p., 1960), 49.
2. Ibid.
3. William Palmer, in Van Cott, *Generations of Websters,* 61–62; see also David O. McKay, "Pioneer Women," *Relief Society Magazine,* Jan. 1948, 8.
4. LeRoy R. Hafen and Ann W. Hafen, *Handcarts to Zion: The Story of a Unique Western Migration* (Lincoln: University of Nebraska Press, 1960), 12.
5. Hinckley, "True to the Faith," *Ensign,* May 1997, 66.
6. Gordon B. Hinckley, *Discourses of President Gordon B. Hinckley, Volume 1: 1995–1999* (Salt Lake City: Deseret Book, 2005), 366.

CHAPTER 1
FROM ENGLAND TO IOWA CITY

Hinckley, dedicatory prayer at Rock Creek, Wyoming, 23 July 1994; used by permission of the Office of the President; see also *Church News,* 30 July 1994, 11.

1. See John Jaques, *Salt Lake Daily Herald,* 12 Jan. 1879, 1.
2. *Millennial Star,* 26 July 1856, 478.
3. James G. Willie Emigrating Company journal, 10 May 1856; Archives of The Church of Jesus Christ of Latter-day Saints (Church archives), Salt Lake City, Utah.
4. Willie company journal, 20 May 1856; see also *Millennial Star,* 26 July 1856, 479.
5. *Millennial Star,* 26 July 1856, 478.
6. Willie company journal, 8 May 1856.
7. Stegner, *The Gathering of Zion: The Story of the Mormon Trail* (Lincoln: University of Nebraska Press, 1964), 228.
8. In *Among the Mormons,* ed. William Mulder and A. Russell Mortensen (New York: Alfred A. Knopf, 1958), 336–37.
9. *Millennial Star,* 7 July 1855, 421–22.
10. *Treasures of Pioneer History,* comp. Kate B. Carter, 6 vols. (Salt Lake City: Daughters of Utah Pioneers, 1952–57), 5:253; *Journey to Zion: Voices from*

the Mormon Trail, comp. Carol Cornwall Madsen (Salt Lake City: Deseret Book, 1997), 636.

11. *Millennial Star,* 26 July 1856, 478–79.

12. *New York Herald,* in Journal History, 14 June 1856, Church archives.

13. Journal History, 14 June 1856.

14. *Millennial Star,* 26 July 1856, 478.

15. Willie company journal, 20 Oct. 1856.

16. Kimball, "Eastern Ends of the Trail West," *Ensign,* Jan. 1980, 31.

17. "Sail and Rail Pioneers," *BYU Studies,* Spring 1995, 30–31.

18. Willie company journal, 21 June 1856.

19. See James G. Willie History, Church archives, Salt Lake City, Utah, 2; see also Journal History, 9 Nov. 1856.

CHAPTER 2
THE CALL TO GATHER

1. History of Thomas and Janet McNeil, DUP archives, Salt Lake City, Utah, 5. The McNeils were among the approximately 250 Saints on the *Thornton* who did not become part of the Willie handcart company. Their sacrifices after arriving in America were also considerable. As counseled by President Franklin D. Richards, they went to St. Louis and prepared to finish the journey to Utah the next year. In 1857, however, they were called to help fulfill Brigham Young's plan to establish settlements along the trail. Their first destination was 100 miles west of Florence, Nebraska, where they established Genoa. In 1859 they were sent another 100 miles to the west to establish the settlement of Wood River. The family finally reached Utah later in 1859. Thomas and Janet McNeil are great-great-grandparents of Elder M. Russell Ballard.

2. *Millennial Star,* 15 Mar. 1848, 84.

3. *Messages of the First Presidency of The Church of Jesus Christ of Latter-day Saints,* comp. James R. Clark, 6 vols. (Salt Lake City: Bookcraft, 1965–75), 2:33.

4. *Millennial Star,* 22 Sept. 1855, 603.

5. Ibid., 1 Dec. 1855, 765.

6. *Deseret News,* 26 Nov. 1856, 300–301.

7. *Millennial Star,* 26 Jan. 1856, 51–52.

8. *The Mormon,* 30 Aug. 1856, 2.

9. *Millennial Star,* 18 Aug. 1855, 522.

10. Hafen and Hafen, *Handcarts to Zion,* 21, 27.

11. Stegner, *Gathering of Zion,* 222.

12. *Millennial Star,* 11 Aug. 1855, 506.

13. See *Church History in the Fulness of Times,* 2d ed. (Salt Lake City: The Church of Jesus Christ of Latter-day Saints, 2003), 356; Franklin L. West, *Life of Franklin D. Richards* (Salt Lake City: Deseret News Press, 1924), 132.

14. Hafen and Hafen, *Handcarts to Zion,* 28.

15. *Millennial Star,* 22 Sept. 1855, 601, 602.

16. Ibid., 601.

17. Betsey Smith Goodwin, "The Tired Mother: Pioneer Recollections," *Improvement Era,* July 1919, 781.

18. *Millennial Star,* 23 Aug. 1856, 542.

19. Ibid., 26 Jan. 1856, 52.

20. Ibid., 5 Jan. 1856, 12–13.

CHAPTER 3
THE HANDCART PLAN

Hinckley, "True to the Faith," 66.

1. *Millennial Star,* 26 Jan. 1856, 51.

2. See *Millennial Star,* 18 Aug. 1855, 518–19; 20 Oct. 1855, 667; 17 Nov. 1855, 730, 732; Leonard J. Arrington, *Great Basin Kingdom* (Cambridge: Harvard University Press, 1958), 148–50.

3. Orson F. Whitney, *History of Utah,* 4 vols. (Salt Lake City: George Q. Cannon and Sons, 1892–1904), 1:547; Arrington, *Great Basin Kingdom,* 151.

4. *Millennial Star,* 26 July 1856, 476–77.

5. Ibid., 14 Feb.1857, 97.

6. Ibid., 26 Jan. 1856, 51.

7. Ibid., 52.

8. Ibid., 51.

9. Eugene England, "Brigham's Gospel Kingdom," *BYU Studies,* Spring 1978, 349; Carter, *Treasures of Pioneer History,* 5:230.

10. See Arrington, *Great Basin Kingdom,* 156.

11. *Millennial Star,* 26 Jan. 1856, 54.

12. Ibid., 22 Dec. 1855, 813–14.

13. Ibid., 26 Jan. 1856, 54; see also 23 Feb. 1856, 122.

14. Franklin D. Richards said the carts would carry 500 or 600 pounds (see *Millennial Star,* 22 Dec. 1855, 810), but in reality they were not designed to hold that much weight, and pulling such a heavy load would have been too burdensome. It is unlikely that any of the carts were loaded so heavily even after bags of flour were added in Florence.

15. According to John Jaques, the light loading of the carts for the journey across Iowa was to allow the emigrants to get used to the method of travel "without a great deal of toil all at once"; see *Millennial Star,* 14 June 1856, 370.

16. *Deseret News,* 26 Nov. 1856, 300.

17. *Millennial Star,* 24 Nov. 1855, 745, 747.

CHAPTER 4
ADVANTAGES AND MISGIVINGS

1. *Millennial Star,* 22 Dec. 1855, 813; see also 26 Jan. 1856, 54.
2. Ibid., 22 Dec. 1855, 810.
3. Ibid.
4. Ibid.
5. Ibid., 26 Jan. 1856, 54.
6. Ibid., 22 Dec. 1855, 810.
7. Ibid., 814.
8. See Stegner, *Gathering of Zion,* 219–20; *Millennial Star,* 26 July 1856, 466.
9. *Millennial Star,* 26 Jan. 1856, 54; see also Brigham Young to Franklin D. Richards, in England, "Brigham's Gospel Kingdom," 350.
10. *Millennial Star,* 22 Dec. 1855, 810.
11. *The Mormon,* 26 Apr. 1856, 2; see also *Millennial Star,* 14 June 1856, 378.
12. *Millennial Star,* 2 Aug. 1856, 489; see also 29 Dec. 1855, 823.
13. Ibid., 22 Dec. 1855, 809.
14. John Chislett, "Mr. Chislett's Narrative," in T. B. H. Stenhouse, *The Rocky Mountain Saints: A Full and Complete History of the Mormons* (New York: D. Appleton and Co., 1873), 313.
15. *Millennial Star,* 22 Dec. 1855, 809.
16. Ibid., 23 Feb. 1856, 124.
17. Chislett, "Narrative," 313.
18. *Millennial Star,* 2 Feb. 1856, 75.
19. Patience Loader Rozsa Archer, "Recollections of Past Days," Church archives, Salt Lake City, Utah, 52.
20. *Millennial Star,* 26 Jan. 1856, 54.
21. Ibid., 1 Mar. 1856, 138.
22. Ibid., 22 Dec. 1855, 811.
23. Ibid., 1 Mar. 1856, 138.
24. Ibid., 14 June 1856, 369.
25. Ibid.
26. Ibid.
27. Ibid., 370.
28. Ibid., 372.
29. Ibid., 370.
30. Ibid.
31. Archer, "Recollections," 50–51.
32. *Millennial Star,* 14 June 1856, 372.
33. Ibid., 371.
34. Ibid., 372.
35. Ibid., 371.
36. Ibid., 377.
37. Archer, "Recollections," 52.
38. Ibid., 52.

Chapter 5
An Enthusiastic Response

1. *Deseret News,* 15 Oct. 1856, 252–53.
2. In *Representative Women of Deseret,* comp. Augusta Crocheron (n.p., 1884), 82.
3. Ibid., 83.
4. Ibid., 84.
5. Ibid.
6. Ibid.
7. Ibid., 85.
8. Ibid.
9. *Pioneer Women of Faith and Fortitude,* comp. Daughters of Utah Pioneers, 4 vols. (Salt Lake City: Daughters of Utah Pioneers, 1998), 1:690.
10. *An Enduring Legacy,* comp. Daughters of Utah Pioneers, 12 vols. (Salt Lake City: Daughters of Utah Pioneers, 1978–89), 9:45–46.
11. Ibid., 9:46.
12. Ibid., 9:47.
13. Ibid., 2:363.
14. *I Walked to Zion: True Stories of Young Pioneers on the Mormon Trail,* comp. Susan Arrington Madsen (Salt Lake City: Deseret Book, 1994), 64.
15. *Pioneer Women of Faith and Fortitude,* 2:1470.
16. Rowley, "Autobiography of Ann Jewell Rowley," in *Some Early Pioneers of Huntington, Utah, and Surrounding Area,* comp. James Albert Jones (n.p., 1980), 242.
17. Ibid., 241.
18. Ibid., 242.
19. Goodwin, "Tired Mother," 775.
20. Ibid.
21. Ibid.
22. Ibid., 778.
23. *Our Pioneer Heritage,* comp. Daughters of Utah Pioneers, 20 vols. (Salt Lake City: Daughters of Utah Pioneers, 1958–77), 14:293.
24. Ibid., 14:293.
25. George Cunningham, "Autobiography of George Cunningham," Church archives, Salt Lake City, Utah, 1.
26. Carter, *Treasures of Pioneer History,* 5:253.
27. Cunningham, "Autobiography," 1.
28. Ibid.
29. "The Gadd Family," in Gadd Family Histories, Church archives, Salt Lake City, Utah, 1.
30. James Henry Linford, *Autobiography of James Henry Linford* (n.p., 1919), 12.
31. Ibid., 2.
32. Ibid., 6.
33. Ibid.

34. Ibid., 7.
35. In Albert R. Lyman, "Bishop Jense Nielson: A Brief Biography," Church archives, Salt Lake City, Utah, 2.
36. Ibid.
37. Ibid.
38. Ibid.

CHAPTER 6
MAKING PREPARATIONS

Hinckley, "True to the Faith," 66.

1. *Millennial Star,* 5 July 1856, 427.
2. Ibid., 2 Feb. 1856, 73–74.
3. Ibid., 14 June 1856, 377; 23 Aug. 1856, 542; Chislett, "Narrative," 313.
4. *Millennial Star,* 14 June 1856, 377.
5. Ibid., 5 Apr. 1856, 218.
6. Ibid., 12 Jan. 1856, 24.
7. Ibid., 5 Apr. 1856, 218.
8. Chislett, "Narrative," 340.
9. *Millennial Star,* 5 Apr. 1856, 218.
10. Ibid., 23 Aug. 1856, 542.
11. Ibid., 22 Dec. 1855, 814–15.
12. Madsen, *Journey to Zion,* 590–91.
13. *Church History in the Fulness of Times,* 348; Arrington, *Great Basin Kingdom,* 79.
14. Delna Swapp Powell, *James McGaw: Eleventh Pioneer Emigration Company 1852* (n.p., 2002), 12; Conrey Bryson, *Winter Quarters* (Salt Lake City: Deseret Book, 1986), 104.
15. Don H. Smith, "The Rest of the Story" (Mormon History Association paper), 26 May 2006, 2.
16. See *Millennial Star,* 3 May 1856, 281.
17. Journal History, 4 Apr. 1856.
18. *Millennial Star,* 24 May 1856, 333.
19. John Taylor, *The Mormon,* 26 Apr. 1856, 2; 21 Feb. 1857, 2.
20. Journal History, 12 Apr. 1856.
21. William Kimball, journal, Church archives, Salt Lake City, Utah.
22. *Millennial Star,* 23 Feb. 1856, 122.
23. Spencer, journal, 24 Apr. 1856, Church archives, Salt Lake City, Utah.
24. *Millennial Star,* 23 Feb. 1856, 127–28.
25. William G. Hartley and A. Gary Anderson, *Iowa and Nebraska,* vol. 5 of *Sacred Places,* ed. LaMar C. Berrett (Salt Lake City: Deseret Book, 2006), 168.
26. *The Mormon,* 26 Apr. 1856, 2.
27. *Millennial Star,* 2 Aug. 1856, 490.

28. *The Mormon,* 26 Apr. 1856, 2.

29. See *Millennial Star,* 23 Feb. 1856, 127.

30. Spencer, journal, 24 Apr. 1856.

31. Woodward, journal, 3 June 1856, Church archives, Salt Lake City, Utah.

CHAPTER 7
CHALLENGES FOR THE WILLIE COMPANY IN IOWA CITY

1. Woodward, journal, 25 June 1856; Hafen and Hafen, *Handcarts to Zion,* 82, says June 28.

2. Journal History, 11 June 1856; see also Daniel Spencer to Franklin D. Richards, in *Millennial Star,* 2 Aug. 1856, 489.

3. *Deseret News,* 6 Aug. 1856, 173; see also *Millennial Star,* 2 Aug. 1856, 490.

4. *The Mormon,* 26 Apr. 1856, 2.

5. Young, *Journal of Discourses,* 4:68–69.

6. Chislett, "Narrative," 313–14.

7. Cunningham, "Autobiography," 2.

8. Willie company journal, 28 June 1856.

9. Ibid., 2 July 1856.

10. Ibid., 6 July 1856.

11. Cunningham, "Autobiography," 2.

12. Stegner, *Gathering of Zion,* 229.

13. Goodwin, "Tired Mother," 775.

14. Ibid.

15. Stegner, *Gathering of Zion,* 221.

16. Ibid., 222.

17. In Lyman, "Bishop Jense Nielson," 4.

18. Jay P. Nielson, "Glorious Victory," 3 (unpublished manuscript; copy in author's possession); also quoted in Glazier and Clark, *Journal of the Trail,* 29.

19. Rowley, "Autobiography of Ann Jewell Rowley," 243–44.

20. Willie company journal, 12 July 1856.

21. See Marilyn Austin Smith, "Faithful Stewards: The Life of James Gray Willie and Elizabeth Ann Pettit," Church archives, Salt Lake City, Utah.

22. See Andrew Jenson, *LDS Biographical Encyclopedia,* 4 vols. (Salt Lake City: Publishers Press, 1901–36), 1:633–34.

23. See *Levi Savage, Jr., Journal,* comp. Lynn M. Hilton (n.p., 1966).

24. *Millennial Star,* 8 Sept. 1855, 574.

25. Levi Savage, journal, 11 July 1856, Church archives, Salt Lake City, Utah.

26. John Ahmanson, *Secret History,* trans. Gleason L. Archer (Chicago: Moody Press, 1984), 27.

27. Ibid., 28.

28. Ibid., 29.

CHAPTER 8
FROM IOWA CITY TO FLORENCE, NEBRASKA

1. See William Woodward to Wilford Woodruff, 17 Feb. 1857, in Journal History, 9 Nov. 1856; see also Ahmanson, *Secret History,* 29, 31.
2. Willie company journal, 16 July 1856.
3. Chislett, "Narrative," 319.
4. Willie company journal, 20 July 1856.
5. Ibid., 23 July 1856.
6. *Deseret News,* 26 Nov. 1856, 300–301.
7. Hartley and Anderson, *Iowa and Nebraska,* 172.
8. Savage, journal, 24 July 1856.
9. Willie company journal, 25 July 1856.
10. Savage, journal, 3 Aug. 1856.
11. *Deseret News,* 26 Nov. 1856, 300–301.
12. Cunningham, "Autobiography," 2.
13. Ibid.
14. See James G. Willie History, 3; see also Journal History, 9 Nov. 1856.
15. Chislett, "Narrative," 316.
16. Savage, journal, 24 July 1856.
17. Chislett, "Narrative," 316.
18. In Journal History, 26 Sept. 1856.
19. Chislett, "Narrative," 318.
20. *Pioneer Women of Faith and Fortitude,* 4:3458.
21. Stegner, *Gathering of Zion,* 232.

CHAPTER 9
DIFFICULT DECISIONS IN FLORENCE

1. Stegner, *Gathering of Zion,* 233.
2. Madsen, *I Walked to Zion,* 57.
3. In Crocheron, *Representative Women of Deseret,* 86.
4. See Hafen and Hafen, *Handcarts to Zion,* 66; Journal History, 14 Aug. 1856.
5. See Journal History, 14 Aug. 1856; see also John H. Latey to John Taylor, in *The Mormon,* 30 Aug. 1856, 2.
6. See Woodward, journal, 13–14 Aug. 1856.
7. Richard E. Bennett, *Mormons at the Missouri, 1846–1852: "And Should We Die"* (Norman, Okla.: University of Oklahoma Press, 1987), 137.
8. Chislett, "Narrative," 316.
9. Willie company journal, 12 Aug. 1856.
10. Ibid., 13 Aug. 1856.
11. Savage, journal, 13 Aug. 1856.
12. Chislett, "Narrative," 317.
13. Cunningham, "Autobiography," 2; see also Madsen, *Journey to Zion,* 636;

Carter, *Treasures of Pioneer History,* 5:252–53; for a similar recollection from Emma James, see Madsen, *Journey to Zion,* 625.

14. Savage, journal, 13 Aug. 1856.

15. Chislett, "Narrative," 331; Woodward, journal, 12 Aug. 1856; Cunningham, "Autobiography," 2.

16. According to Don H. Smith, the handcart Saints had little opportunity to stay in Florence—and probably would have been worse off if they had tried to do so. The Church's campsite contained only about eight acres of deeded land, and expansion would have been difficult because most of the property in the region was claimed by the Florence Land Company. A second problem was employment. The entire population of the county was only about 3,000 at the time; it is questionable whether employment could have been found for a sudden influx of 1,000 to 1,500 emigrants. Most employment that could have been found would have been seasonal, but agriculture was still limited in the area. A third problem was fuel. Despite the arrangements William Kimball made for wood, Smith feels that the Saints would have had difficulty getting permission to harvest enough timber for the winter. Another problem was food. The Church stores of food in Florence would not have been sufficient for the winter, and obtaining additional food would have been difficult because of a poor harvest in the area. Yet another problem was that the winter of 1856–57 was unusually cold, causing many deaths. Smith concludes, "Given the circumstances found in Nebraska in 1856, the emigrants had the choice to go on or face a greater tragedy by staying" ("Rest of the Story," 6–7).

17. Madsen, *Journey to Zion,* 625.

18. Savage, journal, 15 Aug. 1856.

19. Chislett, "Narrative," 316–17.

20. Ahmanson, *Secret History,* 29–30.

21. Chislett, "Narrative," 319.

22. Stegner, *Gathering of Zion,* 239.

23. Chislett, "Narrative," 317.

24. Ibid.

25. Ibid.

CHAPTER 10
FROM FLORENCE TO FORT LARAMIE

1. Willie company journal, 16 Aug. 1856; Franklin D. Richards and Daniel Spencer to Brigham Young, in *Deseret News,* 22 Oct. 1856, 22; Woodward to Woodruff, 17 Feb. 1857, in Journal History; Chislett, "Narrative," 331.

2. See James G. Willie History, 3; see also Journal History, 9 Nov. 1856.

3. With the four independent Siler wagons, a total of 11 wagons left Florence with the Willie company; see Willie company journal, 16 Aug. 1856.

4. In *Millennial Star,* 18 Oct. 1856, 667–68.

5. Chislett, "Narrative," 317–18.

6. Willie company journal, 17 Aug. 1856.

7. Goodwin, "Tired Mother," 775.

8. *Heart Throbs of the West,* comp. Kate B. Carter, 12 vols. (Salt Lake City: Daughters of Utah Pioneers, 1939–51), 4:79.

9. Hartley and Anderson, *Iowa and Nebraska,* 200.

10. Savage, journal, 16 Sept. 1856; see also 10, 13, 15, 17, and 21 Sept. 1856.

11. Willie company journal, 17 Sept. 1856.

12. Ibid., 4 Sept. 1856.

13. Savage, journal, 4 Sept. 1856. William Woodward concurred that the cattle were lost by stampede during the night: "More than half of our cattle were gone this morning—they had stampeded through the night"; see Woodward, journal, 4 Sept. 1856.

14. Savage, journal, 3 Sept 1856.

15. Madsen, *Journey to Zion,* 626.

16. Ibid., 626–27; see also William Woodward letter to Joseph F. Smith, 1907, Church archives.

17. Willie company journal, 4 Sept. 1856.

18. Ibid., 5 Sept. 1856.

19. Cunningham, "Autobiography," 4.

20. Later, on Rocky Ridge Andrew Smith would be one of the heroes who carried others who faltered. After the trek he continued a life of selfless service. He became a bodyguard for Presidents Brigham Young, John Taylor, Wilford Woodruff, Lorenzo Snow, Joseph F. Smith, and Heber J. Grant.

21. Franklin D. Richards and Daniel Spencer to Brigham Young, *Deseret News,* 22 Oct. 1856, 258; see also Ahmanson, *Secret History,* 31.

22. In Glazier and Clark, *Journal of the Trail,* 36.

23. Chislett, "Narrative," 318.

24. Rowley, "Autobiography of Ann Jewell Rowley," 244.

25. Ibid.

26. Savage, journal, 8 Sept. 1856.

27. Chislett, "Narrative," 318.

28. Willie company journal, 7 Sept. 1856.

29. Ibid.

30. Savage, journal, 1 Oct. 1856; see also Willie company journal, 30 Sept. 1856.

31. Chislett, "Narrative," 318.

32. Smith, "Rest of the Story," 3–4.

33. Savage, journal, 15 Sept. 1856.

34. *Millennial Star,* 25 Oct. 1856, 683–84.

35. Chislett, "Narrative," 318.

36. Willie company journal, 12 Sept. 1856.

37. Ibid.

38. Chislett, "Narrative," 319.

39. *Deseret News,* 15 Oct. 1856, 252–53.

40. Stegner, *Gathering of Zion,* 243.

41. Ibid., 240–41.
42. *Millennial Star,* 25 Oct. 1856, 682.
43. Savage, journal, 13 Sept. 1856.
44. Ibid.
45. Woodward, journal, 13 Sept. 1856; Chislett, "Narrative," 319.
46. Chislett, "Narrative," 319.
47. Cunningham, "Autobiography," 4.
48. *Deseret News,* 22 Oct. 1856, 258.
49. Joseph B. Elder, journal, 11 Apr. 1856.
50. Ibid., 12 Apr. 1856.
51. Ibid., 14 Apr. 1856.
52. Ibid., 25 Apr. 1856.
53. Ibid., 15 Aug. 1856.
54. Elder, journal, 21 (no date).
55. Ibid., 26 (no date).

Chapter 11
From Fort Laramie to Independence Rock

1. See Willie company journal, 3–22 Sept. 1856.
2. Savage, journal, 27 Sept. 1856.
3. Chislett, "Narrative," 316.
4. *Millennial Star,* 22 Dec. 1855, 813.
5. John Jaques, *Salt Lake Daily Herald,* 8 Dec. 1878, 1.
6. Daniel Spencer to Brigham Young, *Deseret News,* 6 Aug. 1856, 173.
7. Chislett, "Narrative," 317; Savage, journal, 17 Aug. 1856.
8. Chislett, "Narrative," 317.
9. Savage, journal, 17 Aug. 1856.
10. See Chislett, "Narrative," 319.
11. In Hafen and Hafen, *Handcarts to Zion,* 273.
12. Brigham Young to Orson Pratt, *Millennial Star,* 11 Oct. 1856, 651.
13. Chislett, "Narrative," 319.
14. Savage, journal, 29 Sept. 1856.
15. Chislett, "Narrative," 319.
16. See Josiah Rogerson, *Salt Lake Tribune,* 30 Nov. 1913, 11; George Cunningham, in Madsen, *Journey to Zion,* 637; Dan Jones Emigrating Company journal, 29 Aug. 1856, Church archives, Salt Lake City, Utah; the typescript in the archives differs in wording but not generally in substance; Chislett, "Narrative," 316.
17. See Jesse Haven, journal, 5 Dec. 1856, Church archives, Salt Lake City, Utah.
18. *Millennial Star,* 22 Dec. 1855, 814.
19. Chislett, "Narrative," 320.
20. Savage, journal, 4 and 6 Oct. 1856.
21. *Deseret News,* 22 Oct. 1856, 258.

22. Ibid.
23. Ibid.
24. Ibid.
25. Journal History, 9 Nov. 1856, 33.
26. Robert T. Burton, journal, 13 Oct. 1856, Church archives, Salt Lake City, Utah.
27. *Deseret News,* 6 Aug. 1856, 173.
28. Savage, journal, 1 Oct. 1856.
29. Willie company journal, 2 Oct. 1856.
30. Chislett, "Narrative," 319.
31. Willie company journal, 1 Oct. 1856.
32. Elder, journal, 21.
33. Savage, journal, 4 Oct. 1856.
34. Madsen, *I Walked to Zion,* 64–65.
35. Alfred Gadd diary, 4 Oct. 1856, Church archives, Salt Lake City, Utah.
36. Ibid., 9 Oct. 1856.
37. *Our Pioneer Heritage,* 2:331.
38. Savage, journal, 8 Oct. 1856.
39. Willie company journal, 11 Oct. 1856.
40. Savage, journal, 11 Oct. 1856.
41. See Samuel Openshaw, journal, 24 Aug. and 5 Sept. 1856, Church archives, Salt Lake City, Utah; see also *Enduring Legacy,* 4:203, 204.
42. Rowley, "Autobiography of Ann Jewell Rowley," 244.
43. Ibid.

Chapter 12

The Rescue Begins

Hinckley, "Reach with a Rescuing Hand," *Ensign,* Nov. 1996, 86.
1. "The First Handcart Companies," *Deseret News,* 1 Oct. 1856, 236–37.
2. *Millennial Star,* 13 Dec. 1856, 794–95.
3. Young to Orson Pratt, 30 Oct. 1856, in *Millennial Star,* 14 Feb. 1857, 99.
4. Journal History, 4 Oct. 1856.
5. Rebecca Bartholomew and Leonard J. Arrington, *Rescue of the 1856 Handcart Companies,* rev. ed. (Provo, Utah: Brigham Young University, Charles Redd Center for Western Studies, 1993), 7.
6. *Deseret News,* 15 Oct. 1856, 252.
7. Ibid., 252–53.
8. Ibid., 252.
9. Ibid., 256.
10. "Original Historical Narrative of Lucy Meserve Smith," Church archives, Salt Lake City, Utah.
11. Hafen and Hafen, *Handcarts to Zion,* 124–25.
12. Stegner, *Gathering of Zion,* 222.
13. Young to Orson Pratt, 30 Oct. 1856, in *Millennial Star,* 14 Feb. 1857, 97.

14. Young, *Journal of Discourses,* 4:67.
15. *Millennial Star,* 14 Feb. 1857, 97.
16. Hafen and Hafen, *Handcarts to Zion,* 124.
17. See Wilford Woodruff, in Hafen and Hafen, *Handcarts to Zion,* 130.
18. Daniel W. Jones, *Forty Years among the Indians* (Salt Lake City: Bookcraft, 1960), 61; Bartholomew and Arrington, *Rescue of the 1856 Handcart Companies,* 10.
19. Jones, *Forty Years among the Indians,* 62.
20. Burton, journal, 14 Oct. 1856; Reddick Allred, journal, Church archives, Salt Lake City, Utah.

CHAPTER 13
From Independence Rock to Fifth Crossing

1. See Savage, journal, 15 Oct. 1856; Willie company journal, 15 Oct. 1856.
2. Chislett, "Narrative," 320.
3. Ibid., 321.
4. Cunningham, "Autobiography," 4–5.
5. Stegner, *Gathering of Zion,* 244.
6. Ibid., 245.
7. Chislett, "Narrative," 320–21.
8. "Laleta Dixon's History of Her Ancestor William James of the Willie Handcart Co.," Church archives, Salt Lake City, Utah, 4.
9. Madsen, *Journey to Zion,* 628.
10. Ibid.
11. Madsen, *I Walked to Zion,* 65.
12. Chislett, "Narrative," 321–22.

CHAPTER 14
The Rescuers Arrive

1. Chislett, "Narrative," 322.
2. Willie company journal appendix, 53.
3. Chislett, "Narrative," 322. The fourth man in this express team, not mentioned by either William Woodward or John Chislett, was Abel Garr.
4. Chislett, "Narrative," 323.
5. Mary F. Kelly, "Emily Hill Woodmansee, Poetess," *Young Woman's Journal,* Feb. 1907, 52; see also *Pioneer Women of Faith and Fortitude,* 4:3452.
6. Chislett, "Narrative," 323.
7. Woodward letter to Smith.
8. Chislett, "Narrative," 323.
9. Ibid.
10. Ibid.
11. Ibid., 323–24.
12. Ibid., 324–25.

13. Willie company journal, 21–23 Oct. 1856.
14. In Linford, *Autobiography,* 55. "Skilly" was a thin gruel of flour and water.
15. Eliza M. Linford Denio, "John Linford," DUP archives, Salt Lake City, Utah, 3.
16. John Linford diary, Church archives, Salt Lake City, Utah.
17. Cunningham, "Autobiography," 5.
18. Savage, journal, 20 Oct. 1856.
19. Elder, journal, 22.
20. Ibid.
21. Ibid. Rescuer Harvey Cluff said the Willie company was 25 miles away from the rescuers' camp; see Harvey Cluff, journal, Church archives, Salt Lake City, Utah, 17.
22. Cluff, journal, 17; see also Hafen and Hafen, *Handcarts to Zion,* 213.
23. Chislett, "Narrative," 325.
24. Bartholomew and Arrington, *Rescue of the 1856 Handcart Companies,* 11.
25. Cluff, journal, 19–20; see also Hafen and Hafen, *Handcarts to Zion,* 233–34.
26. Jones, *Forty Years among the Indians,* 62.
27. Chislett, "Narrative," 325–26.
28. In James G. Willie History, 12.
29. Chislett, "Narrative," 325–26.
30. Ahmanson, *Secret History,* 33.
31. *Millennial Star,* 1 Dec. 1855, 765.
32. Stegner, *Gathering of Zion,* 250; Eugene England also refers to "rescuers like Kimball" as heroes; see "Brigham's Gospel Kingdom," 353.
33. *Millennial Star,* 1 Mar. 1856, 138.
34. Chislett, "Narrative," 326–27.
35. Ibid., 326.
36. Hinckley, dedicatory prayer for the Willie company rescue site monument, 15 Aug. 1992; used by permission of the Office of the President; see also *Church News,* 22 Aug. 1992.

CHAPTER 15
CROSSING ROCKY RIDGE

Faust, "A Priceless Heritage," *Ensign,* Nov. 1992, 84.
1. Willie company journal, 22 Oct. 1856; Savage, journal, 22 Oct. 1856.
2. Savage, journal, 22 Oct. 1856.
3. There is some discussion among trail historians about whether the rescuers took the Willie company to Rock Creek or to Willow Creek, three miles to the west. After examining the evidence, I believe that Rock Creek is the site of this camp. By the time the Willie company got to Rock Creek, they had already traveled 16 miles in arctic conditions. It seems unlikely that the rescuers would pass by a campsite that offered good shelter and make the people travel at least another three miles to Willow Creek.
4. Ahmanson, *Secret History,* 33.

5. Elder, journal, 22.

6. Madsen, *Journey to Zion,* 629.

7. *Our Pioneer Heritage,* 14:294.

8. Madsen, *Journey to Zion,* 629–30.

9. *Our Pioneer Heritage,* 14:294.

10. Chislett, "Narrative," 327–29.

11. Savage, journal, 23 Oct. 1856.

12. Rowley, "Autobiography of Ann Jewell Rowley," 242.

13. Ibid., 245–46.

14. Ibid., 245.

15. Ibid.

16. Ibid., 245–46.

17. William and Ann Jewell Rowley Family Organization, *Rowley Family Histories* (n.p., 1992), 61–62.

18. In *Remember: The Willie and Martin Handcart Companies and Their Rescuers—Past and Present,* comp. Riverton Wyoming Stake (n.p., 1997), 137–38.

19. Carter, *Treasures of Pioneer History,* 5:455; see also *Emigrating Journals of the Willie and Martin Handcart Companies and the Hunt and Hodgett Wagon Trains,* comp. Lynne Slater Turner (n.p., 1996), 220.

20. Lyman, "Bishop Jense Nielson," 7–8.

21. In ibid., 7.

22. Faust, "Priceless Heritage" (1992), 84–85; see also James E. Faust, "A Priceless Heritage," *Ensign,* July 2002, 4; Hinckley, "True to the Faith," 66.

23. Faust, "Priceless Heritage" (1992), 85; see also Faust, "Priceless Heritage" (2002), 4.

24. Chislett, "Narrative," 327–29.

25. Allred, journal, 19 Oct. 1856; see also Carter, *Treasures of Pioneer History,* 5:345.

26. Allred, journal, 23 Oct. 1856.

27. Ibid., 24 Oct. 1856; see also Carter, *Treasures of Pioneer History,* 5:345.

28. Allred, journal, Nov. 1856.

29. Eyring, "Finding Safety in Counsel," *Ensign,* May 1997, 26.

30. Allred, journal, 17 Nov. 1856.

31. Ibid., 8 Oct. 1856; see also Carter, *Treasures of Pioneer History,* 5:345.

32. Allred, journal, 13 Oct. 1856.

Chapter 16
From Rock Creek to Fort Bridger

1. Woodruff to George A. Smith, in Journal History, 31 Oct. 1856.

2. Chislett, "Narrative," 330.

3. Ibid.

4. Willie company journal, 31 Oct. 1856.

CHAPTER 17
ACCUSATIONS AND REPRIMANDS IN SALT LAKE CITY

1. Kimball, *Journal of Discourses,* 4:64; or *Deseret News,* 12 Nov. 1856, 283.
2. Kimball, *Journal of Discourses,* 4:64.
3. Ibid., 4:65.
4. Young, *Journal of Discourses,* 4:66.
5. Ibid., 4:67.
6. Ibid., 4:68.
7. Ibid., 4:67.
8. Ibid., 4:68.
9. Ibid., 4:69.
10. Ibid., 4:66–70.
11. Ibid., 4:66–67.
12. England, "Brigham's Gospel Kingdom," 354.
13. *Millennial Star,* 26 Jan. 1856, 54.
14. Ibid.; see also 20 Oct. 1855, 666–67.
15. Orson Pratt, *Millennial Star,* 9 Aug. 1856, 505.
16. West, *Life of Franklin D. Richards,* 102.
17. Ibid., 70.
18. Ibid., 71–72.
19. Ibid., 133–34.
20. See *Life History and Writings of John Jaques,* comp. Stella Jaques Bell (Rexburg, Idaho: Ricks College Press, 1978), 172.

CHAPTER 18
FROM FORT BRIDGER TO SALT LAKE CITY

1. Chislett, "Narrative," 330.
2. Ibid., 331.
3. Willie company journal, 5 Nov. 1856.
4. Ibid., 3–4 Nov. 1856.
5. Howard Christy, "Weather, Disaster, and Responsibility: An Essay on the Willie and Martin Handcart Story," *BYU Studies* (1997–98): 51; James Willie put the number at 77 (Journal History, 9 Nov. 1856); John Chislett put the number at 67 ("Narrative," 331).
6. Hosea Stout, *On the Mormon Frontier: The Diary of Hosea Stout,* ed. Juanita Brooks, 2 vols. (Salt Lake City: University of Utah Press, 1964), 2:605.
7. Willie company journal, 9 Nov. 1856.
8. Chislett, "Narrative," 331.
9. Elder, journal, 23.
10. Ahmanson, *Secret History,* 35.

Chapter 19
After the Trek: Difficulties and Blessings

Snow, *Hymns* (Salt Lake City: The Church of Jesus Christ of Latter-day Saints, 1948), no. 21.

1. See Smith, "Faithful Stewards," 118.
2. Ibid.
3. Cunningham, "Autobiography," 5.
4. In James G. Willie History, 12.
5. Smith, "Faithful Stewards," 169.
6. Ibid., 172.
7. Ibid.
8. Ibid.
9. Ibid., 182.
10. Savage, journal, 25 Oct. 1856.
11. See England, "Brigham's Gospel Kingdom," 353; Christy, "Weather, Disaster, and Responsibility," 54.
12. Chislett, "Narrative," 317.
13. Woodward letter to Smith.
14. See Stegner, *Gathering of Zion,* 240.
15. Savage, journal, 10 Mar. 1857.
16. Ibid., 14 Feb. 1857.
17. Ibid., 12 Apr. 1857.
18. Ibid., 22 Apr. 1857.
19. Hilton, *Levi Savage,* xv.
20. Ibid., 117.
21. Heber J. Grant, *Gospel Standards,* comp. G. Homer Durham (Salt Lake City: Improvement Era, 1941), 294–95.
22. Chislett, "Narrative," 312, 313, 314, 322.
23. Ibid., 322.
24. Ahmanson, *Secret History,* 36.
25. See Charles W. Martin, "John Ahmanson vs. Brigham Young: A Nebraska Legal Controversy, 1859–1861," *Nebraska History,* Spring 1983, 16.
26. Ahmanson, *Secret History,* 33.
27. See Carter, *Treasures of Pioneer History,* 6:38.
28. In Crocheron, *Representative Women of Deseret,* 86–87; see also Carter, *Treasures of Pioneer History,* 6:38–39.
29. Crocheron, *Representative Women of Deseret,* 87.
30. Ibid., 89.
31. Carter, *Heart Throbs of the West,* 4:79.
32. *Enduring Legacy,* 9:46–47.
33. Ibid., 9:47.
34. Ibid., 9:47–48; see also Madsen, *Journey to Zion,* 634.
35. *Enduring Legacy,* 9:48.
36. Ibid.

37. Ibid., 9:47.
38. Smoot, "Developing Inner Strength," *Ensign,* May 2002, 13.
39. See Madsen, *I Walked to Zion,* 66.
40. In James G. Willie History, 12.
41. In La Preal Wight, "If You Keep My Commandments," *Improvement Era,* Aug. 1953, 571.
42. In James G. Willie History, 12.
43. Ibid.
44. See Wight, "If You Keep My Commandments," 571.
45. *Pioneer Women of Faith and Fortitude,* 4:3359.
46. Wight, "If You Keep My Commandments," 598.
47. Ibid.
48. *Pioneer Women of Faith and Fortitude,* 2:1470.
49. Rowley, "Autobiography of Ann Jewell Rowley," 246.
50. William and Ann Jewell Rowley Family Organization, *Rowley Family Histories,* 146.
51. Ibid., 149.
52. Ibid., 169–70.
53. Ibid., 196.
54. Rowley, "Autobiography of Samuel Rowley," in *Some Early Pioneers of Huntington, Utah, and Surrounding Area,* comp. James Albert Jones (n.p., 1980), 250.
55. Goodwin, "Tired Mother," 778.
56. Ibid.
57. Ibid., 781.
58. Ibid.
59. Madsen, *Journey to Zion,* 630.
60. *Our Pioneer Heritage,* 14:293.
61. Ibid.
62. Madsen, *Journey to Zion,* 625.
63. Ibid., 629.
64. Ibid., 630.
65. Ibid., 631.
66. Madsen, *Journey to Zion,* 631.
67. *Our Pioneer Heritage,* 14:295.
68. Cunningham, "Autobiography," 5.
69. Ibid., 6.
70. Ibid.
71. Cunningham, missionary journal, 22 Aug. 1885, Church archives, Salt Lake City, Utah.
72. Ibid.
73. Carter, *Treasures of Pioneer History,* 5:256.
74. Mable Gadd Kirk, "Biography of Eliza Chapman Gadd," in Gadd Family Histories, Salt Lake City, Church archives, 2.
75. "Gadd Family," 2.

76. Kirk, "Biography of Eliza Chapman Gadd," 4.
77. "Gadd Family," 3.
78. Kirk, "Biography of Eliza Chapman Gadd," 3.
79. Darline Tolley Simmons, "Samuel Gadd," in Gadd Family Histories, 3.
80. Golden C. Linford, *Linford Family Heritage* (n.p., 1995), 231–32.
81. Linford, *Autobiography,* 40–41.
82. Robert Kirkwood biography, DUP archives, Salt Lake City, Utah, 3.
83. Joseph Smith Kirkwood biography, DUP archives, Salt Lake City, Utah, 2.
84. In Lyman, "Bishop Jense Nielson," 7.
85. Ibid., 12.
86. Ibid., 16.
87. In Kumen Jones, "A Short History of Elsie Rasmussen Nielson," Church archives, Salt Lake City, Utah, 2.

CHAPTER 20
REMEMBER

Hinckley, "True to the Faith," 66–67.
1. Hinckley, "Reach with a Rescuing Hand," 86.
2. Hinckley, dedicatory prayer at Rock Creek Hollow, Wyoming, 23 July 1994; used by permission of the Office of the President; see also *Church News,* 30 July 1994, 11.
3. Goodwin, "Tired Mother," 778.
4. West, *Life of Franklin D. Richards,* 71–72.

CHAPTER 21
FAREWELL TO THEE, ENGLAND

Hinckley, dedicatory prayer for the Martin's Cove monument, 15 Aug. 1992; used by permission of the Office of the President; see also *Church News,* 22 Aug. 1992, 10.
1. *Our Pioneer Heritage,* 17:303.
2. Ibid.
3. *Millennial Star,* 23 Aug. 1856, 542.
4. Ibid.
5. Hafen and Hafen, *Handcarts to Zion,* 27, 34.
6. *Millennial Star,* 22 Dec. 1855, 184; see also 26 Jan. 1856, 52.
7. Ibid., 28 June 1856, 448.
8. Ibid., 413.
9. Bell, *John Jaques,* 95.
10. Beecroft, journal, 8 and 11 June 1856, Church archives, Salt Lake City, Utah.
11. *Millennial Star,* 28 June 1856, 411.
12. John Jaques, *Salt Lake Daily Herald,* 1 Dec. 1878, 1.
13. Openshaw, journal, 4 June 1856.

14. *Millennial Star*, 30 Aug. 1856, 555.
15. Samuel Taylor Coleridge, *The Rime of the Ancient Mariner*, lines 115–18.
16. *Millennial Star*, 30 Aug. 1856, 555.
17. Bell, *John Jaques*, 98.
18. *Millennial Star*, 28 June 1856, 412.
19. Ibid.
20. Openshaw, journal, 9 June 1856.
21. *Millennial Star*, 28 June 1856, 412.
22. Ibid., 30 Aug. 1856, 555.
23. Ibid., 28 June 1856, 412.
24. Bell, *John Jaques*, 106.
25. Haven, journal, 24 June 1856.
26. Mary Dalley Simkins, History of Mary Ann Barton Allen, DUP archives, Salt Lake City, Utah, 1.
27. Bell, *John Jaques*, 105.
28. Beecroft, journal, 5 June 1856.
29. Bell, *John Jaques*, 98.
30. *Millennial Star*, 28 June 1856, 413.
31. Bell, *John Jaques*, 95.
32. Beecroft, journal, 18 June 1856.
33. Bell, *John Jaques*, 101.
34. Beecroft, journal, 28 June 1856.
35. Haven, journal, 29 June 1856.
36. Bell, *John Jaques*, 101.
37. Ibid., 106.

CHAPTER 22
FROM BOSTON TO IOWA CITY

1. Nathaniel Felt to John Taylor, in *The Mormon*, 12 July 1856, 3.
2. Beecroft, journal, 2 July 1856.
3. Ibid., 4 July 1856.
4. Ibid.
5. *Millennial Star*, 24 Nov. 1855, 747; 26 July 1856, 465.
6. Unpublished paper by Don H. Smith; copy in author's possession.
7. Bell, *John Jaques*, 103.
8. Haven, journal, 7 July 1856.
9. Openshaw, journal, 3 July 1856; see also *Enduring Legacy*, 4:198.
10. Openshaw, journal, 4 July 1856; see also *Enduring Legacy*, 4:198.
11. *Salt Lake Daily Herald*, 5 Jan. 1879, 1.
12. Southwell, Autobiographical Sketch, Church archives, Salt Lake City, Utah, 10.
13. *Salt Lake Daily Herald*, 5 Jan. 1879, 1.
14. Binder, journal, DUP archives, Salt Lake City, Utah, 8.
15. Ibid.

16. Haven, journal, 9 July 1856.
17. Ibid., 12 July 1856; see also Bell, *John Jaques,* 118.
18. Haven, journal, 25 July 1856.
19. *Our Pioneer Heritage,* 12:355.
20. Ibid.
21. Ibid., 12:356.
22. Ibid., 12:356–57.
23. Edward Martin correspondence, Church archives, Salt Lake City, Utah.
24. Ibid., 27 Apr. 1853.
25. Ibid., 1 Sept. 1854.
26. Ibid., 28 July 1854.
27. Ibid., 29 Dec. 1852.
28. Ibid., 29 Sept. 1855.
29. Edward Martin, journal, 17 May 1855, Church archives, Salt Lake City, Utah.
30. *Millennial Star,* 14 June 1856, 377.
31. The source of some of the information in this section is "The Life of Edward Martin," a brief biography by Arline Pavich, a great-granddaughter, Church archives, Salt Lake City, Utah.
32. Haven, journal, 5 Dec. 1852.
33. Ibid., 1 Jan. 1853.
34. Ibid., 10 Mar. 1853.
35. Ibid., 14 Mar. 1853.
36. Ibid., 16 Mar. 1853.
37. Ibid., 23 Mar. 1853.
38. Ibid., 24 Mar. 1853.
39. Ibid., 4 Apr. 1853.
40. Carter, *Treasures of Pioneer History,* 6:241.
41. Ibid., 6:242.
42. Ibid., 6:241.
43. For a reproduction of this pamphlet, see David J. Whittaker, "Early Mormon Imprints in South Africa," *BYU Studies,* Spring 1980, 410–14.
44. Carter, *Treasures of Pioneer History,* 6:246–47.
45. Ibid., 6:247.
46. *Millennial Star,* 14 June 1856, 377.

Chapter 23
An Enthusiastic Response

Hinckley, "The Faith of the Pioneers," *Ensign,* July 1984, 5.
1. *Encyclopedia of Mormonism,* ed. Daniel H. Ludlow et al., 5 vols. (New York: Macmillan, 1992), 2:572.
2. Josiah Rogerson, *Salt Lake Tribune,* 4 Jan. 1914.
3. Richards, in Journal History, 4 Oct. 1856.
4. Bell, *John Jaques,* 108–9.

5. Joseph Beecroft wrote longer, more detailed entries in his journal, but he left the company in mid-August because of poor health.

6. Bell, *John Jaques,* 18.

7. Ibid.

8. Ibid., 19.

9. Ibid.

10. See John Jaques collection, Church archives, Salt Lake City, Utah.

11. Bell, *John Jaques,* 21.

12. Ibid., 31.

13. Ibid., 27, 28.

14. Ibid., 29.

15. *Millennial Star,* 15 Feb. 1852, 60.

16. Bell, *John Jaques,* 53.

17. Ibid., 46.

18. Ibid., 46–49.

19. *Millennial Star,* 14 June 1856, 377.

20. Bell, *John Jaques,* 50.

21. *Millennial Star,* 24 Nov. 1855, 749.

22. Bell, *John Jaques,* 55.

23. Jaques to James Loader, *Millennial Star,* 14 June 1856, 370. This letter and the circumstances that prompted it are detailed on pages 31–35 of this volume.

24. Bell, *John Jaques,* 55.

25. Ibid.

26. Ibid., 84.

27. *Millennial Star,* 30 Aug. 1856, 553–54.

28. Archer, "Recollections," 3.

29. Ibid., 19–20.

30. Ibid., 28–29.

31. Ibid., 29.

32. Bell, *John Jaques,* 81.

33. Archer, "Recollections," 43.

34. Ibid.

35. Ibid., 46.

36. Ibid.

37. Ibid., 47.

38. Ibid., 48.

39. *Millennial Star,* 14 June 1856, 369.

40. Archer, "Recollections," 50; see also 90.

41. *Millennial Star,* 14 June 1856, 377; see also 369–72.

42. Archer, "Recollections," 52.

43. In Van Cott, *Generations of Websters,* 49.

44. William Palmer, in Van Cott, *Generations of Websters,* 55–56.

45. Bell, *John Jaques,* 84.

46. Langley Allgood Bailey, Reminiscences and Journal, Church archives, Salt Lake City, 3.
47. Ibid.
48. Autobiographical Sketch of James Mellor, DUP archives, Salt Lake City, Utah, 2.
49. Ibid.
50. Ibid.
51. Ibid., 3.
52. Ibid., 4.
53. *Our Pioneer Heritage,* 17:303.
54. Mary Goble Pay, "History of Mary Goble Pay," Church archives, Salt Lake City, Utah, 4.
55. Ibid., 2.
56. Autobiographical Sketch of Alice Walsh Strong, Church archives, Salt Lake City, Utah, 1.
57. The Life of Sarah Franks Mackay, DUP archives, Salt Lake City, Utah, 1.
58. Ibid., 2.
59. Elizabeth Horrocks Jackson Kingsford, *Leaves from the Life of Elizabeth Horrocks Jackson Kingsford* [1908], 1–3.
60. Ibid., 1.
61. Johnson, *Deseret News,* 29 June 1897, 8.
62. Elizabeth Sermon Camm, letter to her children, 16 Mar. 1892, Church archives, Salt Lake City, Utah, 2.
63. Ibid.
64. Ibid.
65. Ibid.
66. Ibid., 3.
67. *Our Pioneer Heritage,* 13:359.
68. Autobiography of Heber Robert McBride, Church archives, Salt Lake City, Utah, 1.
69. *Our Pioneer Heritage,* 13:360.
70. McBride, Autobiography, 5–6.
71. Lynne Jorgensen, "The Martin Handcart Disaster: The London Participants," *Journal of Mormon History,* Fall 1995, 175, 176.
72. Autobiography of Margaret Ann Griffiths Clegg, DUP archives, Salt Lake City, Utah, 1.
73. Autobiographical Sketch of William L. Binder, DUP archives, Salt Lake City, Utah, 2.
74. Ibid., 4.
75. Ibid.
76. William Binder papers, Church archives, Salt Lake City, Utah.
77. Jorgensen, "Martin Handcart Disaster," 179.
78. James Bleak, journal, 24 Feb. 1855; Church archives, Salt Lake City, Utah.
79. Scribo (pseudonym of James Bleak), "An Item of Handcart Experience," *Juvenile Instructor,* 15 June 1902, 365.

80. Ibid., 365–66.
81. *Millennial Star,* 1 Mar. 1856, 140.

CHAPTER 24
FROM IOWA CITY TO FLORENCE, NEBRASKA

1. Bell, *John Jaques,* 109.
2. Jaques, *Salt Lake Daily Herald,* 1 Dec. 1878, 1.
3. Franklin D. Richards and Daniel Spencer to Brigham Young, in *Deseret News,* 22 Oct. 1856, 258.
4. Ibid.
5. Ibid.
6. See Samuel Openshaw, in *Enduring Legacy,* 4:200–202.
7. Haven, journal, 27 July 1856.
8. Openshaw, journal, 7 Aug. 1856; see also *Enduring Legacy,* 4:200–201.
9. Southwell, Autobiographical Sketch, 11.
10. Ibid.
11. Jaques, *Salt Lake Daily Herald,* 19 Jan. 1879, 1.
12. Southwell, Autobiographical Sketch, 11.
13. Beecroft, journal, 3 Aug. 1856.
14. Binder, journal, 10.
15. Bell, *John Jaques,* 120.
16. Openshaw, journal, 3 Aug. 1856; see also *Enduring Legacy,* 4:200.
17. *Millennial Star,* 23 Feb. 1856, 124.
18. *Salt Lake Daily Herald,* 5 Jan. 1879, 1. According to Lyndia Carter, John Jaques was telling this story about himself. See "The Mormon Handcart Companies," *Overland Journal,* Spring 1995, 8.
19. Dan Jones Emigrating Company journal, 11 Aug. 1856.
20. Ibid., 20 Aug. 1856.

CHAPTER 25
DIFFICULT DECISIONS IN FLORENCE

1. See Hafen and Hafen, *Handcarts to Zion,* 66; Journal History, 14 Aug. 1856.
2. Haven, journal, 21 Aug. 1856.
3. Binder, journal, 12.
4. *Millennial Star,* 25 Oct. 1856, 683–84.
5. Haven, journal, 22 Aug. 1856.
6. Ibid.
7. Binder, journal, 13.
8. Autobiography of Benjamin Platt, Church archives, Salt Lake City, Utah, 3.
9. Southwell, Autobiographical Sketch, 12.
10. Haven, journal, 24 Aug. 1856.
11. Ibid., 4 Sept. 1856, 10 Nov. 1856.
12. Ibid., 19 July 1856.

13. Young, *Journal of Discourses,* 4:66–70.
14. Bennett, *Mormons at the Missouri,* 137.
15. Josiah Rogerson, papers, Church archives, Salt Lake City, Utah.
16. *Millennial Star,* 14 Feb. 1857, 97; *Journal of Discourses,* 4:66–67.
17. Bell, *John Jaques,* 122.
18. Haven, journal, 24 Aug. 1856.
19. Bleak, journal, 24 Aug. 1856.
20. Openshaw, journal, 24 Aug. 1856; see also *Enduring Legacy,* 4:198.
21. Binder, journal, 13.
22. Jaques, *Salt Lake Daily Herald,* 1 Dec. 1878, 1.
23. Ibid.
24. John Bond, *Handcarts West in '56* (n.p., 1970), 12.
25. Josiah Rogerson, *Salt Lake Daily Herald,* 27 Oct. 1907, 11; see also Rogerson, papers.
26. Platt, Autobiography, 3.
27. *Deseret News,* 15 Oct. 1856, 252–53.
28. Young, *Journal of Discourses,* 4:68.
29. *The Mormon,* 21 Feb. 1857, 2.
30. Richards to James Little, from Florence, 3 Sept. 1856, in *Millennial Star,* 25 Oct. 1856, 682–83.
31. Wheelock to James Little, from Florence, 2 Sept. 1856, in *Millennial Star,* 25 Oct. 1856, 682.
32. *Millennial Star,* 23 Feb. 1856, 122.
33. Bailey, Reminiscences and Journal, 5.
34. Ibid.
35. Ibid.
36. Nadauld, "Follow the Light," *Ensign,* May 1999, 95.
37. Ibid.

Chapter 26
From Florence to Fort Laramie

1. Hunt company journal, 30 Aug. 1856.
2. Haven, journal, 31 Aug.–5 Oct. 1856.
3. Nathan Porter, Reminiscences, Church archives, Salt Lake City, Utah, 96.
4. *Millennial Star,* 25 Oct. 1856, 685.
5. Openshaw, journal, 9 Sept. 1856; see also *Enduring Legacy,* 4:205.
6. Openshaw, journal, 16 Sept. 1856; see also *Enduring Legacy,* 4:206.
7. Openshaw, journal, 13 Sept. 1856; see also *Enduring Legacy,* 4:205.
8. Openshaw, journal, 24 Sept. 1856; see also *Enduring Legacy,* 4:207.
9. Binder, journal, 17–18.
10. Ibid., 18.
11. Ibid.
12. Madsen, *I Walked to Zion,* 44.
13. *Salt Lake Daily Herald,* 19 Jan. 1879, 1.

14. Southwell, Autobiographical Sketch, 12.

15. Rogerson, papers.

16. Jaques, *Salt Lake Daily Herald,* 19 Jan. 1879, 1.

17. Southwell, Autobiographical Sketch, 13.

18. Jaques, *Salt Lake Daily Herald,* 12 Jan. 1879, 1.

19. Bleak, journal, 21–29 July 1856.

20. *Millennial Star,* 22 Dec. 1855, 810.

21. Jaques, *Salt Lake Daily Herald,* 1 Dec. 1878, 1; 5 Jan. 1879, 1; see also Southwell, Autobiographical Sketch, 13.

22. See Albert Jones, handcart notes (1918), Church archives, Salt Lake City, Utah, 5.

23. Whitney, *History of Utah,* 1:547; *Millennial Star,* 26 July 1856, 476.

24. Rogerson, papers.

25. Southwell, Autobiographical Sketch, 13.

26. Platt, Autobiography, 4.

27. Bell, *John Jaques,* 306–7.

28. Ibid., 129, 306.

29. Annie B. Tanner, Sarah Ellen Ashton Beckstead Biographical Sketch, DUP archives, Salt Lake City, Utah, 1.

30. Archer, "Recollections," 52.

31. Ibid., 50.

32. Bell, *John Jaques,* 88.

33. *Millennial Star,* 25 Oct. 1856, 684; Bell, *John Jaques,* 133.

34. Archer, "Recollections," 58–59.

35. Ibid., 59–60.

36. Ibid., 60. Concerning the denial of a request to ride with the sisters in the sick wagon, Sandra Petree wrote: "Patience's distress seems warranted. However, in fairness to Edward Martin, . . . his concerns necessarily had to focus on the pressing need to get the main body of the company moving and keep it moving as rapidly as possible. Unfortunately, there would have been little room in the sick wagon to accommodate ministering relatives" (*Recollections of Past Days: The Autobiography of Patience Loader Rozsa Archer* [Logan, Utah: Utah State University Press, 2006], 211).

37. Ibid.

38. Stegner, *Gathering of Zion,* 241. Stegner attributes this service to William Cluff because Patience Loader gives his name in her account. However, the benefactor may have been Moses Cluff, who was returning from a mission to England.

39. Archer, "Recollections," 69.

40. Ibid., 70.

41. Ibid., 71–72.

42. Ibid., 72.

43. Bell, *John Jaques,* 306; see also 140.

44. *Salt Lake Daily Herald,* 5 Jan. 1879, 1.

45. Simkins, History of Mary Ann Barton Allen, 2.

46. McBride, Autobiography, 10–11.
47. Camm, letter, 16 Mar. 1892, 3.
48. Ibid.
49. Ibid.
50. Ibid., 3–4.
51. *Our Pioneer Heritage,* 17:305.
52. Brigham Young to Orson Pratt, 30 Oct. 1856, in *Millennial Star,* 14 Feb. 1857, 99.
53. *Deseret News,* 15 Oct. 1856, 256.
54. Hafen and Hafen, *Handcarts to Zion,* 124.
55. See chapter 12 for a more detailed account of the call to rescue.

Chapter 27
From Fort Laramie to the Last Crossing of the Platte River

1. Jaques, *Salt Lake Daily Herald,* 8 Dec. 1878, 1.
2. See chapter 11 for an analysis of the resupply problems.
3. Jaques, *Salt Lake Daily Herald,* 8 Dec. 1878, 1; 12 Jan. 1879, 1.
4. Bond, *Handcarts West in '56,* 21.
5. Ibid., 20.
6. Ibid., 22.
7. McBride, Autobiography, 11.
8. Bond, *Handcarts West in '56,* 21.
9. Archer, "Recollections," 93.
10. Bell, *John Jaques,* 144.

Chapter 28
Last Crossing of the Platte River

1. Bell, *John Jaques,* 144.
2. Binder, journal, 20.
3. *Deseret News,* 8 Oct. 1856, 243.
4. Hinckley, "Our Mission of Saving," *Ensign,* Nov. 1991, 53.
5. *Salt Lake Tribune,* 30 Nov. 1913, 11.
6. Kingsford, *Leaves,* 7.
7. *Our Pioneer Heritage,* 13:362.
8. Bond, *Handcarts West in '56,* 23.
9. Carter, *Heart Throbs of the West,* 6:378.
10. Bond, *Handcarts West in '56,* 22, 23.
11. Dan Jones Emigrating Company journal, 19 Oct. 1856.
12. Jaques, *Salt Lake Daily Herald,* 8 Dec. 1878, 1.
13. Kingsford, *Leaves,* 5.
14. Ibid., 6–7.
15. Rogerson, *Salt Lake Tribune,* 4 Jan. 1914, n.p.

16. Archer, "Recollections," 73.
17. Camm, letter, 16 Mar. 1892, 4.
18. Ibid., 6.
19. Hinckley, "Our Mission of Saving," *Ensign,* Nov. 1991, 53–54.
20. *Our Pioneer Heritage,* 17:304.
21. In Lloyd Bartholomew, "Brief Sketches from the Life of James Mellor," DUP archives, Salt Lake City, Utah, 47.
22. Pay, "History of Mary Goble Pay," 3.
23. Ibid., 3–4.

CHAPTER 29
SNOWBOUND AT RED BUTTES

Jones, "Utah Heroes Who Pulled Their All across the Plains," *Deseret Evening News,* 1 Sept. 1906, 20.
1. Haven, journal, 23 Oct. 1856.
2. William Binder, reminiscences, Church archives, Salt Lake City, Utah, 3.
3. Ibid.
4. *Our Pioneer Heritage,* 13:362.
5. McBride, Autobiography, 12.
6. Ibid.
7. Ibid., 12–13.
8. Madsen, *I Walked to Zion,* 45.
9. Ibid., 45–46.
10. McBride, Autobiography, 13.
11. Archer, "Recollections," 74–78.
12. Jaques, *Salt Lake Daily Herald,* 15 Dec. 1878, 1.
13. Bond, *Handcarts West in '56,* 20.
14. Ibid., 23.
15. Ibid., 26–27.
16. Ibid., 23.
17. Ibid., 24.
18. Kingsford, *Leaves,* 8.
19. Ibid., 8.

CHAPTER 30
THE RESCUERS ARRIVE

Hinckley, "Charity Never Faileth," *Ensign,* Nov. 1981, 97.
1. Burton, journal, 26 Oct. 1856.
2. Ibid.
3. Jones, *Forty Years among the Indians,* 64.
4. Ibid.
5. Ibid.
6. Ibid.

7. Ibid.

8. Ibid.

9. Ibid.

10. Binder, reminiscences, 3.

11. John Kirkman, Sketch of the Life of Mary Lawson Kirkman, DUP archives, Salt Lake City, Utah, 1.

12. Bond, *Handcarts West in '56,* 25.

13. Archer, "Recollections," 79.

14. Camm, letter, 16 Mar. 1892, 6.

15. Ibid.

16. Ibid.

17. *Our Pioneer Heritage,* 17:305.

18. Jones, "Utah Heroes Who Pulled Their All," 20.

19. Jones, *Forty Years among the Indians,* 65.

20. Bartholomew and Arrington, *Rescue of the 1856 Handcart Companies,* 22–23.

21. Jaques, *Salt Lake Daily Herald,* 5 Jan. 1879, 1.

22. Solomon F. Kimball, "Belated Emigrants of 1856," *Improvement Era,* Jan. 1914, 204.

23. Jones, *Forty Years among the Indians,* 65.

24. Ibid., 66; see also 65.

25. Kimball, "Belated Emigrants of 1856," 204.

26. Jones, *Forty Years among the Indians,* 66.

27. *Enduring Legacy,* 4:208.

28. Jones, *Forty Years among the Indians,* 66–67.

29. Archer, "Recollections," 80.

30. Bond, *Handcarts West in '56,* 31.

31. Jaques, *Salt Lake Daily Herald,* 15 Dec. 1878, 1.

32. Archer, "Recollections," 81.

33. Ibid., 82.

34. Jaques, *Salt Lake Daily Herald,* 15 Dec. 1878, 1.

35. Jorgensen, "Martin Handcart Disaster," 191.

36. *Utah Pioneer Biographies,* Family History Library, Salt Lake City, Utah, 28:96–97.

37. Clegg, Autobiography, 3.

38. Dan Jones Emigrating Company journal, 3 Nov. 1856.

Chapter 31

At Devil's Gate

1. *Enduring Legacy,* 4:208.

2. Dan Jones Emigrating Company journal, 3 Nov. 1856.

3. Strong, Autobiographical Sketch, 3.

4. Archer, "Recollections," 84.

5. Ibid., 84–85.

6. Ibid., 85.

7. *Deseret News,* 19 Nov. 1856, 293.

8. Ibid.

9. Bell, *John Jaques,* 169.

10. Carter, *Treasures of Pioneer History,* 6:7.

11. Jones, *Forty Years among the Indians,* 68.

12. Compiled from notations at the beginning of Robert T. Burton's journal.

CHAPTER 32
TAKING SHELTER IN MARTIN'S COVE

McBride, Autobiography, 14–15.

1. Bailey, Reminiscences and Journal, 6.

2. Jaques, *Salt Lake Daily Herald,* 15 Dec. 1878, 1.

3. Ibid., italics added.

4. Archer, "Recollections," 86.

5. Jaques, *Salt Lake Daily Herald,* 15 Dec. 1878, 1. Some accounts identify this couple as James and Elizabeth Bleak; see Jorgensen, "Martin Handcart Disaster," 192–93; Madsen, *Journey to Zion,* 584.

6. Jaques, *Salt Lake Daily Herald,* 15 Dec. 1878, 1.

7. Ibid.

8. Ibid., 19 Jan. 1879, 1.

9. Archer, "Recollections," 86–87.

10. Kimball, "Belated Emigrants of 1856," *Improvement Era,* Feb. 1914, 288.

11. Solomon Kimball, "Our Pioneer Boys," *Improvement Era,* July 1908, 679. Although neither recollection of a statement by Brigham Young mentions Stephen W. Taylor and others who assisted the Martin company at the crossing of the Sweetwater, that omission should not be perceived as deliberate. Nor should it be perceived to minimize the sacrifice or continued faithfulness of Stephen W. Taylor or others.

12. Kimball, "Belated Emigrants," Feb. 1914, 288.

13. Burton, journal, 6 Nov. 1856.

14. Kirkman, Sketch of the Life of Mary Lawson Kirkman, 1.

15. Kingsford, *Leaves,* 10.

16. Elizabeth Sermon Camm, "History of Elizabeth Sermon's Emigration and Journey across the Plains," 6, in Joel Edward Ricks, Cache Valley Historical Material, Church archives, Salt Lake City, Utah.

17. Camm, letter, 16 Mar. 1892, 6.

18. Ibid., 7.

19. Bailey, Reminiscences and Journal, 6.

20. Simkins, History of Mary Ann Barton Allen, 3.

21. Bleak, journal, 5 Nov. 1856.

22. Jones, "Utah Heroes Who Pulled Their All," 20.

23. Archer, "Recollections," 50, 90.

24. Ibid., 89.

25. Ibid., 89–90.

26. In *Remember,* 206.
27. Thomas Mackay Family Organization, *Descendants of Thomas Mackay—Utah Pioneer,* 2 vols. (n.p., 1964), 1:54.
28. *Remember,* 206.
29. Pay, "History of Mary Goble Pay," 3.
30. Ibid., 8.
31. Ibid., 4–5.

CHAPTER 33
LEAVING MARTIN'S COVE AND DEVIL'S GATE

1. Journal History, 13 Nov. 1856.
2. Dan Jones Emigrating Company journal, 5 Nov. 1856.
3. Kimball, "Belated Emigrants of 1856," *Improvement Era,* Feb. 1914, 288.
4. Burton, journal, 7 Nov. 1856.
5. Jaques, *Salt Lake Daily Herald,* 22 Dec. 1878, 1.
6. Strong, Autobiographical Sketch, 3.
7. Archer, "Recollections," 87.
8. Bailey, Reminiscences and Journal, 6; see also Glazier and Clark, *Journal of the Trail,* 113.
9. Christy, "Weather, Disaster, and Responsibility," 51, 73.
10. Jones, *Forty Years among the Indians,* 69.
11. Ibid., 70.
12. Bond, *Handcarts West in '56,* 33.
13. Stegner, *Gathering of Zion,* 260.
14. Jones, *Forty Years among the Indians,* 19.
15. Ibid., 18–19.
16. Ibid., 28.
17. Ibid., 29.
18. Stegner, *Gathering of Zion,* 261.
19. Jones, *Forty Years among the Indians,* 70.
20. Bell, *John Jaques,* 157.
21. Ibid., 158.
22. Stegner, *Gathering of Zion,* 263–64.
23. Jones, *Forty Years among the Indians,* 79–80.
24. Ibid., 80.
25. Ibid., 82.
26. Stegner, *Gathering of Zion,* 265.
27. Ibid.
28. Ibid., 266.
29. Ibid.
30. Bell, *John Jaques,* 157.
31. Jones, *Forty Years among the Indians,* 104–5.
32. Ibid., 105.
33. Stegner, *Gathering of Zion,* 272.

34. Jones, *Forty Years among the Indians,* 115.

35. Ibid., 117.

36. Ibid., 110.

CHAPTER 34
HELP FROM EPHRAIM HANKS

1. Sidney Alvarus Hanks, *The Tempered Wind: The Life Story of Thisbe Read Hanks* (Salt Lake City: Salt Lake Times, 1956), 37.

2. Ibid.

3. The date of this event is established in the journal of Robert T. Burton. On the morning of November 11, he left the Hunt company and overtook the Martin company. He recorded that Ephraim Hanks was with the Martin company at that time.

4. Sidney Alvarus Hanks and Ephraim K. Hanks, *Scouting for the Mormons on the Great Frontier* (Salt Lake City: Deseret Book, 1948), 133.

5. Ibid.

6. Ibid., 134.

7. Ibid., 134–36.

8. Ibid., 138.

9. Ibid., 139.

10. Ibid., 140.

11. Hanks, *Tempered Wind,* 40.

12. Ibid., 39.

13. Arza Hinckley, Reminiscences, Church archives, Salt Lake City, Utah, 12–13 (typescript, 2).

14. Bartholomew and Arrington, *Rescue of the 1856 Handcart Companies,* 31.

15. Earl S. Paul, "The Handcart Companies of 1856 and Arza Erastus Hinckley," Church archives, Salt Lake City, Utah, 9.

16. Ibid., 16.

17. Ibid., 17–21.

18. Ibid., preface, 3.

CHAPTER 35
SOME OF THE RESCUERS TURN BACK

1. Jones, *Forty Years among the Indians,* 62–63.

2. Bartholomew and Arrington, *Rescue of the 1856 Handcart Companies,* 32–33.

3. Stout, *On the Mormon Frontier,* 2:605.

4. Allred, journal, 13 Nov. 1856.

5. Stout, *On the Mormon Frontier,* 2:605; "The Companies Yet on the Plains," *Deseret News,* 26 Nov. 1856, 301.

6. Stout, *On the Mormon Frontier,* 2:605–6.

7. Ibid., 2:606.

8. Bell, *John Jaques,* 169.

9. Stout, *On the Mormon Frontier,* 2:606.

10. See Bartholomew and Arrington, *Rescue of the 1856 Handcart Companies,* 34.

Chapter 36
From the Plains of Wyoming to the Mountains of Utah

1. Jaques, *Salt Lake Daily Herald,* 22 Dec. 1878, 1.
2. Burton, journal, 16 Nov. 1856.
3. Ibid.
4. In Duane Call, "Anson Call and His Contributions toward Latter-day Saint Colonization" (Master's thesis, Brigham Young University, 1956), 117.
5. Call, Autobiography and Journal, Church archives, Salt Lake City, Utah, 57.
6. Burton, journal, 18 Nov. 1856.
7. Allred, journal, 17 Nov. 1856.
8. Ibid., 18 Nov. 1856.
9. Madsen, *I Walked to Zion,* 46.
10. Camm, letter, 16 Mar. 1892, 7.
11. Camm, "History of Elizabeth Sermon's Emigration," 7–8.
12. Ibid., 8.
13. Jaques, *Salt Lake Daily Herald,* 22 Dec. 1878, 1.
14. Archer, "Recollections," 90.
15. Jaques, *Salt Lake Daily Herald,* 5 Jan. 1879, 1.
16. Ibid.
17. Archer, "Recollections," 90–91.
18. Ibid., 91.
19. Stout, *On the Mormon Frontier,* 2:607.
20. Jaques, *Salt Lake Daily Herald,* 5 Jan. 1879, 1.
21. Ibid., 22 Dec. 1878, 1.
22. Ibid.
23. Ibid.; see also Archer, "Recollections," 92.

Chapter 37
Arrival in Salt Lake City

Hinckley, "Charity Never Faileth," 97.
1. Jaques, *Salt Lake Daily Herald,* 22 Dec. 1878, 1.
2. Bailey, Reminiscences and Journal, 7.
3. *Deseret News,* 10 Dec. 1856, 320.
4. Strong, Autobiographical Sketch, 4.
5. *Deseret News,* 10 Dec. 1856, 320.
6. Allred, journal; see also Glazier and Clark, *Journal of the Trail,* 185.
7. Ibid.
8. Haven, journal, 15 Dec. 1856.
9. Rogerson, *Salt Lake Tribune,* 30 Nov. 1913, 11.
10. Jaques, *Salt Lake Daily Herald,* 22 Dec. 1878, 1; see also B. H. Roberts,

A Comprehensive History of the Church, 6 vols. (Salt Lake City: Deseret News Press, 1930), 4:101–2.

11. Christy, "Weather, Disaster, and Responsibility," 51, 73.
12. Ibid., 51.
13. Rogerson, *Salt Lake Tribune,* 30 Nov. 1913, 11.

CHAPTER 38
AFTER THE TREK: DIFFICULTIES AND BLESSINGS

Hinckley, "True to the Faith," 66.

1. Rogerson, papers.
2. Ibid.
3. Madsen, *I Walked to Zion,* 44.
4. In Bond, *Handcarts West in '56,* 24.
5. *Pioneer Women of Faith and Fortitude,* 3:1887; Pavich, "Life of Edward Martin."
6. The accounts that say Edward and Eliza were married before 1863 also say that their first baby died in 1857 in Utah and that they had two other children before they were sealed.
7. Martin blessing; copy in author's possession.
8. Haven, journal, 15 Dec. 1856.
9. Ibid., 23 Jan. 1860.
10. "History of Morgan County," *Morgan County News,* 21 Mar. 1947; *Deseret News,* 16 Aug. 1876; *Our Pioneer Heritage,* 5:103.
11. *Millennial Star,* 14 June 1856, 370.
12. Jaques, *Salt Lake Daily Herald,* 19 Jan. 1879, 1.
13. Archer, "Recollections," 93.
14. Bell, *John Jaques,* 172.
15. Ibid., 196.
16. Ibid., 248.
17. Ibid., ix.
18. Ibid., 216.
19. Ibid.
20. Ibid.
21. Ibid.
22. Ibid., 215.
23. Ibid., 222.
24. Ibid., 239.
25. Ibid., 240.
26. *Salt Lake Daily Herald,* 19 Jan. 1879, 1.
27. Ibid.
28. Ibid.
29. Jaques to Willard Done, 18 Mar. 1897, in John Jaques collection; see also Bell, *John Jaques,* 181.
30. Bell, *John Jaques,* 196.

31. Ibid., 284.

32. Ibid., 284–85.

33. Ibid., 284.

34. *Deseret News,* 4 June 1900, 4.

35. Bell, *John Jaques,* 310.

36. Ibid., 175–76.

37. *Salt Lake Daily Herald,* 5 Jan. 1879, 1.

38. Archer, "Recollections," 93.

39. Ibid., 93.

40. Ibid., 147–48.

41. Ibid., 164.

42. Ibid., 166.

43. Ibid., 167–68.

44. Ibid., 169.

45. *Our Pioneer Heritage,* 14:267.

46. Archer, "Recollections," 88.

47. Autobiographical Sketch of Tamar Loader Ricks, DUP archives, Salt Lake City, Utah, 2.

48. Bell, *John Jaques,* 173.

49. John T. Smellie, "History of Tamar Loader Ricks," in Wanda Ricks Wyler, *Thomas E. Ricks, Colonizer and Founder* (n.p., 1989), 212.

50. Bell, *John Jaques,* 94.

51. In Van Cott, *Generations of Websters,* 49.

52. Ibid., 50.

53. Ibid., 73.

54. Amy L. Van Cott, "Life of Francis Webster," DUP archives, Salt Lake City, Utah, 2.

55. In Van Cott, *Generations of Websters,* 61–62; see also David O. McKay, "Pioneer Women," *Relief Society Magazine,* Jan. 1948, 8.

56. "Faith in Every Footstep: The Epic Pioneer Journey," *Ensign,* May 1997, 63; see also James E. Faust, "The Refiner's Fire," *Ensign,* May 1979, 53.

57. Hinckley, "Our Mission of Saving," *Ensign,* Nov. 1991, 55.

58. William R. Palmer, "She Stood Tall on Her Knees," *Instructor,* July 1956, 197; see also William R. Palmer, "Pioneers of Southern Utah," *Instructor,* Apr. 1944, 152–55.

59. Hinckley, "Our Mission of Saving," *Ensign,* Nov. 1991, 55.

60. Palmer, "She Stood Tall on Her Knees," 196–97.

61. Carter, *Heart Throbs of the West,* 9:419.

62. Palmer, "She Stood Tall on Her Knees," 197.

63. Alice Huntington, History of Mary Barton Allen, DUP archives, Salt Lake City, Utah, 6.

64. Ibid.

65. Bailey, Reminiscences and Journal, 7.

66. Ibid.

67. Ibid.

68. Ibid.
69. Ibid., 7–8.
70. Ibid., 8.
71. Virginia Bowles Keeler, A Life History of Jane Allgood Bailey, DUP archives, Salt Lake City, Utah, 4.
72. Ibid.
73. Bailey, Reminiscences and Journal, 10.
74. Melburn Beckstead Ellis, History of Sarah Ellen Ashton Beckstead, DUP archives, Salt Lake City, Utah, 3.
75. *Our Pioneer Heritage,* 17:306.
76. In Laurie Ellen Werner Castillo, History of James Mellor Sr., DUP archives, Salt Lake City, Utah, 5.
77. History of James Mellor and Mary Ann Payne, DUP archives, Salt Lake City, Utah, 22.
78. *Deseret Weekly,* 8 Feb. 1896, 30.
79. *Our Pioneer Heritage,* 17:306.
80. Lula Clark Wagner, Biographical Sketch of Louisa Mellor Clark, DUP archives, Salt Lake City, Utah, 6.
81. In Bartholomew, "Brief Sketches from the Life of James Mellor," 50.
82. History of Charlotte Elizabeth Mellor Roper, DUP archives, Salt Lake City, Utah, 1.
83. Pay, "History of Mary Goble Pay," 5–7.
84. William Goble, DUP archives, Salt Lake City, Utah, 4.
85. Ibid.
86. Pay, "History of Mary Goble Pay," 8.
87. Ibid., 9.
88. Ibid., 16.
89. Ibid.
90. Ibid., 17.
91. Ibid., 18.
92. Ibid.
93. Hinckley, "Faith of the Pioneers," 6.
94. Strong, Autobiographical Sketch, 4.
95. Alice Walsh Strong Biography, DUP archives, Salt Lake City, Utah, 2.
96. Strong, Autobiographical Sketch, 1, 4.
97. "Our Gallery of Pioneers: Mrs. Alice Walsh Strong," copy in DUP archives, Salt Lake City, Utah.
98. Obituary, DUP archives, Salt Lake City, Utah.
99. Strong, Biography, 2.
100. Daisy Duncombe, Sketch of Thomas Sloan Mackay, DUP archives, Salt Lake City, Utah, 27.
101. Life of Sarah Franks Mackay, 3–4.
102. Kingsford, *Leaves,* 7.
103. Ibid., 1.
104. Ibid., 11.

105. *Deseret News,* 29 June 1897, 8.

106. Ibid.

107. Ibid.

108. Ibid.

109. Carter, *Treasures of Pioneer History,* 6:53.

110. Ibid., 6:53.

111. Ibid.

112. Camm, letter, 16 Mar. 1892, 3.

113. Ibid., 2.

114. Ibid., 8.

115. Ibid.

116. Ibid., 9.

117. Ibid., 5.

118. Ibid., 2, 5.

119. Ibid., 9.

120. McBride, Autobiography, 15.

121. *Our Pioneer Heritage,* 13:363.

122. In Margaret Ann Howard McBride Ferrin biographical sketch, DUP archives, Salt Lake City, Utah, 4.

123. In Kathy Hancock, Jenetta Ann McBride Ferrin biographical sketch, DUP archives, Salt Lake City, 4.

124. McBride, Autobiography, 45.

125. Ibid., 6.

126. Heber McBride to Zelma McBride Ririe West, DUP archives, Salt Lake City, Utah.

127. In Darvil and Bruce McBride, *Chariots of Hope* (Pasadena, Calif.: Pacific Book and Printing, 1983), 200.

128. Jane Griffiths Fullmer, in Ella Campbell, "An Earlier Pioneer History" (1914), Church archives, Salt Lake City, Utah, 3.

129. Clegg, Autobiography, 4.

130. Ibid.

131. Ibid., 6; Mabel Clegg Harris, Biographical Sketch of Margaret Ann Griffiths Clegg, DUP archives, Salt Lake City, Utah.

132. Autobiography of Jane Griffiths Fullmer, DUP archives, Salt Lake City, Utah, 3–4.

133. Fullmer, Autobiography, 4.

134. Ruth E. Newbold and Beth G. Knudsen, Henry Squires biographical sketch, DUP archives, Salt Lake City, Utah, 3.

135. Grace K. Thurgood et al., Echo Squires Kirkham DeLee biographical sketch, DUP archives, Salt Lake City, Utah, 3.

136. Jones, handcart notes, 7.

137. Binder, journal, 9.

138. Binder, reminiscences, 4.

139. Binder, papers.

140. Jenson, *LDS Biographical Encyclopedia,* 1:642.

141. Jorgensen, "Martin Handcart Disaster," 183.
142. Mary Groom, "History of My Great-Grandfather, Robert Clifton" (1954), DUP archives, Salt Lake City, Utah, 3.
143. Jones, "Utah Heroes Who Pulled Their All," 20.
144. Bleak, journal, 15 Sept. 1856.
145. Scribo (Bleak), "Item of Handcart Experience," 366–67.
146. Bleak, journal, 30 Nov. 1856.
147. Ibid., 8 Apr. 1857.
148. Ibid., 9 Apr. 1857.
149. Caroline Addy, "James Godson Bleak, Pioneer Historian of Southern Utah" (M.A. thesis, BYU, 1953), 20.

CHAPTER 39
THE HEARTS OF THE FATHERS

1. Edward Martin correspondence, 29 Sept. 1855.

CONCLUSION: A TRAIL OF TEARS, A TRAIL OF HOPE

1. Nathan Porter, "Reminiscences," 98; Church archives, Salt Lake City, Utah.
2. In Merrill J. Mattes, *Platte River Narratives* (1988), 130.
3. Faust, "Priceless Heritage" (2002), 5.
4. *Enduring Legacy,* 9:47.
5. Kingsford, *Leaves,* 10.
6. Ibid., 7.
7. Archer, "Recollections," 88–89.
8. *Deseret News,* 26 Nov. 1856, 300–301.
9. Faust, "Priceless Heritage" (2002), 5.
10. Hinckley, dedicatory prayer, 23 July 1994; used by permission of the Office of the President; see also *Church News,* 30 July 1994, 11.
11. Palmer, in Van Cott, *Generations of Websters,* 61–62; see also McKay, "Pioneer Women," 8.
12. Kingsford, *Leaves,* 7.
13. Crocheron, *Representative Women of Deseret,* 89.
14. Goodwin, "Tired Mother," 778.
15. Johnson, *Deseret News,* 29 June 1897, 8.
16. DeNio, "John Linford," 3.
17. In Ron Ray, *The Crossing: Trials of 1856* (n.p., 1997), 78
18. In Madsen, *Journey to Zion,* 631.
19. *Enduring Legacy,* 9:47; italics added.
20. Hafen and Hafen, *Handcarts to Zion,* 193.
21. See William W. Slaughter and Michael Landon, *Trail of Hope: The Story of the Mormon Trail* (Salt Lake City: Deseret Book, 1997), 136.

SOURCES

BOOKS

Addy, Caroline. "James Godson Bleak, Pioneer Historian of Southern Utah." Master's thesis, Brigham Young University, 1953.

Ahmanson, John. *Secret History: A Translation of "Vor Tids Muhamed."* Trans. Gleason Archer. Chicago: Moody Press, 1984.

Archer, Patience Loader Rozsa. *Recollections of Past Days: The Autobiography of Patience Loader Rozsa Archer.* Edited by Sandra Ailey Petree. Logan, Utah: Utah State University Press, 2006.

Arrington, Leonard J. *Great Basin Kingdom: An Economic History of the Latter-day Saints, 1830–1900.* Cambridge: Harvard University Press, 1958.

Bartholomew, Rebecca, and Leonard J. Arrington. *Rescue of the 1856 Handcart Companies.* Rev. ed. Provo, Utah: Brigham Young University, Charles Redd Center for Western Studies, 1993.

Bell, Stella Jaques. *Life History and Writings of John Jaques.* Rexburg, Idaho: Ricks College Press, 1978.

Bennett, Richard E. *Mormons at the Missouri, 1846–1852: "And Should We Die."* Norman, Oklahoma: University of Oklahoma Press, 1987.

Berrett, LaMar C., and A. Gary Anderson. *Wyoming and Utah.* Vol. 6 of *Sacred Places* series. Edited by LaMar C. Berrett. Salt Lake City: Deseret Book, 2006.

Bond, John. *Handcarts West in '56.* N.p., 1970.

Bryson, Conrey. *Winter Quarters.* Salt Lake City: Deseret Book, 1986.

Call, Duane. "Anson Call and His Contributions toward Latter-day Saint Colonization." Master's thesis, Brigham Young University, 1956.

Carter, Kate B., comp. *Heart Throbs of the West.* 12 vols. Salt Lake City: Daughters of Utah Pioneers, 1939–51.

———. *Treasures of Pioneer History.* 6 vols. Salt Lake City: Daughters of Utah Pioneers, 1952–57.

Chislett, John. "Mr. Chislett's Narrative." In T. B. H. Stenhouse. *Rocky Mountain Saints: A Full and Complete History of the Mormons.* New York: D. Appleton and Co., 1873.

Church History in the Fulness of Times Student Manual. 2d ed. Salt Lake City: The Church of Jesus Christ of Latter-day Saints, 2003.

Clark, James R., comp. *Messages of the First Presidency of The Church of Jesus Christ of Latter-day Saints.* 6 vols. Salt Lake City: Bookcraft, 1965–75.

Crocheron, Augusta, comp. *Representative Women of Deseret.* N.p., 1884.

Encyclopedia of Mormonism. Edited by Daniel H. Ludlow et al. 5 vols. New York: Macmillan, 1992.

Enduring Legacy, An. 12 vols. Salt Lake City: Daughters of Utah Pioneers, 1978–89.

Glazier, Stewart E., and Robert S. Clark, comps. *Journal of the Trail.* N.p., 1997.

Grant, Heber J. *Gospel Standards.* Compiled by G. Homer Durham. Salt Lake City: Improvement Era, 1941.

Hafen, LeRoy R., and Ann W. Hafen. *Handcarts to Zion: The Story of a Unique Western Migration, 1856–1860.* Lincoln: University of Nebraska Press, 1960.

Hanks, Sidney Alvarus. *The Tempered Wind: The Life Story of Thisbe Read Hanks.* Salt Lake City: Salt Lake Times, 1956.

Hanks, Sidney Alvarus, and Ephraim K. Hanks. *Scouting for the Mormons on the Great Frontier.* Salt Lake City: Deseret Book, 1948.

Hartley, William G., and A. Gary Anderson. *Iowa and Nebraska.* Vol. 5 of *Sacred Places* series. Edited by LaMar C. Berrett. Salt Lake City: Deseret Book, 2006.

Hinckley, Gordon B. *Discourses of President Gordon B. Hinckley, Volume 1: 1995–1999.* Salt Lake City: Deseret Book, 2005.

Hymns. Salt Lake City: The Church of Jesus Christ of Latter-day Saints, 1948.

Jenson, Andrew W. *LDS Biographical Encyclopedia.* 4 vols. Salt Lake City: Publishers Press, 1901–36.

Jones, Daniel W. *Forty Years among the Indians.* Salt Lake City: Bookcraft, 1960.

Journal of Discourses. 26 vols. London: Latter-day Book Depot, 1854–86.

Linford, Golden C. *Linford Family Heritage.* N.p., 1995.

Linford, James. *Autobiography of James Henry Linford.* N.p, 1919.

Madsen, Carol Cornwall, comp. *Journey to Zion: Voices from the Mormon Trail.* Salt Lake City: Deseret Book, 1997.

Madsen, Susan Arrington, comp. *I Walked to Zion: True Stories of Young Pioneers on the Mormon Trail.* Salt Lake City: Deseret Book, 1994.

———. *The Second Rescue: The Story of the Spiritual Rescue of the Willie and Martin Handcart Pioneers.* Salt Lake City: Deseret Book, 1998.

Mattes, Merrill J. *Platte River Road Narratives.* Urbana and Chicago: University of Illinois Press, 1988.

McBride, Darvil, and Bruce McBride. *Chariots of Hope.* Pasadena, Calif.: Pacific Book and Printing, 1983.

Mulder, William, and A. Russell Mortensen, eds. *Among the Mormons: Historic Accounts by Contemporary Observers.* New York: Alfred A. Knopf, 1958.

Our Pioneer Heritage. 20 vols. Salt Lake City: Daughters of Utah Pioneers, 1958–77.

Pioneer Women of Faith and Fortitude. 4 vols. Salt Lake City: Daughters of Utah Pioneers, 1998.

Powell, Delna Swapp. *James McGaw: Eleventh Pioneer Emigration Company 1852.* N.p., 2002.

Remember: The Willie and Martin Handcart Companies and Their Rescuers—Past and Present. Compiled by Riverton Wyoming Stake members. N.p., 1997.

Roberts, Brigham H. *A Comprehensive History of The Church of Jesus Christ of Latter-day Saints.* 6 vols. Salt Lake City: Deseret News Press, 1930.

Slaughter, William W., and Michael Landon. *Trail of Hope: The Story of the Mormon Trail.* Salt Lake City: Deseret Book, 1997.

Sonne, Conway B. *Saints on the Seas: A Maritime History of Mormon Migration, 1830–1890.* Salt Lake City: University of Utah Press, 1983.

Stegner, Wallace B. *The Gathering of Zion: The Story of the Mormon Trail.* Lincoln: University of Nebraska Press, 1964.

Stout, Hosea. *On the Mormon Frontier: The Diary of Hosea Stout, 1844–1861.* Edited by Juanita Brooks. 2 vols. Salt Lake City: University of Utah Press, 1964.

Thomas Mackay Family Organization, comp. *Descendants of Thomas Mackay— Utah Pioneer.* 2 vols. N.p., 1964.

Turner, Lynn Slater, comp. *Emigrating Journals of the Willie and Martin Handcart Companies and the Hunt and Hodgett Wagon Trains.* N.p., 1996.

Tyler, Daniel Watts. *A Concise History of the Mormon Battalion in the Mexican War.* Chicago: Rio Grande Press, 1881.

Utah Pioneer Biographies. 44 vols. N.p., 1935–64. Family History Library, Salt Lake City, Utah.

Van Cott, Amy. *Generations of Websters.* N.p., 1960.

West, Franklin L. *Life of Franklin D. Richards.* Salt Lake City: Deseret News Press, 1924.

Whitney, Orson F. *History of Utah.* 4 vols. Salt Lake City: George Q. Cannon and Sons., 1892–1904.

William and Ann Jewell Rowley Family Organization, comp. *Rowley Family Histories.* N.p., 1992.

Wyler, Wanda Ricks. *Thomas E. Ricks, Colonizer and Founder.* N.p., 1989.

PERIODICALS

Carter, Lyndia McDowell. "The Mormon Handcart Companies." *Overland Journal* 13, no. 1 (1995): 4–18.

Christy, Howard A. "Weather, Disaster, and Responsibility: An Essay on the Willie and Martin Handcart Story." *BYU Studies* 37, no. 1 (1997–98): 7–74.

Deseret News. Salt Lake City, Utah.

Deseret Weekly. Salt Lake City, Utah.

England, Eugene. "Brigham's Gospel Kingdom." *BYU Studies* 18, no. 3 (1978): 328–76.

Eyring, Henry B. "Finding Safety in Counsel." *Ensign.* May 1997, 24–26.

Faust, James E. "Faith in Every Footstep: The Epic Pioneer Journey." *Ensign.* May 1997, 62–64.

————. "A Priceless Heritage." *Ensign.* Nov. 1992, 84–86.

Goodwin, Betsey Smith. "The Tired Mother: Pioneer Recollections." *Improvement Era.* July 1919, 774–81.

Hinckley, Gordon B. "The Faith of the Pioneers." *Ensign.* July 1984, 3–6.

————. "Our Mission of Saving." *Ensign.* Nov. 1991, 52–59.

————. "True to the Faith." *Ensign.* May 1997, 65–67.

Jorgensen, Lynne. "The Martin Handcart Disaster: The London Participants." *Journal of Mormon History* 21, no. 2 (1995): 171–200.

Kelly, Mary F. "Emily Hill Woodmansee, Poetess." *Young Woman's Journal.* Feb. 1907, 51–55.

Kimball, Solomon F. "Belated Emigrants of 1856, Part I." *Improvement Era.* Nov. 1913, 3–15.

————. "Belated Emigrants of 1856, Part II." *Improvement Era.* Dec. 1913, 108–17.

————. "Belated Emigrants of 1856, Part III." *Improvement Era.* Jan. 1914, 201–11.

————. "Belated Emigrants of 1856, Part IV." *Improvement Era.* Feb. 1914, 287–99.

————. "Our Pioneer Boys." *Improvement Era,* July 1908, 679.

Kimball, Stanley B. "Eastern Ends of the Trail West." *Ensign.* Jan. 1980, 30–33.

————. "Sail and Rail Pioneers before 1869." *BYU Studies* 35, no. 2 (1995): 7–42.

Latter-day Saints' Millennial Star, The. Liverpool, England.

McKay, David O. "Pioneer Women." *Relief Society Magazine.* Jan. 1948, 4–9.

Martin, Charles W. "John Ahmanson vs. Brigham Young: A Nebraska Legal Controversy, 1859–61." *Nebraska History* 64 (Spring 1983), 1–20.

Morgan County News. Morgan County, Utah.

The Mormon. New York City, New York.

Nadauld, Margaret. "Follow the Light." *Ensign.* May 1999, 94–96.

New York Herald. New York City, New York.

Palmer, William. "She Stood Tall on Her Knees." *Instructor.* July 1956, 196–97.

Ray, Ron. *The Crossing—Trials of 1856.* N.p., 1997.

Salt Lake Daily Herald. Salt Lake City, Utah.

Salt Lake Tribune. Salt Lake City, Utah.

Scribo (James Bleak). "An Item of Handcart Experience." *Juvenile Instructor.* 15 June 1902, 365–67.

Whittaker, David J. "Early Mormon Imprints in South Africa." *BYU Studies* 20, no. 4 (1980): 404–16.

Wight, La Preal. "If You Keep My Commandments." *Improvement Era.* Aug. 1953, 571, 598.

Selected Unpublished Journals, Diaries, Papers, and Recollections

Archival sources that lack a formal title or an identifiable author are not included in this bibliography. Information about the repositories of these sources is provided in the notes.

Allred, Reddick. Journal. LDS Church Archives, Salt Lake City, Utah.

Archer, Patience Loader Rozsa. "Recollections of Past Days." LDS Church Archives, Salt Lake City, Utah.

Bailey, Langley Allgood. Reminiscences and Journal. LDS Church Archives, Salt Lake City, Utah.

Beecroft, Joseph. Journal. LDS Church Archives, Salt Lake City, Utah.

Binder, William. Journal. Daughters of Utah Pioneers History Department, Salt Lake City, Utah.

———. Papers. LDS Church Archives, Salt Lake City, Utah.

———. Reminiscences. LDS Church Archives, Salt Lake City, Utah.

Bleak, James. Journal. LDS Church Archives, Salt Lake City, Utah.

Burton, Robert T. Journal. LDS Church Archives, Salt Lake City, Utah.

Call, Anson. Autobiography and Journal. LDS Church Archives, Salt Lake City, Utah.

Camm, Elizabeth Sermon. Letter to her children, 16 Mar. 1892. LDS Church Archives, Salt Lake City, Utah.

Campbell, Ella. "An Earlier Pioneer History." LDS Church Archives, Salt Lake City, Utah.

Cluff, Harvey. Journal. LDS Church Archives, Salt Lake City, Utah.

Cunningham, George. Autobiographical Sketch. LDS Church Archives, Salt Lake City, Utah.

———. Journal. LDS Church Archives, Salt Lake City, Utah.

Dan Jones Emigrating Company Journal. LDS Church Archives, Salt Lake City, Utah.

Dixon, Laleta. "Laleta Dixon's History of Her Ancestor William James of the Willie Handcart Co." LDS Church Archives, Salt Lake City, Utah.

Elder, Joseph B. Journal. LDS Church Archives, Salt Lake City, Utah.

Gadd, Alfred. Diary. LDS Church Archives, Salt Lake City, Utah.

Gadd Family Histories. LDS Church Archives, Salt Lake City, Utah.

Haven, Jesse. Journal. LDS Church Archives, Salt Lake City, Utah.

Hinckley, Arza. Reminiscences. LDS Church Archives, Salt Lake City, Utah.

James G. Willie Emigrating Company Journal. LDS Church Archives, Salt Lake City, Utah.

James G. Willie History. LDS Church Archives, Salt Lake City, Utah.

Jaques, John. John Jaques Collection. LDS Church Archives, Salt Lake City, Utah.

Journal History of The Church of Jesus Christ of Latter-day Saints. LDS Church Archives, Salt Lake City, Utah.

Kimball, William. Journal. LDS Church Archives, Salt Lake City, Utah.

Kingsford, Elizabeth Horrocks Jackson. *Leaves from the Life of Elizabeth Horrocks Jackson Kingsford.* Ogden, Utah, 1908.

Levi Savage Jr. Journal. Comp. Lynn M. Hilton, 1966. LDS Church Archives, Salt Lake City, Utah.

Lyman, Albert R. "Bishop Jense Nielson: A Brief Biography." LDS Church Archives, Salt Lake City, Utah.

Martin, Edward. Correspondence. LDS Church Archives, Salt Lake City, Utah.

———. Journal. LDS Church Archives, Salt Lake City, Utah.

McBride, Heber. "Autobiography of Heber Robert McBride." LDS Church Archives, Salt Lake City, Utah.

Nielson, Jay P. "Glorious Victory." Copy in author's possession.

Openshaw, Samuel. Journal. LDS Church Archives, Salt Lake City, Utah.

Paul, Earl S. "The Handcart Companies of 1856 and Arza Erastus Hinckley." LDS Church Archives, Salt Lake City, Utah.

Pavich, Arline. "The Life of Edward Martin." LDS Church Archives, Salt Lake City, Utah.

Pay, Mary Goble. "History of Mary Goble Pay." LDS Church Archives, Salt Lake City, Utah.

Platt, Benjamin. Autobiography. LDS Church Archives, Salt Lake City, Utah.

Porter, Nathan. Reminiscences. LDS Church Archives, Salt Lake City, Utah.

Rogerson, Josiah. Papers. LDS Church Archives, Salt Lake City, Utah.

Rowley, Ann Jewell, "Autobiography of Ann Jewell Rowley," in *Some Early Pioneers of Huntington, Utah, and Surrounding Area.* Compiled by James Albert Jones. 1980.

Rowley, Samuel, "Autobiography of Samuel Rowley," in *Some Early Pioneers of Huntington, Utah, and Surrounding Area.* Compiled by James Albert Jones. 1980.

Savage, Levi. Journal. LDS Church Archives, Salt Lake City, Utah.

Smith, Don H. "The Rest of the Story: Blight on Mormon Emigration History." Unpublished paper presented at the conference of the Mormon History Association, Casper, Wyoming, 26 May 2006.

———. "Thomas Tennant." Unpublished paper.

Smith, Lucy Meserve. "Original Historical Narrative of Lucy Meserve Smith." LDS Church Archives, Salt Lake City, Utah.

Smith, Marilyn Austin. "Faithful Stewards: The Life of James Gray Willie and Elizabeth Ann Pettit." LDS Church Archives, Salt Lake City, Utah.

Southwell, John. Autobiographical Sketch. LDS Church Archives, Salt Lake City, Utah.

Spencer, Daniel. Journal. LDS Church Archives, Salt Lake City, Utah.

Strong, Alice Walsh. Autobiographical Sketch. LDS Church Archives, Salt Lake City, Utah.

Woodward, William. Journal. LDS Church Archives, Salt Lake City, Utah.

Index

Ahmanson, Johan: asks for help for the poor, 47; background of, 69–70; on William H. Kimball, 83, 142; on first impression of Salt Lake Valley, 176; after handcart trek, 186–87

Alexander, Thomas, 374

Allen, John, 429

Allen, Mary Barton: healed by blessing, 223–24, 256; on father's failing health, 307; trials of, 307–8; on Martin's Cove, 363–64; after handcart trek, 428–29

Allred, Reddick: takes charge of relief station, 131, 159–62, stays true to assignment, 211, 392; Ephraim Hanks camps with, 382; on leaving for Salt Lake City with the Martin company, 393; returns to Salt Lake City, 400

Andrews, Sarah. See Bailey, Sarah Andrews

Archer, John, 418

Archer, Patience Loader Rozsa: misgivings of, 30, 32, 252–54; conversion of, 249–50; photographs of, *250, 419;* on journey on *John J. Boyd,* 251–52; on father's failing health, 302–3; on wolves, 303; on father's burial, 305; on tent pins, 306; on health of Zilpah Jaques, 315; on crossing Platte River, 322–23; on experience at Red Buttes, 331–33; on arrival of rescuers, 341; on David Blair family, 347–48; on meeting rescue

wagons, 349; on need for warmth, 354–55; on crossing Sweetwater, 359; on rescuers crossing Sweetwater, 360; on mother's dance, 366–67; on mother riding in wagon, 371; on sleeping in wagon, 394–95; on kindness of rescuers, 395; on Salt Lake City, 415; marries Sergeant John Rozsa, 415; goes to Washington, D.C., 416; prays for soldier husband, 416; on death of husband, 417; consoled by young son, 417–18; service of, 418–19; testimony of, 419; on God's sustaining power, 473

Ashton, Betsy, 433

Ashton, Elizabeth, 257

Ashton, Mary. See Wardle, Mary Ashton

Ashton, Sarah Ann, 257–58, 301, 433

Ashton, Sarah Ellen. See Beckstead, Sarah Ellen Ashton

Ashton, William: story of, 257–58; returns to England, 301, 433, reunites with Sarah Ellen, 434

Atwood, Millen: on gathering poor, 15–16, 26; background of, 66–67; on Saints leaving company, 72; on Iowa residents, 72–73; on "grumblers," 87; on Rocky Ridge, 151; after handcart trek, 184; on divine strength, 473

Bailey, Jane Allgood: faith of, 256–57; keeps son alive, 293–94; Margaret Nadauld on, 294; keeps husband from dying, 363, 468; strength of,

429–30; after handcart trek,
430–32

Bailey, John: story of, 256–57; wife of,
will not let him die, 363, 468; in
Martin's Cove, 430; after handcart
trek, 429–32

Bailey, Langley: embarrassed in England,
257, 429–30; struggles of, 293–94;
on father almost dying, 363; on
leaving Martin's Cove, 371; on
arriving in Salt Lake City, 398; after
handcart trek, 430–33; Mary Goble
Pay reminisces with, 441

Bailey, Sarah Andrews, 432

Bailey, Sarah Emma Warner, 432

Bailey, Thomas, 431

Bailey, William, 256–57

Bain, May, 42

Barnes, George, ix, 467

Barton, Elizabeth, 256, 307

Barton, Francis, 256, 307, 428

Barton, Mary. See Allen, Mary Barton

Barton, Mary Ann Taylor, 256, 307–8,
428

Barton, William, 256, 307–8

Bastian, Andrew, 195

Beckstead, Sarah Ellen Ashton, 433–35

Beckstead, Thomas, 433–34

Beecroft, Joseph: on meetings aboard
ship, 224; on living below deck,
225; on arrival in America, 225; on
train ride, 227; on Thomas
Tennant, 227; sickness of, 276–77;
on meteor, 279

Binder, Eliza Camp, 268–69, 460–62

Binder, William: on mob in Chicago,
229; background of, 268–69; on
meteor, 279; on combining of
Haven and Martin companies, 284;
on meeting in Florence, 286; on
Indians, 296; on burning blankets,
316; on pulling handcarts through
storm, 327; on deaths at Red
Buttes, 328; on arrival of rescuers,
340; after handcart trek, 460–62

Births: at sea, 9, 11–12, 14, 221, 303; on
the trail, 40, 396

Blair, David, Jr., 270

Blair, David, Sr., 269–70, 383–84,
462–63

Blair, Deborah (daughter), 270

Blair, Deborah (mother), 269–70, 463

Blair, Elizabeth, 270

Bleak, Elizabeth Moore, 270–72, 464,
465–66

Bleak, James: background of, 270–72,
463; photograph of, 271; on
meetings in Florence, 286; on guard
duty, 299; and reduced rations,
364, 467–68; on Arza Hinckley,
387; blesses son, 464; after handcart
trek, 464–66

Bleak, Thomas, 464

Blessings: through faith, 3; after
tribulation, 474–77; to handcart
participants, 475–76; to posterity,
476–77; to others in future
generations, 477. See also Testimony

Blessing(s), priesthood: given to Francis
Webster, 2; given to Mary Barton,
223; given to Langley Bailey, 293;
given to James Loader, 302; given
to David Blair, 383–84; Ephraim
Hanks gives, 383–84; given to
Thomas Bleak, 464

Bond, John: on Franklin D. Richards in
Florence, 287–88; on condition of
Martin company near Laramie
Peak, 313–14, 314–15; on crossing
of Platte River, 318; on Red Buttes
camp, 334–35; on arrival of
rescuers, 340–41; on Sermon
family, 348; on Daniel W. Jones,
372–73

Branch presidents, 266–72, 456–66

Brimley, Rachel. See Martin, Rachel
Brimley

Bunker, Edward, 57–58

Bunker handcart company, 114, 310

Burns, Ruth. See McBride, Ruth Burns

Burton, Robert T.: on rescue teams
turning around, 108; on difficulty
of rescue trip, 139; keeps count of
items, 357; on weather at Devil's

Gate, 370; left in charge at Big
    Sandy, 395–96
Bryant, Ann, 102

Caldwell, Agnes, 77
Call, Anson, 391–92
Call, Emma Summers, 392
Call, Margaretta Clark, 392
Camm, Elizabeth Sermon: background
    of, 264–65; bears heavy burden,
    308–9; at last crossing of Platte,
    323; on arrival of rescuers, 342; on
    death of husband, 362–63; after
    husband's death, 393–94; Edward
    Martin shows empathy to, 405;
    after handcart trek, 449–51; faith
    of, 450
Camm, Robert, 450
Camp, Eliza. See Binder, Eliza Camp
Camp Floyd, 416
Chapman, Eliza. See Gadd, Eliza
    Chapman
Chimney Rock, 307
Chislett, John: criticizes idealizing of
    handcart plan, 29–30; on
    inadequate preparations, 61;
    background of, 68–69; photograph
    of, 69; on beginning journey, 71;
    on kindness of Iowa residents,
    73–74; on flour rations, 74–75; on
    breakdowns of handcarts, 75; on
    Levi Savage's plan to wait out
    winter, 81; on emigrants' trust in
    leaders, 83; on good spirits of Willie
    company, 87; on continuing
    without cattle, 90–91; on
    complaining, 91; on resilience of
    emigrants, 92; on Franklin D.
    Richard's company, 93; on
    reprimand of Levi Savage, 96; on
    lack of resupply, 106; on rationing
    meeting, 110; on challenges along
    Sweetwater, 126, 127–28; on
    husbands and fathers, 126–27; on
    effects of deaths, 130; on arrival of
    rescuers, 132, 141; on renewed
    hope, 133; on deaths during storm,

134, 135–36; on waiting for supply
    train, 135; on rescuers' delay, 139;
    on William Kimball and George
    Grant, 142; on deaths after rescuers'
    arrival, 144–45; on division of
    rescue team, 145; on crossing
    Rocky Ridge, 149–52; on burying
    dead, 157–58, 164; on reaching
    Fort Bridger, 172; on arriving in
    Salt Lake City, 174–75; on Levi
    Savage, 181; after handcart trek,
    185–86
Clark, Louisa Mellor: in England,
    217–18; on leaving grandfather,
    259; prays and finds pie, 309–10;
    crosses Platte River, 324–25; on
    arrival of rescuers, 342–43; on
    Cyrus Wheelock, 435; after
    handcart trek, 437
Clark, Margaretta. See Call, Margaretta
    Clark
Clayton, Alice. See Martin, Alice Clayton
Clegg, Henry, 456–57
Clegg, Margaret Ann Griffiths: on
    father's service, 267; looks for
    father, 351–52; after handcart trek,
    456–59; photograph of, 457
Clifton, Ann, 269, 462
Clifton, Mary, 269, 462
Clifton, Rebecca, 269, 462
Clifton, Robert, 269, 462
Clifton, Sophia, 269, 462
Cluff, Harvey, 138–39, 140
Cluff, William, 304
Conversion: of Emily and Julia Hill,
    37–38; of Susanna Stone, 39; of
    Ann Rowley, 41; of constable and
    spies, 41; of William James family,
    42–43; of Linford family, 45; of
    Nielson family, 46–47; of John
    Jaques, 245; of Mellor family,
    258–59; of Alice Walsh, 260–61;
    of Sarah Franks, 261; of William
    Binder, 268; of Daniel W. Jones,
    373–74
Cooper, Ann. See Savage, Ann Cooper
Cowley, Emily Wall: background of, 39;

pulls brother in handcart, 88; after handcart trek, 189–91; stays at Brigham Young's home, 400

Cowley, William, 190

Cram, Abby. *See* Haven, Abby Cram

Cunningham, Andrew, 52

Cunningham, Elizabeth, 43, 201

Cunningham, George: on arriving in New York City, 11; childhood of, 43–44; on storms in Iowa City, 62; on enduring ridicule, 73; on Levi Savage's plan to wait, 81; on supplies running out, 90; on reprimand of Levi Savage, 96–97; on sacrifices, 127; on death, 137; on James Willie, 178; after handcart trek, 199–201

Cunningham, James, 43

Cunningham, Mary Wrigley, 200–201

Curtis, George, 9, 130

Curtis, Rachel, 9, 14

Dana, C. R., 55–56

Death(s): total number of, 3, 470; at Rock Creek, 7; at sea, 8, 9; of animals, 21; main causes of, 60; on journey across Iowa, 76; on journey to Fort Laramie, 102; along Sweetwater, 126–27, 129–30; during storm, 134; George Cunningham on, 137; at Rocky Ridge, 148–49, 150, 154, 157–58; in Willie Company, 172; on rail journey of Martin company, 228; on *Horizon*, 251; on *John J. Boyd*, 251; in Martin company, 301, 401–2; at Red Buttes, 328, 335; at Martin's Cove, 361–68; wishing for, 394

DeLee, David, 460

DeLee, Echo Squires Kirkham, 396, 460

Devil's Gate, 337–39, *338*, 370

Dickens, Charles, 9–10

Disease: at sea, 8; on Mississippi and Missouri Rivers, 28; in Iowa City, 62–63; along trail, 128.

Dove, George, 318

Elder, Joseph: left behind to search for cattle, 90; photograph of, *98*; background of, 98–99; joins Willie company, 99–100; willingness of, to serve, 100–101; on deserters, 110; leaves to find rescuers, 135, 138; on crossing Rocky Ridge, 147; on first impression of Salt Lake Valley, 175–76

Ellsworth, Edmund, 57, 317

Ellsworth handcart company, 114, 310

Emigration: "fire of," 14–15; push and pull for, 15–16; benefits of, 17–18; of poor, 18–20; cost of, 23–24; by handcart, 24–26; preparations for, 48–57. *See also* Zion

Emigration agents: oversee gathering, 48–57; duties of, 51, 52; zeal of, 83; emigrants trust, 83; Brigham Young reproves, 166–67, 291; and blame, 339

Empy, Jesse, 102

Eyring, Henry B., 160–61

Faith: blessings from, 3; true to, 7; and endurance, 30–31; of Jens Nielson, 64–65; of Reddick Allred, 161; role of, 167; stories teach, 211; of Dan Jones, 376; of emigrants, 403, 442; of Patience Loader, 419; Gordon B. Hinckley on, 442; of Elizabeth Sermon, 450–51; seeing with eye of, 472

Faust, James E.: on Rocky Ridge, 146; on Bodil Mortensen, 156; on James and Joseph Kirkwood, 157; on Sarah Franks and George Padley, 367; on refiner's fire, 424–25; asks why, 471; on suffering, 475

Ferguson, James, 122, 173, 389

Ferrin, Jacob, 451, 452–53

Ferrin, Jenetta McBride: becomes family's caretaker, 308, 314, 451; death of father of, 329–31; after handcart trek, 451–53; testimony of, 453

Ferrin, Samuel, 451

Florence, Nebraska: organization in, 52; William Kimball prepares, 53–54; Willie company in, 77–85; delays in, 78–79, 282; Martin company in, 282–94; as important stop, 282. *See also* Winter Quarters

Flour: rations of, 74–75, 364, 467–68; diminishing supply of, 104; price of, 106

Ford, Ann Rowley Bastian: background of, 41–42; gives up feather bed, 65; on loss of cattle, 91; feeds family with two biscuits, 113; on crossing Rocky Ridge, 153–54; after handcart trek, 195–96

Ford, Luke, 196

Fort Bridger, 172, 396

Fort Laramie, 102–3, *103*, 105–6

Fort Seminoe, 337–38

Franklin, Thomas, 318

Franks, Sarah. *See* Mackay, Sarah Franks

Fullmer, Almon, 458

Fullmer, Jane Griffiths, 267, 456–59

Gadd, Alfred, 111–12, 202

Gadd, Daniel, 111

Gadd, Eliza Chapman: not member of Church, 44; trials of, 112; after handcart trek, 201–3; photograph of, *201*; remembering, 210

Gadd, Isaac, 202

Gadd, Martha Paxman, 202

Gadd, Mary Ann. *See* Rowley, Mary Ann Gadd

Gadd, Mary Ann Hobbs, 202

Gadd, Samuel, 44, 111–12, 201

Gadd, Samuel, Jr., 112, 201, 210

Garr, Abel: in express team of rescuers, 123, 339; and Hunt company, 346; on express journey to Salt Lake, 355; reports on Martin company, 390

Goble, Caroline, 368

Goble, Edith, 368, 440

Goble, Edwin, 368

Goble, Fanny, 260

Goble, James, 368

Goble, Mary (daughter). *See* Pay, Mary Goble

Goble, Mary (mother), 260, 325–26, 438–39

Goble, Susanna Patchet, 440

Goble, William: background of, 260; trials of, 325–26; and death of wife, 439; after handcart trek, 440

Gold Rush, 1, 31, 254, 422

Good, Charles, 73

Goodwin, Betsey Smith: on self reliance, 19, 42; gets scarlet fever, 62–63; helps brother, 87–88; on Marjorie Smith's faith, 196–97; remembering, 212; on goodness of God, 476

Goodwin, Isaac, 197

Gourley, Nicholas, 351

Grant, George D.: makes arrangements for emigration, 53; favors leaving Winter Quarters, 82–83, 289; leads rescue mission, 121–23, 311; photograph of, *122*; establishes relief station, 131, 159; John Chislett praises, 142; greets Reddick Allred, 161, 392; sends news to Brigham Young, 355–56; has wagons emptied, 369–70; assigns Daniel W. Jones to stay at Devil's Gate, 372–73; dedication of, 390; goes on express journey, 395

Grant, George W., 354–55, 360–61

Grant, Heber J., 184, 194

Gray, Jane. *See* Martin, Jane Gray

Greasewood Creek, 348–49, *349*

Griffiths, Elizabeth Webb. *See* Keddington, Elizabeth Webb Griffiths

Griffiths, Herbert, 267, 350

Griffiths, Jane. *See* Fullmer, Jane Griffiths

Griffiths, John, Jr., 267

Griffiths, John, Sr., 267, 350–52

Griffiths, Margaret (daughter). *See* Clegg, Margaret Griffiths

Griffiths, Margaret (mother), 267

Griffiths, Thomas, 267, 456

Guard duty, 299–301, 461

Haigh, Sarah Ann, 318
Haines, George, 318
Haley, William, 102
Hall, Martha. *See* Haven, Martha Hall
Hampton, Ben, 374
Handcarts: cost of, 1, 29; and exposure
    to extremities, 2; ten companies of,
    3; decision to use, 21–26; speed of,
    27, 28; ease of, 27–28; and health,
    28; preparing to use, 51; examined
    by Daniel Spencer, 55; challenges in
    building, 55–57; not ready in time,
    57–61; illustration of, *74;*
    breakdowns of, 75, 91; repairing, in
    Florence, 78–79; weight limits for,
    273; left on plains, 370–71
Handcart plan: description of, 25–26,
    247–48; promotion of, 29–30,
    168–69; and divine inspiration, 29,
    411–12; reservations about, 30–35;
    triumphs of, 470–71; blessings
    from, 474–77; continuance and end
    of, 477–78
Hanks, Ephraim: photograph of, *381;*
    meets Martin company, 381–83;
    blesses David Blair, 383–84,
    462–63; helps those with frozen
    limbs, 384–85; marries Thisbe
    Read, 385
Hanks, Thisbe Read, 385
Haven, Abby Cram, 236
Haven, Jesse: leads half of Martin
    company, 59; company of,
    combined with Martin company,
    87, 283–84; appointed as
    counselor, 219; blesses sick girl,
    223; speaks to youth, 224; on
    arrival in America, 226; as leader of
    company, 230; background of,
    235–42; experience of, in
    Philadelphia, 237; resolutions of,
    237; as missionary, 237–42;
    faithfulness of, 238; discouragement
    of, 238–39; as writer, 241; leaves
    Iowa City, 274; on criticism in
    company, 275–76; travels with
    Hodgetts company, 284; on

meeting in Florence, 286; on
    arriving in Salt Lake City, 401; after
    handcart trek, 407–8
Haven, Jesse, Jr., 408
Haven, Martha Hall, 236, 408
Haven, Sarah Taylor, 407–8
Haven handcart company: combines
    with Martin company, 87, 283–84;
    organized, 230; leaves Iowa City,
    274; crosses Iowa, 275–81; conflict
    in, 275–77; arrives in Florence,
    282;
Higbee, Isaac, 373–74
Hill, Emily. *See* Woodmansee, Emily Hill
    Mills
Hill, Julia. *See* Ivins, Julia Hill
Hinckley, Arza, 385–87
Hinckley, Gordon B.: on tragedy of
    handcart companies, 3, 403;
    dedicatory prayer of, at Rock Creek,
    7, 211–12, 475; and Perpetual
    Education Fund, 20; on gratitude
    for pioneers, 209; on remembering,
    211–12; dedicates Martin's Cove
    Monument, 217; on power of faith,
    243; on crossing Platte River,
    317–18; on heroic rescue, 337; on
    members taking in emigrants, 398;
    on Pucell orphans, 425, 426; on
    story of Mary Goble Pay, 442
Hinckley, Marjorie Pay, 260
Hobbs, Mary Ann. *See* Gadd, Mary Ann
    Hobbs
Hodgetts, Benjamin, 274, 380
Hodgetts wagon company: Ahmanson
    family in, 69–70; Siler company
    joins, 92, 186–87; Saints from
    Horizon join, 230; leaves Iowa City,
    274; crosses Iowa, 280–81; arrives
    in Florence, 282; leaves Florence,
    295; crosses Platte River, 319; fights
    through storm, 327; in Red Buttes
    camp, 327, 334–35; rescuers
    approach, 340; arrives at Devil's
    Gate, 353; leaves behind
    possessions, 369; arrives in Salt

Lake City, 400–401; mortality rate in, 401

Horizon: departure of, 217; number of passengers on, 219; crosses Atlantic, 220–25; captain of, 221, 224, 226; births and deaths on, 221; seasickness on, 222; spiritual outpouring on, 223–24; arrives in Boston, 225–26

Hunt, John, 274

Huntington, C. Allen, 360–61

Hunt wagon company: Saints from *Horizon* join, 230, 260; leaves Iowa City, 274; crosses Iowa, 280–81; arrives in Florence, 282; leaves Florence, 295; crosses Platte River, 319; rescuers find, 346; dissension in, 352; reaches Devil's Gate, 353; arrives in Salt Lake City, 400–401; mortality rate in, 401

Hurren, Eliza Reeder, 41, 193–95

Hurren, Emma: 41, 76, 193, 195

Hurren, James, 41, 193–95

Hurren, Mary. *See* Wight, Mary Hurren

Hurren, Sarah, 41, 193, 195

Hurren, Selina, 76, 193

Hyde, Orson, 39, 189, 231

Hymns, 191, 246, 325, 472

Ice Slough, 132

Independence Rock, 123, 124, *124*

Ingra, Elizabeth, 102

Iowa City: emigrants arrive in, 2, 12–13; as key venue, 52; Daniel Spencer in, 55; Willie company in, 57–70; delays in, 57–61; living conditions in, 61–63; Martin company in, 230

Ivins, Israel, 187

Ivins, Julia Hill: background of, 36–38; photograph of, *37;* after handcart trek, 187–89

Jackson, Aaron: background of, 262; at last crossing of Platte, 320; death of, 320–22, 335; remembering, 468

Jackson, Elizabeth. *See* Kingsford, Elizabeth Jackson

James, Emma. *See* Rowley, Emma James Johnson

James, Jane: background of, 43; and death of husband, 148–49, strength of, 197–99; after handcart trek, 199; remembering, 209–10

James, John, 149

James, Mary Ann, 43, 148–149, 198

James, Reuben: stays with dying father, 148–49, 151–52, 198, 210

James, Sarah. *See* Johnson, Sarah James

James, William: background of, 43; failing health of, 128–29; at Rocky Ridge, death of, 148–49, 151–52, 197–98; remembering, 210

Jaques, Alpha, 410, 414

Jaques, Flora: 35, 248, 396, 409

Jaques, John: letter of, to in-laws, 32–35, 253; in home of Franklin D. Richards, 171; on board *Horizon,* 220–21; on pace of *Horizon,* 221–22; on sight of ocean, 222; on seasickness, 222–23; on meeting of Saints, 223, 224; on community of Saints, 224; on Irish emigrants, 225; on arrival in Boston, 225; on Captain Reed's visit to Salt Lake City, 226; on rail journey, 229; on rudeness of some Americans, 229; on dilemma of emigration officials, 243–44; as writer, 244, 246–47; as missionary, 244–46; photograph of, *245;* testimony of, 245–46; marriage of, 247; emigration of, 247–48; on handcart plan, 247–48; on leaving belongings behind, 273; on heat, 278; on man carrying woman, 279–80; on meeting in Florence, 286, 287; on George Waugh, 297, 298; on cornet, 298–99; pulls Tamar Loader in handcart, 302; tribute of, to James Loader, 306; on reduced rations, 312–13; weakness of, 315; on crossing Platte River, 319; on Red Buttes camp, 333–34; on emigrants' trauma, 345; on meeting rescue wagons, 348; on camping near Independence Rock, 350; on crossing Sweetwater, 359–60; on gathering wood, 360; on determining who should ride, 370; on sleeping in wagons, 394; on finding warm sleeping spot, 395; and death of Flora, 396, 467; on wagon wheels on snow, 396; on birth at Echo Canyon, 396; on company's arrival in Salt Lake City, 398; on death toll, 401; after handcart trek, 408–13; as newspaper editor, 409–10; family of, 410–11; on death of Rose, 410; looks back on handcart trek, 411–13; testimony of, 412–13; tributes to, 413–14; on Amy Loader, 415

Jaques, Zilpah Loader: marries John Jaques, 247–48; leaves England, 251; gives birth, 303; helps pull handcart, 315; family of, 410–11; after husband's death, 413–14

Johansen, Maren. *See* Parsons, Mary Johnson

John J. Boyd, 250–52

Johnson, Aaron, 199

Johnson, Dan, 386

Johnson, Lorenzo, 199

Johnson, Mary. *See* Parsons, Mary Johnson

Johnson, Sarah James: background of, 43; on poor health of father, 128–29; on death of father, 148–49; after handcart trek, 198–99

Johnston's Army, 415, 461

Jones, Albert: on fathers, 327; on arrival of rescuers, 343; William Binder pulls cart for, 461; on David Blair, 462–63

Jones, Dan, 274, 380

Jones, Daniel W.: on condition of Willie company, 140–41, 339; on finding Martin company, 343; on condition of Martin company, 347; on

inadequacy of rescue team, 356–57; assigned to stay at Devil's Gate, 372–73; background of, 373–74; conversion of, 373–74; hunger of, at Devil's Gate, 374–78; faces attack, 378; false accusations against, 378–79; Brigham Young writes letter exonerating, 379–80; on other rescue teams, 388

Jones, Samuel S., 364–65

Jones, William, 476–77

Keddington, Elizabeth Webb Griffiths, 267, 456–59

Keddington, William, 459

Kimball, David P., 360–61

Kimball, Heber C.: on hard winter, 22; receives letter about handcart companies, 109–10; on criticism against Brigham Young, 166; baptizes Margaret McBride, 266; blesses Reddick Allred, 400

Kimball, William H.: on emigration, 15; photograph of, *53;* prepares Florence, 53–54; purchases cattle, 54; favors leaving Winter Quarters, 82–83, 287; praises Joseph Elder, 101–2; in rescue mission, 122; John Chislett praises, 142; resentment toward, 142–43; tireless work of, 142–43, 173; leads Willie company into Salt Lake, 172; sent to find Martin company, 173; in express courier, 389–90, 395–96

Kingsford, Elizabeth Jackson: photograph of, *262;* background of, 262; at last crossing of Platte, 320–22; on death of husband, 320–21; on Red Buttes camp, 335–36; on Martin's Cove, 362; testimony of, 445, 476; after handcart trek, 446; remembering, 468; on God's sustaining power, 472–73

Kingsford, William, 446

Kirkham, Reuben, 460

Kirkman, John, 340, 361

Kirkwood, Alice Pulley, 205–6
Kirkwood, James, 46, 156–57, 205, 210
Kirkwood, Joseph Smith, 46, 156–57, 205, 210
Kirkwood, Margaret, 46, 156–57
Kirkwood, Robert, 46, 156–57, 205
Kirkwood, Thomas, 46, 156–57, 205
Knowles, Mary. *See* Mellor, Mary (Polly) Knowles

Lajuenesse, Basil, 338
Lajuenesse, Charles, 338
Latey, John H., 16, 318
Laurey, John, 332–33
Leason, William, 102
Leavitt, Mary Horrocks, 320
Lewis, Laura. *See* McBride, Laura Lewis
Linford, Amasa, 137, 205
Linford, George, 204–5
Linford, James, 45–46, 204
Linford, John: background of, 45–46; death of, 136–37, 203; monument to, 205; takes long-range view, 476
Linford, Joseph, 205
Linford, Maria. *See* Rich, Maria Linford
Linford, Mary Rich, 205
Linford, Miranda Savage, 205
Lloyd, Susanna Stone: photograph of, *39;* background of, 39–40; on divine help, 191–92, 472; after handcart trek, 192–93; strength of, 193; descendants of, 477
Lloyd, Thomas, 192
Loader, Amy: reservations of, 31–35; meets up with John and Zilpah Jaques, 248; conversion of, 249; poor health of, 253, 302; photograph of, *365;* strength of, 365–66, 414; dances, 366–67, 468; after handcart trek, 414–15
Loader, Ann, 422
Loader, James: son-in-law's letter to, 31–35; meets up with John and Zilpah Jaques, 248; conversion of, 249; determination of, 253, 302–4, 414; death of, 304–5, 414; makes tent pins, 306

Loader, Jane, 251, 421–22
Loader, John, 251, 416–17, 421
Loader, Maria, 251, 331–32, 421–22
Loader, Marshall, 414
Loader, Patience. *See* Archer, Patience Loader Rozsa
Loader, Robert, 251, 421–22
Loader, Sarah, 251, 421–22
Loader, Tamar. *See* Ricks, Tamar Loader
Loader, Zilpah. *See* Jaques, Zilpah Loader

Mabey, Charles, 424
Mackay, Sarah Franks, 261, 367–68, 444–45
Mackay, Thomas, 444
Martin, Alice Clayton, 231, 405–6
Martin, Edward: as leader of handcart company, 2, 219, 404–5; background of, 230–35; photograph of, *231;* in Mormon Battalion, 232; faith of, 233; as missionary in England, 233–34; writes to daughter, 234–35, 468; in Emigration Department, 235; after handcart trek, 404–7; leadership of, 404–5; shows empathy toward Elizabeth Sermon, 405; family life of, 405–6
Martin, Eliza Salmon, 406
Martin, Jane Gray, 406
Martin, Mary Ellen, 231, 233–35, 405
Martin, Rachel Brimley, 406
Martin handcart company: route of, *xii–xiii, xiv;* Francis Webster joins, 2–3; and Willie company, 13; delays in starting, 57–61; in Iowa City, 59–60; arrives in Florence, 87; Reddick Allred assists, 160–62, 392–93; Edward Martin appointed leader of, 219; and Perpetual Emigration Fund, 219–20; demographics of, 243; leaves Iowa City, 274; crosses Iowa, 275–81; delays of, 275; arrives in Florence, 282; combines with Haven company, 283–84; decision of, to

leave Florence, 285–87; leaves
Florence, 295; crosses Nebraska,
295–97; guard duty in, 299–301;
deaths in, on journey to Fort
Laramie, 301; arrives in Fort
Laramie, 312; rations reduced in,
312–14; crosses Platte River,
317–26; at Red Buttes, 327–36;
express rescuers find, 339–43;
condition of, at rescuers' arrival,
345–46; rescue wagons meet,
348–49; arrives at Devil's Gate,
353; crosses the Sweetwater,
358–61; in Martin's Cove, 361–68;
leaves Martin's Cove, 369–72;
crosses Rocky Ridge, 391; enters
Utah, 391–97; arrives in Salt Lake
City, 398; deaths in, 401–2. *See also
Horizon*

Martin's Cove: monument in, 217; and
Red Buttes camp, 328; location of,
358; photograph of, *362;* conditions
in, 361–68; deaths at, 371–72

Mathers, Jane. *See* Savage, Jane Mathers

McArthur, Daniel, 57, 75

McArthur handcart company, 114, 310

McBride, Ether, 455

McBride, Heber: and love of ocean, 265,
453; background of, 265–66;
becomes caretaker, 308, 314, 451;
death of father of, 329–31; on
Martin's Cove, 358; after handcart
trek, 453–54; testimony of, 454

McBride, Jenetta. *See* Ferrin, Jenetta
McBride

McBride, Laura Lewis, 455

McBride, Maggie, 452, 455

McBride, Margaret: background of,
265–66; sickness of, 308, at Red
Buttes, 329–31; after handcart trek,
451–52

McBride, Peter: on receiving
missionaries, 266; remembers
Indians, 296; on father crossing
Platte, 318; at Red Buttes, 330–31;
on riding in wagons, 393; on
leadership of Edward Martin, 405;

on conditions of home in Utah,
451; after handcart trek, 454–55

McBride, Robert; background of,
265–66; sickness of, 308; crosses
Platte, 318; death of, 329–30;
remembering, 468

McBride, Ruth Burns, 454–55

McGaw, James, 52–53, 82–83

McNeil, Janet, 9, 14

McNeil, Thomas, 9

McPhail, Archibald, 154–55

McPhail, Henrietta, 154–55, 400

McPhail, Jane, 154, 155

Mellor, Charlotte Elizabeth. *See* Roper,
Charlotte Elizabeth Mellor

Mellor, James: carries wife aboard ship,
218–19; background of, 258–60;
after handcart trek, 435–37; as
missionary, 436

Mellor, John, 436

Mellor, John Carlos, 435

Mellor, Louisa. *See* Clark, Louisa Mellor

Mellor, Mary Ann: gives birth before
Horizon sails, 217–18; begins
journey in poor health, 218–19;
background of, 258–60; receives
divine help, 309–10; crosses Platte
River, 324–25; after handcart trek,
435–37

Mellor, Mary (Polly) Knowles, 436

Missionary work: Brigham Young on,
17–18; in Britain, 18; and
emigration, 48–50, 52–54; of
Franklin D. Richards, 169–70; of
Edward Martin, 233–34; of Jesse
Haven, 237–42; in South Africa,
239–42; of James Mellor, 436; of
James Bleak, 465–66

Mitchell, Euphemia, 42

Moore, Elizabeth. *See* Bleak, Elizabeth
Moore

Mormon Battalion, 67, 170, 232

Mormon Grove, 262–64, 446

Mormonism: power in, 15; opposition
to, 38, 45, 46; promise of, 63; and
rescue effort, 119; blessings of,
188–89; and economic classes, 227

Mortensen, Bodil, 46, 155–56, 194, 210
Mulliner, Samuel, 458

Nielson, Elsie: background of, 46–47; sacrifices savings, 64–65; at Rocky Ridge, 155–56; after handcart trek, 206–8; remembering, 210
Nielson, Jens: background of, 46–47; sacrifices savings, 64–65; at Rocky Ridge, 155–56; after handcart trek, 196, 206–8; remembering, 210
Nielson, Niels, 46–47, 155–56, 210

Oakey, Rhoda Rebecca, 173–74
Openshaw, Samuel: on progress of *Horizon*, 221; on seasickness, 222; impressed by America, 228, 277; on meeting in Florence, 286; on landscape, 296; on Indians, 296; on resuming trek to Devil's Gate, 347; on arriving at Devil's Gate, 353

Padley, George, 261, 367, 444, 468
Parsons, Ann Elizabeth. *See* Webster, Ann Elizabeth (Betsy) Parsons
Parsons, Elijah, 447–48
Parsons, Mary Johnson: becomes orphan, 262–63; in Brigham Young's home, 400, 447; suffers frostbite, 446–47; marriage and adult life of, 447–49; tribute to, 448; faith of, 476
Patchet, Susanna. *See* Goble, Susanna Patchet
Paxman, Martha. *See* Gadd, Martha Paxman
Pay, Mary Goble: background of, 260; gets lost in snow, 325–26; on leaving baby sister's grave, 368; on death of brother, 368; on mother's death, 438; suffers frostbite, 439; marriage and adult life of, 440–41; as grandmother of Marjorie Pay Hinckley, 442
Pay, Richard, 440–41
Perpetual Education Fund, 20
Perpetual Emigration Fund: purpose of, 19–20; number of emigrants using, 21; goes into debt, 24, 218;

Brigham Young sells property to replenish, 26, 218; need for, 50–51; Mellor family relies on, 218; and Martin company, 219–20
Philpot, Eliza, 144
Platt, Benjamin, 284, 290, 301
Platte Bridge, 317
Platte River, 88, 317–26, *317, 328*
Poor, 15–16, 18–20, 64, 255. *See also* Perpetual Emigration Fund
Porter, Nathan, 295
Pratt, Orson, 120, 171, 238
Prayer: Reddick Allred and, 161; for suffering emigrants, 185–86; of Marjorie Smith, 197; of missionaries, 240; of Louisa Mellor, 309–10; of Dan Jones and men, 375
Pucell, Ellen. *See* Unthank, Ellen Pucell
Pucell, Margaret (daughter), 256, 324, 425, 428
Pucell, Margaret (mother), 255–56, 324, 468
Pucell, Samuel, 255–56, 324, 468
Pulley, Alice. *See* Kirkwood, Alice Pulley

Read, Thisbe. *See* Hanks, Thisbe Read
Red Buttes, 327–28
Reed, Captain, 221, 224, 226
Reeder, Caroline, 40, 129–30, 193–94
Reeder, David, 40; death of, 111, 129, 193–94
Reeder, Lydia Wilkinson, 193
Reeder, Robert: background of, 40; on ocean voyage, 40; on death of father, 111; on death of sister, 129–30; after handcart trek, 193
Rescue mission: beginning of, 116–19, 121–23; urgency of, 120–21, 310–11; members of, 121–23; of 1865, 453–54; and divine influence, 471; miraculous timing of, 473–74
Rescuers: meet Willie company, 131–45; John Chislett on, 132, 141; William Woodward on arrival of, 132; James Willie and Joseph Elder

search for, 134–35, 138; Mary
Hurren on arrival of, 141–42;
divide, 145; meet Martin and
Hodgetts companies, 339–40;
William Binder on, 340; John Bond
on, 340–41; Patience Loader on,
341, 395; Elizabeth Sermon on,
342; Joseph Sermon at arrival of,
342; Louisa Mellor on, 342–43;
Albert Jones on, 343; find Hunt
company, 346; in wagons, meet
Martin company, 348; cross
Sweetwater, 360–61; some turn
back, 388–89
Resupply teams, 105–9
Rich, Joseph, 203
Rich, Maria Linford, 45–46, 203–4
Rich, Mary. *See* Linford, Mary Rich
Richard, Jean Baptiste, 317
Richards, Franklin D.: as mission
president, 7–8, 9; photograph of, *8,
283;* and Willie company, 13; on
commandment to gather, 15, 17;
on preparing for emigration, 18;
promotes handcart plan, 27–29,
168–69; responds to reservations,
30–31; instructs missionaries about
emigration, 48–49; meets with
Willie company, 92–98; reprimands
Levi Savage, 95–97; on company's
morale, 97–98; estimates meeting
points for resupply, 106–7, 122–23;
tells Brigham Young about
remaining companies, 115–16,
310; speaks in general conference,
117, 290; refers to manna, 143–44;
assessment of efforts of, 168–72;
background of, 169–71; faith of,
170, 212; appoints Edward Martin,
219; on demographics of Martin
company, 243; appoints John
Jaques assistant editor, 246;
combines Haven and Martin
companies, 282–85; encourages
Martin company forward, 287–88,
290–92; on spirit of handcart

pioneers, 292; takes in Jaques
family, 409
Richards, Jane, 170
Richards, Wealthy, 169–70
Ricks College, 421
Ricks, Tamar Loader: leaves young man,
251; illness of, 302–4; after
handcart trek, 414, 419–21
Ricks, Thomas E., 420–21
Rock Creek Hollow: dedicatory prayer
at, 7, 211–12, 475; trek reenactments end at, 146; photograph of,
158; monument at, 158–59,
209–12
Rocky Ridge: ascent of, 146; crossing,
146–62; photograph of, *147;* as
triumph, 147; William James family
at, 148–49; John Chislett's account
of, 149–52; Levi Savage's account
of, 152–53; Ann Rowley's account
of, 153–54; Archibald McPhail at,
154–55; Jens Nielson family at,
155–56; Bodil Mortensen at, 156;
James Kirkwood at, 156–57
Rogerson, Josiah: on decision to leave
Florence, 285, 288–90; on George
Waugh, 297–98; on guard duty,
300; on crossing Platte River, 318;
on Aaron Jackson's death, 321–22;
on death toll in Martin company,
401, 402; on leadership of Edward
Martin, 404–5
Roper, Charlotte Elizabeth Mellor, 310,
324–25, 437–38
Roper, Henry, 437–38
Roper, Susannah, 437–38
Rowley, Ann. *See* Ford, Ann Rowley
Bastian
Rowley, Elizabeth, 41–42
Rowley, Emma James Johnson: family of,
43; on parents' determination, 82;
on buffalo, 89; on storm, 89–90;
on hitching milk cows to wagons,
90; marries John Rowley, 196;
on mother's strength, 198, 477
Rowley, John, 41–42, 154, 196, 199
Rowley, Louisa, 41–42

Rowley, Mary Ann Gadd, 112, 196, 202

Rowley, Samuel, 41–42, 196

Rowley, Thomas, 154, 196

Rowley, William, 41

Rozsa, Amy Rosalie, 417, 418–19

Rozsa, Frank, 417–18

Rozsa, John, 415–18

S. Curling, 10–11, 380

Sacrifice: willingness to, 36; obedience better than, 47, 64; of Nielson family, 64–65; in preparing for journey, 64–65; required by the rescue, 118–19, 474; of Francis Webster, 254–55; of James Bleak, 271; of personal belongings, 273

Salmon, Eliza. *See* Martin, Eliza Salmon

Salt Lake Valley: Willie company arrives in, 172; kindness of Saints in, 173–75; engraving of, *175;* initial reactions to, 175–76. *See also* Zion

Savage, Ann Cooper, 183

Savage, Jane Mathers, 67, 180

Savage, Levi: photograph of, *67;* background of, 67–68; on residents of Iowa, 72; on flour rations, 74; urges company to wait out winter in Florence, 80–82, 181; experience of, 84–85; loyalty of, 84–85; on lost cattle, 89; on Platte Valley sand, 89; optimism of, 91; reprimanded by Franklin D. Richards, 95–97; on elderly, 102; on shortage of flour, 104; on lack of resupply, 106; on cost of crackers, 109; on death of oxen, 112; on weakness of emigrants, 125; gives up flour, 137; on Rocky Ridge, 146, 151; on crossing Rocky Ridge, 152–53; oversees animals, 164–65; after handcart trek, 180–83; as hero, 181; character of, 181–83

Savage, Levi Mathers, 67

Savage, Miranda. *See* Linford, Miranda Savage

Scott, Joseph, 340

Scott, Mary, 340–41

Seasickness, 222–23

Self-reliance: Franklin D. Richards teaches, 18–19, 95; James Willie on, 20; Betsey Smith on, 42, 197; Brigham Young and, 121, 167

Seminoe Cutoff, 162

Sermon, Elizabeth. *See* Camm, Elizabeth Sermon

Sermon, John, 394

Sermon, Joseph: background of, 264–65, 449; attitude of, 308–9; at arrival of rescuers, 342; death of, 362–63, 449

Sermon, Robert, 393

Ships. *See Horizon; John J. Boyd; S. Curling; Thornton*

Siler, Andrew, 86

Siler wagon company, 86, 92

Simmons, Joseph, 173, 389

Smith, Andrew, 90, 490

Smith, Alexander, 42, 87–88

Smith, Betsey. *See* Goodwin, Betsey Smith

Smith, Jane, 42, 197

Smith, John, 107

Smith, Joseph, 184, 229, 231

Smith, Joseph F., 207, 413

Smith, Leonard, 236, 239–42

Smith, Marjorie, 42, 196–97

Smith, Mary, 42

Smith, William, 107

Smoot, Abraham, 107

Smoot wagon company, 107–8

South Africa, 236–42

Southwell, John: on mob in Cleveland, 229; on opposition in Iowa, 277–78; on thunderstorms, 278; on combining of Haven and Martin companies, 284; on George Waugh, 297; on cornet, 298; on guard duty, 300–301

Spencer, Claudeus, 160

Spencer, Daniel: arrives in Iowa City, 54–55; sends John Van Cott for lumber, 56; knows of numbers in handcart company, 58; speaks in general conference, 117; organizes companies, 230

Squires, Echo. *See* DeLee, Echo Squires Kirkham

Squires, Henry: background of, 267–68; finds clothing for newborn daughter, 396; after handcart trek, 459–60; remembering, 467

Squires, Sarah, 267–68, 396, 459–60

Stegner, Wallace: on Mormon emigrant ships, 9–10; on gathering, 17; on Iowa heat, 62; on emigrants' lack of experience, 63; on deaths along trail, 76; on benefits of walking, 77; on zeal of emigration leaders, 83; on promises of Franklin D. Richards, 94–95; on rescue effort, 119; on weakness of travelers, 127; on William Kimball, 143; on Loader family, 304; on Daniel W. Jones, 373–74; on hunger of men at Devil's Gate, 375, 376, 377

Stephens, Evan, 454

Stevens, Selena. *See* Wall, Selena Stevens

Stockdale, Mary Ann, 69

Stone, Susanna. *See* Lloyd, Susanna Stone

Storms: first, of winter, 132, 317–18; descriptions of, 278–79, 362

Stout, Hosea: assigned to find Martin company, 173, 389; on rescuers turning back, 389; in express team, 395–96

Strong, Alice Walsh: background of, 260–61; photograph of, *261;* on husband's death, 353–54; on riding in wagon, 370–71; on arrival in Salt Lake City, 400; after handcart trek, 442–43; testimony of, 443

Strong, Jacob, 442

Suffering: lessons learned in, 2–3; compensation for, 212; and gratitude, 443; and sanctification, 445; God often does not take away, 474

Summers, Emma. *See* Call, Emma Summers

Sweetwater River: location of, 124; challenges along, 126, 127–28; deaths along, 126–27, 129–30; crossing, 148–49, 359; bravery of rescuers crossing, 360–61

Tait, Anna: gratitude of, 8; on captain of ship, 9, 11; on arriving in New York City, 11; on demographics of emigrants, 12; journey of, 12

Taylor, John: and the Loader family, 33; directs affairs in New York City, 52; on estimating number of handcarts, 56; gives instructions for no delays, 59

Taylor, Mary Ann. *See* Barton, Mary Ann Taylor

Taylor, Sarah. *See* Haven, Sarah Taylor

Taylor, Stephen W., 132, 360, 510

Temple: building, 17; work, 42, 446, 452

Tennant, Thomas: buys home from Brigham Young, 26, 227–28; Joseph Beecroft writes about, 227; and Jesse Haven, 285; cattle of, 300

Testimony: of Francis Webster, 2–3, 423–24, 475–76; of Millen Atwood, 184; of James Linford, 204; of Jens Nielson, 208; of Edward Martin, 233; of John Jaques, 245–46, 412–13; of Patience Loader, 419; of Alice Walsh, 443; of Elizabeth Jackson, 445–46; of Jenetta McBride, 453; of Heber McBride, 454; of Jane Griffiths, 458

Thornton: leaves England, 7–8; captain of, 9, 11; arrives in New York City, 11–12

Trials. *See* Suffering

Turner, Richard, 102

Tyler, Daniel, 305, 383

Unity, 241–42

Unthank, Ellen (Nellie) Pucell: family of, 256; is orphaned, 324; Francis Webster mentions, 424; after handcart trek, 425–28; sculpture of, *427,* 427–28

Unthank, William, 426–27

Van Cott, John: and Daniel Spencer, 55; sent for lumber, 56; favors leaving Winter Quarters, 82–83; and Claudeus Spencer, 160; turns rescuers back, 389

Wagons: cost of, 1, 21; in handcart companies, 26; hitching milk cows to, 90; riding in, 370–71, 393; sleeping in, 393, 394–95; used in "down-and-back years," 478

Walker, William, 236, 239–42

Wall, Emily. *See* Cowley, Emily Wall

Wall, Joseph: background of, 39; pulled by sister in handcart, 88; after handcart trek, 189–91

Wall, Selena Stevens, 190–91

Walsh, Alice. *See* Strong, Alice Walsh

Walsh, John, 443

Walsh, William, 260–61, 442

Wardle, Isaac J., 293, 433

Wardle, Mary Ashton, 433

Warner, Sarah Emma. *See* Bailey, Sarah Emma Warner

Waugh, George P., 219, 223, 297–98

Webb, Chauncey, 56, 122, 289

Webster, Ann Elizabeth (Betsy) Parsons: sails with last large group, 1–2; and childbirth, 2; background of, 254; after handcart trek, 422–25

Webster, Francis: and Gold Rush, 1, 254; pays fare for others, 1, 254, 422; goes to Cedar City, 2; remains obedient, 2; and frozen feet, 2, 255, 422; sickness of, 2–3, 255, 422; recalls experience, 2–3, 423–24, 475–76; background of, 254–55; rebaptism of, 270; after handcart trek, 422–25

Wheelock, Cyrus: as rescuer, 122; blesses Mary Ann Mellor, 219; speaks on *Horizon,* 255; speaks for leaving Florence, 289; on spirit of handcart pioneers, 292–93; at Martin's Cove,

370; meets Martin company in Utah, 435

Wight, Joseph M., 194

Wight, Mary Hurren: family of, 41; on arrival of rescuers, 141–42; pays tribute to James Willie, 179; survives trek, 193; suffers frostbite, 194–95

Wilkinson, Lydia. *See* Reeder, Lydia Wilkinson

Willie, Elizabeth Pettit, 66, 178

Willie, James G.: appointed company leader, 7; prays at sea, 9; on poverty of emigrants, 19–20; background of, 66; photograph of, *66;* on kindness of Iowa residents, 73; urges company to start journey, 80, 81–82; on complainers, 91–92; reproves Levi Savage and Millen Atwood, 96–97; proposes rationing, 110; leaves to find rescuers, 134–35, 138; after handcart trek, 178–80; leadership of, 178

Willie, William, 178

Willie handcart company: route of, *xii–xiii, xiv;* suffers tragedy, 3; and Martin company, 13; in Iowa City, 58–59; delays in starting, 57–61; formal organization of, 65–70; travels to Florence, Nebraska, 71–76; members of, leave, 71–72, 110–11; crossing Iowa, 72–74; quality of handcarts in, 75–76, 91; in Nebraska, 77–85; trusts in leaders, 82–83; trusts in Lord, 82–83; leaves Winter Quarters, 86; loses cattle, 89–92; Franklin D. Richards visits, 92–98; arrives at Fort Laramie, 102; food supply of, 103–5; gets no resupply, 105–9; rationing in, 110, 125; stealing in, 111; animals in, 112–13; rescuers meet, 131–45; crosses Rocky Ridge, 146–58, 329; monument to, 158–59; travels to Fort Bridger, 163–65; deaths in, 172; arrives in

Salt Lake City, 172–76; mortality rate in, 401. *See also Thornton*

Winter Quarters: use of, 52; establishment of, 79, 285; difficulties of staying at, 82, 291–92. *See also* Florence, Nebraska

Woodmansee, Emily Hill Mills: background of, 36–38; photograph of, *37;* on difficulties of walking, 77–78; receives onion, 132–33; after handcart trek, 187–89; testimony of, 476

Woodmansee, Joseph, 188

Woodruff, Wilford: Rowley family hears, 41; on arrival of first handcart companies, 114–15; on condition of Willie company, 163; John Jaques as secretary of, 410; and James Bleak, 466

Woodward, William: on chopping logs, 56; expected Willie company, 58; background of, 68; on repairing handcarts, 78; on death of oxen, 112; on rescuers' arrival, 132; on sleeping in snow, 133; on Rocky Ridge, 151; on exposure, 172; on Levi Savage, 181; after handcart trek, 185

Wrigley, Mary. *See* Cunningham, Mary Wrigley

Wyoming pioneer trail, *xiv*

Young, Brigham: calls for emigration, 14, 16; concern of, for poor, 16; envisions Zion, 17; on Perpetual Emigration Fund, 19; decides to use handcarts, 21–26; engraving of, *23;* on financial problems, 24; on handcart plan, 24–25; sells property to replenish Perpetual Emigration Fund, 26; promotes handcart plan, 27–29, 77, 168–69; responds to reservations, 30–31; on wood for handcarts, 56; on arrogance, 95; and suggested rations, 104; receives

letter about handcart companies, 109–10; meets first two handcart companies, 114; hears report of Franklin D. Richards, 115–16, 310–11; calls for rescuers, 116–18, 310–11; counts cost of rescue, 119–20; prophetic foresight of, 120–21, 471; and self-reliance, 121; speaks against criticism, 166–68; on faith and good judgment, 167; requests that John Jaques emigrate, 247; reprimands emigration leaders, 291; photograph of, *311;* on rescuers crossing Sweetwater, 360–61; and Daniel W. Jones's hearing, 378–79; writes letter exonerating Daniel W. Jones, 378–79; sends rescuers back, 389; gives instructions on care for emigrants, 399; takes in emigrants, 400; Mary Goble on emotions of, 438–39; promises Mary Goble her feet would be saved, 439; and James Bleak's ring, 464–65

Young, Joseph A.: in first rescue team, 122, 311; gives onion to Emily Hill, 132–33; photograph of, *133;* on express journey from Devil's Gate, 339; on express journey to Salt Lake City, 355; on discarding heavy items, 369; reports on Martin company, 390; packs snow, 397

Zion: gathering to, 1, 7, 14–20; desire to reach, 14–16, 36, 137, 199, 243–44, 265, 441; building, 16, 199, 409–10; Brigham Young envisions, 17; impressions of, 175–76, 430–31; hard times in, 188, 196, 206, 403, 440; expectations about, 189, 199, 430–31; as work in progress, 189, 199, 431; sticking with, 412–13; blessings of living in, 457, 476–77. *See also* Emigration; Salt Lake Valley